The Chairmaker's Workshop

The Chairmaker's Workshop

Handcrafting Windsor and Post-and-Rung Chairs

DREW LANGSNER

Lark Books

To the memory of Ruedi Kohler, 1901-1995,
a Kufermeister (master cooper) in the Swiss Alps,
who made beautiful chairs and was my first woodworking teacher and a wonderful friend

---

Published in 1997 by Lark Books
50 College Street
Asheville, North Carolina, U.S.A., 28801

© 1997 by Drew Langsner

Editor: Bobbe Needham
Design and production: Elaine Thompson
Production assistant: Bobby Gold
Photography: Drew Langsner with photographic assistant Kenneth Kortemeier;
    cover photo and photos on pages 5, 10, 12b, 67–70, 84, 122b, 123–24, 127, 128a, b, 129, 140,
    169, 204, 209, 213, 219, 232, 237, 238, 246, 252, 261b, 269, 281–82, 287 by Evan Bracken;
    back cover photo by Grant Libramento
Line drawings and fig. 6.4: Kay Holmes Stafford
Chair view plans and drawings on pages 268, 272, 279, 280, 284–85: Don Osby

Library of Congress Cataloging-in-Publication Data
Langsner, Drew.
    The chairmaker's workshop : handcrafting Windsor and post-and-rung chairs /
Drew Langsner.
        p.   cm.
    Includes bibliographical references and index.
    ISBN 1-887374-34-5
    1. Chairs.   2. Windsor chairs.   3. Furniture making.   I. Title.
TT197.5.C45L36   1997
684.1'044--dc21   97-8054
                                                                   CIP

10 9 8 7 6 5 4 3 2 1

First Edition

Distributed by Random House, Inc., in the United States, Canada, the United Kingdom,
    Europe, and Asia
Distributed in Australia by Capricorn Link (Australia) Pty Ltd.,
    P.O. Box 6651, Baulkham Hills Business Centre, NSW 2153, Australia
Distributed in New Zealand by Tandem Press Ltd., 2 Rugby Rd.,
    Birkenhead, Auckland, New Zealand

The written instructions, photographs, designs, patterns, and projects in this volume
are intended for the personal use of the reader and may be reproduced for that purpose only.
Any other use, especially commercial use, is forbidden under law without written permission
of the copyright holder.

Every effort has been made to ensure that all the information in this book is accurate. However, due
to differing conditions, tools, and individual skills, the publisher cannot be responsible for any injuries,
losses, or other damages that may result from the use of the information in this book.

Printed in Hong Kong by Oceanic Graphic Printing Productions Ltd.

ISBN 0-8873-7434-5

For information about Country Workshops' hands-on courses and woodworking tools:
Drew Langsner, 90 Mill Creek Road, Marshall, North Carolina, 28753; phone, 704/656-2280.
Web site: //countryworkshops.org   E-mail: langsner@countryworkshops.org

CONTENTS

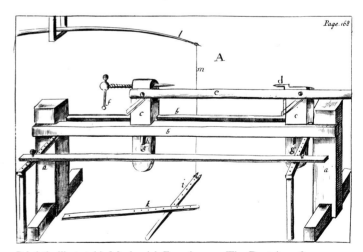

Pole lathe illustrated in Mechanick Exercises: or, The Doctrine of Handy-Works, *by Joseph Moxon (1703).*

The author, boring stretcher mortises in the legs of an American Windsor

ACKNOWLEDGMENTS

I could not have undertaken a book of this scope without help from many friends.

I would particularly like to thank John D. Alexander and Dave Sawyer. John taught me the basics of making a post-and-rung chair in 1978. He started Country Workshops' classes in ladder-back chairmaking and has continually supported our efforts. Dave Sawyer showed me how he makes a Windsor chair in 1983. Many of the techniques that I use are still based on Dave's methods.

For the history of chairmaking, I drew on two primary researchers whom I also met through Country Workshops, Nancy Goyne Evans and Dr. Bernard D. Cotton; both were more than generous in sharing information and answering my questions about their specialties, which are American Windsors and British regional chairs, respectively.

Throughout the writing I was in contact with a number of chairmaker friends. Welsh chairmaker John Brown shared his ideas and photographs of many old stick Windsors from Wales and Ireland. Dan Mayner agreed to my request to draw plans of one of his comfortable post-and-rung rockers for the project section of the book. Thomas Donahey and Carl Swensson were extremely helpful in developing the section on genuine rush seating. Mark Taylor made the reproduction slant-back Shaker chair expressly at my request. Other chairmaker friends who helped—by answering questions or loaning slides of their work—include Mike Abbott, Brian Boggs, Curtis Buchanan, Mike Dunbar, Peter Follansbee, Peter Murkett, Mario Rodriquez, Dan Stalzer, and Don Weber.

I was also able to borrow photographs of historic chairs and chairmakers from several sources. The Philadelphia comb-back Windsor is from the collection of Marilyn and James Flowers. The Rhode Island sack-back Windsor is owned by Edward and Helen Flanagan. The Shaker rocker is from the Shaker Village of Pleasant Hill, Harrodsburg, Kentucky. The other eighteenth-century American Windsors are from a private collection.

King-Thomasson Antiques (Asheville, North Carolina) generously loaned me a lovely pass-arm Sussex rush-bottomed chair for photographing and study of construction details. Photos of the other English chairs are courtesy of Dr. Bernard D. Cotton. The Irish Gibson chair was photographed courtesy of the Irish Agricultural Museum, Wexford, Ireland. Photos of the antique Welsh chairs were provided by the Museum of Welsh Life, Cardiff, Wales. The Swedish stick Windsor is in the collection of Katarina Agren, editor of *Hemsloyd* magazine. Wille and Gunnel Sundqvist own the six-leg reclining rocker from Sweden.

An Irish stick Windsor; this style is known as a "Gibson chair." The extreme slouch angle of the back makes this a comfortable lounging chair.

The etching "Men Shoveling Chairs" is from the Robert Lehman Collection, Metropolitan Museum of Art, New York. Photos of the English Windsor chairmaker Jack Goodchild appear courtesy of the Rural History Centre, University of Reading, England. The historic photo of the Kentucky chairmaker Henderson Mullins is used with the special permission of Berea College and the Doris Ulmann Foundation.

Most of the black and white photographs are the fruit of a shared undertaking by myself and Kenneth Kortemeier. Marlin Mathiesen took the photo sequence on saddling a Windsor bow-back seat, and Evan Bracken took most of the studio photos of the project chairs.

The book could not have been written without the encouragement of my publisher at Lark Books, Rob Pulleyn. Bobbe Needham was my patient editor.

I want to thank all of these friends and colleagues for hanging tight with me during the writing and production of this book.

FOREWORD

When I became interested in Windsor chairs twenty years ago there was very little literature on the subject available. Two volumes by Ivan Sparkes, the curator of the High Wycombe chair museum, were mainly historical and, apart from a chapter on American Windsor chairs in each book, confined to locally produced items. In the United States at about that time a facsimile of the original 1917 edition of *A Windsor Handbook* by the Reverend Wallace Nutting was printed. There was little else, and no how-to books.

This was the period of the first rumblings of interest in chairs, both Windsor and ladder-back. Concurrently, but quite separate from this interest in chairs, another movement was underway. Using ancient techniques—hand splitting logs; cleaving with axe, froe, and drawknife; and reinventing the shaving horse and pole lathe—the "woodland men" were on the march.

It was in an alternative bookshop, in, of all places, Regent Street, London, that I came across a book called *Country Woodcraft* by Drew Langsner. Although this book was not directly connected with making chairs, what it did do was bridge the gap between the woods and the workshop. *Country Woodcraft* is an accessible and inspirational book, covering a wide range of crafts, and to this day it is in pride of place on my bookshelf.

Chairmaker John Brown

At about the time I was struggling over my first chair, Drew and Louise, just married, were on a tour of Europe. In Switzerland the seminal moment occurred when Drew met Ruedi Kohler, one of the last master coopers working in the Swiss Alps. Drew put in two spells in Ruedi Kohler's workshop learning to make traditional coopered containers. This is a bit like starting at the end and working backwards, for any kind of coopering is a highly skilled job and requires that combination of technical knowledge and "eyeball" ability that takes time to master.

On returning home, the Langsners bought their farm in North Carolina. The message was clear—organic homesteading and making what you need. A chance meeting with like-minded individuals was the catalyst for the birth of their crafts school, Country Workshops. In the meantime Drew had met John Alexander, the author of *Make a Chair from a Tree*, and an interest in chairs was established.

The courses at Country Workshops are now well established. The location in the Smoky Mountains is beautiful and provides a perfect environment for the classes that take place there. Since the start, a variety of teachers from all over America and Europe has been invited to teach not only chairmaking, but such skills as timber framing, carving Swedish woodenware, toolmaking for woodworkers, and many others.

Over the years, Drew has acquired a vast fund of knowledge of different chairmaking techniques, old and new, which he is now making available to us in *The Chairmaker's Workshop*. A great strength in Drew's own work is that he is not restricted to traditional styles. I have seen one chair—a cross between English Wycombe and Philadelphia Windsors, flavored with Langsner—a very worthy chair, comfortable to sit in, and lovely to look at. Skills plus imagination is art—Drew Langsner is an artist.

A visit to Country Workshops, whether as a student or teacher, is an experience. In 1995 I spent a very happy time there with twelve students. There was an inspirational atmosphere that led me to believe anything could be achieved. The courses are a treasure. They are not only a thorough grounding on the technicalities of making a Windsor or ladder-back chair, but all the peripheral questions are answered—alternative materials, where to find the right tools, in fact an encyclopedic knowledge of anything to do with building wooden chairs. If only such a course had been available when I was searching for chairmaking information, I could have saved much time and sweat.

Now Drew has distilled his experience and scholarship into this new book. I am happy to endorse it and wish him, the book, and Country Workshops well, and a long life.

John Brown
Newport, Pembrokeshire, Wales

Part One:
Getting Set Up

CHAPTER 1

Welcome to My Workshop

A corner of the author's workshop

I work in an old tobacco-curing barn that has gradually been converted into a well-equipped chairmaker's workshop. There's a large central area with workbenches, several lathes, and a fine view of Sugarloaf Mountain. This is where I teach classes in traditional chairmaking for Country Workshops, a small handcrafts school that I started in 1978.

WINDSOR AND POST-AND-RUNG CHAIRS

The chairs I make are related to two basic styles—post-and-rung chairs, and Windsors. Historically, most of the parts for both types were turned on a lathe—picture the legs and stretchers of a Windsor chair. Turned parts lend themselves to having round, cylindrical tenons (the projection on a piece of wood that is fitted into a mortise—a cavity— to make a joint). Matching round mortises are quickly bored with a drill. In my chairs, I often use parts shaved with a drawknife instead of turned with a lathe. I enjoy this way of working wood, and I like the resulting appearance of the handwork.

A third type of chair, using rectangular mortise-and-tenon construction, is made by a branch of traditional woodworking known as joinery. Joined chairs are generally made from rectilinear rails (crosspieces) and stiles (posts or legs), with flat surfaces that form 90-degree angles, instead of the cylindrical shapes and myriad angles of Windsors and post-and-rung chairs. Joined chairs were first made at the same time as turned post-and-rung chairs, but usually by different craftspeople. I don't cover traditional joined chairmaking in this book.

You can recognize post-and-rung chairs by their four-sided framework composed of cylindrical parts. Continuous

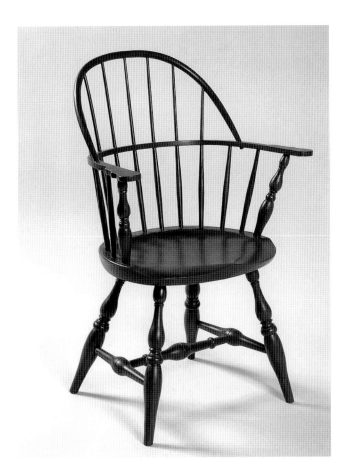

posts serve as rear legs and uprights for the back support, which can be slats, vertical spindles, or woven fiber. Post-and-rung chairs usually have a seat of flat splints, rush, or fiber woven across the upper round of cross rungs. Although I have never made a wooden seat, these may also be used. Six to eight cross rungs located below the seat strengthen the lower part of the frame.

Windsor chairs usually are made entirely of wood, with a solid plank seat and independent leg and back support systems that are bored into the seat at compound angles. The back support and optional armrests typically consist of an array of turned or shaved spindles mortised into the seat, and one or more bent hardwood bows that serve as a frame for the back support and armrests. The legs and their connecting stretchers are usually turned, often with decorative detailing.

Several other traditional chair styles share the Windsor's construction, among them Welsh stick chairs, Irish hedge chairs, and the Swedish pinnar. The common Boston rocker was a commercially popular, late nineteenth-century Windsor. In this book, I call all of these related chairs "Windsors."

Windsor and post-and-rung chairs have several characteristics in common. Unlike most furniture, the parts of these chairs can be made from split sections of a straight-grained log, instead of from milled lumber. This splitting process is called riving. Rived components are often superior to similar parts produced by sawing, because rived

wood follows the natural fiber configuration of the wood, whereas sawing severs the fibers at an angle. Rived parts are usually stronger (for their weight or mass), and they will bend easier than sawn parts. The basic post-and-rung chair is simpler than a Windsor, so I always suggest that chairmaking novices start by producing at least one post-and-rung chair. Without significant differences in tools and equipment, you can produce both types in the same workshop.

There are several basic types of post-and-rung chairs. The simplest is a stool with four legs and eight to twelve cross rungs. The basic post-and-rung dining chair, or side chair, has two or more cross slats for a back support and no armrests. The slats are usually horizontal, but they can also be vertical, mortised between lower and upper crosspieces. For comfort, the backrest should be bent, forming an angle of about 102 degrees between the seat and back. The seat design for most of these chairs is a trapezoid, with the front wider than the back. Post-and-rung construction is also commonly used for armchairs and rocking chairs.

The post-and-rung chair projects in this book were made with shaved parts, but they can also be turned on a lathe. Turning is the more common, traditional approach. A basic, inexpensive lathe is suitable for most chair work, but you can also make your own lathe for almost no cash outlay. (I've included plans for building a spring-pole lathe in Part 4.) Turning wet wood is almost as much fun as shaving wet wood.

Part of the appeal of the Windsor style is that you can easily modify the construction and embellishments to suit your own taste or that of a buyer. The gallery sections of this book include a variety of old and contemporary Windsors and post-and-rung chairs.

My personal interest in chairmaking has focused on teaching rather than production. While I appreciate the proficiency that is achieved only by production work, I find that in teaching I am constantly learning more about the chairs and how to make them. There is always a challenge in explaining concepts and methods to students who come to class with a wide range of expertise and talents. In many instances, I've picked up an idea or a different method from one of my students. My chairmaking is limited to producing several chairs a year. These can be post-and-rung chairs or Windsors, depending on the orders I receive.

Occasionally I have time to make a chair chosen by whim. My first original chair design was the post-and-rung youth chair, in Chapter 11. Two more recent chairs that I designed are the high-back stick Windsor in Chapter 8 and the double-bow English-style Windsor in Chapter 17.

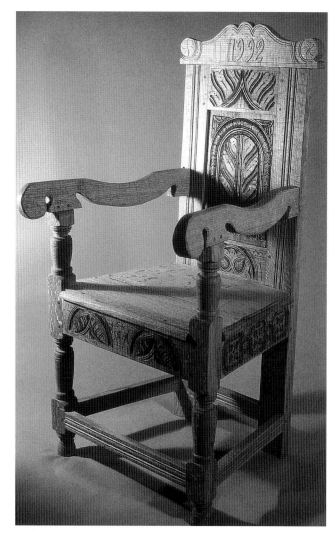

A contemporary interpretation of a seventeenth-century joined chair, made by Peter Follansbee

Two versions of a classic American bow-back Windsor, both made by the author

COUNTRY WOODCRAFT AND GREEN WOODWORKING

John Alexander, a fellow chairmaker and the author of *Make a Chair from a Tree*, once commented on my calling our craft *country woodcraft*. He said that these craft traditions had both urban and rural roots, that chairmaking, for instance, was often the work of highly skilled urban joiners and turners. John had coined a new term, *green woodworking*, as a contemporary conceptualization of an old way of working wood. Green woodworkers generally go directly to the forest for their materials. Logs are split with wedges into billets that are shaped into parts for chairs, baskets, and other useful objects—quite a different story from woodworking that relies on lumber that is milled and kiln-dried into uniform sizes before woodworkers gets their hands on it.

But *country woodcraft* is correct also. As the industrial system developed, many traditional handcrafts were abandoned. Surviving practitioners were often rural craftspeople, living in the poorer, backwater areas where progress and development were slow. In many cases craft techniques were lost or forgotten. Lon Reid, a mountain chairmaker in the original *Foxfire* book, shaved chair posts and rungs with a drawknife. His father and grandfather, also chairmakers, used a lathe. When the lathe broke down, it wasn't repaired. Lon Reid made do.

These rural woodworkers often produced chairs, kitchen woodenware, and other crafts with a direct sense of design, artistry, and honesty lacking in the more pretentious, fashionable products created by urban craftspeople or in factories. Welsh stick Windsors are one example. These chairs are handmade, country versions of English Windsors. The best Welsh chairs use direct, visible construction, displaying a directness of approach and simplicity of design that I admire. Perhaps more important is the element of personal connection and character found in crafts work that is truly handmade.

Tools for green woodworking tend to be simple and straightforward. The craft is especially satisfying because the work is a direct result of one's hand skills, the condition of one's tools, and the wood being worked— a distinct contrast to setting up and operating a piece of machinery that does the actual woodworking. Green woodworking is also in harmony with a philosophy of caring for our environment and personal health. It calls for local, natural materials. Electricity plays a minor role. Its waste products are mostly wood shavings, rather than sawdust and fine airborne particles of wood dust and toxic finishes.

Green woodworking techniques are great for shaping wood, but green (wet) wood is not suitable for chair joinery. Like many water-saturated materials, green wood shrinks as it dries. This means that joints made with wet wood will fall apart when the wood dries. Chair assembly is done after the wood has been dried to the appropriate moisture content for the various parts. (I discuss this in detail in Chapter 4.)

My interest in green woodworking began in 1972, when I apprenticed to a cooper in the Swiss Alps. Before then, I had little experience using traditional hand tools. For coopering I used a shaving horse and acquired a froe, drawknife, side hatchet, spokeshave, brace, and auger bit. All are greenwood chairmaker's tools also.

LADDER-BACKS AND STICK WINDSORS

In 1979 John Alexander came to our North Carolina farmstead to teach Country Workshops' first course in ladder-back chairmaking. At that time, John didn't know how to teach the making of a post-and-rung chair within the five-day time frame of the class we offered; instead he taught how to make post-and-rung stools. They're simpler and yet provide many of the challenges of making a chair. Now we've refined our Ladder-Back Chairmaking course

Continuous-arm Windsors, being made by Dave Sawyer

to the point where we teach a two-slat ladder-back with bent back posts—the chair that I explain in Chapter 6. To give you an idea of how long it takes a novice to make such a chair, working at it full time, the course is now six days long and includes weaving a Shaker-tape seat on each completed frame.

The chairmakers' network is a small one. Vermont chairmaker Dave Sawyer, who has taught the Ladder-Back

An inspirational stick Windsor, from the collection at the Museum of Welsh Life, Cardiff, Wales.

A BRIEF HISTORY OF THE CHAIRMAKER'S CRAFT

I am not an authority on the history of making chairs. However, I have always been interested in this subject and have picked up bits and pieces over the years. When I started writing this book, I decided to learn more about the development of the chairs I've been making.

The earliest and best-known American books on Windsor chairs are Wallace Nutting's *A Windsor Handbook* (1917) and his *Furniture Treasury* (1928). Thomas Hamilton Ormsbee's *The Story of American Furniture* (1943) also includes an extensive section on Windsor chairs. Both writers hypothesized an evolution of design and artisanship that begins with simple or "primitive" chairs. Step by step, the classic American Windsor design takes shape. Strange-looking English Windsors precede the more sophisticated and perfectly proportioned Windsors made by North American craftspeople in the mid–eighteenth century.

As a chairmaker, for me these books raised serious questions—and some doubts. Through Country Workshops I have been fortunate to meet several people who have seriously investigated the chairmaking story. John Alexander told me about Nancy Goyne Evans when we were planning our first Windsor chairmaking class in 1987. Nancy Evans has been investigating Windsor chair history for more than thirty years, researching documents such as inventories and probate records, as well as journals and old artworks. Her article "A History and Background of English Windsor Furniture," published in *Furniture History* in 1979, and recent correspondence have been major sources for my information about early Windsor chairs. (Nancy Goyne Evans's magnum opus, *American Windsor Chairs*, was published by Hudson Hills in 1996.)

My other major source of scholarly chairmaking history has been Bernard Cotton, whose hands-on study of English woodland crafts and chairmaking went forward under the tutelage of Fred Lambert, the almost legendary craftsman who wrote *Tools and Devices for Coppice Crafts*, first published in 1957. Bill Cotton has two advanced degrees in social science from London University and is the author of numerous articles and several books on vernacular English furniture. His comprehensive work *The English Regional Chair* is the authoritative study on English ladder-back, spindle-back, and Windsor chairs. Where Nutting was driven by subjective judgment to develop design standards for determining a fine-quality Windsor, contemporary researchers like Evans and Cotton are engaged in combining verifiable facts and supporting evidence into an accurate, and often complex, history of chairmaking.

I met Bill Cotton during Country Workshops' first tour of England and Wales, when he and his wife, Gerry, hosted our group with a traditional plowman's lunch, followed by a slide lecture on Philip Clissett, a nineteenth-century rural

Chairmaking workshop several times, in 1983 coached me through his methods for making a continuous-arm Windsor. While writing this book I visited Dave; his methods still form the foundation to my approach in making a Windsor.

In the spring of 1993 an English colleague, Mike Abbott, visited us. We had corresponded for several years, since the publication of Mike's book, *Green Woodwork*. Mike had agreed to be the guide for Country Workshops' upcoming crafts tour of England and Wales. During his visit, Mike showed me a new book, *Welsh Stick Chairs*. John Brown makes chairs deeply rooted in the Welsh stick Windsor tradition that also express his personal interpretation of the style. During our tour of England and Wales I had the pleasure of meeting John Brown and seeing his chairs, as well as some of the old chairs at the Museum of Welsh Life.

This was my introduction to vernacular Windsors made by countryside woodworkers. It turns out that stick Windsors were also made in Ireland, parts of England, and even in the southern tip of Sweden.

"Men Shoveling Chairs" by a Master at Flanders, c. 1445. A rare chance to study a selection of realistically rendered period chairs.

chairmaker who influenced William Morris and others in the English Arts and Crafts movement. For this book, Bill Cotton has graciously loaned me several color plates of outstanding English chairs.

I also recommend *American Seating Furniture*, by Benno M. Forman, which includes several in-depth essays on the methods used by furniture historians as well as on the development of various chair styles and how they are interrelated.

The history of post-and-rung and Windsor chairmaking turned out to be more complex than I had anticipated, with many gaps still to be filled in—the fabric of this story is a weave of known and as yet unfound threads in which exceptions seem to accompany most statements of fact. Much of what I say is still speculative, or in the realm of generalization.

Because wood decays and burns, the study of very early furniture depends largely on artworks and documents in which chairs play an incidental role. Surviving artworks clearly show that wooden chairs were being made three or four thousand years ago. The basic wooden-seating concept, a stool consisting of a plank seat housing three or four socketed legs, occurs in a few examples traced to Thebes, Egypt (about 1,400 BC). This is the same construction method used in Windsor chairs. Examples of rectangular rush-seated stools have been dated before the

birth of Christ. We also know that wooden stools, chairs, and tables were made by the Romans and throughout the Middle Ages, but no pieces are known to survive. A few artworks from the thirteenth to the fifteenth centuries depict furniture and woodworkers using tools very like the traditional hand tools that we are familiar with.

In a pen, ink, and chalk drawing from Flanders dated about 1445, "Men Shoveling Chairs," men with long-handled wooden shovels are piling a variety of period seating into a heap. Most of the chairs were turned, although several plank stools also appear in the picture. Quite a few of the turned stools in the picture have three legs, and there are also several folding chairs. A joined chair with woven seat and backrest is at the top of the pile.

A guild of turners formed in London in the early fourteenth century lists, in Article 4 of its 1608 ordinances, wares commonly produced by turners at that time, including chairs and spinning wheels. These were mostly post-and-rung chairs, with rush or plank seats. An engraving from about 1635, "The Turner" by the Flemish artist Jan van Vliet, depicts a craftsman at his spring-pole lathe. Against the back wall we clearly see a conventional post-and-rung chair with a solid plank seat, and in the foreground a spinning wheel appears prominently.

No research has yet convincingly explained why Windsor chairs are called "Windsors." According to Nancy Evans,

"The Turner," by Jan van Vliet, c. 1635, one in a series of illustrations depicting early seventeenth-century Flemish trades

The earliest known written references to Windsor chairs predate the oldest provenanced Windsors by several decades. In 1718, Stephen Switzer wrote a treatise on rural gardening where he described "a large Seat, call'd a Windsor Seat, which is contriv'd to turn round any way, either for the Advantage of the Prospect, or to avoid the Inconveniences of Wind, the Sun, &c." Daniel Defoe wrote about a chair he saw at Windsor Castle in 1725 "with a high Back, and Cover for the Head, which turns so easily, the whole being fix'd on a Pin of Iron, or Brass of Strength sufficient, that the Persons who sit in it, may turn it from the Winds." Defoe describes the construction as being similar to an open box, with board sides, back, and top. The chair does not begin to resemble what we call a Windsor.

The earliest Windsors were most likely fairly elaborate chairs. The post-and-rung chairs and spinning wheels produced by the master guild turners were the work of skilled artisans. There is no reason to suppose that these turners would produce primitive furniture.

While old, vernacular Windsor-type chairs with plain legs and simple lines do exist, they are impossible to date. According to Evans, it is almost certain that stick Windsors and other vernacular chairs were not progenitors of the Windsor style but rural versions of fancier chairs made by contemporary professional turners—yet this remains an open question. Leg angles and other details of existing old stick Windsors suggest that these chairs were generally made by part-time woodworkers. Construction and materials indicate that they were made by and for members of the lower economic classes. This perspective in no way lowers the value of the stick Windsors and other rural variations.

The industrial revolution created the factory production system beginning in the eighteenth century. High Wycombe, in Buckinghamshire, England, was an early center of factory-made Windsors. The needed wood was available nearby, and the major market —London—is not far to the east. These chair factories were among the first to organize production by specialized division of labor and use of interchangeable parts. Depending on the size of the factory, there were turners, seat saddlers, fret workers (who sawed intricate patterns in the central back splats common to English Windsor chairs), assemblers, finishers, and so on. Production was done on a piecework basis, with craftspeople usually working as independent contractors. The business was highly competitive, with long hours and low pay, and factory owners were constantly looking for ways to lower production costs. According to Bill Cotton, by the mid-1870s High Wycombe had nearly a hundred chair factories, producing more than four thousand chairs a day.

Several English books on rural crafts tend to romanticize early Windsor chairmaking history, especially the role of itinerant woodland turners, known as "bodgers," who set up temporary shelters in the beech woodlands and used homemade spring-pole lathes to produce Windsor turnings as piecework. (Bill Cotton has researched the term *bodger*, a

it is almost certain that the first Windsors were made by master turners in London, not in the small town of Windsor, based on the following findings: The earliest provenanced Windsor-style chairs do not appear until the mid-eighteenth century. In the early 1720s the registers of apprenticeship indentures listed twenty-eight master turners in London. The town of Windsor is located in county Berkshire, about thirty miles west of London. Four parents living in county Berkshire sent their sons away for training as turners. Two boys went to London, one went to the Reading (slightly west of Windsor), and the other went to East Sussex, which is directly south of London. It is therefore probable that there were few, if any, turners living in Windsor during the formative years of the English Windsor chair style.

My own hunch is that a decline in the sale of turned spinning wheels plays an important part in the story. The development of the Windsor style coincides with the beginnings of industrialization. The early development of woolen mills resulted in a rapid decline in home spinning, which had been an important cottage industry throughout much of rural Britain. As a woodworker, when I look at a spinning wheel, I see little technical difference from a Windsor chair. Both consist of turned legs, spindles, and other cylindrical parts that intersect a tilted central plank at myriad angles. I believe that some of the craftspeople who had been making spinning wheels turned to making Windsor chairs.

word apparently first used by journalists in the early twentieth century to refer to woodland turners; it seems to be a derogatory term, deriving from *botcher*.) A pole lathe is driven by a cord wound around the turning and pulled downward by a foot treadle. An overhead spring pole pulls the cord back after each downward stroke. That the action is reciprocal, rather than continuous, limits the speed of work, as half the time—when the turning is spinning in reverse—no cutting is done. Although the method is inefficient, an accomplished pole-lathe turner can produce quality turnings at an impressive rate. But—as distinct from these romanticized "bodgers"—most of the High Wycombe area turners actually worked in sheds next to their village homes (not under trees), and they generally used treadle lathes, which turn continuously in one direction and are therefore more efficient than pole lathes.

In the 1600s, North American craftspeople were making chairs in a variety of styles. Turners made both spindle-back and slat-back post-and-rung chairs. "Great chairs"—joined chairs with arms—were prominent household furnishings, but simple side chairs and benches were more common. The seats could be planking, rush, cane, or flat woven splints. Joined chairs tended to have solid plank seats, but some were upholstered with leather, or "turkey work," a woven ruglike fabric. Joined chairs commonly featured decorative turned elements worked between the rectangular mortise-and-tenon construction. Caned chairs were apparently among the types made by the first artisans who called themselves "chairmakers." According to Benno Forman, high-style caned chairs peaked in popularity for the several decades that preceded the rise of the Windsor style, in the mid-1700s.

No one is sure when the first Windsor chairs were made in the North American colonies. By the late 1700s, most Windsors made in the young United States were produced in factories, using interchangeable parts and specialized division of labor. Many early chairmakers were actually entrepreneurs, not master artisans working with an apprentice or two. In 1775, Francis Trumble advertised in the *Pennsylvania Gazette* that he had 1,200 available chairs in stock. On October 22, 1801, James Hallett Jr. placed this ad in the *New York Gazette*: "For Sale 5,000 windsor chairs of various patterns, prepared for a Foreign market of the very best materials and workmanship."

Still, handmade chairs continued to be produced in small quantities in England and the United States. In general, one-person shops were more likely to produce post-and-rung chairs than Windsors, probably because almost all parts of a post-and-rung chair can be made on a lathe. In contrast, producing a Windsor requires mastery of a wide range of craft skills. It is likely that many craftspeople who could single-handedly make fine Windsor chairs were mostly occupied with repair work. This would explain the individual, sometimes eccentric, quality of many older, handmade Windsors that survive today.

English Windsor chairmaker Jack Goodchild at work in Naphill, Buckinghamshire, c. 1950. His methods and finished chairs were very similar to English Windsors made in the late eighteenth century.

Windsor and post-and-rung chairs should not be stereotyped as either urban or country furniture. Although the first Windsors seem to have been produced in London, rural and village workshops were soon turning out similar chairs. Chairs made in factories and by individual craftspeople could be of high quality or quickly produced for the lower-priced markets.

The interpretive Windsor history writings of Nutting and Ormsbee appear to go off track when they describe the evolution of the American Windsor as a refinement of the English Windsor style. I agree that the best American Windsors made between 1775 and 1825 are elegant pieces of furniture, but I do not find the American Windsor style superior, or more refined. While working recently on my first English-style—or perhaps English-inspired—Windsor (a project chair in Chapter 17), I developed new respect for the old English chairmakers. It may be that many characteristics of American Windsor chairs were originally developed by a desire to produce more quickly a more competitive chair, and perhaps something different for the market—the American Windsor style tends to be considerably lighter than English Windsors, and the angles used for boring legs and back bows are dramatic.

Eighteenth-century American Windsors were commonly painted black or green. To the uninitiated, painting a wooden chair often seems like sacrilege. However, painted wooden furniture was very popular from the seventeenth into the nineteenth centuries. While the English often made Windsors from wood species chosen for their

Jack Goodchild dipping finished chairs in a vat of stain, which would be followed by a coat of shellac varnish

required to build up a substantial amount of color, giving the finish a rich depth not found in modern paints, which use much higher concentrations of pigment but no lead. According to Nancy Evans, the deep forest green commonly associated with American Windsors was not commonly used until well into the nineteenth century. The recipe combined blue, red, and yellow pigments with lampblack.

English and American Windsors of similar basic construction commonly go by different names. To confuse matters, the names of English and American Windsor back styles are not consistently used either from one area to another or among the craftspeople who make them. I've compiled a few of these confusing English and American Windsor names (for consistency, in this book I use the names that are followed by the asterisk).

American Windsor Names	English Windsor Names
Comb-back,* great Windsor	High-back, comb-back
Bow-back,* hoop-back, loop-back, oval-back, side bow-back	Low-back, hoop-back
Sack-back,* bow-back	Low-back, high hoop-back, high stick-back, double bow-back,* smoker's high-back, high stick-back, low stick-back
Low-back,* captain's chair	Low bow-back, smoker's bow-back, library chair
Continuous arm,* one-piece bow and arm	Continuous arm (produced in southwest England, mid-1800s)
Fan-back	Comb-back

appearance, American Windsor chairmakers commonly used woods that served their special construction purposes but were not aesthetically compatible. Painting tied the chair together visually. And here's a secret from the old workshops: Painting also helps to conceal errors in craftsmanship, hiding repairs and sometimes defects. Early American Windsors were painted with oil colors that were quite similar to artists' oils used for pictures. Completed chairs were primed with linseed oil and lead-based grey paint, then finished with several thin coats based on a mixture of linseed oil, pigment, lead, varnish, and sometimes turpentine.

The green paint popular for eighteenth-century American Windsors was based on verdigris, a toxic pigment obtained by the reaction of acetic acid on copper. The color resembles that of oxidized copper (sometimes Prussian blue was added). An unstable substance, verdigris reacts with other chemicals that it contacts, and the actual hue can range from turquoise green to bright blue. Several coats were

The Swedish Windsor Tradition

The Swedes have their own version of Windsor chairs, *pin-nar*. "Pin" is a derivative of "spindle." Although it seems unlikely, it is apparently true that Windsors came to Sweden from America, not from England. As I recently discovered when I had a chance to examine a large number of Swedish pin chairs in the warehouse of the Nordic Museum, the turning patterns of their legs and stretchers are based on American patterns, which differ considerably from most English Windsor turnings. Most Swedish pinnar were inexpensive side chairs produced in factories, but many were also made by individual craftspeople. Popular about 1900, low-backs and small fan-back side chairs are the most common styles.

A stick Windsor from the southern tip of the Swedish coast. A baby seal-skin fur belongs in the hollow part of the seat.

The Swedish Windsor rocker, a very comfortable recliner popular in the early 1900s. The curved seat and backrest are similar to those of Boston rockers, made about the same time.

The Swedes also invented a unique Windsor recliner, derived from the American "Boston rocker," with the same generous S-profile seat, tall back, and large comb at the head of the spindles. But the Swedish version has a backrest that slouches at a very wide angle and six legs (three to each rocker). You can't sit up in this chair; it's designed to rock gently back to a restful position — something like floating in a Windsor water bed.

In rural parts of Sweden's south coast, the chairmaking tradition produced chairs very similar to Welsh stick Windsors. They tend to be low-backs, with bows made from naturally crooked tree parts, and plain, shaved legs. Like the Welsh chairs, every one is different; designs are a marriage of available materials, basic tools, and the maker's notion of a chair. Some are quite beautiful.

Pinnar—*Swedish Windsor chairs*—*ready for hand sledding to market, about the turn of the nineteenth century*

HOW TO USE THIS BOOK

This is a handbook for making post-and-rung and Windsor chairs. My approach emphasizes efficiency and accuracy, but not speed or production. The processes that I use interweave craft skills, hand tools, and wood as the chair is developed. I enjoy making chairs by hand; one of the goals of this book is that you find the work enjoyable too.

My personal interest lies in making a high-quality chair that combines comfort, structural integrity, and pleasing appearance. In my chair shop, I use the best tools, techniques, and materials that I know of. I also try to use local materials. While I employ a few power tools, most of the work stems from the traditional craft, performed with simple hand tools—I do not emphasize historic methods using period tools.

I chose chairs for this book based on designs that I enjoy making. The patterns are not reproductions of specific historic chairs, but my interpretations of traditional styles. The American Windsor drawings, for example, are close to chairs made about 1800. I suggest that you consider the designs and measured drawings as good starting points; for instance, seat sizes and shapes can be modified easily, while leg and backrest angles are more complex (the Appendix includes tables that can be used for modifying the complex leg and spindle angles of Windsor chairs).

I think of green-wood chairmaking as a living, growing tradition, and so I hope you will consider nothing in this book the only way to do it. Although I have written this book as a complete introduction for novice green-wood chairmakers, I expect advanced amateurs, and even professional chairmakers, to find useful ideas here. My detailed instructions are intended primarily for beginning chairmakers. If you're experienced at chairmaking, I am sure you do some of this work differently. (In fact, I've changed some of my methods while writing this book.) There are many good ways to construct these chairs.

If you are a novice chairmaker, I suggest you read Chapters 1-5, then step back in ambition and start out by making a post-and-rung stool (Chapter 10). A handsome and useful piece of furniture, this stool is much easier to make than a post-and-rung chair with a bent back. The main difference in construction is that the stool consists of all 90-degree angles, whereas the ladder-back chair is based on a trapezoid-shaped seat and includes the added complexities of the bent back posts and mortised back slats. Also, the ladder-back chair requires straighter and longer wood than the stool does. If you're a novice primarily interested in making Windsors, I still recommend making a simpler post-and-rung chair before tackling an American or English Windsor; both are quite complex artistically and technically.

Chapters 2 to 4 cover basic but essential information on tools, setting up a shop, sharpening, and chairmaking woods and wood preparation. This material is based on my experience in green woodworking for more than twenty years.

In Part 2, I deal in Chapter 5 with basic riving techniques. In the remainder of Part 2 and in Part 3, the basic reference and tutorial sections, Chapters 6 through 9, I guide you step by step through the making of three sample chairs: a two-slat ladder-back post-and-rung chair, a stick Windsor, and an American bow-back Windsor, all projects I have taught at Country Workshops. Chapter 7 focuses on three methods for seating post-and-rung chairs.

In Chapters 10 through 17, Part 4, you'll find plans and materials lists for a variety of post-and-rung and Windsor chairs. I've kept the text in these chapters brief, limited to specific details that distinguish these chairs from those in the tutorial chapters.

Part 5 includes plans for a shaving horse, a chairmaker's workbench, a spring-pole lathe, and two simple wood kilns. In the Appendix on designing a chair, I've included two tables that can be helpful in dealing with boring compound angles. (I know that some woodworkers will frown on this mathematical approach, but I invite skeptics to try this system.)

Four sections of color photographs show you a sampling of old and contemporary chairs that are outstanding variations of the project chairs. I hope you'll be inspired by what has been done in various chairmaking traditions and will borrow elements or derive ideas for your own chairmaking projects.

Finally, as I do with my students, I must emphasize the importance of safety in the workshop. Chairmaking, like other woodworking, involves the use of sharp, potentially dangerous, tools and machinery. As I write this, I am taking a course of antibiotics to combat a staph infection on my left index finger caused by a slight slip of a very sharp chisel. Contrary to what many old-timers have said, I firmly believe that sharp tools are far more dangerous than dull ones.

Home workshops are often located in confined, multi-purpose quarters. An excellent safety measure is simply to keep an orderly workshop. Put away tools that are not in use. Wear eye and ear protection, following recommended safety procedures. Move heavy weights (timber or machinery) properly. Don't work with edged tools when you're tired. Always watch out for the safety of visitors or others in your workshop.

A few other safety tips to keep in mind for any woodworking shop:

- Do not rush. I find I accomplish my best work when I aim for steady, thoughtful progress.

- Many wood finishes are hazardous. Rags soaked with linseed oil or tung oil can spontaneously combust as they dry. Other finishes release toxic fumes during application and drying. (Read labels.)

- Wood dust generated when making shaved chairs is much less noxious than the dust created in a shop that uses production sanding equipment. But most chairs require some sanding. Microscopic wood-dust particles are now officially rated as carcinogenic. When sanding, wear a properly fitted dust mask.

- Make small mistakes. This bit of advice may seem obvious, but I think it is an essential element of woodshop wisdom. Small mistakes are much easier to correct than major errors, which can lead to disasters.

Finally, have fun!

CHAPTER 2

A Chairmaker's Toolkit

The workshop I describe here is a hybrid of my personal shop and the facility Country Workshops classes use, a well-equipped but not elaborate chairmaker's workshop that combines traditional and contemporary tools and equipment for making post-and-rung and Windsor chairs. If you're making chairs one at a time, or in small batches, you won't require a large work area. My personal shop space is 9 by 28 feet, and I've worked in smaller places with few problems. It's also nice to have an outdoor area for splitting logs, and a separate area for storing wood.

Chairmaking equipment and tools often differ from those used for making most other kinds of furniture, although Windsors and post-and-rung chairs call for most of the same tools. Finding specialty hand tools for chairmaking can be a challenge. Some tools discontinued by manufacturers a hundred years ago have become collectors' treasures, and mass-marketed hand tools can be of poor quality or inappropriate. But if you're going to enjoy working wood with hand tools, you need good ones—properly designed, manufactured, and sharpened. You can make some of these yourself, and for not much expense. (I include details on how to make several chairmaking tools in this chapter, and in Part 5 I explain how to make a shaving horse, chairmaker's workbench, kiln, and spring-pole lathe.)

WORK AND STORAGE SPACES

Although it's not a necessity, you'll appreciate having a sturdy workbench, outfitted with at least one good, strong vise. I've made and used a variety of workbenches during the past twenty years. While a large, European-style joiner's bench is impressive, I've come to realize that it's not ideal for chairmaking. I now prefer a much smaller

My design for a chairmaker's workbench. The vise on the right will hold a chair seat between the twin screws, which are 28 inches on center.

workbench—my newest is only 2 feet wide and 4 feet long (see Chapter 19). Because I want to be able to work around all sides of a chair without moving it, I've designed my workbench to be positioned several feet from any wall. My new workbench can be bolted to the shop floor, so that it can't move when I'm aggressively inshaving or drawknifing the seat of a Windsor chair. I've also chosen to forego a tool well; I'd rather be able to use the full width of the workbench and have a flat surface when I'm working on chair assembly or finishing.

I generally use a shaving horse to hold wood for shaping with a drawknife and spokeshave (see Chapter 18)—especially for most drawknife work, a shaving horse is much more convenient than a vise. A low, shop-made bench, it has a vertical swinging clamp operated by foot. The two traditional shaving-horse constructions are the Swiss-German "dumb head" and the English "bodger's" bench. I prefer the dumb-head shaving horse, which has a central swinging unit with clamping jaws on either side of the head. The bodger's shaving horse consists of a framework that straddles the low bench and work platform; wood to be shaved is inserted beneath the jaw, which also serves as a cross-brace. Both styles perform the same function.

For axe work, you'll need a large hardwood hewing stump in the shop or work yard. Since you'll often be striking this valuable piece of equipment with an axe, which you want to keep very sharp, when you're not using it you should cover the stump top with a shallow inverted box to keep off dirt and grit. This is important because it's quite natural to rest one's foot on or to stand on a convenient log stump—and shoes carry grit.

You should have a separate work area for grinding and sharpening. Sharpening is a messy process, and grinding produces minute metallic particles that should be kept away from your workbench. You'll also appreciate having a sink and running water nearby, for washing hands and tending water stones. You can put a dedicated sharpening workbench together using 2 by 4s, screws, and construction-grade lumber. The bench surface should be large enough to mount a machinist's vise and a grinder, with enough room left for honing and other handwork. Be sure to include shelving and several electric receptacles within easy reach.

You also need a place to dry wood, so that the moisture content of chair parts is relatively correct before you start putting them together. If your output is low, you can rig a rack above a furnace or make space behind a woodstove. If you need to speed up the process, a simple kiln helps (see Chapter 20).

How you light your work area is important. I prefer natural light, with windows that I can also open for ventilation. Overhead fluorescent lights do a good job of providing general, even lighting when the sun isn't shining. For task lighting, incandescent machinist's lamps and other fixtures on flexible arms are very useful. Directional light-

A Zug Stuhl *(pull bench), a Swiss-style shaving horse*

ing works well for providing a low-angled, raking light, which you'll appreciate when shaping round work at the lathe or shaving horse, or examining an edge that you're sharpening.

About tool storage. I keep tools I seldom use on overhead shelves, easy to get to but out of the way. I keep my chair-making tools in a rolling cabinet with lots of drawers. Mine is a professional mechanic's tool cabinet, but you can make something similar from wood. Large tools that don't easily fit in a toolbox should have edge guards—to protect the tool, yourself, and shop visitors. Edge guards need to fit well and be easy to take on and off. I like leather guards with snap tabs for closures, but effective guards can be made from many materials. Sections of an old hose make fine guards for axes and drawknives. You can also make guards from canvas, cardboard, and even wood.

TOOLS FOR LOGGING, SPLITTING, AND RIVING

Since green woodworking begins with a log, you'll need special tools to cut and move these big fellows. A saturated oak log can weigh nearly 90 pounds per cubic foot. A log 18 inches in diameter at the butt end and 12 feet long could measure 14 cubic feet, depending on the taper toward the small end. This log will weigh about 1,200 pounds. That's a lot of weight to deal with. **Safety note: You need to be extremely careful whenever moving, cutting, or splitting large logs.**

Crosscut and Chain Saws

The first tool you'll need is a saw for cutting logs. Today most logs are cut with a chain saw, but you can use an old-fashioned two-person crosscut saw or even the smaller one-person versions. A two-person crosscut saw is a pleasure to use, if it's a good one, properly sharpened. The newer two-person crosscuts that I've tried are inferior to the better old saws. Look for an old saw with a crescent, tapered-ground blade. (This means that the saw teeth are thicker than the back of the blade, and that the thickness milling follows the curve of the teeth; only the best crosscut saws were made this way.)

Crosscut saws combine two types of teeth in a repeated pattern. Condition and sharpening seem to be more important than the specific tooth pattern (for complete details on sharpening a two-person saw, see Warren Miller's *Crosscut Saw Manual* in the Bibliography). Although I own several of these saws, I use them mostly for teaching and demonstrations. In real life I almost always use a chain saw to cut logs.

A chain saw and a hard hat that combines eye and ear protection. A cant hook leans against the tote box, used to haul wedges, gluts, and a hatchet.

Log splitting tools, left to right: *cant hook, 8-pound sledge hammer, two conventional steel wedges, narrow-angle starting wedge, glut, hatchet*

Safety note: If you're ready to buy a chain saw, here are two recommendations. First, realize that chain saws are very dangerous tools; learning and following the manufacturer's safety rules is imperative. Read the manual that comes with your saw, and then follow the instructions. Second, select a small-engine shop that you can trust for advice and service. There are a number of excellent chain-saw manufacturers. Avoid the smallest saws offered by many makers, which are generally cheap consumer-grade weekend tools. For general use, select a chain saw with an engine displacement of 3 to 3-1/2 cubic inches. This saw will have enough power to cut through a twenty-four-inch oak, and yet will not be expensive or too heavy to carry in the woods. After deciding on the make and model, select the bar length for the chain. A 3-cubic-inch engine can handle a 16- to 20-inch bar.

I also use an electric chain saw in and around the shop for cutting logs and split bolts to length. It's comparatively quiet and very reliable, always starting in even the coldest weather.

Wedges and Sledge Hammers

Cheap plastic wedges are very useful for felling and some crosscutting tasks. For splitting logs you need several steel wedges. Along with any other tools you take into the woods (like a maul and an axe), paint these red or bright blue, so they won't get lost. A flat, narrow-angle wedge works especially well for starting a split. I pound steel wedges with a sledge hammer, which is much more effective than using a wooden maul. An 8-pound sledge is a good weight. If you saw the handle down to 24 inches, it will be much easier to wield for this kind of work. **Safety note: Be sure to wear safety glasses when striking steel against steel.**

You also need two or three large wooden wedges, called gluts. These you make yourself, from hardwood saplings or even old hardwood timber. You'll need a wooden maul for striking a froe, or the back of a polled axe, when it's used as a wedge.

Axes

You will need a woods axe when splitting a log with wedges and gluts, either a short-handled hatchet or a larger polled axe. A polled axe has a single blade and a flat surface above the eye. Double-bit axes have great balance, but they are dangerous, so I seldom use one. An axe used during splitting should be fairly sharp. An ordinary axe head with symmetrical bevels works fine.

Hooks and Tongs

Peaveys and cant hooks are used to roll and lever heavy logs. The difference between these two tools is at the working end. A peavey has a pointed spike; a cant hook has a small row of teeth perpendicular to the handle. Old-time loggers seem to prefer one or the other. I like using a short cant hook (2 feet) and a hefty peavey (4 to 5 feet).

Hand tongs that resemble the old iceman's carriers, or huge ice-cube tongs, are very useful for carrying logs and split wood about 6 to 10 inches in diameter and 4 to 8 feet long. Tongs are especially helpful if you store green wood underwater. You can order them from a chain-saw shop.

Making Gluts, Mauls, and Froe Clubs

You can make gluts, mauls, and froe clubs from straight limbs or saplings of any heavy hardwood species. I generally use hickory, oak, or dogwood.

A glut is an oversized wooden wedge, used to continue the splitting process after a split in a log has widened past the point where steel wedges are effective. Gluts are 3 to 4 inches around and about 15 inches long. You can rough out the working end of a glut with a hatchet and then finish it with a drawknife. The enclosed angle of the wedge bevels should be about 30 degrees, and the splitting edge about 60 degrees. To prevent its early destruction from pounding, the head end should have a chamfer around the perimeter.

Froe clubs and other mauls (used to strike gluts or the back of a polled axe) can be made from a sapling or a root node. Saplings are easier, because using a root node involves working very irregular grain and cleaning away a lot of dirt and grit. Even then, you can expect some damage to edges of cutting tools. However, from a dogwood root node you can make an almost indestructible club or maul.

If you're using a sapling or limb, look for a straight one with a clear section for the handle and a knotty section for the hitting area. It's easier to shape a longer piece, so crosscut the sapling or limb a foot longer than the length for the finished club. As the green wood dries, splits known as checks will form at both ends. After drying, the checked ends can be sawed off.

The blank for a froe club starts out 30 inches long (a). The finished (dry) handle should be about 12 to 15 inches long and 1-1/2 inches in diameter. You can form the froe club handle in several ways (b). You can rough it out with an axe and then finish it using a drawknife (as for the gluts). Or you can saw some kerfs around

Steps in making a froe club: a, Select a sapling 3 to 4 inches in diameter, about 30 inches long. Knots at one end help to prevent splitting during use; b, shape handle, smooth the head area, and coat ends to minimize checking during drying; c, after drying, saw off checked ends—finish length is about 20 inches.

the handle area, and then split off the waste wood. Using either method, form a smooth transition area from the striking section to the handle. (If the head section ends with an abrupt angle, the forces from pounding will concentrate at the transition area; you want maximum pounding force transmitted to the section that actually strikes the froe.)

I like the finished, dry head of a froe club to be about 3-1/2 inches in diameter and about 10 inches long (c).

I suggest making several gluts and a pair of froe clubs at one time, using green wood. Since you'll use up these green-wood tools quite quickly, the extra gluts and clubs can dry out and harden while you're using the others.

Mauls for striking polled axes are made exactly like froe clubs, only mauls are considerably larger. The finish length of my favorite maul—made from a dogwood root node—is about 30 inches. Its dry weight is about 10 pounds. I've used it for nearly twenty years.

Froe, with froe club made from a hickory sapling

Froes

Riving is a controlled method of splitting wood with hand tools. You rive out parts as close as you dare to the actual size of your chair parts. For riving you need a froe and a froe club (see the sidebar "Making Gluts, Mauls, and Froe Clubs"). The froe is a splitting tool that consists of a straight double-bevel blade with a perpendicular round wooden handle secured at one end by a ferrule (a metal ring). A good-sized froe for chairmaking has a blade 10 to 12 inches long, and a handle that extends 12 to 16 inches above the ferrule.

You can sometimes find old froes at places that sell antique tools, although most used froes are beaten up pretty badly, and many were not made very carefully to begin with. The details of design and tuning for even a tool this simple make the difference between mediocrity and efficiency. Occasionally, a nice old froe does show up; buy it.

The froe I use has several refinements. The enclosed blade angle at the edge is about 35 degrees. A smooth transition is ground between the bevels and the sides of the blade. The blade is thick in width and short in depth compared to most older froes, stubby proportions that increase leverage. Blacksmith-made froes have a forged ferrule, which is seldom really round. I prefer a ferrule made of a length of steel tubing, welded to the blade. (The advantage of using a tubing ferrule is that it's truly round, making it easy to properly fit a tight handle. Using tubing also means the ferrule can be deeper than the width of the blade, which helps to keep the handle in its socket.) Regular mild steel is adequate for froe blades, which are not heat treated.

Other Riving Equipment

Riving equipment can include a homemade brake, used to secure four-to-six-foot pieces of wood that are awkward to split. A basic brake consists of a forked tree trunk supported above ground level by a pair of opposing poles slipped between the branches of the fork. A brake is not a necessity, but it does make riving big stuff more manageable.

To complete the riving kit you'll need a hatchet, a pencil, and a few common measuring tools. You'll use the hatchet to sever connecting cross fibers during the wedging stage

of splitting, and sometimes to hew off dirty bark. Pencils are required for marking out saw cuts and riving divisions. Water-soluble pencils mark nicely on wet wood. You'll need a tape measure or a folding rule. A 6-inch pocket ruler is handy for figuring out where to draw splitting lines. At times I've use straight-leg dividers to mark off even-width divisions on the end of a really large log.

Tools for Shaving Wood

A good drawknife and spokeshave are necessities. Even if you turn your chair parts at a lathe, a drawknife will be useful to prepare turning stock by shaving it into an octagonal section, and for shaping other parts, such as back slats.

Drawknife

The efficiency and control that can be achieved with a drawknife are the result of the tool's geometry—the two handles at right angles to the length of the blade. You can pull a drawknife with considerable force and still control the blade for exacting cuts and delicate work. Skillful use comes from practice and from having a drawknife that is properly sharpened.

Drawknives are made with blades in various shapes and sizes. Blade lengths range from 4 to 6 inches for fine detailing work to 24 inches for debarking logs. The blade may be flat and straight, curved (as viewed from above), or bowed (as viewed from the edge). Properly sharpened, a flat, straight blade is efficient for most drawknife work and is much easier to sharpen than a curved or bowed blade. Most pre–twentieth-century drawknives were handmade and have curved blades. Old drawknives were made with curved blades mainly because the shape is much easier for a blacksmith to forge.

Most drawknife blades are flat on one side, with a bevel on the other. Although some experts may disagree, I find that a drawknife can be efficiently used with the bevel up or down. It all depends on edge geometry, sharpening, handle angles, and what you are doing. I suggest buying a drawknife with a flat,

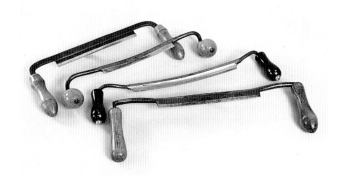

Chairmaker's drawknives. The drawknife with a straight, flat blade is recommended for general use.

straight blade. These were commonly available in hardware stores until about 1970—now you need to search used-tool shops and garage sales for them. Blades can be 8 or 10 inches; length doesn't seem to make any difference for most work.

Specialized drawknives with bowed blades, a configuration sometimes found in old hand-forged drawknives, are used for shaving flat areas, such as post-and-rung chair slats—a good tool for a chairmaker to own.

Inshave

To hollow the concave surface of Windsor seats (after the initial roughing out work, done with a hollowing adze), you'll need an inshave, a drawknife with the blade forged into a U-shape.

The inshave I prefer has handles angled upward to about 135 degrees from the plane formed by the blade, instead of the more common handles set at right angles to the blade. The high handles make the inshave harder to control until you get the knack of using the tool, but I found an inshave with right-angled handles barked my knuckles when I took any but the most shallow shavings.

Spokeshaves

Spokeshaves are mutant hand planes with very short soles and with handles that protrude on both sides, and their working geometries are similar. The flat steel blade, supported by a frog, is held in place by a simple chip breaker held fast with a thumbscrew or a central screw flanked by two depth-adjustment screws. You'll usually use a spokeshave after drawknife work to take fine, controlled-thickness cuts—you regulate the depth of cut exactly as you do with a hand plane. Spokeshaves are made in many styles, with various blade/sole configurations and blade depth–setting systems.

Wooden-body spokeshaves, the oldest style, use a blade that has two tangs bent at right angles to the cutting edge. Mortised through the wooden body, the tangs are held in place by friction or threaded adjusting nuts. The advantage of a wooden-body spokeshave lies in the extremely low cutting angle of its blade, useful when shaving highly figured wood or the end grain of hardwoods. One problem with wooden-body spokeshaves—especially when used to shave cylindrical stock—is that the sole wears into a hollow configuration. This results in an enlarged and irregular throat opening, which can offset the advantage of having a low cutting angle. (One remedy is to inlay a brass sole plate just in front of the throat opening.)

An iron-body spokeshave with a flat sole (and matching straight blade) is excellent for general work. While steel castings can be pot iron or malleable iron, it's worth spending the few extra dollars for malleable iron; a pot-iron spokeshave can break if it's dropped. Most new spokeshaves will work quite nicely after you've sharpened them. With a tune-up—which can include a higher-quality replacement blade—spokeshaves can be used for very impressive work. The single thumbscrew models are more difficult to adjust,

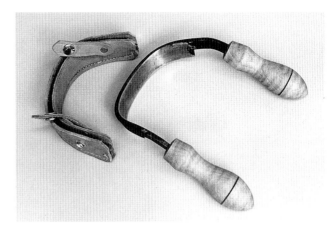

An inshave, used for saddling Windsor seats. Note the obtuse angle between the blade area and the handles.

Spokeshaves, from top: *standard spokeshave with flat sole and twin-blade adjusting screws; a basic spokeshave without adjusters holds blade setting better but is more difficult to adjust; a small flat spokeshave with excellent balance for shaving cylindrical chair parts; Brian Boggs's concave spokeshave, designed for finish work on post-and-rung chair legs; shop-made travisher made from a standard spokeshave.*

but they tend to hold the blade more securely than the twin-screw adjustment models.

Besides flat-soled spokeshaves, concave, convex, and round-soled spokeshaves are available—I've never had much success with the round-soled variety. Used for rounding chair legs and similar stock, concave spokeshaves have a sole that is semi-circular from side to side, and flat from nose to heel. The flat blade is ground to a matching concave configuration. Convex spokeshaves (with a lengthwise convex edge) are intended for shaping hollow areas, such as Windsor chair seats. Commonly available ones have too much curvature for most work, although they could be modified to shave the deeply dished rear section of a hollowed seat.

A more useful convex spokeshave, with a fairly shallow curvature, is variously known as a chairmaker's shave, travisher, or bottom shave. It's usually a shop-made tool with a wooden body and a tang-style blade. In the past, chairmakers bought blades in various curvatures from a local blacksmith and then made their own bodies. Commercially manufactured antique travishers are rare finds.

Making a Travisher

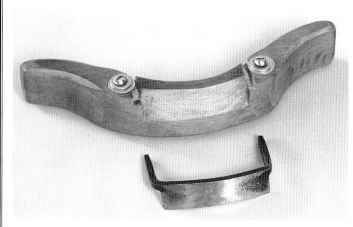

Shop-made travisher, with 01 tool-steel blade

A variation of convex spokeshave with a shallow curvature, a travisher is almost a necessity for smoothing Windsor chair seats.

Start by making the tanged blade. This can be forged using standard blacksmithing techniques. Or you can make the blade from cold, flat tool-steel bar stock. Most of the shaping is done with a hacksaw, grinder, and file while the blade is flat. Heat is required for bending the tangs and the curvature of the blade.

I've made several travisher blades from a tool-steel alloy called 01 flat stock, available from machinist supply companies and preannealed, that is, softened for forming cold. You can get 3/16-inch by 3/4-inch stock in 18- and 36-inch lengths. The travisher blade in the drawing requires about 5-3/4 inches.

You can pencil layout lines on the surface of the steel, but more exact markings can be scratched in if you coat the surface with machinist's bluing or the ink from a permanent felt marker. The tangs should be about 1-3/8 inches long; 3 inches is a good length for the blade (a).

Hacksaw the blade to overall length. Then drill 1/4-inch holes at the tangent of the tang/blade corners. Hacksaw the tangs (1/4 inch wide) and the ends of the blade. Clean up saw cuts with a file. Grind and file the bevel to an enclosed angle of 30°.

The bending can be done at a forge or with an oxyacetylene welding outfit. Using a welder, arrange a steel plate, with two crosspieces to support the blade about 1/4 inch above the plate. (The supports can be two bolts or pieces of scrap.) Lay the flat blade across the supports. Apply heat to the bottom of the plate with a cutting attachment. When the center of the blade is red hot, pick it up with locking pliers. Hammer the blade curvature using a 2-inch steel pipe or other rounded surface for an anvil. A curve with a rise of 3/8 inch at the center of a 3-inch blade is about right for most Windsor seat work. The bevel should be on the concave side of the curve (b).

Reheat the blade before attempting to bend the tangs. The red-hot tangs can be bent close to shape using pliers. Fine-tune the bends by tapping against an anvil. (The anvil section of a machinist's bench vise will work.) The tangs must be in line and parallel to each other.

Harden and temper the blade following the instructions in the sidebar "Making a Tapering Plane" in this chapter.

You can make the wooden travisher body from any dry, dense, short-grained hardwood, such as beech or hard maple. The stock is 1-1/2-inches thick. Saw the outline of the travisher body on the flat stock.

There are two ways to mount the blade. Traditionally, the bent tangs are slightly tapered and secured by friction into matching tapered mortises in the wooden body. A simpler method is to cut slots that match the tangs into the back of the travisher body (c). The blade is held in place using washers and small bolts that pass through the wooden body (d). In either case, you must be careful when excavating the cavity for the blade and escape for the shavings. This is careful chisel and file work. The throat (the opening just ahead of the protruding blade) should be kept quite narrow, about 1/16 inch. The escape for the shavings should be large enough for shavings to exit without jamming in the wooden body (e).

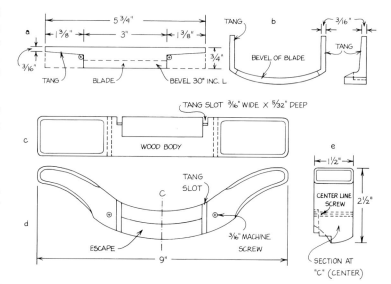

An alternative to making a wooden-body travisher is to modify a flat-soled iron-body spokeshave. Start with a spokeshave that has upswept handles. (A flat-handled spokeshave would be impossible to hold onto when working a hollowed surface.) Use a grinder and then a file to reshape the sole to a uniform end-to-end curve. Regrind the flat blade so that the edge matches the curve of the sole. Hacksaw off the ends of the handles where they begin to curve downward. Then use a grinder and file to round the edges of the amputated handle ends.

TOOLS FOR HEWING

Hewing refers to removing chips of wood by swinging an axe or adze into the material being shaped. (An axe blade is in line with the handle, while an adze blade is perpendicular to the axis of the handle.) Axes are generally used to hew flat or convex shapes. Adzes are made to hew flat shapes and to hollow out cavities, such as Windsor chair seats.

Green-wood chairmakers use axes during riving, to sever stubborn cross fibers in a log being split, and sometimes to hew away stock that is too thick. An axe can also be used for special purposes, such as hewing the armrests of a post-and-rung rocker.

Hatchets and Axes

Standard polled hatchets and axes are used out in the woods and for splitting, as discussed earlier in this chapter. For hewing, use a broad hatchet (a one-handed axe with a flat side and a single bevel to the outside of your swing) or a well-balanced double-beveled hatchet. For good balance, the axis of the handle should be in line with the center of gravity of the axe head. (Balance is less important with a broad hatchet.) The inner bevel of a double-beveled hatchet must be flat; an axe with a rolled bevel will tend to glance off the work being hewed.

Hollowing Adzes

A hollowing adze is the traditional tool chairmakers use to begin roughing out the cavity of Windsor chair seats. This adze can have a short, medium, or full-length handle, depending on the adze head and the user's preference. In the past, chairmakers did their roughing out, or saddling, by standing on the plank and using an adze with a full-length handle. This is my preference; it's efficient and safe if you're careful. Novices are often more comfortable using an adze with a short or medium-length handle. (Seat blanks can also be clamped flat on a workbench or secured vertically in a bench vise.)

The edge of a hollowing adze should be 2 to 4 inches across, and it must have an exterior bevel, or the adze will dig into the wood and tend to get stuck. My Swedish friend Hans Karlsson makes an elegant adze head that is 2-1/4 inches across. The curve of the blade is somewhat flattened in the center area; this shape leaves a gently scalloped surface.

My own adze, designed especially for hollowing Windsor seats, has an edge 3-1/2 inches across, and the head weighs about 50 percent more than the Hans Karlsson adze head. The adze edge is ground with a continuously variable bevel. The exterior bevel in the center section gradually shifts to an interior bevel at each side. The variable bevel improves a cut's control and efficiency with no bouncing or resistance at the sides of the upswept blade.

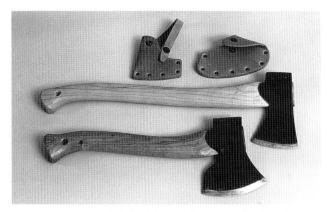

Shop axes: top, *axe used during riving work;* bottom, *a Swedish "sloyd" (handcraft) axe useful for hewing*

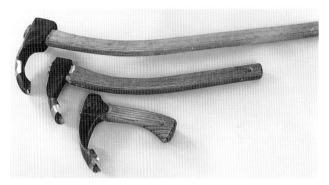

Hollowing adzes, from top: *chairmaker's saddling adze with 30-inch handle, designed by the author; Swedish hollowing adzes with 20-inch handle and with short handle*

TOOLS FOR BORING AND TENON MAKING

I group boring and tenon making together because you'll use cylindrical mortise-and-tenon construction for most of the socket joinery in post-and-rung and Windsor chairs.. (For information on standard boring tools used in green-wood chairmaking, refer to general texts on woodworking.) Socket joinery is fast, accurate, and relatively easy.

Bit Braces

You'll find a bit brace and standard auger bits useful, although variations and substitute tools are available.

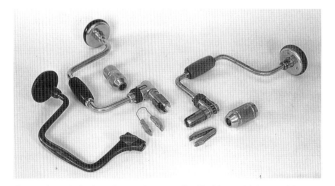

Braces, from left: *late nineteenth-century Spofford brace; bit brace with a universal chuck; bit brace with alligator chuck*

Several types of braces exist, with the usual range in quality and cost. Conventional bit braces are designed to hold standard auger bits with a tapered square lug at the attachment end. However, many bits have a straight cylindrical or hexagonal shank intended for use with electric drills that have a Jacobs chuck (the chuck is the mechanism that holds the bit). Since chairmakers sometimes need to use one of these drill bits with an old-fashioned bit brace, get a brace with a "universal" chuck, whose construction allows it to grab bit shanks that are round or hexagonal in addition to the standard tapered square lug. The jaws of a universal chuck pivot at their midsection; these can hold most drills. The other standard brace chuck has "alligator jaws" and can be used only with augers with a tapered square lug at the end. Look for a brace with a chuck that does not wobble.

In terms of size, chairmaking requires a brace with an 8- or 10-inch sweep (brace "sweep" refers to the rotation diameter of the crank).

I don't often advocate using antique tools, but one I especially like is called a Spofford brace, made in the late nineteenth century, just a few years before the modern types of brace chuck were invented. The chuck of a Spofford brace is simply a split chunk of steel with negative cavities that match a tapered square lug; the halves are tightened using a large wing nut. Spofford braces really do the job, with no wobble or play in the attachment mechanism. Used-tools dealers generally price them quite reasonably.

Electric Drills

With increasing frequency, green-wood chairmakers are using hand-held electric drills. Their attraction for me is not speed; drilling wood by muscle power is usually fast enough. One advantage lies in the drill's chuck. Because it holds cylindrical and hexagonal drill shanks, it opens the way for using a wide range of drill bits. Another advantage is that being able to hold the drill with only one hand frees your other hand for another task, such as supporting or backing up the work. Also, an electric drill can be operated in almost any body position. Finally, the sensitive trigger of a good-quality, variable-speed electric drill allows drilling at controlled, slow speeds, a great advantage. I like the cordless models.

Although some chairmakers love their drill presses, I usually prefer using a hand-held drill. Consumer-grade drill presses often have excessive quill runout—they don't turn in an accurate circle. Because of vibration, they don't make a clean, accurately sized hole, even with good jigging or a clamp. I also find mortising with drill-press jigs boring, compared to working with hand-held tools.

Wood Bits

Conventional auger bits made for use with bit braces have a cutting geometry that consists of a central lead screw, two circumferential scoring nibs at the perimeter, and two crosswise cutters that span the lead screw and scoring nibs. Of the two types of auger bit, Jennings augers have a fine-threaded lead and a double-spiral shank with no central shaft, while Irwin augers have a coarser lead thread and a single spiral winding around a central shaft. With a Jennings auger you must be careful not to bend the double-spiral, shaftless shank. An occasional problem with Irwin bits is that the lead screw can pull the drill downwards faster than you want to work. Both styles are easy to sharpen.

Auger bits are made in sizes from 1/4 to 2 inches in diameter. The conventional sizing system uses increments of 1/16 inch (number 5 means 5/16 inch). Augers above 1 inch in diameter are available in increments of 1/8 inch but are still specified in sixteenths, so a number 20 auger is 1-1/4 inches in diameter.

Spoon Bits

A spoon bit is shaped like a half cylinder, with a cutting end that approximates the shape of half of a dome. Since such bits can be made by a blacksmith, they were made long before bits with auger shanks and complicated multipart cutters and were used in many pre–factory era chairs.

Although they look primitive, spoon bits are effective boring tools with some unique characteristics. They cut clean holes and will bore at an angle. Some Windsor chairmakers prefer spoon bits because they can bore a hole with a neck that is smaller in diameter than the bottom of the hole. This shape results from wobble inside the hole, as it deepens. A matching bulbous tenon forced into such a swollen hole will not easily come out. Still, I'm not convinced that this is a superior joint. It's difficult to make a bulbous tenon that closely matches the enlarged inner hole. Also, if the joint eventually loosens, I want to be able to take it apart for repairs.

The ability to bore at an angle is not unique to spoon bits. Most of the angled borings in the stick Windsor (Chapter 8) and the bow-back Windsor (Chapter 9) are made with conventional auger bits, powerbore bits, and ordinary twist bits.

In my opinion, the time to use spoon bits is when you're making authentic reproductions, copied from originals made with spoon bits. And spoon bits are fun to play with.

Five-eighths-inch boring bits: a, spade or paddle bit; b, Jennings auger bit; c, Irwin auger bit; d, "electrician's" auger bit; e, rare forstner bit with tapered lug; f, powerbore; g, powerbore with shortened lead point; h, high-speed twist bit; i, auger bit file, for sharpening

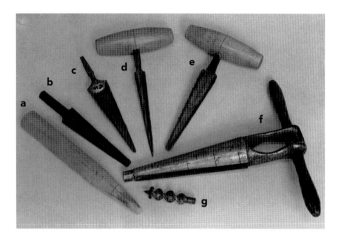

Reamers: a, dummy tapered tenon, for test fitting while reaming mortises; b, fluted machinist's reamer; c, 10-degree reamer with tapered lug; d, narrow-angle reamer; e, nineteenth-century 8-degree reamer; f, cast-steel reamer, with removable auger, g, to start hole

Even though auger bits bore a clean hole, they present a few problems: (1) In cylindrical stock, the lead screw or scoring nibs can inadvertently break through the back of the hole; (2) the actual diameter of most auger bits is 1/64-inch larger than the nominal size, a problem if you want to use a fixed-size tenon cutter; and (3) because of their tapered square shank, conventional auger bits cannot be used with a Jacobs chuck or with most bit extensions, which are used as aids in horizontal boring.

Designed for use with a drill press, *forstner bits* can also be used with a hand-held electric drill or even with a bit brace (if you can find a forstner with a tapered square lug at the end). Forstner bits have a short lead point and scoring nibs that are shallow in depth, lengthened to extend about one-fourth of the way around the perimeter of the head. This construction lessens the danger of boring through the back side of a small diameter cylindrical chair part. In use, a forstner bit rides on the extended nibs. Like an auger bit, forstners have two cutters that span between the lead point and side nibs; there is no spiral on the shank to help remove the cuttings. Although forstners cut a very clean hole, extensions are not generally available for these bits.

For post-and-rung chairmaking, I use a variation of the forstner bits, such as Stanley powerbore bits. These have only one cutter and one side nicker, both too long for many chair borings but easily filed down. A major advantage is that the shank accepts extensions that are manufactured for spade bits, the cheap, flat "paddle" bits made for electric drills.

I sometimes use ordinary machinist's twist bits with a variable-speed electric drill. These are especially useful for boring into end grain on the steep sides of a Windsor bow.

Reamers

Reamed mortises are required when you use tapered cylindrical tenons for Windsor legs and the ends of back bows. Usually you'll bore a round hole first, then shape the conical interior with a reamer. The converging sides of a reamer should be straight, forming a half cone, with a lug at the end that fits a brace or is permanently attached to a wooden T-handle.

For a good tapered joint in wood, the inclusive angle of the reamer can be 8 to 12 degrees. (The inclusive angle of a reamed mortise must match the inclusive angle of the tapered tenon.) Wider inclusive angles won't hold the tapered tenon as well.

Tenon Formers

For durable post-and-rung chairs, you make tenons from fully dry wood that fit extremely tightly into their bored mortises. I try to make tenons 1/100 inch oversize, so they must be pounded in or pulled with clamps into their matching mortises. For sizing, I use test holes in dry hardwood and dial calipers that measure tenon dimensions in thousandths of an inch.

I like and use a variety of tools and methods for making cylindrical and tapered tenons. In the ladder-back chair project (Chapter 6), for instance, the six side-panel rungs are tenoned using a spokeshave, then sanded to size; the front and back rung tenons are made with a tenon maker designed by Brian Boggs. The tenons in the stick Windsor project (Chapter 8) are formed with a tenon former and a tapering plane, while the bow-back Windsor project (Chapter 9) uses leg and stretcher tenons made on a lathe and spindle tenons made with a tenon cutter, or simply shaved and sanded. (For a photograph of tenon-forming tools, see the sidebar "Alternate Tenon-Making Tools and Methods" in Chapter 6.)

Making a Tapering Plane

Shop-made tapering plane—a rounder for making tapered tenons

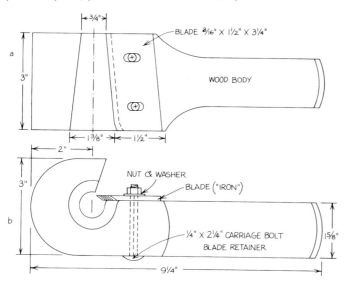

You can make rounders for cutting tapered tenons in any dimensions. The plans here are for a large tapering plane used to cut tapered tenons for Windsor chair legs. The tapered hole must match an available reamer. This plane can also be used to make cylindrical tenons whose diameter matches the small end of the cutter. Some adjustment in sizing is possible.

The wooden tapering plane shown here is made from a dry hickory block 3 by 3 by 9-1/4 inches. Elm, beech, and rock maple are also ideal. Square up the block, then bore a pilot hole for the tapered hole. (Drill across the growth rings if possible.) Ream the hole to desired dimensions. Saw the flat area that accepts the blade and the escape for the shavings. Don't shape the handle section until all the working parts are finished.

Make the blade from preannealed 01 tool steel, available in various sizes from machinist's supply houses. This steel can be hacksawed, filed, and drilled as a cold material. Note the slight curve at the end of the blade bevel that goes over the entry end of the plane (a).

To harden the blade, heat it red hot in a forge or with a gas welder. (The steel will lose magnetism at the exact correct temperature.) Quench in vegetable oil. Temper by "soaking" in an oven at 375 to 400 degrees for thirty minutes.

Bore 1/4-inch holes for the carriage bolt blade retainers (b). Test the cutter. You may have to modify the blade bevel or the exact height of the blade. (If necessary, the blade can be raised with paper shims.)

Shape the handle to your own satisfaction.

Tenon formers: a, dowel pointer; b, A.A. Woods hollow auger; c, Boggs tenon former; d, shop-made tapering plane; e, commercial production tenon cutter

A tenon former that's not used in these projects but that you might find useful is the hollow auger. Tuning up one of these old tools can be challenging, but some cut nicely. To use one, you need to locate a boring bit that is properly sized for the tenons made by the hollow auger. (We're considering increments of much less than 1/100 inch here.) Antique A. A. Woods hollow augers are adjustable, with a continually variable diameter, plus other features for fine-tuning the cut.

You can make your own tenon former or tapering plane from a wooden block and a spokeshave or plane blade (see the sidebar "Making a Tapering Plane" in this chapter). Both tools are sometimes called "rounders." Rounders can have a set diameter for making cylindrical tenons, or the blade can be skewed for making conical, tapered tenons. The rounder is rotated while the wood being shaped into a tenon is held in a vise.

You can also buy commercially manufactured tenon cutters. Although designed for use with a drill press, these can also

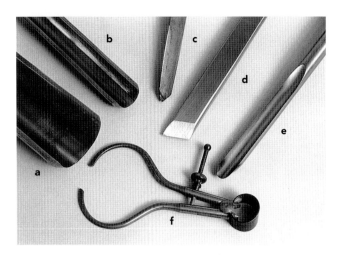

Basic chairmaker's turning tools: a, *2-inch roughing gouge;* b, *1-inch roughing gouge;* c, *1/8-inch parting tool, ground from an old file;* d, *skew chisel;* e, *5/8-inch spindle gouge (with ladyfinger grind);* f, *small pair of outside calipers*

Making a Scratch Beading Tool

You'll use this simple scratch beading tool to make decorative beads (incised grooves) along the front edge of D-section Windsor bows. Usually, two beads are cut in the bow front, each spaced about 3/16 inch in from the bow corners.

Shop-made scratch beader

The body of the beader is made from a single piece of close-grained hardwood, as shown in the figure. The easiest way to make the slot for the blade is to saw a kerf along the full length of the upper part of the blank. Then insert wooden shims, of a thickness to match the blade, at both ends of the kerf.

Make the blade from an old plane iron or any other flat steel stock that is about 3/32 inch thick. The bead is shaped with files. The edges of the bead must be squared to cut well. I angled the edges in slightly toward the back, which improves the cutting in one direction but precludes using the tool in both directions. Hardening and tempering isn't necessary.

Secure the blade in position with two 3/16-inch machine bolts, nuts, and flat washers.

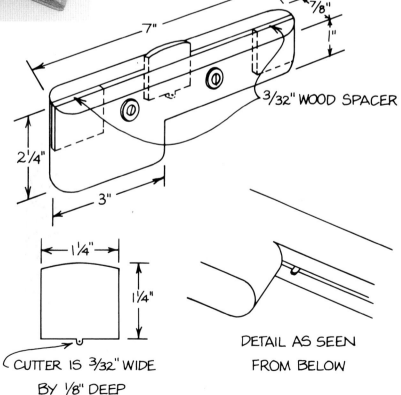

7"

7/8"

1"

3/32" WOOD SPACER

2 1/4"

3"

1 1/4"

1 1/4"

CUTTER IS 3/32" WIDE BY 1/8" DEEP

DETAIL AS SEEN FROM BELOW

be used with a hand-held electric drill or a bit brace. Tenon formers are available in 1/8-inch-diameter increments from 3/8 to 1 inch.

Most tenon formers require a slight chamfer (groove or bevel) at the tenon ends in order to get the cutter started. This chamfer can be formed with a dowel pointer turned with a bit brace, or it can be whittled or filed.

TOOLS FOR TURNING

Lathes

In chairmaking, work done on a lathe is referred to as *spindle turning*. For green-wood chairmakers, the lathe can be the heart of the shop, can be used selectively, or can be no part of the shop at all. The tutorial Windsor and other project chairs can be made without any lathe work. Or you may choose to use a lathe more than I do, turning parts that I prefer to shave. It's a matter of preference.

For chairmaking, you don't need an expensive lathe, and you may choose to use a shop-made spring-pole lathe (see Chapter 21). A basic electric lathe, like the old ones made by Delta and Record for use in home shops, is well suited for most spindle turning. Avoid the very cheapest imported lathes; they weigh too little and will vibrate excessively.

For Windsor turnings I like a lathe tool rest at least 22 inches long, a length that saves a lot of time moving the tool rest along the bed. You can make one from hardwood lumber and a strip of steel available at any hardware store.

Lathe Tools

Chairmaking calls for only a few turning tools. I like the hefty ones made from high-speed steel. A basic set includes four: A 1-1/4- to 2-inch roughing gouge for rounding turning blanks and shaping simple turnings, a 1/2-inch spindle gouge for shaping more ornate bends and coves, a 1-inch skew chisel to cut nodes on bamboo turnings and to make final cuts on parts of baluster turnings, and a 1/8-inch-wide parting tool to cut grooves into turned cylinders.

You'll need several outside calipers so that you can measure different diameters while turning a set of legs and stretchers. You'll also need a full-face shield that should be used during initial rounding of parts.

OTHER TOOLS FOR GREEN-WOOD CHAIRMAKING

I'll include a basic selection of saws and measuring tools here and discuss other common tools as they are called for in the tutorial chapters.

Saws

For many light sawing tasks I often use a handsaw that combines Japanese-style saw teeth with a Western panel-saw blade.

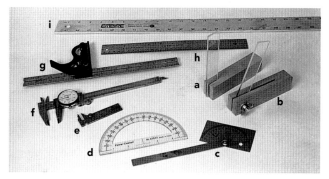

Measuring tools: a, *shop-made try square;* b, *shop-made sliding bevel gauge;* c, *mechanic's protractor;* d, *inexpensive drafting protractor;* e, *inside-outside calipers that measure in units of 1/32 inch;* f, *dial-gauge inside-outside calipers that measure in units of .001 inch;* g, *combination square;* h, *12-inch ruler;* i, *48-inch aluminum ruler*

For rough cutoff work, it's quick and very useful. Finding a good-quality dovetail or back saw—a small saw with a reinforced back and at least twelve teeth per inch—is not easy; consider using a Japanese dozuki saw as an alternative.

You can make your own turning saw, a traditional bow saw with rotating end pieces that you can use to saw the outline of Windsor seat planks (see the sidebar "Making a Turning Saw"). A basic 14-inch band saw is very useful (although not essential) for sawing the outline of Windsor seats and all manner of cut-off work. I also use it to resaw rivings when splitting isn't fully predictable.

Measuring and Layout Tools

For chairmaking measurements, I find good-quality tools are usually good enough. I see no advantage in getting the finest or fanciest measuring tools.

A 6-foot tape or folding rule with extender is useful for measuring between legs, such as for Windsor stretchers. I like flexible, stainless-steel, 6- and 12-inch rulers with cork backing, which are available at office-supply stores—1/16-inch increments are small enough. I prefer rulers that start at the end, rather than those that start 1/4-inch or so in from the ends. I also use a 2-inch-wide, 24-inch aluminum ruler. A combination square combines a 12-inch steel ruler with a sliding square and miter gauge.

The adjustable shop-made bevel gauge used in the tutorial stick Windsor project (Chapter 8) is in some ways superior to the ones for sale. Shop-made bevel gauges have at least three advantages: (1) The wooden base is about 50 percent wider than those on commercial bevel gauges, which makes it easy to balance and keeps it from tipping over; (2) the adjustable arm is low enough to place underneath a bit brace without getting knocked over; and (3) its translucent plastic arm allows you to align it with the center of the part you're gauging it against. A carpenter's framing square, 18 by 24 inches, is useful for Windsors. (Avoid professional builders' framing squares with scales in 1/10- and 1/12-inch increments, which can cause slipups unless you're very familiar with them.)

Making a Turning Saw

Once you start using a band saw, it's easy to forget how useful and efficient a homemade turning saw can be. Used for centuries, this variant of the bow saw can be custom made for a variety of sawing chores. Unlike an ordinary bow saw, it has pivoting knobs on both ends of the frame that allow you to rotate the blade to any angle. You can then tilt the frame to one side so that you can saw deep cuts and most types of curves.

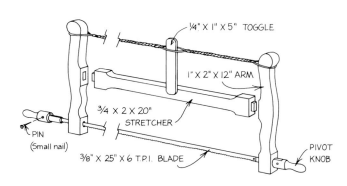

Shop-made bow saw, with knobs for rotating the blade

You can make the arms for the frame from any strong, air-dried hardwood. The pivoting knobs are generally turned on a lathe, but they could be rectangular—these knobs are for rotating the blade only, not for handles when you saw. Blades are made from standard band-saw stock, readily available. If you expect to cut out Windsor seats with your turning saw, I recommend 3/8-inch-wide blade stock, with six teeth per inch.

The turning saw in the figure uses two arms shaped from 1-by-2-by-12-inch stock; at the bottom of the arms, holes 1/2 inch in diameter house the pivoting knobs. The 1/2- by-1-inch rectangular mortises for the stretcher tenons are only 1/2 inch deep. Shape the arms so that they are comfortable to hold.

Make the stretcher from a 3/4-by-2-by-20-inch piece of any straight-grained wood. Hardwood is not necessary, and you can have a lighter weight tool if you use a softwood, such as spruce.

The pivoting knobs have a lengthwise slit for the saw blade and a small hole that houses a cross pin to secure the blade in place. The cross pins are small box nails cut to length.

Since a frame saw cuts on a pull stroke, the blade must be tensioned. My saw blade is tightened with several winds of linen cord, but any stout cord will work. Make the toggle from a piece of scrap hardwood.

Band-saw blade stock can be cut to length with ordinary tin snips. Since band-saw blades are hardened, you will have to anneal (soften) the ends of the blades to drill holes for the cross pins. Annealing is a simple process: Heat the blade ends with a propane torch or over a kitchen gas stove until the ends become red hot. Then set the blade ends aside to cool slowly (do not quench). Use a center punch to mark a dimple at each end of the blade for the cross-pin holes. The distance between end dimples must be based on the finished length of the stretcher, two arm widths, and the location of the cross pins on the pivoting knobs. Drill 3/32-inch holes at the dimples for the cross pins.

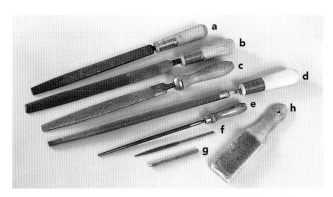

Rasps and files: a, *10-inch flat bastard file;* b, *12-inch half-round file;* c, *10-inch hand-cut pattern-maker's rasp;* d, *5/8-by-14-inch rat-tail file;* e, *5/16-by-8-inch rat-tail file;* f, *riffler;* g, *broken rat-tail file for use with electric drill;* h, *file card.*

To measure in hundredths or thousandths, you can use a 6-inch dial gauge, much easier to read than vernier gauges or micrometers. Most dial gauges can also measure the depth of a hole.

Finally, add an inexpensive colored plastic protractor (less likely to get lost than the clear plastic); an orange plastic drafting triangle, 30 to 60 degrees; a 9 mm mechanical pencil, with "hb" lead (no more pencil sharpening!); an awl for marking centers and other tasks; a sturdy compass for scribing the bottom of chair legs (get one that can hold an extended pencil); and straight-leg dividers.

A scale or moisture meter, while not essential, comes in handy for determining the moisture content of rungs and other chair parts. I use an inexpensive digital scale that measures in 2-gram and 1/10-ounce increments.

Abrasives and Finishing Tools

I try to keep sanding and finishing as simple as possible. Even though sharp-edged tools create very smooth wood surfaces, some scraping and sanding seems inevitable. A 5-inch-diameter random- orbit sander, while not useful with post-and-rung chairs, works well on Windsor seats. (I'll discuss finishes, paints, and other finishing supplies in the tutorials.)

My favorite flat scraper is four-sided, with a curve on one long side. A supply of 80-, 120-, and 220-grit sheets of sandpaper will take care of most sanding chores. I find that cloth-backed sandpaper lasts longer and has better abrasion.

I find half-round rasps very useful; the best are called pattern-maker's rasps. Good ones are expensive but will last for years if you prevent them from contacting other rasps and files during storage. Be sure to put a handle on any tanged rasp or file. Bastard-cut half-round machinist's files are good for detailing tenons. Rat-tail rasps are often useful in fitting Windsor spindles; the most useful sizes are 5/16, 3/8, and 1/2 inch.

You'll need on hand supplies of disposable gloves for finishes and if you use polyurethane glue; clean white rags torn into pieces about 5 by 10 inches; 1-1/2-inch, good-quality sash brushes for Windsors (saw off the handle to a total length of about 8 inches).

I recommend wearing a dust mask for sanding and when you're using some finishing materials. If you're particularly sensitive to dust or fumes you should consider buying an air helmet, which has a high-quality filter and a small pump that supplies continuous clean air behind a full-face shield attached to a plastic hard hat. You'll also need safety glasses for splitting, when striking steel against steel, and when working at a band saw or other power tool.

I know that novice chairmakers may find this list rather long and somewhat daunting. Finding good tool suppliers may be a challenge, and the expense is considerable. One solution is to begin by taking a course or workshop where specialty tools are supplied. When you do buy tools, I recommend that you buy good ones; cheap substitutes are generally disappointing.

Making a Chairmaker's Bevel Gauge

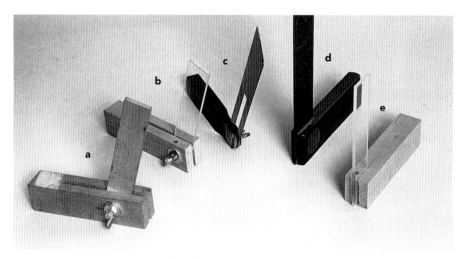

Bevel gauges and try-squares: a, b, and e are shop-made versions with superior stability.

Standard sliding bevel gauges have several faults that make them less than ideal for chairmaking, problems you can avoid by making your own bevel gauge. Make the base and arm from any dry hardwood. I used maple and made the base stock and slot for the arm with a table saw.

The base is 1 inch wide, 1-1/4 inches high, and 4-3/4 inches long. The arm is 3/16 inch thick, 1 inch wide, and 5-3/4 inches long. The fastener is a 5/16-by-1-1/2-inch carriage bolt, combined with a flat washer and a wing nut. I offset it from the center of the base to increase end grain beyond the hole in the arm. (An improved version of the bevel gauge employs a translucent plastic arm, especially useful when gauging turnings or tapered chair parts that don't have parallel sides.)

Make two bevel gauges, for simultaneous use with front and side angles. You can also make a nicely balanced try square following the same specifications.

Making a Spindle Scraper

Shop-made spindle scraper

No matter how carefully you finish a spindle with a spokeshave, you'll find yourself creating narrow, flat facets. The quickest way to round a spokeshaved spindle is to use a scraper made especially for the purpose.

Square up a 9- to 12-inch block of dry hardwood 1-1/8 inches on each side. To shape the handles, turn the block on a lathe or whittle and rasp them to shape. Saw and chisel a housing across the center for the removable blade clamp and shaving escape. Make the blade clamp from another piece of hardwood. Shape the scrapings escape as shown. Drill and countersink holes for the two 1/4-by-1-inch machine screws that secure the blade clamp to the main body section. Countersink housings for the 1/4-inch nuts.

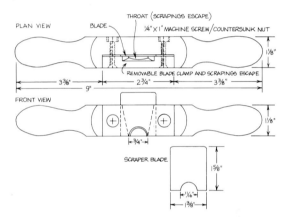

Shape the concave, 3/4-inch diameter half-circle cutout on the bottom of the scraper with a large, rat-tail rasp.

Hacksaw the scraper blade from an abandoned handsaw. Form the 11/16-inch- diameter cutout with a round file. Put a burr on the edge by burnishing at an angle with a hard rod, such as the shank of a screwdriver.

CHAPTER 3

Sharpening Your Tools

Sharpening a 5/8-inch powerbore bit with an auger bit file. Use the file only on the underside of the cutter and the inside of the side nicker.

A sharp tool is something like a fine racing horse—it promises great performance, but taking care of it and allotting time for training come with the territory. In spite of the old saw that "a sharp tool is a safe tool," its very sharpness makes a sharp tool not only cut wood more easily and efficiently than a dull one, but also far more dangerous. When using sharp tools, you need to be very careful to protect both yourself and their delicate edges.

One reason many woodworkers gravitate toward power tools is that they have never had the satisfaction of using properly sharpened hand tools or of seeing the fine work such tools produce. Also, the selection of tools and abrasives available for grinding and honing a fine edge can be confusing at best, daunting at worst. During the years that I've been working green wood, I've had the good fortune to learn about sharpening from several woodworkers who maintain and use extremely sharp tools. In this chapter I'll pass that knowledge along to you, explain several concepts about sharpening, and then get to the specifics of sharpening some of the specialized tools used by chairmakers.

Sharpening is a three-step process: (1) Developing the correct geometry for the type of tool, usually by grinding or otherwise shaping; (2) sharpening the edge, often referred to as honing, usually with bench stones; and (3) polishing, which may include buffing.

CUTTING-EDGE GEOMETRY

Through experience, I've come to agree with master wood-carver, teacher, and turner Wille Sundqvist that "the bevel is more important than the edge." What does this mean? No matter how sharp a tool's edge, it will fail you if its geometry is inappropriate for the tool or for the task you're asking it to do. For example, a 90-degree edge can be made very sharp, but it won't slice wood. Or the bevel of a sharp edge might be slightly convex (or *dubbed*), so that you have to lift the tool so high to cut with it that it's inefficient.

The first thing to remember is that a cutting edge has two sides—it is a juncture of two intersecting planes. In geometry, such a juncture is called an *arris*. A tool's edge may be formed by the junction of a single bevel and the back (flat) side of a blade (as in plane blades and chisels) or by the junction of two bevels (as in knives and most axes) (see fig. 3.1).

An edge's sharpness is only as good as the surface of the rougher of the two sides at the arris. If you look at a tool edge through a 10-power hand lens, you will see minute scratches on both planes and tiny serrations at the arris. When you hone and polish a tool, the surfaces and the arris grow smoother. A sharp edge in tool steel has a highly polished surface on both sides of the arris.

For most cutting tasks, a low *included angle*—the angle at the arris—cuts best, but a wider angle holds up better. The optimum included angle for woodworking tools varies from about 20 to as much as 45 degrees for certain turning tools. For the hardwoods used to make chairs, I sharpen most hand tools at an included angle of 25 to 35 degrees. In addition to a tool's cutting geometry, the appropriate included angle is determined by the type of steel the tool is made of, the steel's hardness at the edge, the hardness of the wood to be worked, and personal woodworking habits.

Sharpening, especially honing, is an ongoing process. For good work you will need to do touch-up sharpening periodically.

Hollow-Ground Bevels

Often to sharpen a tool you'll want to make the bevel either absolutely flat or slightly concave (slightly *hollow ground*, that is, ground until a hollow appears along the center of a bevel). It's much easier to create a slightly rounded, convex (rolled) surface than a flat one (see fig. 3.2).

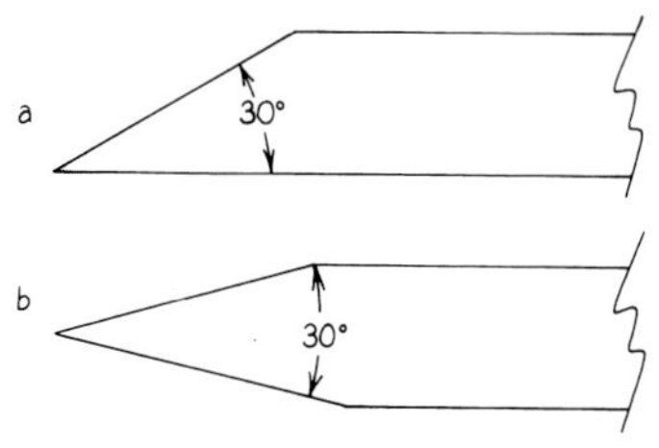

For a hollow-ground bevel, a grinding wheel is used for shaping; the result is a "heel and toe" configured bevel (see fig. 3.3a). The hollow reduces the bevel surface area to be honed and polished, which means faster honing. During honing on a flat stone, you can register the honing angle by clicking against the heel and toe of the bevel. This helps to prevent rocking, which will either result in a rounded, convex bevel or cause you to lose control of the bevel angle.

One important point to remember when hollow grinding is to leave very narrow bevel flats at the heel and toe. The *too-narrow* included angle of a full-hollow grind (see fig. 3.3b) can be corrected by honing either a microbevel or new heel and toe flats that correspond to the desired angle. A full-hollow grind made with a high-speed bench grinder also increases the risk of overheating at the edge, resulting in a loss of temper.

To strengthen a full-hollow grind by honing a microbevel, you readjust the honing angle, forming a narrow band just behind the cutting edge (fig. 3.3c). Advocates of microbevels point out that resharpening is faster than honing the full bevel and that the larger bevel angle is stronger than the original ground angle. However, I generally avoid microbevels; to speed up honing I prefer a slight hollow grind along the bevel; that way I'm sure to maintain the cutting angle I want. Particularly for the chairmaking tools that you'll use with the bevel side down, where the bevel acts as a guide or register for the cutting action, a microbevel is too narrow to be effective. For instance, a microbevel makes a drawknife useless for bevel-down shaving. Microbevels are fine on plane blades and chisels that are used exclusively bevel side up, as long as the included cutting angle is low enough.

Rolled Bevels

Rolling or dubbing either side of an edge generally increases the included angle. With drawknives and inshaves a small amount of rolling or dubbing is not only acceptable, but actually desirable in order to control depth of cut. Unlike a plane or spokeshave, a drawknife has no mechanical "fence" to control tool depth. You control the depth of your cut by making frequent, subtle adjustments in tool angle as the cut progresses. A drawknife used bevel up to shave hardwood will invariably have some rounding across the back (flat) side of the blade. Similarly, a drawknife used bevel down on hardwood requires some rounding across the bevel. (When shaving softwood, a drawknife will often work fine shaving bevel up with a very flat back side on the blade; softwoods compress somewhat during a cut.) The danger in forming a roll across either side of a drawknife blade is that the included cutting angle (at the edge) quickly increases, especially if both sides are rolled.

To judge the included angle of a dubbed bevel on any tool, but particularly a drawknife, you need to take a very close look at the bevel configuration. If the dubbing extends

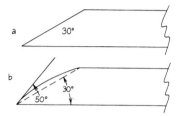

FIG. 3.1. Cutting-edge geometry for typical hand tools— an included angle of 30 degrees is common: *a*, single bevel, as in chisel, drawknife, and plane blades; *b*, double bevel, as in knife and axe blades

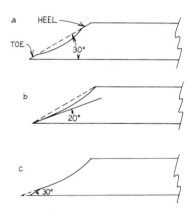

FIG. 3.2. A, perfect example of conventional bevel with 30 degree included angle; *b*, rolled bevel resulting in a 50-degree included angle at the cutting edge

FIG. 3.3. A, Hollow grind centered on a 30-degree bevel; *b*, hollow grind extending from bevel toe to heel, resulting in a weak 20-degree included angle; *c*, 30-degree microbevel ground at the edge of a 20-degree hollow grind

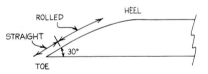

FIG. 3.4. Suggested drawknife bevel geometry—the bevel is rolled above the 30- degree included cutting angle.

from cutting edge to heel, it becomes very difficult to determine the true included angle. But if dubbing begins slightly beyond the cutting edge and then extends back to the heel, you can maintain the desired included angle and use the dubbed section of the bevel for controlling the cut (fig. 3.4).

With spindle-turning gouges, bevels should be fully hollow ground so that the bevel actually rubs against the turned wood. This rubbing bevel action allows you to control the tool, which is cutting a cylindrical surface.

Besides bevel geometry, factors that come into play in evaluating cutting effectiveness are the angle of blade to wood (the actual cutting angle), the direction the blade moves in, and the width of a tool's throat (the opening in front of the protruding blade). When a blade is held at an angle to the path of the cut—called *skewing*—the effective cutting angle

A Prairie slow-speed water grindstone; the purchaser mounts a 1,725 rpm motor to the jack shafts. The jigs are for sharpening plane/chisel blades and knives.

is lower than the included angle measured perpendicular to the edge. This effect of skewing is easy to understand if you compare a road that goes straight up a hill to a road that approaches a hill at an angle. By skewing, a 40-degree included angle may actually cut at 30 degrees or less. A lower cutting angle almost always makes a finer, smoother cut. I often recommend skewing when a cut is difficult.

Moving the blade sideways as the cut progresses—*slicing*—has a similar effect. I can press a very sharp knife edge directly against my finger without getting cut. If I pull the knife slightly sideways, the edge will slice through my flesh. If you use slicing, skewing, or both with a well-sharpened tool, you can make a glassy smooth cut on many highly figured hardwoods.

Finally, a narrow throat opening on a plane or spokeshave always improves the quality of a cut and results in a smoother surface.

EQUIPMENT FOR SHARPENING

Sharpening equipment can be categorized into the three sharpening stages: (1) Shaping and grinding implements, which determine the geometry of the edge and blade, include grinders, belt sanders, files, and the coarsest hand-held stones; (2) honing tools, with which sharpening actually begins, which include bench stones, shaped slips, and the finer-grit wheels; and (3) polishing stones and compounds, used on buffing wheels, strops, or some other matrix. Choosing what equipment to buy or use can be confusing; personal preference, budget, and availability are important considerations.

Motor-Powered Wet Grinders

Motor-powered slow-speed grinders that run in a water bath are safer and easier to use than high-speed conven-

tional bench grinders. Since they produce no sparks, you don't have to worry about fire risk or shielding your eyes. Unlike the old water-lubricated grinding wheels made from quarried sandstone, which cut slowly and might freeze and crack when saturated, vitrified aluminum-oxide water wheels are fast cutting. Most are designed to rotate between 90 and 120 rpm. (Constant immersion will soften these wheels; they should be removed from the water when not in use.)

A very basic wet grinder, such as the Prairie, uses a quick-cutting vitrified wheel that needs careful truing with a diamond dresser or carbide stick before it can be used. Since the axles are mounted in a cast-aluminum housing without bearings, you must oil the axles before each grinding session. This grinder can be purchased with a factory-mounted motor or with jack-shaft speed-reduction pulleys for a purchaser-installed motor. (The motor should be mounted so that the wheel turns away from the tool rest—if it's set up to turn toward the tool rest, a copious amount of water will ride over the wheel, over the tool being ground, and onto the floor. Grinding with the wheel turning away from the tool rest is disconcerting at first, but it's not difficult to learn.)

I also use a higher-quality wet grinder made for serious tool sharpening, such as the Swedish Tormek. This unit offers both a 10-inch grinding wheel and a removable stropping wheel mounted on the other side of the housing. In contrast to the three o'clock grinding position of most water and high-speed grinders, the adjustable tool rest is positioned so that you grind almost at the top of the wheel. This twelve-o'clock grinding position causes water to flow back into the trough and makes the unit more steady to operate. This grinder requires a low supporting workbench. A wide range of sharpening jigs is available, including a diamond truing tool and a jig for planer and jointer blades that works perfectly for grinding flat, straight drawknives.

Most Japanese wet grinders grind on the side of a horizontal wheel, available in various grits and made with materials similar to Japanese water stones. Working on the side of the wheel, however, makes hollow grinding impossible. These grinders come with an attachment for grinding wide planer and jointer blades. They do a fine job once all the adjustments are correctly set.

Conventional Bench Grinders

Conventional bench grinders that operate at 3,450 rpm work well for many grinding tasks. But bench grinders are tricky to use; they make it very easy to overheat a tool edge, causing loss of temper (indicated when the tool edge suddenly turns blue). Bench grinders also produce copious sparks, which can cause eye injury, damage eyeglasses, or start a fire. The tool rests that come with most bench grinders are flimsy and difficult to adjust.

I'm comfortable using a bench grinder to shape plane and chisel blades, which are relatively narrow and flat. But I have never been able to get consistently ground bevels on gouge, axe, or adze blades with a high-speed grinder. Drawknife blades present a particular problem, due to their length and their handles, which invariably bump into the grinder's motor housing. Carving knives with blades that curve up toward the tip (such as Swedish "sloyd" knives) are among the most difficult tools to grind with a bench grinder. However, if you are unusually skillful, a bench grinder may still be the most versatile tool to use for shaping the bevels of many hand tools.

Should you elect to use a bench grinder, I recommend some adaptations. White and pink crystalon wheels cut cooler than the standard grey silicon carbide wheels that come with bench grinders. Crystalon wheels wear quickly, constantly exposing new abrasive particles. For grinding tools, use a 80- or 120-grit wheel. (Finer-grit wheels tend to glaze with metal fragments and are more likely to overheat the tool being ground.) You can replace the flimsy tool rest that comes with home-shop bench grinders with a bench-mounted, shop-made tool rest, or an aftermarket tool rest, which is easy to set up at various angles to the wheel.

When you use a bench grinder, you must cool the edge being ground by frequent dipping in water or with a continuous spray. A hand-held, trigger spray bottle works fine if you have an assistant to operate it; machinist's cooling-mist devices are operated with an air compressor.

Safety note: Be sure to use approved eye protection when working with a bench grinder. Grinder guards and safety shields should always be in place.

Hand-Cranked Grinders

An alternative to the high-speed bench grinder is a wheel you turn with a hand crank. Some woodworkers rig up a hand-cranked grinder to a shop-made tool rest, a combination that offers precise grinding, if you can crank with one hand and smoothly move a plane blade or chisel across the tool rest with the other. The gearing on the best hand-cranked grinders turns the wheel at an impressive 2,000 rpm. However, you must maintain a very light grinding touch against the wheel, since torque at that speed is very limited.

Another type of hand-cranked grinder uses direct drive, without any gearing. These are slow-speed wet grinders, which offer you adequate torque but limited wheel speed, resulting in much slower grinding. At least one manufacturer offers a jack shaft and pulley kit, so that the hand-cranked unit can be converted for use with an electric motor.

Sanders

You can also shape tools with motorized sanders. Heat buildup is considerably less than with a bench grinder, more than with a water wheel. You can use belt sanders to flatten the back sides of blades, and with some belt sanders you can create a hollow grind by sanding where the belt runs around the wheels. Bench- and floor- mounted belt

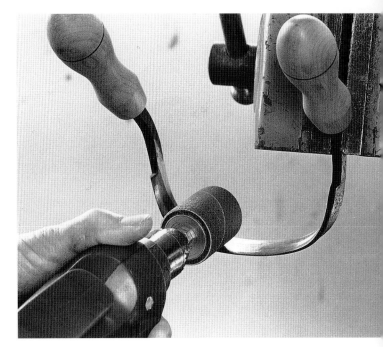

Grinding an inshave with a small drum sander mounted to an electric drill

sanders often have adjustable tool supports. For occasional use, you can clamp a hand-held belt sander upside down on a workbench. **Safety note: You must orient belt sanders so that the belt runs away from the cutting edge of the tool; if you sand toward the tool, the edge could catch in the belt, causing a tear and loss of control of the tool.**

Especially for shaping curved edges, I make extensive use of small drum sanders that consist of a sanding sleeve, rubber cylinder, and 1/4-inch shaft. These can be mounted to an ordinary electric-drill chuck. Dusting talcum powder on the rubber drum helps with fitting on the preformed sanding sleeves. (I've found the drums designed for use with ordinary sandpaper disappointing.)

It's easy to see why drum sanders work well on the inside of a curve, such as the horseshoe-shaped blade of an inshave or adze. But I also drum sand the exterior of curved blades. Because the sander itself is curved, I can see under the drum, where the sanding is taking place.

Bench Stones

When steel is soft, you can make good progress using an ordinary file. However, most blade tools are tempered to a hardness that makes filing ineffective. Shaping with coarse sharpening stones is realistic when there's not much metal to remove. The fastest-cutting abrasives are coarse- and medium-grit synthetic diamond stones, which are definitely superior to the coarse crystalline oil stones and water stones previously used. I consider diamond stones a good value, even though they eventually break down in use (since they are a surface coating applied to a steel or plastic matrix, their life span is shorter than that of other abrasives).

Honing stones and accessories: a, *cone-shaped waterstone;* b, *shop-made extension for holding spokeshave blades;* c, *monocrystaline diamond hone;* d, *shop-made base to secure honing stones;* e, *Japanese waterstone;* f, *1-1/2-by-2-inch sleeve sander;* g, *slip-shaped waterstone*

Because polishing-grade water stones are considerably softer than the coarse- and medium-grit stones, they require special care; a sharpened tool edge can unexpectedly plow into the stone and gouge a trough in the surface. I find special paste nagura stones helpful for keeping the surface of polishing stones in good condition.

With use, any bench stone tends to dish, forming a low area in the middle. Water stones dish very quickly. For sharpening plane and chisel blades, their surface must be flattened, a process that usually takes just a few minutes. To do this, you need wet-dry sandpaper and a piece of plate glass about 6 by 12 inches and at least 3/8 inch thick. Sprinkle water on the glass and over the sandpaper surface. Then rub the stone back and forth over the sandpaper until it is flat. Rinse the resultant slurry off the stone before using it. I use 120-mesh wet-dry paper to flatten 800- to 1,200-mesh stones, and 180- or 220-mesh paper for 4,000- to 8,000-mesh stones. Wet-dry sandpaper is available at stores that sell paint and body-repair supplies for cars, and in most good hardware stores.

A set of bench stones is a substantial investment, so you want to know what you're buying. For general use, I prefer 2-by-8-inch stones, which work well for most tools. An alternative is a combination 1,000/6,000 water stone. For curved-edge tools, such as gouges and inshaves, I often use water-stone slips and cones.

The two basic types of synthetic diamond stones use monocrystalline diamonds and the less expensive polycrystalline diamonds. Polycrystalline diamond stones go through a break-in period. Initial sharpening is extremely aggressive, but diamond particles will fracture from the surface, leaving a slower-cutting but still impressive honing tool. Monocrystalline diamonds outlast their less-expensive competitors and ultimately represent a better value. The finest-grit diamond stones are rated at 1,200 mesh.

EQUIPMENT FOR HONING AND POLISHING

Since the early 1980s, synthetic Japanese water stones have been the choice of most woodworkers who take sharpening seriously. These products work much faster than the natural stones lubricated with light oil Western woodworkers have used. (Although quarried Japanese water stones are available, they tend to be expensive, and I'm not convinced that they offer advantages.) Using Japanese water stones is messy, but cleanup with water is quick and easy, and the results make the extra trouble worthwhile.

Common Japanese water stones are available in three grit ranges. The coarsest, 180- 250 mesh, are intended for shaping work. These wear down quickly, and I've been disappointed with their performance. Medium-grit water stones, 800-1,200 mesh, work very effectively and can be kept in a water bath unless freezing temperatures threaten, which will result in cracking. Fine-grit polishing water stones, 4,000-8,000 mesh, are both more expensive and more effective.

Basic Selection of Bench Stones

Shaping	2-by-8-inch coarse monocrystalline diamond	220 or 325 mesh
Honing	2-by-8-inch medium monocrystalline diamond or Japanese water stone	800-1,200 mesh
	2-by-4-inch Japanese water slip stone	1,000 mesh
Polishing	2-by-8-inch Japanese water stone	4,000-8,000 mesh
	2-by-4-inch Japanese water slip stone	4,000 or 6,000 mesh

Strops and Buffers

Besides the fine-grit Japanese polishing stones, you can also use strops, buffing wheels, and lapping compounds for polishing, the final step in sharpening.

Polishing a curved edge on a flat stone is inefficient because there is minimal point of contact with the abrasive. Strops and buffing wheels have some give to their surface, which makes them particularly useful for polishing tools with curved or bowed edges. Usually made of leather or very coarse cloth, strops can be stretched end to end across an I-shaped wooden frame or over a wheel. Although hard felt buffing wheels cost several times more than cloth wheels, they are superior for precision buffing; cloth buffing wheels are too soft for effective control of the buffing action. With both strops and wheels, you use a fine, abrasive compound packaged in a stick or tube. White aluminum oxide, sometimes labeled stainless-steel buffing compound, works fine for polishing steel tools.

You can also polish specially shaped tools, such as gouges, using a wooden matrix as a buffer and applying the same compounds used on buffing wheels and strops.

An ordinary lathe will power wooden disk-and-spindle buffers. Del Stubbs, well known as a turner, is also an accomplished toolmaker who uses a round softwood disk, with various configurations turned on the perimeter, for polishing his carving and turning tools. For larger curved tools, you can turn a tapered softwood spindle mounted between centers into an effective buffer.

Approach all buffing with caution. Polishing can occur so fast, especially at the edge, that you may find you've rounded a carefully shaped bevel before you know it.

Safety note: Buffing into an edge is extremely dangerous. The slightest inaccuracy in tool position can cause a catch, throwing a very sharp tool out of control. Always buff with the wheel turning away from the edge. If a buffing wheel is mounted to a conventional forward-turning grinder, buff by holding the tool below the three o'clock position, with the tool edge directed down toward the bench surface.

Diamond Slurry

Polycrystalline diamond slurry compounds in an oil base may be the ultimate in polishing abrasives; 5-micron diamond slurry will quickly bring a well-honed surface to a high polish. Using diamond slurry requires an appropriately shaped matrix, which can be iron, wood, or a proprietary product. You transfer a small dab of slurry to the matrix, thin it with an oily solvent, and polish as with any other honing compound. The problem that I've had with diamond slurries has been quick wear-down of the matrix plate. But their polishing speed is awe inspiring.

SHARPENING ACCESSORIES

If you intend to do any serious tool sharpening, you'll need a few accessories at your sharpening bench. I use a wooden block with a cutout center section as a shop-made holder to secure stones so that they don't scoot about during use. The

Sharpening aids, from left: machinist's bluing, mechanic's protractor, machinist's try square, wide-nib permanent felt marker (substitute for bluing)

holder I use for most of my stones, which are 2 by 8 inches, secures them by a wedge at one end and supports the stones at the ends; an open gap beneath the center section of the stones drains any slurry that otherwise might collect and contaminate the stone or cause it not to seat flat in the holder. For sharpening drawknives, the holder needs to be at least 4 inches high to insure clearance between the drawknife handles and bench surface.

At my sharpening bench I have two vises. I find a generic Chinese machinist's vise very useful for securing odd-shaped tools such as an inshave or the head of an adze; it swivels around its base, and the jaw assembly rotates 360 degrees on its own axis. A standard woodworker's vise, which can be an inexpensive one, secures the wooden stone holder I use with the 2-by-8-inch honing stones and when the jaws of the machinist's vise are too high for comfortable use.

For examining the edge of sharp tools, I recommend a gooisenecked incandescent lamp that produces a bright, point-source light. An inexpensive, 10-power hand lens, a 30-power hand-held microscope, or both, make it possible to really see an edge. To check for flatness, you'll need 6- and 12- inch steel straightedges; they can be inexpensive ones for this level of work. Machinist's bluing and wide felt markers are useful for inking surfaces to be sharpened; honing off the ink allows you to see exactly where sharpening is taking place. I use a steel machinist's square to check 90-degree angles and a stainless-steel mechanic's protractor with a pivoting leg to measure bevel angles. You can buy a bevel-angle notch gauge with notches at 5-degree-angle intervals or you can make your own gauges from plastic or sheet metal to the exact included angles that you use. For honing plane and chisel blades, a honing guide maintains a consistent angle as you hone. (Because I sharpen so many different-shaped tools, I've concentrated on developing freehand sharpening skills, so I don't use a honing guide.)

To keep water stones wet, I use lidded plastic food-storage containers. (Don't allow saturated stones to freeze.) If you use oil stones, you'll need honing oil, which you can mix yourself using one part 30-weight automotive oil and three parts kerosene. Keep rags or paper towels on hand. A sink nearby with mechanic's lanolin hand cleaner will be helpful.

SHARPENING CHISELS

A chisel is an example of an edged tool that combines a flat side (the back) and a bevel side (the face). In making chairs, you'll use chisels to chop slat mortises for the backs of post-and-rung chairs, and to dress spindle wedges on Windsor bows. Plane blades are sharpened exactly like chisel blades.

Grinding the Bevel

Check the included angle of the bevel; 25 to 30 degrees is fine for most uses. Regrind the bevel if necessary. If you decide to create a slight hollow grind in the center of the bevel, which I recommend, be careful not to grind the heel or toe of the bevel—these will be helpful when you're honing the bevel later.

Testing for Sharpness

How do you know when an edge is really sharp? Looking directly at the edge under good light is one of the best methods. Very slight dullness will show up as a slim glimmer on the edge. You should not be able to see the actual edge. The sides of the edge adjacent to the arris should be highly polished. A matte sheen indicates that sharpening could be better.

It's also helpful to examine the edge with a 10-power loupe or a hand-held 30-power microscope, although these limit your field of view, and you may miss a small dull area or microchip.

Although the classic test for sharpness is shaving the hair on one's forearm, the range of hair consistency makes this an inexact test. Another subjective test is to set the sharpened edge across a fingernail and observe how far you can tip the nail toward vertical before the tool slips; this becomes quite a useful gauge after you've done it a few times.

In my opinion the best sharpness test is to try the edge on the same material that you will use the tool on, which is also the best way to check edge geometry. If sharpness and geometry are correct, you should be able to create a glassy smooth surface with each pass of the tool. (You may need to skew or slice on figured hardwood.) Micro-chipouts, which can occur easily when an edge is very sharp, will show up as tiny ridges on the wood surface. Dull areas of the edge create a matte surface on the wood.

Be fussy setting up the grinder's tool rest. If you use a high-speed bench grinder, I recommend an 80-mesh crystalon wheel; with this grinder, you'll need to cool the chisel in water whenever the edge warms to the touch. Be sure the wheel's grinding surface is clean and flat across the width. As you grind, move the chisel sideways across the wheel. Use very light pressure against the wheel.

Conditioning the Back

Before proceeding, be sure that your bench stones are flat. Chisel and plane blades cannot be properly sharpened using dished or concave bench stones.

After grinding the bevel, check the back side of the blade for flatness. Start with a visual check using a straightedge. Flatness should extend at least half an inch behind the edge. A slight, almost imperceptible, hollow behind the edge is permissible, but don't accept any convexity. If necessary, flatten the back using coarse or medium diamond honing stones. (An equivalent oil stone, though much slower cutting, would be a coarse crystalon.) Do not lift or roll the chisel during flattening. You can use machinist's bluing or a wide-tip felt marker to track progress.

Continue until you can feel the formation of a burr, also called a wire edge, when you pass a finger lightly across the edge. The *burr* is a minute band of metal that is actually pushed over to the opposite side of the arris. Do not try to create a heavy burr. Quit when the burr extends the full length of the arris.

Here is where I depart from the procedure used by many woodworkers: I prefer to polish the back side of the blade before honing the bevel side. The idea, which is borrowed from traditional Japanese woodworking, is to prepare the back side to a polished finish just once. From then on, most honing and polishing is done on the bevel side. There are two reasons for this: (1) Every time you hone the back side, you make the blade a little thinner, and thus a little weaker; honing the bevel only reduces the length of the blade; (2) by continuing on the flat side, you reduce the thickness of the attachment point of the burr. Burrs are like scabs; you shouldn't pick them off. The idea is to wear away the burr by continuing with a finer honing stone on one side of the edge.

Once you have a burr, switch to a medium-grit 800- to 1,200-mesh diamond or water stone. Continue rubbing on the flat, back side of the blade. Press the blade quite firmly on the stone. You are transforming the visibly striated surface left by the original, coarse stone into a flat grey surface—you can actually feel the medium stone abrading the surface left by the coarser stone. Learning when to stop honing with the medium-grit stone takes some practice. The feeling becomes smoother when you're done with the medium stone; don't stop until the flat grey color runs right up to the edge.

Polishing the Back

Polish the back side of the blade with a 4000- to 8000-mesh water stone, or a hard black Arkansas stone. You will feel a transition from a smooth surface with obvious friction to one that seems almost greasy. Stop when you see a polished surface across the full width of the edge.

Honing the Bevel

Start honing the bevel with a fine diamond stone, an 800- to 1200-mesh water stone, or a fine India oil stone. Rub the chisel bevel back and forth over the length of the stone. The trick is to maintain the same angle as you rub. This is where a slight hollow grind is useful. The two-point contact of the heel and toe of the hollow grind gives you positive angle registration. And the hollowed-out section makes the process faster, since there is less metal to hone away.

Skewing the chisel bevel at an angle on the stone will make it easier to keep a consistent angle as you rub back and forth.

Use considerable downward pressure for initial honing. (Light pressure drags the process out and increases the likelihood that you'll change the angle and thus round off the bevel.) Continue until you feel a burr across the flat side of the blade.

Polishing the Bevel

Polish the bevel exactly as you polished the flat side. If the steel is fairly hard, the burr will waste itself off as you polish the bevel. If a very faint burr is now perceptible on the flat side of the blade, lightly polish the flat side to remove this burr. If a new burr develops on the bevel side, remove it by polishing the bevel very lightly.

SHARPENING SPOKESHAVES

You sharpen a straight, flat spokeshave blade almost exactly as you sharpen a chisel or plane blade. These tools share the blade geometry of a flat back side, and a single, sometimes hollow-ground, bevel.

Sharpening a spokeshave blade presents two challenges. First, a common spokeshave blade is about 1/2 inch wider than a 2-inch-wide honing stone. Instead of buying wide, expensive stones, skew the blade at an angle of about 30 degrees across the width of a 2-inch stone, which creates a longer contact path across the bevel. This also makes it considerably easier to maintain the correct honing angle when you rub back and forth. Skewing is particularly useful with thin blades that have a narrow bevel.

The second challenge lies in the difficulty of holding the short spokeshave blade securely while rubbing back and forth on the honing stone. An effective spokeshave honing aid suggested by John Alexander is a blade-extension stick. You can make one quickly from a reject rung or spindle about 3/4 inch in diameter and 6 to 8 inches long. Saw a kerf in one end of the stick to hold the spokeshave blade. Bevel one side of that end, so that the stick can be used at a close angle to the honing stone. Drill a hole through the stick to accept a 3/16-inch machine bolt, washer, and a wing nut.

As you follow the same steps used for sharpening a chisel, keep in mind that standard spokeshave blades are quite soft. Use very light pressure during polishing, or you will spend an excessive amount of time flipping the blade from one side to the other to remove the wire edge.

FINE-TUNING SPOKESHAVES

Tuning up a spokeshave can improve its performance greatly, ensuring that it will take much finer shavings, leave a smoother wood surface, and hold a better edge. The procedure is basically the same as tuning a hand plane. The first step is deciding on what style spokeshave body to work with—a standard spokeshave with twin-blade adjustment screws, a spokeshave with a single friction-screw blade adjustment, or one of many older designs which you may already own or purchase used. The adjustment nuts and slots in the blade on a twin-screw spokeshave are generally poorly mated, so making a fine adjustment can be frustrating.

Most original spokeshave blades are too soft to take or hold a fine edge, and so thin they are hard to sharpen and tend to vibrate in use. You probably will want to replace the original spokeshave blade with a thicker (1/8 inch), harder tempered one made from better tool steel. Aftermarket replacement blades are available from some specialty mail-order tool suppliers. You can also make your own blade from flat, preannealed O1 tool steel. Sharpen your new blade following the standard procedure for single-bevel blades.

Your replacement blade is likely to be too thick to fit through the throat of the iron body, but it's also important to keep the throat opening as narrow as possible—no wider than 1/20 inch for fine work. (As the throat opening gets larger, shavings start to lift off the wood in front of the cutting edge of the blade; the shaving is not cut, but split.) Before opening the throat directly, check the sole and the *frog* (the part of the body that supports the blade) of the spokeshave for flatness—flattening these will open the throat to some extent. If necessary, flatten the sole with a file or diamond stone, then shape a slight upwards curve at the leading and trailing edges of the sole. Flatten the frog with a flat mill file. It's important that the blade lie flat, with no wobble. You can open the throat farther by filing along the leading edge of the opening.

If you're tuning a spokeshave with the original blade, the throat opening will be too large. Place a paper shim behind the blade to reduce the effective throat opening. You may need to experiment with different kinds of paper or light cardboard to find the appropriate thickness.

You also need to tune the *chip breaker* (the flat cap that secures the spokeshave iron to the frog), whose lower edge must maintain continuous contact with the upper side of the iron. Use a file to make any necessary corrections. You should also elongate the center screw hole with a round file. Relocate the edge of the chip breaker about 1/16 inch beyond the edge of the blade.

SHARPENING DRAWKNIVES

A drawknife is the major tool you'll use for shaping greenwood chair parts that aren't turned on a lathe. These instructions are for sharpening a flat, straight drawknife with a blade 8 to 10 inches long and with perpendicular handles in line with the blade, a considerably easier task than sharpening one with a bowed or curved blade. The technique must be modified when sharpening a curved drawknife.

The first step when conditioning a new or used drawknife is to slightly round the extreme corners of the blade to about 1/8-inch radius with a coarse honing stone or a grinding wheel. A drawknife never cuts wood at the ends of the blade, but these corners cause most of the accidental cuts that people get when using this tool.

You can tune a flat, straight drawknife for use with the bevel facing down or up. The secret is in understanding how a drawknife is controlled during a cut. For shaving hardwoods I generally work bevel down. If the drawknife is to be used bevel up, you may want to bend the handles downwards about 30 degrees in relationship to the plane of the blade. (*Warning:* Bending cold handles isn't always possible. Depending on the hardness of the metal, handles could snap off instead of bend. Heating the handle corners with an oxyacetylene torch will prevent such breakage.)

Unlike plane and chisel blades, the side of the drawknife blade in contact with the wood requires a very slight curvature perpendicular to the cutting edge. This curvature, known as a *rolled edge*, or *dubbing*, can be on the flat, bevel, or both sides of the blade. Dubbing should start slightly behind the cutting edge, so that the curvature doesn't increase the included angle of the blade.

To examine the geometry of the blade, use a straightedge to check the back side of the blade and the bevel. Hold the straightedge perpendicular to the edge. For use with the bevel up, the flat side can have some slight curvature perpendicular to the edge, but the section immediately behind the edge should be flat. Next, use a mechanic's protractor or notch gauge to check the included angle, which should be 25 to 30 degrees; regrind, if necessary (fig. 3.4).

If you have an old drawknife whose edge is chipped or uneven along its length, you need to joint (that is, straighten) the edge before proceeding with grinding or honing. Secure the drawknife edge-side up in a vise. To clean up and straighten the edge, hold a diamond hone 90 degrees to the back and rub back and forth the length of the blade. This seems drastic, but it's the correct first step in conditioning a worn or misused blade. Stop when the edge is straight and free of nicks or pits.

Preparing the Flat Side

To monitor honing, coat the back side and bevel with machinist's bluing or a magic marker. Secure bench stones in a holder tall enough to create clearance for the drawknife handles. If the back side of the blade is close to flat, you can dress it with an 800- to 1,200-mesh diamond or water stone. Be sure to keep the back of the blade flat on the honing stone; don't lift or tip it! Hone right up to the edge. Flatten the back of wavy, curved, or pitted blades with a coarse diamond stone or stationary belt sander. For belt sanding, orient the drawknife so that the belt turns away from the edge. This is a tricky operation. Use a light touch, and check progress constantly. After belt sanding or milling, hone the back side with a medium diamond stone or an 800- to 1,200-mesh water stone. Finally, polish the back with a 4,000- to 8,000-mesh water stone. The polished area must extend the full length of the edge.

Preparing the Bevel

You'll need to grind the bevel when the included angle requires modification, or if dubbing on the bevel is extreme. While it's possible to grind a drawknife bevel freehand, I prefer to use a jig. The long bevel requires a precise grind along its full length. For jigged grinding you first have to check and possibly straighten the rear edge of the blade, which works as a register for the jig. Use a diamond hone or a stationary belt sander.

Slow-speed water grinders are excellent for jig grinding drawknives. With most grinders, I use two spring clamps to secure a stop block on the tool rest. The angle of the tool rest combined with the exact placement of the stop block determines the grinding angle (see fig. 3.5). To prevent spilling water, the Prairie wet grinder must turn away from the tool rest. With the Tormek grinder, remove the leather-

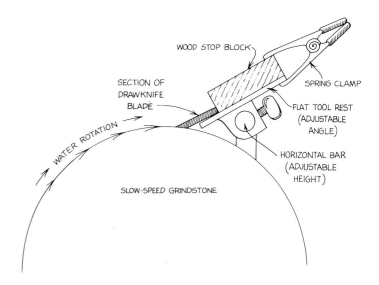

Fig. 3.5. Schematic for grinding a drawknife with a flat, straight blade using a slow-speed wet grinder. The back edge of the drawknife is supported by the tool rest and stop block.

Grinding a drawknife that has a flat, straight blade

The ground drawknife edge

faced stropping wheel to make clearance for the drawknife handles. Clamp a stop block to the flat aluminum jig designed for grinding turning tools. Try to keep water off the rubber-rimmed drive wheel. The drive wheel will slip if the surface gets wet. The Tormek planer-jointer blade jig can also be used. This is an expensive accessory, but excellent for grinding drawknives with straight, flat blades.

Grind by moving the drawknife sideways along the full bevel until you feel a burr on the full length. If you don't grind the full length, the edge will develop a curvature, which you don't want.

For honing the bevel side of the drawknife blade, mount an 800- to 1,200-mesh water stone in a wooden holder, which in turn is secured in a bench vise or with wedges on the bench top. Position yourself at the end of the stone, so that you look down its length. Begin honing by placing the right end of the blade across the far end of the stone. Follow the bevel angle, or double click on the heel and toe of a newly ground hollow bevel. Pull the drawknife at a diagonal along the length of the stone, so that at the near end the stone is in contact with the left end of the drawknife blade. Maintain the bevel angle and push the drawknife across the stone diagonally. Stop at the far end in the original position (see fig. 3.6). Continue honing in both directions until you have a burr along the full length of the edge.

Fig. 3.6. Honing a drawknife. To wear the drawknife and stone evenly, rub the bevel for the full length of the stone in both directions.

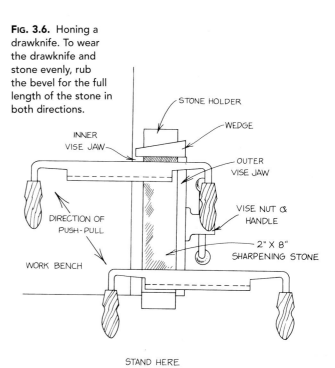

In most cases, sufficient dubbing (rolling the bevel) occurs by itself during freehand honing. On a recently ground blade with a distinct hollow grind, the heel of the bevel will act as the control fulcrum when shaving with the bevel down. This is acceptable if the bevel is not too wide.

Choosing a Stone to Start Honing

You know that you should sharpen your tools when they begin to get dull, but how do you determine which stone to use at the beginning of a sharpening session? It depends on how dull the edge is.

If the edge is still quite sharp, start with a polishing stone. Work for no more than one minute. Check for a very fine wire edge (burr). If there is no wire edge, and it doesn't appear to be imminent, put the polishing stone away. Then try honing with an 800- 1,200-mesh water stone, again for about one minute. As before, check for a wire edge. If you have a wire edge on most but not all of the edge, continue with the same stone. If no wire edge is apparent, drop back to a coarser mesh, such as a 225- to 350-mesh diamond stone. Then work up to a fine honing stone. Always end by polishing.

It's just common sense. You could start sharpening a very dull tool with a polishing stone, but it would be time wasted. And if you start sharpening a slightly dull tool with a medium diamond stone, you needlessly wear away the tool and the stone, along with squandering your valuable time.

Honing and polishing a drawknife

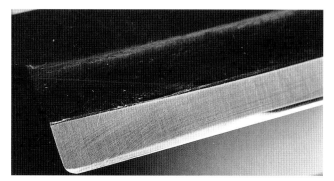

The polished drawknife edge

Control will be a little skittery working bevel down until you've honed off the hollow grind. Keep dubbing to the minimum curvature required for controlling a cut. (With overdubbing, you will have to hold the drawknife at a steep angle before it begins to cut.)

Polish the bevel with a 4,000- to 8,000-mesh water stone until you can see a polished surface adjacent to the arris along the entire bevel. Finish by lightly polishing the flat side of the blade. You may not raise a distinguishable burr with the polishing stone. With a good light source, you should see a polished surface just beyond the arris along the full length of the flat side of the blade. Without magnification you should not be able to see the actual edge.

SHARPENING INSHAVES

You'll use this special-purpose horseshoe-shaped drawknife to hollow Windsor chair seats, a process called *saddling*, after initial hollowing with an adze.

Looking at Blade Geometry

The geometry of an inshave blade and the angle of its handles greatly affect this tool's usefulness. With a curve that is rather flat in the middle, and with tighter curves blended into each end, you can take a wide, shallow cut in the middle of the seat and still work the steeper contours at the back of the seat. You need a distinct bevel on the outside of the blade, and handles that angle upward (about 135 degrees) so that they do not bump into the seat blank.

Measure the included angle of the edge, which should be close to 30 degrees. For control in use, the exterior bevel should be about 3/8 inch wide. (A narrower width doesn't provide enough registration to control the cut.) Examine the interior side along the edge. Often, the interior of an inshave blade is roughly ground, with striations that intersect the arris. Remember that any edge is the result of two intersecting planes. The interior surface at the edge of an inshave must be just as smooth and polished as the bevel. As an aid in seeing exactly where you're sharpening, apply machinist's bluing to the interior surface and the exterior bevel.

Grinding an Inshave

To grind an inshave blade, I use 120-mesh cylindrical sanding sleeves 1-1/2 inches in diameter and 2 inches long that I can mount to an electric drill. These sanding sleeves remove metal quickly, without creating the heat associated with grinding stones. During sanding you can look almost under the rotating cylinder, so it's easy to see what you're doing. Because there is good contact area, these sleeves cut very rapidly on the inside of the curve. I also use them on the outside curve. (It may take you awhile—it did me—to work up to running the drill at full speed with confidence and good control.)

Secure the inshave so that you can work on the interior side of the blade (usually there is no interior bevel). A machinist's bench vise will hold a tang at the section between the blade and handle. Clean up the interior with a sanding sleeve, continuously moving the sander from side to side. Be careful at the right end of the blade. To keep the drum from wrapping around the blade, reverse the direction of the drill. That is, put the drill in reverse when approaching the right end and in forward at the left end. Don't tip the sanding sleeve to get to the edge quickly. Sand until the bluing is removed all the way to the edge. Stop sanding when a burr has formed along the entire exterior (bevel) side of the edge.

Polishing an inshave with a 4,000-mesh water stone. Rub the stone lengthwise along the bevel.

For an inshave, I recommend sanding the exterior bevel before honing and polishing the interior of the blade. Reposition the inshave so that you can get over the exterior bevel with the sleeve sander. Move the electric drill in an arc, with the center located near your chest. Sand the exterior bevel until you can feel a new burr on the inner side of the blade.

Honing

Hone the interior side with 1,000-mesh cone-shaped water or diamond stones. On a curved edge like this, work the honing stones following the length of the blade. (Conventional honing, perpendicular to the blade, results in uneven contact, and maintaining a consistent angle is difficult.) Reposition the inshave so you can hone the exterior bevel. Refine the sanded bevel by rubbing an 800- to 1,200-mesh diamond or water stone along the length of the bevel.

Polish both sides of the edge with a 4,000-mesh water stone or a hard, felt buffing wheel. Polishing the inshave blade with a buffing wheel and white, stainless-steel buffing compound is quick and useful, but also tricky, especially on the interior side of the blade. Before actually trying this, do a dead run, passing the full length of the blade against the buffer with the motor off. Because of the curved blade, much of the buffing will take place on the arris of the wheel. **Safety note: Be sure that the wheel turns *away from* the cutting edge.**

Grinding a hollowing adze with a 3/4-by-2-inch sanding sleeve

Because of the inshave edge's curved shape and blade length, it's easy to leave a section slightly dull. Test the inshave on a piece of softwood, such as a pine board. Use all parts of the edge, observing the hollowed surface created with each section, which should be glassy smooth. If any shaved area is fuzzy or ridged, locate the dull area by examining the edge under good light, then repeat sharpening.

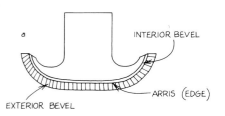

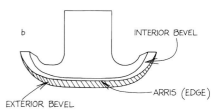

FIG. 3.7. Front view of the edge of a hollowing adze: *a*, conventional exterior bevel; *b*, transitional bevel that combines an exterior bevel in the center section with interior bevels at the upswept lips

SHARPENING HOLLOWING ADZES

Follow the same process for grinding and sharpening a hollowing adze as for an inshave (see fig. 3.7). Be sure to consider tool geometry and how the exterior bevel affects the handle angle. I sometimes do some initial shaping on the exterior bevel of an adze blade with a belt sander. I use a 3/4-by-2-inch sanding sleeve to shape or clean up the interior side, and hone the interior side with cone-shaped water stones.

SHARPENING SHOP KNIVES

I can't imagine making a chair without using one of my many shop knives for the small odd tasks that inevitably arise. For general tasks, like carving dowels to secure the slats of post-and-rung chairs and trimming the many small wedges used during the assembly of Windsor chairs, I use a very sharp knife with a 3- to 4-inch blade. I use a similar knife, which I don't keep as sharp, for splitting small stock such as pegs and wedges by hitting the back of the blade with a hammer. Both are Swedish sloyd (handcraft) knives. I use a very sharp chip-carving knife to carve my initials on the bottom of each Windsor seat.

Knife blades are usually symmetrically beveled. Woodworkers' knives are ground with opposing wide bevels that form an included angle of 20 to 25 degrees. For carving, the bevels must be flat or slightly hollow ground. Use a belt sander or slow-speed water wheel and be patient with yourself—grinding the bevels of a woodworking knife is a difficult skill to master. The included angle is narrow, and the blade is thin and curved along the edge.

Honing and polishing knife blades is less difficult than grinding. Knives with bevels that run parallel to the curve of the blade edge must be honed lengthwise along the bevel, rather than perpendicular to the edge. You need to lift the handle as you swing along the curve toward the tip of the blade.

SHARPENING SHOP AXES

Hand axes for shop use divide generally into axes with symmetrical double bevels, and broad hatchets with a flat side on the inner face and a bevel on the outer face. (In section, a broad-hatchet edge is similar to a chisel.) Some shop axes are ground with a hybrid configuration—a long, shallow bevel on the inside face, and a short, steep bevel on the outside face.

The advantage of the broad-hatchet configuration is that the axe doesn't have to be tilted in order to cut. (When you swing an axe, you don't have much control once you've made contact with the wood). However, a well-balanced, symmetrically beveled axe can be tilted without loss of control. Balance is achieved by aligning the center of balance of the head with the handle, and by correct grinding.

An axe to be used for hewing must have a flat or slightly hollow-ground inner bevel. (If you are right-handed, the inner bevel is the left bevel as you hold the axe.) If the inner bevel is rolled, the edge will not engage the wood unless the axe is tipped at an angle. And once it's tipped, you lose control of the cut because there is no registration against the bevel. In plan view, the axe edge should be curved, which helps to make a slicing cut in the wood. The included-edge angle should be 30 to 35 degrees.

I recommend grinding the edge freehand, using sanding sleeves with an electric drill. Apply machinist's bluing to the bevels before you start, so that you can easily see exactly where grinding takes place. **Safety note: The sander must rotate away from the edge.**

For both honing and polishing, secure the axe in a vise (or with clamps on a bench top), and then work honing stones over the stationary tool. **Honing an axe is dangerous—** with only a slight slip, your fingers can be cut by the exposed stationary blade. For this reason, I use 2-by-8-inch honing stones that are an inch thick. Rub along the length of the bevel, not perpendicular to the edge. Work through successive grits, as with sharpening any other edged tool.

When sharp, your shop axes will have the same polished edge as your other tools, and they deserve the same respect. One mark of this respect is to cover the chopping surface of your chopping stump with a box lid–shaped cover to keep it clean when not in use. I recommend making or buying an edge guard for each sharpened axe.

CHAPTER 4

Chair Wood

Air drying "chairmaker's gold." Shaved front posts and rungs for seven or eight ladder-back chairs. The front posts are tapered at the foot end. All are octagonal in section.

W hat wood to choose for a chair depends on a combination of circumstances: the wood's appearance, availability, and cost, how you're going to build the chair, and—always—understanding the special stresses wooden chairs undergo. Because they are portable, chairs may be left in environments hostile to wood, finishes, adhesives, and joinery. Chair joints are subjected to loading stresses that tend to concentrate in very small areas, as when a chair is tipped onto its rear posts or dragged across an uneven floor. An even more significant stress comes from the continual swelling and shrinking of wood joinery as the humidity changes. (An excellent resource for anyone who uses wood is R. Bruce Hoadley's *Understanding Wood*.)

A CHAIRMAKER'S WOOD PRIMER

On the first morning of a chairmaking workshop, we start by looking at a red oak log, an excellent species for making post-and-rung chairs and most parts of Windsor bows and spindles. From the end view, bark, and other external features, we get a fair idea of the quality of wood the log will yield.

How Trees Grow

A tree grows in diameter by adding *growth rings* in an ever-enlarging concentric pattern around the central *pith*. Each growth ring usually represents one year of growth. Among oaks, each ring has two bands, one representing *early growth* and one *late growth*.

A thin slice of red oak. The large pores forming the light bands (which you can see through) are early wood. The diagonal lines are clusters of ray cells.

Structurally, wood cells resemble bundles of strawlike fibers packed together. In spring and early summer, new fibers grow quickly and are large in diameter (on a red oak, you can often see the hollow ends of individual early-growth fibers with the naked eye). Later in the year, when growth slows, new fibers are relatively small in diameter. For chairmaking from green wood, I try to use logs whose growth rings average 1/8 to 3/16 inch wide.

You can divide hardwoods into three categories by cell porosity. Cell porosity is important to you as a green-wood chairmaker because you want to take every advantage you can of the physical qualities of wood. In *ring-porous* species such as oak, ash, and hickory, it's easy to see the size difference between late- and early-growth fibers. You can distinguish the growth rings of *diffuse-porous* woods, such as cherry, maple, and beech, mainly by color differences, not fiber diameter. Diffuse-porous wood are fine for chairmaking, but do not work well for riving; parts are usually sawed. A third group, the *semidiffuse-porous*—sometimes called *semiring-porous*—species, includes black walnut and butternut. Walnut is an excellent chairmaking wood; it's strong, handsome, and bends easily. Butternut is beautiful but too weak for chair parts.

Ring-Porous Hardwoods

For green-wood chairmaking, it's important to know that most ring-porous hardwoods split readily and predictably—with their large, early-wood cell diameter, they tend to have long, tough fibers. The major exception is elm, a ring-porous wood that often resists splitting; to take advantage of this anomaly, use elm for fine and sturdy Windsor chair seats.

Most ring-porous hardwoods are tough, and the long, straight fibers make them excellent for bending and for shaping with hand tools such as drawknives and spoke-shaves. The large fibers of oak, ash, and hickory, tough in tension and compression, are easy to separate lengthwise, which makes them great as riving woods and for supplying fine splints for basketry and woven chair seats.

Wood from a fast-growing ring-porous hardwood is usually superior in strength and bending qualities to the same species when it grows slower. The explanation lies in the ratio of early wood to late wood for each annual ring. Late wood is stronger than early wood because of its smaller diameter, more densely packed cells. In a fast-growing ring-porous tree, the ratio of late wood to early wood is as much as three times that of slower-growing trees. A slow-growing oak, for example, may actually have a wider band of early wood than of late wood—as a chairmaker, you'll find this wood offers you a lesser chance for successful bends and less strength.

Post-and-rung chair frames and most parts of Windsors require hard, strong woods. Posts and rungs that are rived and shaved should be made with tough, long-fiber hardwoods such as oak, ash, and hickory. Diffuse-porous, short-fiber, dense-grained woods such as hard maple and beech are especially suited for turned parts, since they tool with cleaner detailing, but you may also make turnings from the long-fiber hardwoods. Windsor seats are often made with softwoods, although hardwood seat planks made from such woods as elm or even tulip poplar are structurally superior.

HOW CHAIRMAKERS LOOK AT TREES AND LOGS

Green-wood chairmaking is an intimate dance between raw wood, hand tools, and your body mechanics. Knowing the nature of wood is key to using wood with hand tools.

To make post-and-rung and Windsor chairs, you will rive hardwood, then shave or turn it. For posts, bows, slats, and spindles, look for logs that appear to be free of major knots, with minimal taper, wide growth rings, and pith near the center. Also check the bark furrows, looking for a pattern that runs straight up and down the trunk (without spiral). You are looking for wood that is "perfect," but with no character, such as wavy grain, bird's-eye figures, or other special characteristics.

Not all first-class chairmaking wood is clear, but it must be straight grained. You can use figured wood for chair turnings you don't plan to paint. Traditional English chairmakers commonly used wavy-grained fruit woods and speckled yew to attractive effect. The arms of English Windsors and Welsh stick chairs are sometimes pieced together from planks sawed or hewed from curved trunks and limbs. The spindle crests (or combs) of these chairs can be sawed from timbers that have an attractive grain pattern.

When you look at a cross section of an oak log, working from the outside in, first comes the bark (including an inner layer called *bast*), then a single layer of growing cells called the *cambium*, then an outer zone of *sapwood*, then an inner layer of *heartwood*, and at the very center the *pith*. Sapwood is usually much lighter in color than heartwood (fig. 4.1). As you examine the end of a log, you may also notice purple or black blotches that can indicate buried foreign matter, such as metal fence wire or nails, or color-stain fungi. You can still use these logs, but they often have long stains or blotches running through them. (You can work around stains or use stained wood under seats, for example.)

Bark

Because the bark of a log or standing tree mirrors the wood inside, it can help you decide whether to select a tree for chairmaking or not. Bark often has distinctive, length-wise furrows, caused by splitting as the tree grows in diameter. If the furrows are straight, you can be sure that the wood beneath the bark is also straight. Spiraled bark furrows indicate spiral fiber in the wood. Bark bumps and rough scars (sometimes called cat faces) indicate healing areas where limbs have fallen off the trunk (fig. 4.2). These often persist for many years after a limb has broken away. Limbs inside a log form knots, and as the trunk fibers grow around the knot the surrounding wood becomes distorted, therefore unusable.

The bast of hickories and of some other species makes an excellent material for woven seats of post-and-rung chairs.

Sapwood and Heartwood

Sapwood carries nutrients between a tree's leaves, growing cambium, stem tips, and roots. Nutrients move through a

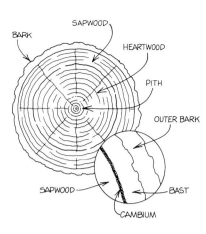

FIG. 4.1.
Section view
of a typical log

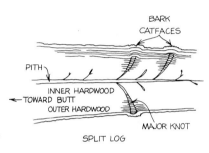

FIG. 4.2.
In a split log, note knots (limbs) originate at the pith, numerous small knots in the inner heartwood, and distorted wood fiber around larger knots. Cat faces telegraph onto bark for many years after a limb and knot have fallen off the trunk.

tree not according to the season but in response to root pressure, atmospheric pressure, specialized metabolic functions, and other variables. The peak time for sap flow in a tree depends on its species and can range from spring through autumn; in terms of when to cut a tree, the state or timing of sap flow makes no difference and needn't be taken into account. All sapwood is susceptible to decay. With oaks, sapwood generally takes up about one-tenth of the radius. With hickory and ash, the area of sapwood is so great some trees have no heartwood at all.

Even in a living tree, heartwood is dead. It is there only for skeletal support. When sapwood changes into heartwood, complex *extractives* deposited in the cells resist decay and sometimes discourage insect attack. Extractives are also responsible for the distinguishing darker color of heartwood.

Pith

Lying at the center of the annual rings, the pith is not really wood but spongy matter like that found in leaf stems. About 1/8 to 1/4 inch across, it represents the tree's earliest stem-tip growth. The pith rots quickly, sometimes leaving a hollow pathway. Wood for chair parts should not contain the pith, which is often a starting place for serious cracking.

The pith of an ideal log for chairmaking lies near the center of the log. When it's off-center, you know that the tree grew on a slope and, to compensate and grow straight up, formed *reaction wood*. Such wood splits and warps unpredictably during shaping processes and drying.

A red oak log, about 20 inches in diameter, that looks promising for green-wood chairmaking. The pith is near the center, growth rings are fairly large, and the band of sapwood is narrow.

Hardwood forest at the author's mountain farmstead—a guest cabin to the left, the family residence at the right.

Uniformity

As a chairmaker, you will generally prefer logs with minimal taper. When riving a 60-inch Windsor bow along the growth rings, you want even growth-ring width from one end to the other. A *butt-cut log*—the bottommost log from a felled tree—often has a considerable amount of reaction wood at the buttress area, near the ground. Buttress wood, which usually runs only a foot or two up the trunk, commonly has wavy grain, is hard to split, and is no fun to work with a drawknife, although it can make excellent Windsor chair seats or armrests for post-and-rung chairs. Usually the trunk straightens out and the wood becomes normal in structure within a few feet of the buttress end.

FINDING WOOD

How Much Will You Need?

You can rive all the parts of post-and-rung chairs from one log. For Windsors you'll need sawed planks for the seats. Turning stock can be rived, which is the best method if you like skinny sections on your turnings, or from clear sections of sawed straight-grain 2 by 2s.

The red oak log that we've been looking at—probably 12 feet long and 24 inches around at the large end—is a butt-cut log. You can expect to get a lot of the clearest, straightest chair wood around from such a large, premium butt log—enough to make ten to fifteen post-and-rung chairs. If you plan to make only a set of six chairs for the family dining table, that's far too much wood.

An oak tree of this size growing in an eastern U.S. forest may have two other good 12-foot logs that taper to a narrower diameter higher in the tree, a more realistic size to use if you're a novice chairmaker. Even though these will have considerably more knots, the price per board foot should be considerably less than for a prime butt log. When I have felled an exceptional quality tree, I often find acceptable chairmaking wood for rungs and front posts more than 30 feet above the stump end.

Cutting Your Own

My family and I live on a 100-acre farmstead that is about three-fourths mixed eastern temperate forest. We have a fair amount of excellent red oak but not much hickory, white oak, or ash. We have lots of tulip poplar and some nice white pine — both species are commonly used for

Windsor seats. For turning stock, there is red maple, some hard maple, beech, and sweet birch. Sometimes when I need chair wood I go out with a chain saw (or axe, maybe) and cut down a tree.

But felling a large tree is a task that I don't take lightly. Although our forest is continually growing, we have a limited supply of trees of high enough quality to make chair parts. In recent years I generally fell a tree for chair wood only if it is dying and I can get to it with my pickup truck or tractor.

While I enjoy the work and challenge of getting timber off our land, I also know that logging is a complex operation and a dangerous one. A freshly felled oak log contains green wood that can weigh more than 75 pounds per cubic foot. When this tree falls, you are dealing with very significant forces and with a stupendous weight when you're moving felled logs on the ground. In addition to getting chairmaking wood, felling entails cutting and hauling all the firewood and, for us, cleaning up the site in the forest. This adds up to a lot of work.

Safety note: Felling trees, cross cutting, and skidding logs are extremely dangerous activities. Felling a tree is something that's best learned by experience in the woods while helping someone who already knows how to do it. There is a good introduction to microscale logging in my earlier book, *Green Woodworking*; if you're serious about logging methods and safety, I recommend *Professional Timber Falling*, by D. Douglas Dent.

Red oak logs stacked at a small local sawmill. Always choose the best, and don't bicker over the asking price.

Buying Logs from Sawmills

The best alternative to doing your own logging is buying logs (and sometimes sawed planks) at a small local sawmill. The advantages of this approach are clear. Before you even pick up a saw, you have an opportunity to look over dozens, if not hundreds of logs. Most mills stack logs in piles by species. You can examine both ends of every log, checking for interior rot, off-center pith, width of growth rings, and so on.

The sawmill can load the log onto your pickup or trailer, or they may be willing to deliver when they aren't too busy. I often bring my chain saw along, so that I can buck the log into convenient lengths that are easy to handle back at the shop.

No matter what a sawmill charges, you will get a bargain if the wood turns out to be of good quality. Our 12-foot sample log, 24 inches around at the butt, may measure 20 inches around at the small end, which is where logs are measured for conversion into board feet. Using a Doyle log rule (one of three standard U.S. log-conversion formulas), this log should yield 192 board feet of lumber. If it is a veneer-grade log, it may wholesale for eighty cents per

Doyle Log Rule Contents in Board Feet					
Dia. Inches (at small end)	Log Length in Feet				
	8	10	12	14	16
6	2	3	3	4	4
7	5	6	7	8	9
8	8	10	12	14	16
9	13	16	19	22	25
10	18	23	27	32	36
11	25	31	37	43	49
12	32	40	48	56	64
13	41	51	61	71	81
14	50	63	75	88	100
15	61	76	91	106	121
16	72	90	108	126	144
17	85	106	127	148	169
18	98	123	147	172	196
19	113	141	169	197	225
20	128	160	192	224	256
21	145	181	217	253	289
22	162	203	243	284	324
23	181	226	271	316	361
24	200	250	300	350	400
25	221	276	331	386	441
26	242	303	363	424	484
27	265	331	397	463	529
28	288	360	432	504	576
29	313	391	469	547	625
30	338	423	507	592	676

Loading a red oak log just over 12 feet long

board foot, a premium price for a log at a sawmill, $154 (in 1996). But I also estimate that this very fine log should contain wood for about fifteen ladder-back chairs, which makes the price of wood per chair $10.24. That's an upper-end price for materials. An excellent quality, non-veneer-grade red oak log that will convert into lots of fine chair wood will probably sell for about fifty cents per board foot. Of course, this price doesn't include the costs of delivery or your time.

And you can usually find smaller diameter logs. A 12-foot log that's 12 inches in diameter—large enough to bust into parts for four post-and-rung chairs—yields 48 board feet. You can anticipate two problems with smaller logs: finding clear wood that is acceptable, and dealing with relatively more waste compared to larger logs.

Sawmills can also be your best source for specialty lumber, such as Windsor seat planking and turning stock. The main problem that I've had when buying chair wood is getting the sawmill owner or sawyer to understand my requirements. For years there seemed to be far too much waste in the freshly milled white pine that I was buying for Windsor seat planks. I eventually took a finished Windsor chair to the mill, so the men could see what I was making. Then I stayed at the mill for most of an afternoon, riding shotgun while they were sawing pine, so I could show the sawyer exactly what I wanted.

My best advice regarding sawmills is always to be very nice to the folks who work there. They are doing you a favor when they stop production to deal with someone who wants to buy a single log once in a while. If you can get them to understand what you're looking for, they may become enthusiastic about your project and be on the lookout for the special logs or boards that you need. I never dicker over prices.

Buying Logs from Small Band Mills

If you live in a rural area where there are forests or farm woodlots, you can be almost certain that someone nearby owns a portable band mill. These mills usually don't stock-pile logs or lumber; everything is custom work. The mill owner may be able to supply the logs you need, or you supply them yourself.

The one disadvantage of most portable band mills is the slowness of their horizontal band saw, compared to commercial sawmills' circular saws. But their advantages are many. The kerf a small band mill makes is typically about 1/16 inch, compared to 1/4 inch for most circular saws; with valuable wood, especially when it's cut into thin boards, that is a very significant saving. Band mills are also comparatively safe, and they can produce highly accurate work. (I've had a log cut into near-perfect 1/8-inch-thick slices.) Since band mills tend to be one- or two-person operations, you'll often be expected to help with the

Portable band mills brought to the site cut slowly but accurately and can be operated by one or two people.

work—your chance to be directly involved with quality control. Smallness is also an advantage if you're requesting a special job, such as sawing a curved tree trunk into bowed planks for chair arms. For example, my Welsh friend John Brown hires a band mill to saw slabs to be converted into flitch-sawed planks for bent arm pieces and other parts of his handsome stick Windsors (see Chapter 8). (Flitch sawing leaves the original wavy back edge on each side of a sawed plank.) If this is done carefully, there is less waste than in riving. John rips the slabs into curved bow sections himself with his shop band saw.

Some band mills can be hauled to a yard close to where the tree was felled—then you don't have to get involved in trucking logs.

Other Sources

You can also get chair wood from firewood dealers, tree trimmers, and maintenance departments for municipal parks, roads, and cities. The big hurdle is getting these folks to understand what you are looking for. Once firewood dealers or tree trimmers realize that for the right stuff you will pay many times the value of firewood, they will go out of their way to be helpful.

HOW TO STORE LOGS AND LUMBER

A common question that I'm asked is, How long will wood stay green in the log? There's no simple answer. It depends on factors like wood species, log size, and weather, as well as a chairmaker's work schedule and storage facility. As green-wood chairmakers we covet freshly felled wood. But in our attempts to keep wood green we also risk development of wood decay. Under most environmental condi-

tions, a freshly felled log begins to dry out immediately and unevenly, resulting in checking at the ends. And we want to avoid even incipient decay that cannot be seen, for it will have already weakened our material.

Wood Decay

To prevent decay, a chairmaker first needs to know how decay works. Decay is the result of fungi growing in the wood, and those fungi thrive only with oxygen, moisture, a moderate temperature, and food. The fungi will not grow in either saturated or dry wood—they like a 30 percent moisture content best. This means that air-dried wood, which typically has a moisture content of 15 to 20 percent, will not decay unless wetted again and kept wet (for example, by frequent rain). Wood-decay fungi's favorite temperature range is 75 to 90 degrees Fahrenheit; most growth stops below 40 and above 105 degrees. Carbohydrates in the wood serve as food for these fungi. While the sapwood of all species is susceptible to decay, the heartwood of many species contains fungi-resistant extractives.

If you convert a log into chair parts shortly after felling, generally speaking you don't have to worry about the wood either drying out too fast or decaying. This is a good idea if you have the energy, if the log is a reasonable size, and if you know what chair parts you need. Be aware of the exceptions. In temperate weather, for instance, the sapwood of some species, most notably red oak, decays within weeks of felling. Unless red oak is logged in winter and used during cold weather, you can't use the sapwood for chairs. In fact, the decay resistance of sapwood is low for all species. And the sapwood of white pine, which you may want to use for Windsor seats, molds and color stains quickly. Some molds physically weaken the wood, although others mainly change the color.

Storing Logs Outdoors

What happens if you just leave a log in your yard? Again, it depends on a variety of factors. I've shaved and bent green-wood chair parts and tool handles from red oak logs that had lain in a yard for more than six months; I had to discard all the sapwood, but the heartwood was still green and sound. Large logs dry much more slowly than do small logs or split logs. Something as simple as keeping the log out of direct sunshine and drafts helps a great deal. For short-term storage I tack a piece of tin or plywood at the end of the log that gets direct sun and wind exposure.

You can also slow the drying process by sealing the exposed wood at the ends. Wood dries much faster

Heartwood Decay Resistance of Wood Species Commonly Used in Green-Wood Chairs

Low Resistance	Moderate Resistance	High Resistance
Alder	Elm	Catalpa
Ash (all)	Fir	Cedars (all)
Aspen	Gum, Red	Cherry
Beech	Hornbeam	Cypress
Birch	Larch, Western	Mulberry
Butternut	Locust, Honey	Oak, White
Cottonwood	Oak, Red	Osage orange
Gum, sweet	Pine, Northern white	Pine, Southern yellow
Hackberry		Redwood
Hickory		Walnut
Linden		Yew
Maple (all)		
Pecan		
Persimmon		
Pine, Southern white		
Poplar, True		
Poplar, Yellow		
Spruce		
Tupelo		
Willow		

Another way you can slow down drying is to cover the log with polysheeting and store it in a cool, shady place to be sure it doesn't get too warm under the plastic. To protect the wood from ground moisture, raise it onto some cross bolsters.

Storing Logs in Water

You can also keep chair wood from drying out by immersing it in still water, as in a pond or tub, which will deprive fungi of needed oxygen. New-felled heavy woods like oak, hickory, and ash will sink. Split logs you plan to store underwater into manageable sections; otherwise fetching them out of the water can be difficult—tongs help.

You can keep large rivings wet and green for about a year. Eventually, a fungus will form, signaled by surface discoloration, which you can shave off. Gradually the wood will weaken and fail when it is bent or subjected to stress. (If you store oak in still water, such as a 55-gallon drum, a slimy algae will develop in the water; hose it off and the wood should be fine.)

Storing Air-Dried Wood

If you have time, the opposite approach to wet storage is to start making chair parts or rivings near chair-part size from green wood as fast as possible. You can bend square or octagonal stock; there's no need to do finish work on bent posts and arm bows with green wood—and square stock bends with fewer failures than round stock. You can rive posts, rungs, and spindle blanks green and allow them to dry as rivings, or you can work to near finish dimensions. Dry wood will tool to a much finer surface quality than will wet wood. Air-dried wood keeps indefinitely and won't deteriorate if you store it with even minimal protection.

If you can't get right to bending and riving, another approach is to cut the log into lengths a bit longer than your longest chair parts. Split these into quarters or eighths, coat the end grain, and set them in a protected place, like a floored shed. Let them dry at their own rate, then use them as you need them.

Green wood that is air drying needs to be kept in a well-ventilated storage area. Stack rivings with space between individual pieces and each row. If the floor is dirt, stacks should begin a foot above ground level. Place wooden 1-inch-by-1-inch spacers, called *stickers*, between the boards at about 4-foot intervals. Placing weights on top of the stack helps to prevent sawed planks from warping during drying (cinder blocks make good weights).

Hardwood that dries too quickly may develop internal hollows, known as honeycombing. Honeycombing develops because wet wood shrinks as it dries, and it dries from the outside in. If drying goes too fast, fibers close to the surface shrink and harden, a process called *case hardening*. When the inner fibers start drying, the outer shell can shrink no further; the inner fibers burst apart from each other and sometimes from the outer fibers, leaving lacy

through severed end grain than along its length. The sealant that I prefer is a water-based paraffin product used by commercial sawmills. It is easy to apply, translucent, and reasonably priced. Latex (acrylic) paint also adheres nicely to wet end grain; let it dry, then brush on another coat. White or yellow glue will work, as will cold black asphalt roofing mastic, which you trowel on with a putty knife. (A disadvantage with mastic is that it obscures the growth rings, so when you're ready to rive parts, you have to saw off a slice from the end to see what you're doing.)

A sealant may work too well. If some moisture can't escape, you may be setting up conditions for fungus development. The paraffin sealants seem to allow enough moisture to escape from end-coated logs. Leaving bark on logs helps slow the drying process in cold weather, but in warm weather bark can hold in the moisture required by decay fungi.

hollows up and down the interior of the piece of wood. Scary stuff for a chairmaker. (I would not have believed this could happen from air drying if I had not seen honeycombing on the insides of chair posts stored in the loft of our shop during a very hot summer.)

Choosing and Storing Seat Planking and Turning Stock

When you get fresh-sawed planking for Windsor seats from the mill, the boards are 12 feet long, at least 2-1/8 inches thick, and roughly 10 inches wide. I prefer flat-sawed stock, not quarter-sawed, which is more likely to split. Your first task is to go through the boards, looking for imperfections and also for very good pieces. You can't use planks that contain the pith; these pieces will almost always split during drying. If you're working with white pine, pay attention to the knots: Look for planks from which you can get two adjacent seat blanks between the knots. I saw the planks into boards 38 to 48 inches long. These are easy to store, and I like joining and gluing up boards of this length.

Two other defects to avoid in seat planking: resin streaking and wind shakes. Resin is often a problem with white pine. You can work with small flecks or streaks, but if you see great canals of the stuff, reject the wood. Wind shakes are generally circumferential splits caused either by storms bending the trunk or by felling; sometimes you won't discover them until the wood dries out, or even until you are carving a seat. Wind shakes commonly run the full length of a 12-foot board. If the boards were sawed from one log, you may be able to trace a wind shake from one plank to another. With wind shakes you have two choices: Junk the wood, or rip it into narrower sound pieces that can be glued back together.

Sawed planks for Windsor seats or pieced arm bows need to be air dried before you use them. Once the wood is dry, you can work either with seat planks that measure a full seat width, or with narrower planks jointed and edge glued. I generally glue up seat blanks from 10-inch wide boards, but I occasionally use three or even four boards.

There is a certain romance to using full-width planks (a single-plank seat is easier to carve and probably a good sales feature if you are going into production), but fresh-sawed planks 2-1/8 inches thick, 18 to 20 inches wide, and 12 feet long are very heavy and cumbersome to move or store during drying. Any modern wood glue will join planks into seats at least as strong as those you make from a single board.

Be sure to end coat all the blanks immediately after they are sawed. Placing 1-inch-by-1-inch stickers between layers of drying planks is imperative.

Examples of honeycombing, the result of drying green wood too rapidly

Examine and store wood sawed into 2 by 2s for turning stock much as you do seat planking. Crosscut the 2 by 2s into turning blanks based on a list of turning-stock lengths. Look for pieces with clear, straight grain and minimal *runout*—grain that angles off the sides of a blank instead of running the full length. For Windsor legs, maximum acceptable runout depends on the style of your turnings. You need straighter wood for fancy ring-and-baluster Windsor legs, which traditionally include a very small diameter hollow cove (a negative half-round in a spindle turning) about halfway up, than for bamboo (double-bobbin) or English-style turnings. Although some Windsor chairmakers use only rived turning stock, I believe that sawed turning stock is fine if you check it carefully. Runout up to 1-inch deflection over a 20-inch post will not weaken even the most daring turnings. Pieces with somewhat more runout can often be used for stretchers or arm posts.

Splitting turning stock may be an easier way to get green wood for turning, but you generally waste more wood by riving than by sawing. You can get more square blanks by sawing a log into a grid than from rived, pie-shaped pieces.

You can keep sawed or rived turning stock green underwater or in a freezer, or you can store it carefully and allow it to dry. Use end-grain sealant and stickers. Turning won't be so easy with air-dried stock, but tooling surface quality will be superior.

DRYING GREEN WOOD FOR CHAIRMAKING

If you understand how wood dries and apply what you know in your chairmaking, your chairs will hold up under long-term environmental stresses and use.

Moisture Content and Wood Shrinkage

The wood in a living tree contains a great deal of water. After a tree is felled, wood generally begins to dry out and shrink. Conversely, dry wood gradually expands in a wet environment. Wood is a hygroscopic material; shrinking or expanding occurs whenever the environmental humidity fluctuates.

Wood *moisture content* (m.c.) is measured as a percentage ratio of the weight of a sample compared to its weight fully dried. For example, a piece of wood that weighs 5 pounds now compared to 4 pounds after drying currently has a moisture content of 25 percent; that is, it weighs 25 percent more now than when it's dry. The green moisture content of a freshly cut piece of oak that weighs 10 pounds and later dries to 5 pounds is 100 percent; it weighs 100 percent more green than dry. The formula for figuring moisture content is

$$\% \text{ mc} = \frac{(\text{initial weight}) - (\text{oven dry weight}) \times 100}{\text{oven-dry weight}}$$

Equilibrium moisture content (e.m.c.) refers to a stable moisture content after adjustment is made for the humidity of the current environment. A 1-inch-thick oak board that has air dried for a year and has leveled out at 20 percent e.m.c. will not be any drier ten years later if the same environmental humidity prevails.

In most cases you do not need to know actual percentages of moisture content. Once you understand the basic concept, experience and rules of thumb are sufficient. A small scale that measures in fractions of an ounce or grams is useful, but not necessary. If you want to collect more data, you can purchase a moisture meter, which measures electrical resistance between two pins inserted in a sample piece of wood.

Think of wood as bundles of parallel straws. Wet wood contains water in the straw tubes (*free water*) and in the walls of the straws (*bound water*). As wood dries, it first loses free water but doesn't shrink. At about 35 percent m.c., the fiber saturation point, wood begins to shrink; it is now losing bound water. Loss of bound water can continue to about 5-6 percent m.c., the moisture content of wood that has been kiln dried, or the equivalent. Air-dried wood ranges from 15 to 25 percent m.c., with variations depending on local environmental conditions.

Dimensional shrinkage varies in direction of measurement and among different species. Shrinkage tangent to the growth rings is about twice the shrinkage parallel to the rays. On the growth-ring plane, dimensional shrinkage for oak can be as much as 10-12 percent. On the ray plane, maximum dimensional shrinkage is 5-6 percent (see fig. 4.3). Maximum lengthwise shrinkage is about one-tenth of 1 percent. For chairmaking, you don't need to take lengthwise shrinkage into account.

Band-milled flitches (planks sawn through-and-through) stacked with 1-by-1-inch stickers for air drying

Joinery and Moisture Content

At the time of assembly, the strongest chair joinery combines air-dried mortises and kiln-dried tenons. Growth-ring alignment also plays a major role. The joints actually tighten after assembly. Under optimal conditions, you can assemble a chair without using glue. The understructure of these traditional chairs lacks triangulation. All the strength is in the joinery itself.

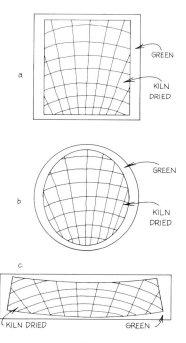

Fig. 4.3. Shrinkage: *a* and *b* both show that shrinkage tangent to the growth rings is approximately twice that of shrinkage in line with the rays; *c*, a sawed board will shrink and warp opposite the curve of the growth rings.

In a post-and-rung chair, the posts (which house the mortises) should be air dried and the rungs (which have tenons at their ends) should be kiln dried. After assembly, the mortise wood will lose some moisture content; the tenon wood will pick up some moisture from the mortise wood and the environment.

By orienting a tenon with the growth rings perpendicular to the mortise wood fiber, you minimize wood movement during fluctuations of humidity. On a post-and-rung chair rung tenons should be oriented with their rays in line with the length of the posts.

You must also consider racking stresses, the load on the joints during use. The chair's challenge doesn't lie in supporting dead weight. Besides changes in humidity, chairs are stressed when sitters lean back and sometimes tip chairs back onto the rear posts.

The same principles apply to Windsor joinery, only the situation is a bit more complex. The legs of a Windsor chair contain mortises (for the side stretchers) and tenons (fitted to the seat). Windsor chair legs should be thoroughly dry (the equivalent of kiln dried) at their tenon ends but air dried in the mortise areas. (The method for doing this is explained in Chapter 8 on making stick Windsors.) You'll also need to consider the orientation of the parts—including the seat plank. In fact, there is some debate among chairmakers regarding optimal orientation for certain joints.

It is also necessary to ask why chairs fall apart. To begin with, very few chairs are assembled following the guidelines in the preceding paragraphs. A properly assembled chair will withstand many years of normal use. Eventually, cyclic changes in humidity will cause most chair joints to fail. In the eastern United States, humid summer weather causes swelling in the tenons. Swelling in a tight joint results in fiber degradation. During dry (winter) periods, the degraded tenons shrink, and joints can loosen. Joints usually fail under dry conditions, but it is continual fluctuations of dryness and wetness that cause the failure. Incidentally, air-conditioning creates a drying environment, just like most heating systems.

Drying Time

Unless you have specialized equipment and expertise, you should dry chair parts slowly. Different wood species, dimensions, and drying environments make rule-of-thumb drying times impossible. Take into account air movement and outdoor temperature—the colder, the slower; once wood freezes, drying ceases.

To prevent checking, which occurs when the porous ends of a piece of wood dry faster than the middle section, coat the ends of green wood with a sealant. While glue and ordinary latex paint work quite well, I use a proprietary paraffin-based sealant formulated for this purpose.

For kiln drying or its equivalent, you can make a special drying device or simply put wood somewhere in your

home or shop that has a good drying environment, like an improvised rack above a furnace or woodstove. In summer, an air-conditioned room will work as a wood drier (see Chapter 20 for plans for shop-made kilns).

Wood-Bending Basics

When a solid piece of wood is bent, the outer part of the curve is stressed in tension, while the inner part is subjected to compression. The effect is similar to what happens when a horizontal beam is loaded between two points. As with the loaded beam, there is a neutral axis along a midarea of the beam (see fig. 4.4).

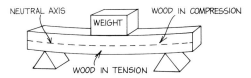

FIG. 4.4. A bent piece of wood acts like a beam in tension. When wood is bent the section on the inside of the bend goes into compression and the section on the outside of the bend goes into tension.

During the bending process, as the wood fibers on the concave side of the curve are compressed, they take on minute, uniform deformations. The fibers in tension on the convex side of the curve actually stretch. When bending a coarse-grained wood like oak, you can watch the grain pattern elongate and stretch out. You can also use a tape measure to see how much stretching occurs on the tension side of a wood bend. In my experience, green wood bends much easier than air-dried stock.

Bent chair parts should be made from wood that is free of defects. Carefully sawed parts, with little fiber runout, will bend just as well as rivings. Transitions in thickness should be gradual, with faired curves. You want to minimize the concentration of forces that occurs at abrupt transitions. All surfaces should be smooth, especially on the tension side of the curve. Rough areas often tear or crumple during bending.

Wood is usually bent following the growth rings, but bends on the ray plane are almost as successful. The back bow of a continuous-arm Windsor requires bends in both planes; the arm bends are at right angles to the back bend.

Wood-Bending Failures

Wood bending is an imprecise technology. Failures can be caused by using inappropriate wood, poor shaping, insufficient steaming, a too severe bend, and faulty bending technique. Failure is more likely as bends get tighter. Similarly, thick-sectioned stock is more prone to failure, as is wood of questionable quality or tree species considered marginal for bending purposes. When possible, the section of a bent piece should be wider than it is thick.

The most common failure is tearout of long fibers on the tension side of the bend. Another type of tension failure can be described as a ragged fissure perpendicular to the surface. This failure is often caused by incipient decay that is invisible to the eye. Unlike long-fiber tearout, these ragged fissure failures are not repairable. A third type of bending failure is buckling on the concave (compression) side of the curve. Buckling failures range from being slightly discernible to severe. Wood with minor buckling failures can sometimes be used. Severe buckling is sometimes accompanied by delamination of the growth rings.

Bends that take the wrong shape can also be considered a type of failure. Irregular bent curves are caused by irregular thicknesses or variation in the wood fiber. A thin area will buckle; a thick area will be stiff and resistant to bending compared to the surrounding wood.

Example of a tension failure on a Windsor bow. The strip can be glued back.

Heating Wood

Heating wood with steam or hot water gives it temporary plasticity—bendability. Steam is usually easier to deal with than boiling, although you can heat thin stock, such as green ladder-back slats, by ladling boiling water over a piece for two or three minutes. Green bows for American Windsors, which are typically 7/8 -1 inch in diameter, should be steamed (or boiled) for thirty or forty minutes; air-dried bows need an hour or more. Although ladder-back posts are heavier, their bend is less severe and the flat relief makes bending easier. The heavy bows of English Windsors and Welsh stick chairs should be steamed or boiled for one to two hours.

Heating and steaming times are approximate. Both too little and too much heating can lead to failures. It's probably safe to leave wood in a steamer for twice the recommended period before significant fiber damage occurs.

Making a Steamer

The steamer that I've used for years is more efficient than typical homemade steamers, a PVC pipe chamber connected to the steam source by a hose. My steam chamber consists of an elongated wooden box made of scrap wood with a gap in the center of the bottom that matches the diameter of the pot used to boil water. Four wooden cross dowels keep the wood being steamed above any condensation that develops on the steamer floor (see

fig. 4.5a). The steamer rests directly on the pot. Two crescent-shaped wooden lids are set on the sides of the pot rim that are not covered by the steamer. Pieces of foam rubber plug each end (see fig. 4.5b).

To increase steaming efficiency, make the box as small as possible. Mine is 68 inches long. Most Windsor bows are no more than 60 inches long, which allows 4 inches for each foam plug. If I have to steam a larger piece, such as a Windsor settee bow, I steam and bend one end at a time. (The center section of the settee bow is straight.)

You don't have to worry about building the box very tight—an airtight steamer would explode,. Also, condensation will develop inside the steamer. When using my steamer outdoors, I let water from condensation drip onto the ground. In the shop, I put a tray on the floor to catch the drips. Insulating the box might help maintain heat and minimize condensation, but I'm also concerned about increasing the risk of fire.

If your water pot is small, the steam chamber, balanced on the pot, could easily be tipped over. For safety, on the sides of the

A ragged fissure failure such as this is usually caused by incipient decay. Discard the piece.

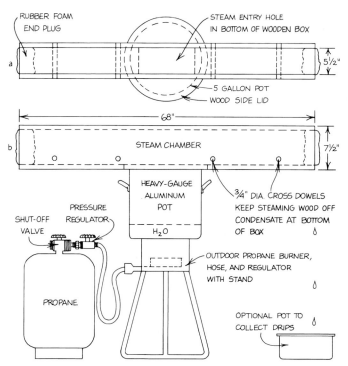

FIG. 4.5. Schematic for Country Workshops steamer. The steam chamber is a simple wooden box, with a hole on the bottom for entry of steam directly from the pot of boiling water.

Country Workshops steamer. The heat source is propane, coupled with a burner made for outdoor cooking. For indoor steaming, use an electric hot plate.

box you can clamp support sticks that extend to the floor. For further stabilization, put a weight on top of the steam box.

I've used several different heat sources. Gas burners work far better than electric hot plates. Camping stoves that burn kerosene or white gas work quite well, as does an ordinary kitchen stove. The best heat source I've found is a propane-fueled burner made for cooking outdoors. For safety, I use it only outside. I use a 5-gallon restaurant-style stock pot for the boiler—two-thirds full it holds enough water to boil for nearly two hours.

Keep your steamer away from your sharpening area. Metal dust in the steamer can cause oak to blacken or turn dark blue.

Before putting wood into the steamer, make pencil marks indicating center lines and direction of bending, something you don't want to deal with when you pull out the hot, steamed wood. Tie a twine tail around one end of each piece of wood going into the steamer, both for identification and to avoid having to reach into the steamer. You can tie knots into the ends of the twine tails to distinguish different pieces in the steam box.

Limbering Wood and Wood-Bending Forms

Bends in heavy wood, such as ladder-back posts, should be limbered immediately after steaming.

To make a limbering fixture, a simple bending brake that exercises the wood in the bending area before you secure it to a bending form, refer to the plans in figure 4.6. You can

also limber the posts using any appropriately distanced space between two fixed stations, such as the jaws of an opened bench vise. The advantage of the jig is that the interior bending surfaces are rounded; limbering with the jaws of a vise may leave indentations in the wood.

For most wood bending, you'll use bending forms, although the thin slats of our tutorial ladder-back are bent without them. I make bending forms the exact size and shape that I want the bent piece to take. You'll know the bend has set if you leave the bent wood on the form until it shrinks a bit and rattles loose.

Spring-back must be considered if one form must be used for many pieces and there is limited time for the bends to set. With a simple bend, such as a Windsor bow-back, it's possible to remove the wood from the form shortly after bending. This type of bend can be held in shape during drying with twine connecting the two ends of the bow.

Typical bending forms for Windsors use a 3/4-inch-thick plywood interior form with extension legs bolted to the back (fig. 4.7). The extension legs are used with removable pegs and wedges to secure the piece being bent against the form. At the top center of the form I often screw a permanent block in place instead of using a removable peg. The bottom of the block is angled to match a wedge. I prefer to make extension legs with scrap oak 1-1/2 to 2 inches thick, with 1-inch-diameter hardwood pegs.

The most elaborate bending form that I use is for the triple bend on the bow of a continuous-arm Windsor.

The form consists of a back bow and two elbow-armrest forms screwed to a plywood backing. I mount the elbow-armrest forms at a divergent angle of about 10 degrees. This requires shaping bending planes at compound angles on the armrest sections of the form. The ends of the bent

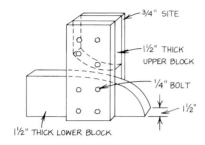

FIG. 4.6.
Limbering jig, used on chair legs after steaming but before putting the piece into the bending form

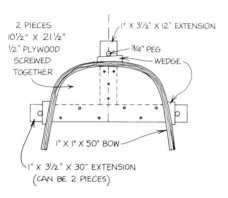

FIG. 4.7.
Bending form for a stick Windsor arm bow, shown with bent bow, pegs, and wedges in place

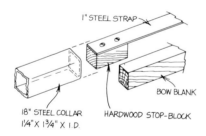

FIG. 4.8.
Bending straps are used to force a piece of bent wood into compression. The steel strap on the outside of the bend takes up the tension.

Steel bending straps help prevent tension failures on heavy bows.

arms are secured against the form with clamps while the bends set.

Bending Straps

Bending straps can dramatically reduce your bending failures when your chances of success look poor. Bends of heavy bows for English Windsors and Welsh stick chairs, particularly, are more likely to succeed if you use straps. The problem is not curvature; the comparatively thick-sectioned stock used for these chairs is much harder to bend than that of most American Windsor chairs.

Make bending straps from 1-inch-wide galvanized steel strapping, as shown in figure 4.8. The end fixtures are 4-inch-long wooden blocks secured at each end of the strap with two 3/16-inch bolts to secure each end block. The space between the blocks is the length of the piece to be bent, plus a gap to allow for a small amount of stretching. (I make the gap about 1/8 inch for a 50-inch piece.)

The strap and end blocks are coupled with sleeves that also act as extensions for leverage during the bend. The sleeves slip over the end blocks and about 6 inches past the ends of the wood being bent. Lengths of rectangular section steel tubing 20 inches long with interior measurements of 1-1/4 by 1-3/4 inches, the sleeves fit snugly over the end blocks (with bolts) and the piece to be bent. The advantage of using rectangular tubing is that you can use its flat sides to prevent or correct any twisting during the bend.

Place the straps over the piece to be bent immediately after steaming. (Prewarm them, if there is significant chance that they will absorb heat.) The bending procedure is the same as when you're not using straps.

CHOOSING AMONG WOOD SPECIES

All the wood species in this section are good choices for post-and-rung and Windsor chairs. I encourage you to try locally available species. Chairmakers in the eastern half of the United States and northern Europe should have little trouble finding excellent chairmaking materials. Chairmakers in the western United States and other areas where the forest is primarily conifers need to be more creative in locating materials. Don Weber, who lives on the Mendocino coast in California, has made and sold English-style Windsors for years, so I know it's possible. Check out fruit and nut woods and yard trees. Yew, for example, which is prized by British chairmakers, is generally not straight and clear, but it bends well and is an attractive wood.

Wood for Rived Posts, Rungs, Bows, and Spindles

Ash (*Fraxinus*) • There are many varieties of *fraxinus*, usually named with a color (white ash, black ash, green ash, etc.). Any *fraxinus* ash that is straight grained and clear will rive, shave, and bend into chair parts. Ash has little color or visual texture, but it is a dependable wood that grows in many areas where oak and hickory aren't available. (On the northwest U.S. coast a little-known species called Oregon ash has proven excellent for chairmaking.) Ash can also be pounded and then divided into splints for basketry and chair seats.

Hackberry *(Celtis occidentalis)* • A cream-colored, ring-porous wood that splits and bends nicely. Not particularly attractive, but very useful where available.

Hickory *(Carya)* • Heavy, tough, and usually easily bent, all of hickory's many subspecies are suitable for chairmaking, excellent for all parts of post-and-rung chairs, and the bows and spindles of Windsors. Hickory sapwood, almost white, mellows to ivory with age. Though the heartwood is often discarded, it is a rich brown that compares favorably with tropical exotics; the heartwood is often missing or splotchy in young trees, and in some subspecies and growing areas. Hickory splints are occasionally used for chair seats. See Chapter 7 for instructions for obtaining and using hickory bast, the inner layer of bark, a premium material for woven post-and-rung chair seats that look like rawhide.

Oak, White *(Quercus alba and others)* • My friend Daniel O'Hagan calls white oak the king of woods, and I believe he's right.

The U.S. lumber trade divides oaks into just two groups, white and red—not botanically correct but practical. The woods of the two are usually easy to distinguish, but not always—some red oak looks quite white, some white oak quite red. For details, refer to R. Bruce Hoadley's *Identifying Wood*.

For chairmaking, white oak tends to be more forgiving and more elastic than red oak. It appears to be less porous. When riving white oak there is often time to make corrections during the splitting process. Red oak tends to pop apart at unpredictable times. Slow-growing white oak sapwood and heartwood can sometimes be rived into fine splints for basketry and chair seating.

Oak, Red *(Quercus rubra and others)* • Both red and white oak are strong and tough. Red oak is usually redder, but the woods often look similar in color when finished with oil and given some age. Dry red oak is considerably easier to work than white, if you're shaving with hand tools, and red oak rives very nicely and bends just about as well as white oak. (Although I love white oak, I use red oak more frequently because high-quality red oaks are easier to find where I live.)

Pecan *(Carya illinoensis)* • Pecan and hickory are members of the same subgroup of the walnut family. In the eastern United States, pecans are native to low-lying areas of the Mississippi drainage and along parts of coastal Maryland, Virginia, and North Carolina. While not commonly used as a chair wood, these trees are available in orchards and yards across the warmer parts of the United States. Pecans planted as yard trees may be the better source, but even orchard trees, which tend to have many branches and little straight grain, may offer some good wood for chair parts. Bast from pecans resembles hickory bast.

Locust, Black *(Robinia pseudoacacia)* • While not commonly used for chairmaking, clear, straight-grained black locust wood is beautiful and can be rived, shaved, and bent into chair parts. Most black locusts have a rather twisted, gnarly shape, and large ones are often hollow in the inner heartwood. It's a species to experiment with if it is available.

Wood for Turned Posts, Rungs, and Spindles

While any of the listed riving woods are also suitable for turning, they won't render the fine detailing of these close-grained, mostly diffuse-porous species. (Turned ash is very common in English post-and-rung chairs.) For comparative bendability, I rank ash, elm, hickory, red and white oak, pecan, and yew as excellent, and beech, birch, cherry, black locust, red and sugar maple, and walnut as fair.

Beech *(Fagus)* • One of my favorite species and often available in log form at low cost, beech has a short, dense grain, and a handsome tawny, speckled appearance. Although not particularly favored in the United States, beech is highly regarded as a turning wood by English chairmakers, perhaps because beeches in England appear to grow cleaner and straighter than their relatives across the Atlantic.

Birch *(Betula)* • Birch wood, though not flashy, turns well and is strong. Birches grow in moist, cool to cold climates. White birch is common throughout northern Europe.

Cherry, Black or Wild *(Prunus serotina)* • A handsome wood that turns with crisp details, cherry can be used for all parts of post-and-rung and Windsor chairs. Pin cherry *(Prunus pensylvanica)*, weaker and a little lighter in color, can be used if parts are made a little thicker.

Mahogany, Central American *(Swietenia)* • Commonly used for all parts of high-quality, early American Windsors, this rich, even-grained, dependable species lacks character. I favor (and lobby for) the use of native hardwoods.

Maple, Red *(Acer rubrum)* • While not a great turning wood like sugar maple, red maple (sometimes called "soft maple") is much harder than silver maple, which I consider useless for chairmaking. Probably not suitable for turning ring-and-baluster Windsor legs, unless you keep the cove bit heavy.

Maple, Sugar *(Acer saccharum)* • Also called "hard maple" and "rock maple," sugar maple is the standard against which chairmakers measure all other turning woods. Black maple *(Acer nigrum)*, which may also be called "hard maple" and "rock maple," is similar.

Pear *(Pyrus communis)* • A European native, pear has been naturalized throughout much of the United States and is a good candidate chair wood for chairmakers in the western part of the country. Chair parts made from "fruit-wood" are often actually pear, which has been a prized furniture wood for centuries.

Yew *(Taxus)* • Medium brown, often fairly gnarly, and sometimes bearing an attractive, abstract speckled pattern, yew bends quite well—it's the only conifer suitable for chair legs, bows, and spindles. Seldom used in U.S. furniture, yew is highly prized by chairmakers in the United Kingdom, where it's most commonly used for Windsor arm and back bows (made from limbs), but also for turnings and even seats. A variety is native to the Pacific Northwest.

Walnut, Black *(Juglans nigra)* • Walnut chairs are mostly a contemporary phenomenon, although a few early American walnut Windsors exist. Walnut turns fairly nicely, and its clear, straight-grained stock is considered a good bending wood.

Elm *(Ulmus americana and others)* • While elm is not generally selected as a turning species, all-elm Windsors are fairly common in England. Elm is almost impossible to split; turning blanks must be sawed out.

Wood for Windsor Seats

Ash *(Fraxinus)* • *Fraxinus* can be used for all-ash Windsors, probably a contemporary concept. Saddling with traditional hand tools would be a chore. Ash is commonly used for factory-made chairs with shallow seats.

Butternut *(Juglans cinerea)* • A soft, open-grain species, beautiful but fragile, butternut is used in Windsors with natural finish.

Cherry *(Prunus serotina)* • Although not a traditional Windsor-seat wood, cherry is strong and beautiful, and all-cherry Windsors are impressive. Not my choice for carving.

Chestnut *(Castanea dentata)* • Occasionally used for seating in old American Windsors, chestnut resembles elm but weighs less and lacks elm's resistance to splitting. The chestnut blight killed *Castanea dentata* throughout North America; the wood is now quite valuable, especially in chair plank dimensions.

Elm *(Ulmus)* • The wood of choice for the seats of unpainted Windsors, elm is gorgeous, especially when slab sawed. A coarse-grained, medium-hard wood, it's not easy to carve and dulls tools quickly. Unfortunately, the great majority of elm trees in the United States and Europe have succumbed to Dutch elm disease, although you can still find elms in some forests or planted as shade trees, scattered almost anywhere.

Linden *(Tilia)* • Also known as basswood, and as lime in the United Kingdom, linden is a white wood slightly harder and more expensive than white pine, and without the resin problem. While it has no visual appeal, it takes paint very nicely and is a favored carving wood.

Maple *(Acer saccharum and A. rubrum)* • For seats, maple is associated with degenerate, factory-made Windsors, but this lovely wood is occasionally used for all parts of handsome, contemporary Windsors.

Oaks • Generally not used for Windsor seats except in cheap factory-made chairs, oak was commonly used in very old Welsh stick Windsors. Wild-grain live oak makes handsome but heavy seats.

Pine, White *(Pinus strobus)* • Commonly used for American Windsors, old and contemporary, pine is a weaker wood than I prefer for a Windsor seat. Almost always painted; stained pine tends to look muddy, although it's easy to carve and fairly available compared to other Windsor-seat species. Resin pockets can be a problem. Conifers in the western United States, such as spruce, western cedars, and many western pines, can be used for Windsor seats. Planks with closely spaced growth rings are preferred for their strength.

Poplar, Tulip *(Liriodendron tulipifera)* • Many of the oldest surviving American Windsors have tulip poplar seats. Also known as yellow poplar, this wood is denser than white pine and harder to carve. Tulip poplar makes a substantial seat; it takes paint nicely and also stains with predictability.

Walnut *(Juglans nigra)* • Like cherry, all-walnut Windsors are a contemporary notion. Gorgeous, of course.

The Project Chairs

All project chairs are made by Drew Langsner, except as noted.

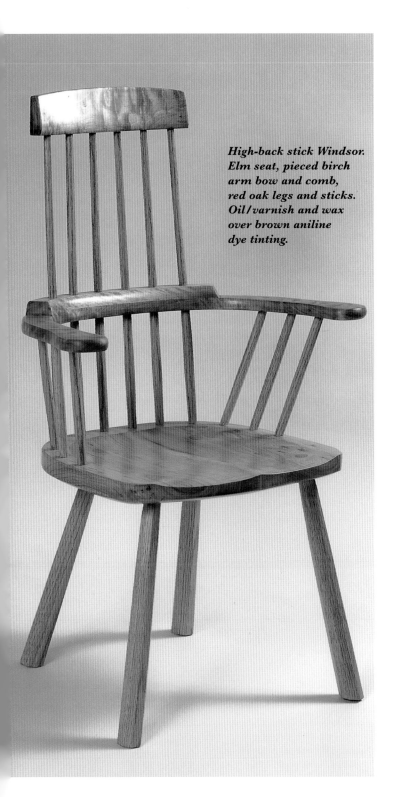

High-back stick Windsor. Elm seat, pieced birch arm bow and comb, red oak legs and sticks. Oil/varnish and wax over brown aniline dye tinting.

Ladder-back side chair. White oak, with hickory-bark seating.

*Sack-back Windsor armchair.
Tulip poplar seat, red oak bows
and spindles, maple turnings.
Alkyd enamel/varnish.*

*Continuous-arm Windsor. Pine
seat, red oak bows and spindles,
maple turnings.*

*Post-and-rung stool.
White oak with
hickory-bark seating.
Penetrating oil finish.*

*Low-back stick Windsor.
Tulip poplar seat, red oak
bow and sticks, maple
legs. Oil/varnish over-
coated with paste wax.*

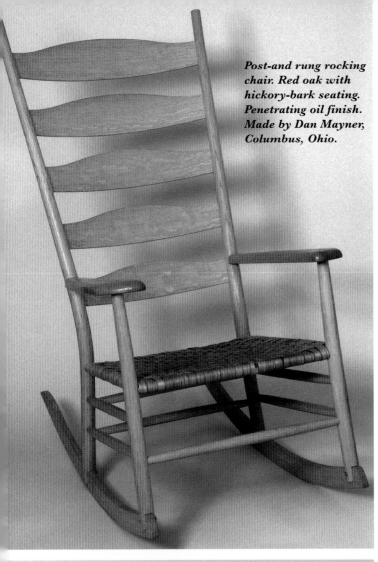

Post-and rung rocking chair. Red oak with hickory-bark seating. Penetrating oil finish. Made by Dan Mayner, Columbus, Ohio.

Post-and-rung youth chair. Red oak with hickory-bark seating. Penetrating oil finish.

Comb-back Windsor armchair. Tulip poplar seat, red oak bows, (bent) comb and spindles, maple turnings. Alkyd enamel/varnish.

Bow-back Windsor side chair. Tulip poplar seat, red oak bow and spindles, maple turnings. Alkyd enamel/ varnish.

Double-bow English-style Windsor. Elm seat, red oak bows and spindles, cherry splat, stretchers, and turnings.

Sack-back Windsor settee. Tulip poplar seat, red oak bows and spindles, maple turnings. Alkyd enamel/varnish.

Part Two:
Post-and-Rung Chairs

Riving the Materials

An English post-and-rung spindle-back rocker, c. 1850. The rush seat is new.

MATERIALS LIST: COUNTRY WORKSHOPS LADDER-BACK

Number of Pieces	Description	Rived Green Dimensions	Shaved Green Dimensions	Finish Dimensions
2	Front posts	1-3/4" sq x 20"	1-3/8" oct x 20"	1-7/16" dia x 18-3/4"
2	Rear posts	1-3/4" sq x 40"	1-3/8" oct x 34"	1-7/16" dia x 34"
3	Front rungs	1" sq x 18+"	3/4" oct x 18+"	11/16" dia x 17"
9	Side/rear rungs	1" sq x 14-1/2+"	3/4" oct x 14-1/2+"	11/16" dia x 14"
1	Upper slat	1/2" x 4 x 17"	3/16+" x 3-1/2" x correct fit	Same as shaved green
1	Lower slat	1/2" x 3-1/2" x 14"	3/16+" x 3-1/4" x correct fit	Same as shaved green

Riving is green-woodworking terminology for splitting wood with care, precision, and control. You want to keep individual rivings minimal in size to keep down waste and to save yourself work shaving parts to size. This riving can be done in a yard or on a sturdy shop floor, which keeps the end grain of the blanks clean.

For riving posts and rungs for the Country Workshops ladder-back, the tools you'll need are

- 2-person crosscut saw or chain saw
- Rough crosscut handsaw
- 1 or 2 wooden gluts
- Froe
- Small side axe
- 6-inch ruler
- Safety glasses
- Pencil
- 2 or 3 steel wedges

- 8-pound sledge hammer
- Froe club
- Chair stick
- Gloves (optional)
- Brake (useful but not necessary)
- Narrow starting wedge (optional)

STUDYING THE LOG

Riving is largely a series of decisions about what to do next. Before you begin, study your log. If you have a big, almost clear log — say 12 feet long with a 20-inch diameter—start by bucking a 40-inch block from the smaller end. If the log has only a 10- or 15-inch diameter and is kind of rough, begin by splitting it in half.

Here's the reasoning behind my choice: The big log probably has wood for many more chairs than you want to make at once; one 40-inch section from the small end may yield excellent wood for several chairs. What remains will comprise two more 40-inch sections, plus a chunk from the butt that may become firewood. (The butt end contains reaction wood, which splits unpredictably and does not shave easily. The butt is usually flared, or curved, so it won't yield the straight rivings required for rungs and most post styles.) On the other hand, the smaller log often has quite a few exterior and interior knots to deal with. Because the knots are at random locations, you can't predict where you'll find the most valuable parts, which you'll use for rear posts and back slats. Once the full-length log is split open, you can see what you're working with.

With the large log, crosscut a 40-inch block using a chain saw or a two-person crosscut log saw. If the log is muddy, axe off the bark at the crosscut section before sawing.

The First Split

- **The first rule in riving wood is that you must follow through with any split that already exists. If you don't, you'll lose control of your split and waste wood.**

The end grain of a log almost always shows some radial splitting that crosses the pith, probably the result of stress or impact when the tree was felled. Based on the first rule of riving, it's important to start with this existing split, even if it's in an undesirable location. If you start a new split at a different location, the original split also opens up, and you lose control of the process.

I don't think it matters which end you split first. (I studied this question when I was splitting about 10,000 shingles for our log house and couldn't find any significant difference.) To mark your intended splitting pattern, pencil a line on the end grain that follows the existing split and continues along a ray line to the bark. I use a water-soluble pencil that marks very legibly on wet wood.

If you don't wear glasses, put on safety glasses. You will be pounding steel wedges with a sledge hammer, and metal fragments may fly loose. A wooden club will be less effective. Do not strike steel wedges with the poll of your axe—this would not only ruin the axe head but increase the risk of flying metal fragments.

The log is usually horizontal, although if it's a short one, you can upend it. I start by scoring with an 8-pound sledge hammer and an ordinary splitting wedge. If you haven't already done so, shorten the handle of your sledge hammer to 20 to 24 inches for better balance.

To save your back, I suggest trying a body posture that has worked well for me and many others. Stand directly over the log, with your back toward the middle of the log. Bend your legs a little, so that your back isn't doing much of the work. With your left hand, hold the wedge on the pencil line. Lightly pound the head of the wedge. Swing the sledge in a direct line with the center of your body. Then move on to an adjacent section of the marked line. Serious splitting begins after scoring the line on both sides of the pith. Use the same body stance. Use a narrow-angled starting wedge, if you have one, placing it on the lower half of the end grain just inside the division between sapwood and heartwood. Again hold the wedge with your left hand and begin pounding with the sledge.

When the wedge begins to bite into the log, release it and hold the sledge with two hands, one hand forward toward the head of the sledge. Your forward arm does most of the lifting while your other arm works as a pivot. Be sure to pound in line with the axis of your body. Remind yourself that accuracy is more important than power—but pound with some gusto. Hit the wedge head square on. Off-center blows can knock the wedge crooked or make it pop out. Poor aim is also more likely to result in flying metal fragments or a broken sledge-hammer handle. When the wedge is started, you can relocate to the side of the log. Continue pounding until only 1 inch of the wedge head remains outside the log, then stop. Always leave this inch of wedge head. It gives you something to work with if the wedge doesn't come loose when you need it.

WARNING! Never put your hands inside the crack of a log to retrieve a wedge or for any other reason. Consider the log a giant spring until it divides into pieces with no connecting tension.

With the first wedge now almost buried in place, put a second steel wedge in the new split in the upper half of the log. Most likely, the first wedge has caused a split to open that follows the initial indentation across the log. Starting the second wedge is much easier. Drive in the second wedge until 1 inch

Before splitting a log, pencil a radial splitting line that extends from any pre-existing split.

Using a standard wedge to score along the penciled line. This small indentation will influence how the split develops.

Using a flat, narrow-angle starting wedge to start the split. The handle of the 8-pound sledge hammer has been cut down to 24 inches.

Leapfrogging a pair of wedges into the developing crack. Always leave 1 inch of wedge head above the bark.

Driving a standard splitting wedge into the bark side of the log. (The starting wedge could have been driven further into the log.)

Using gluts to widen the crack. Never put your hands into the opening; the log is now a giant spring.

of the head remains outside the log. By now, the first wedge may have loosened or fallen free, and you should see a split opening on the upper side of the log. Drive in a third steel wedge, starting along the tighter part of the crack. As before, leave 1 inch of wedge head showing.

Take a free wedge and leapfrog it in front of the most recently driven wedge. Continue leapfrogging wedges to the end of the log. If the log is a good one (and friendly), it will be close to splitting into separate halves. Some logs resist splitting in half because of crossing connective fiber in the inner heartwood—this could turn out to be excellent material.

You can open the crack farther using a homemade wooden glut, which can take a lot of beating if it's used with a little care. Look into the crack to find a clear opening for the glut, without cross fiber connecting the sides. With the glut in place, strike the head end square on. As you drive the glut in, buried wedges should come free, although some may remain.

Roll the log over, so that the lower crack faces up. Find a place along the crack to start a steel wedge or another wooden glut. Leapfrog wedges, gluts, or both. Be careful that newly placed wedges are not driven into any buried wedges on the opposite side—some may not have been released. You've now split the log in half. Examine the crack for buried wedges before axing any connective fiber that remains. If you must axe near a buried steel wedge, position yourself so that the wedge is beyond the arc of your swing. Sever the connective fibers.

I'm always struck by the knowledge that the wood in a freshly split log has never been exposed to light until now. No wood finish can capture this fresh, clean appearance, and it would be hard not to appreciate the tangy smell of a fresh split.

Visualizing Chair Parts

Now you can start thinking about where various chair parts are going to come from.

Look at the interior knots and notice how they all originate at the pith. Look for wavy wood indicating knots beneath the exposed surface, and note that the wavy fiber around a knot must be discarded along with the knots. Observe growth-ring width and where the pith lies.

To divide one of the half logs into quarter sections, use the same basic procedure as for making the original split. This time there will probably be no incipi-

The first view of the split log—a snapshot view of the tree's history, and wood that has never been exposed to dayli[...]

ent cracks to follow when marking out the split. It's usually a good idea to divide the half log into about equal quarter sections. When an even division would create sections that will mean excessive waste as wood is rived further, you can try dividing the half log into three sections. This split will probably run fairly straight, especially with sections only 40 inches long. (Windsor bows, which are commonly 60 inches long, require more nerve and luck throughout the splitting process.)

Splitting down the center of the half log, on the way to splitting it into four bolts, each an eighth of the original log.

Continuing the split into quarter-log bolts.

Locate gluts where cross fibers in the crack won't intercept their leading edge. Scattered cross fibers in the inner heartwood hold the split bolts together. I don't pull the bolts apart until all splits are complete. The heavy half-log is more stable than lighter split out bolts.

Severing connecting fibers in the split half-log with a hatchet. Note that the arc of the swung hatchet cuts away from the iron wedge.

The pieces you're now splitting are known as *bolts*; when they're rived into smaller blanks they're called *billets.*. You don't need to split all the bolts at once. Large chunks (say, half logs) will keep greener than smaller bolts. Since every log is different, you may get a different number of bolts than the log pictured here; for example, a small-diameter log may divide into only four bolts.

Once the log is in bolts, it's time for some serious planning. Most likely some bolts will look better than others. Look over the dimensions and grain configuration of each one. You'll reserve the best bolts for slats and rear posts, which are not only long but bent in the backrest section; these rivings should be as straight as possible.

Think first about the posts, which will be shaved green to 1-3/8-inch squares. Post rivings should be 1-3/4 to 2 inches across if you're a novice, or as narrow as 1-1/2 inches if you're experienced and have very good wood. Consider that all four posts taper to 1 inch in diameter at the foot end. Rear posts also have a long, gradual taper to 1 inch in the upper section. The posts require full dimensions only in the rung cage, the 1-3/8-inch section that will be mortised for the rung tenons.

Front posts start out about 20 inches long; you'll trim them to final length after assembly. The taper on the lower third of the front posts can utilize some natural curvature in the wood. (I explain how to straighten a curved post billet in the section on shaving the front posts in the next chapter.)

For the slats you need to save an 18-inch section of nearly perfect wood. I make the upper slats 3-1/2 inches wide. With oak, I prefer slats that are all heartwood. Oak sapwood is usually discarded, but you can use it if it's sound, and you don't mind having bicolored slats.

Rungs require fairly straight wood. They're split out from stock at least 1/2 inch overlength and trimmed later to 17 inches for front rungs and 14 inches for side and rear rungs. You'll rive rung blanks into 1-inch trapezoids. (If the wood rives really well, you could push down the size to about 7/8-inch trapezoids.) Rungs are shaved green to 3/4-inch squares.

Set aside the best bolts for rear posts and slats. Saw the remaining 40-inch bolts into halves (for front posts and rungs). Wood is inconsistent. You'll find material for long and short rungs in wood that won't make the best front posts. The best course is to make as many long rungs as possible, since you can always make them into short rungs later. You'll start by riving out rungs and front posts for practice before you rive the longer, more demanding rear posts. (The bolt reserved for slats can wait—you

Fine material for making several ladder-back chairs. Note the cant hook, used to turn the log.

won't need it until you've assembled the posts and rungs. If that is likely to be awhile, you can store the slat wood underwater, freeze it, or keep it in a plastic bag in a shady place.)

RIVING AND EXAMINING RUNG STOCK

Let's work with a hypothetical bolt 20 inches long that you're going to rive into long and short rungs. To figure out how to rive this piece into 1-inch "squares" for rungs, first measure with your ruler radially, from the beginning of the heartwood toward the pith. (Unless oak sapwood is 1 inch wide and from a fresh-cut tree, I discard it.) In ash and hickory, which may have almost nothing but sapwood, measure

from the cambium toward the pith. Pencil a line dividing the bolt in half (or thirds, if this is less wasteful). If you draw a chord across the full width, you'll waste a lot of heartwood just inside the cambium. Pencil in radial divisions of 1 inch, from the outside toward the pith, then mark off 1-inch-wide sections (see fig. 5.1). For splitting, you hope for an even number of divisions, but often this is not possible.

You're now ready to rive 1-inch rung billets with a froe and wooden club. The order of riving is important (see fig. 5.2). For the hypothetical bolt you've just marked out, your first riving removes the inner heartwood (fig. 5.2a). Place the froe blade on your riving line—be careful not to tilt the blade just before impact—then hit the back of the froe blade with the club. Be sure that the club comes down on the froe in line with the block of wood, not off to one side.

For rivings less than two feet long, you can use a polled axe instead of a froe. To do this, set the bolt upright on the ground or shop floor. If you're right-handed, use your left hand to hold the axe head in place on the end grain of the bolt. Hold the club with your right hand and smack it down directly onto the axe head. Test with a moderate impact at first, to get an idea of how much force is necessary—a too-powerful blow can drive the axe through the wood and into the floor or knock the axe head toward your leg.

- **The second rule of riving is that most splits should be divisions into halves, with near equal stiffness on each side.**

Layout for rung blanks. The sapwood on this red oak log will be discarded. It's a little too narrow, and already beginning to decay.

FIG. 5.1. Layout for riving 1-inch rung billets from an eighth section of an oak log, about 6 inches wide at the chord crossing the sapwood, which will be discarded. If this were ash or hickory, the divisions would begin at the cambium.

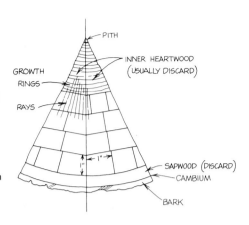

PITH

INNER HEARTWOOD (USUALLY DISCARD)

GROWTH RINGS

RAYS

SAPWOOD (DISCARD)

CAMBIUM

BARK

1"

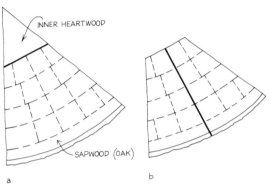

INNER HEARTWOOD

SAPWOOD (OAK)

a

b

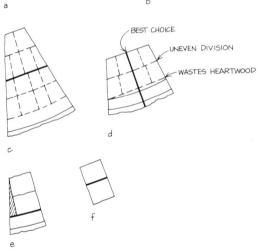

BEST CHOICE

UNEVEN DIVISION

WASTES HEARTWOOD

c

d

e

f

FIG. 5.2. Progression of rivings for rung or post billets: *a*, splitting off the inner heartwood, often discarded; *b*, radial split into divisions of approximate equal area; *c*, splitting tangent to the growth rings; *d*, another radial split; *e*, splitting, hewing, or shaving off the sapwood; *f*, final tangential split into equal billets

Usually the inner heartwood is wavy or contains knots, so you discard it. If it looks usable, set it aside for possible conversion into rungs. The second riving is radial, down the center of the remaining trapezoid (fig. 5.2b). The third riving is tangent to the growth rings (fig. 5.2c). (This riving could run out toward the smaller, inner trapezoid; off-center splits usually run out toward the narrower side because it is comparatively less stiff.) I probably wouldn't use the axe for this riving or for any of the smaller ones that follow.

Striking the head of a polled axe with a dogwood-root maul, an excellent method for riving medium-sized pieces

Riving small pieces with a froe and froe club, usually done on the shop floor, or on top of a chopping stump

Final riving, into rung billets. Note the straight, clear grain on this beautiful red oak.

FIG. 5.3.
Looking at imperfect rung rivings: *a*, "banana" riving; *b*, an S-rung; *c*, long rung with too much taper at one end

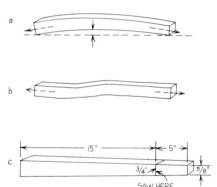

The fourth riving is an easy choice, a radial division into symmetrical sections (fig. 5.2d). Two alternative choices indicated in the figure would either create uneven segments or waste heartwood. The fifth riving separates off the sapwood. This riving will run out, forming a wedgelike chunk of waste. When this happens, turn the piece end for end, and rive off the sapwood from the other end. To help ensure the final split into even halves, use a drawknife to shave away the excess wood in the shaded area (fig. 5.2e). The sixth riving divides the wood into two very tidy rung billets about 1 inch wide on each side (fig. 5.2f). Repeat these six steps to rive the remaining pieces into rung blanks.

From the piece of inner heartwood you may be able to rive two or three rungs. Start riving either radially or on the tangent—the order probably doesn't matter.

As you examine your rung blanks for quality, you'll find some with a slight banana shape; you can use those with

curvatures up to 3/16 inch (fig. 5.3a). You can also use S-shaped rung blanks (fig. 5.3b), if the two ends are more or less in alignment and if you like a rustic look; these can make attractive middle or lower rungs. (You'll sometimes find that a bolt that appears quite straight produces curved rung billets; this curvature develops when riving releases internal tension within the wood.) Also, a long front-rung blank that tapers too much can often be converted into a shorter side or rear rung (fig. 5.3c). The minimum width for a green rung riving is about 13/16 inch: Although the tenons are just 5/8 inch in diameter, you form them after rung stock has dried, and you need some surplus to smooth the rung and to allow for drying shrinkage. Tiny pin knots, about 1/16 inch in diameter, are no problem. (These occur when a solitary leaf cluster develops on the tree trunk.)

Always rive more parts than the chair requires. Some rivings will warp or check during drying, and others may turn into seconds as you work on them. Rive at least sixteen rungs, including five or six long front rungs, and at least three front posts and three rear posts. You can always use the extra stock for test joints and to practice chopping slat mortises. Or on another chair.

RIVING THE POSTS

Rive front-post blanks roughly 20 inches long, even though their trim height is 18-3/4 inches. The ideal post rivings are 1-3/4 inches across (fig. 5.4a), but I often use 2-inch units. One end of the riving can taper to about 1-1/8 inch. You can work with some curvature in the rived front posts, particularly toward only one end (fig. 5.4b), but a front-post riving with a gradual curve along the full length will be a challenge to shave—you will have to deal with descending grain (fig. 5.4c).

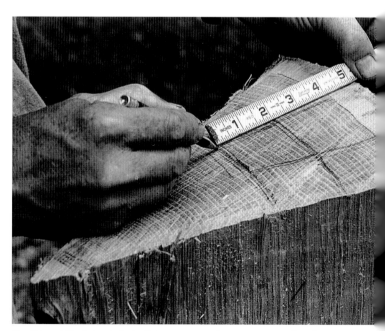

Pencil layout for the posts. I also hope to squeeze a bonus post or two from the inner heartwood.

FIG. 5.4. Front post rivings: *a*, a perfect riving (dashed line indicates shape of post with taper at lower end); *b*, an acceptable riving whose curvature at one end doesn't interfere with shaving a front post; *c*, a riving whose elongated curvature makes shaving a front post tricky but possible

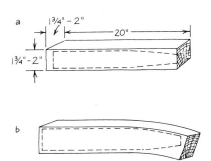

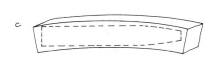

Using a splitting brake, a forked tree trunk supported by opposing poles. The brake steadies the bolt, making precise riving easier.

Splitting the rear posts

Wood for the rear posts is both longer and of better quality than wood for rungs or front posts. The backrest section of the rear posts that takes the bend must be free of defects. Rive the back posts from full-length stock (40 inches)—trim length of the rear posts is 34 inches. Riving longer pieces gives you more choice when it comes to locating the 34-inch posts.

The end-grain layout is the same as for the front posts. Draw out a riving plan on the end of the bolt similar to the rung layout, but with 1-3/4- to 2-inch sides. Start by riving off the inner heartwood, followed by a radial riving down the center. Then you must decide how to proceed, considering the same factors you looked at for riving the rungs.

For riving the rear posts I recommend using a *brake* made from a narrow-forked tree crotch. Place the blank inside the fork, using the near limb as a support. When using a brake, the froe blade is set horizontal across the end of the blank. Center the froe blade on the blank, leaving some free space between the line of the froe handle and the

near edge of the blank. (You don't want the froe handle, or your knuckles, to intercept the riving blank when the froe blade is driven into the wood.) It's also useful to have free space between the froe handle and the wood so that you can pound on the froe blade with a narrow club after the froe has entered the wood. If you don't have a brake, set the wood on end by balancing it or leaning it against something.

Carefully place the froe blade across the end grain and smack the back of the froe blade with your froe club, holding the blade steady. (If after the first smack you decide that the froe blade was not perfectly positioned and you have an incipient crack where you don't want it, remember the first rule of riving! You must finish this riving anyway.)

It may take two or three smacks before the froe enters the end grain; continue until the blade is buried to its full width in the wood. Keep hitting the exposed blade until the back of the froe blade is about 1 inch into the wood.

Continue to open the split by levering the froe with the handle—always downward, or toward yourself. Slip a scrap of wood behind the froe blade to keep the crack open and take pressure off the blade. With the crack held open, slide the froe forward. Repeat by levering and advancing the froe until the piece rives in half. Rive three rear posts for each chair you plan to make.

An alternative to riving along rays and growth rings is to lay out a grid (fig. 5.6), useful when high-grade wood is riving very predictably. You should have less waste, but you will create rivings with a tilted growth-ring–ray orientation. (Discard any grid riving with the pith inside the area of the cylinder to be shaved.)

You sometimes will choose not to divide a section into even halves—when, for example, that would mean excessive waste or when a section contains an intrusive knot. You can sometimes successfully rive large, stiff bolts into thirds. With some bolts, you may choose to rive away waste wood. For instance, if a post riving turns out to be 2-1/2 inches across, you can rive off about 3/4 inch of waste, knowing that the riving will run out toward the narrower side of the crack. The scrap will probably be a long, tapered wedge. Rive off the roughest side, preserving the best original side.

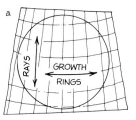
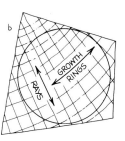

Fig. 5.5. Growth-ring orientation of rived and shaved posts: *a*, conventional riving with placement of shaved cylinder; *b*, skewed or irregular riving—the shaved cylinder remains unaffected.

Placing a piece of scrap behind the split, so that the froe can be moved forward into the riving

RIVING VARIATIONS

In the riving examples so far, the layouts were in trapezoids, generally following the rays and growth rings of the wood (see fig. 5.5a), the obvious path to take when riving parts that resemble pie slices. But rivings can take any configuration. You can skew them at an angle to the rays or growth rings (fig. 5.5b) or even create rivings with five sides. If your goal is to make cylinders, the original rived shape is irrelevant—when you've finished shaving the cylinder, you will still have the conventional ray–growth ring configuration.

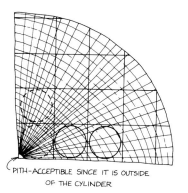

Fig. 5.6. A grid layout for clear, straight-grained wood that is riving perfectly. The yield will be greater than riving trapezoidal billets.

PITH–ACCEPTABLE SINCE IT IS OUTSIDE OF THE CYLINDER

Rived billets for one chair, left to right: three front posts, sixteen rung blanks (all overlength), three rear posts

Correcting Rivings during a Split

A riving often runs to one side of the original blank, because either the froe was misplaced or the stiffness on the sides of the split was uneven. It's sometimes possible to control the direction of runout, especially with the longer rivings.

If you're riving with a brake and the split starts to run toward you (and toward the froe handle), release pressure on the froe. Rotate the blank 180 degrees and resume with the froe, pulling the handle toward the heavier side of the blank. If you're successful, the advancing crack will migrate back toward the thicker section. If the crack passes center, rotate the blank again, so that you can pull toward the side that is now the wider.

• **Riving rule number three: To correct a riving, pull the froe toward the heavier side.**

Correcting a riving is based on the fact that pulling the froe puts tension on the surface of the near side of the split. The fibers in tension begin to tear, making that side narrower.

When you correct a riving, proceed cautiously, a small step at a time. Go easy. Stop often to examine how the crack is developing. Look at both sides of the bolt, and rotate the blank as soon as you see evidence that the crack is wandering.

This riving correction process doesn't always work. For instance, rung pieces may be too stiff and short for directing the split. Correcting a white oak riving is much easier than correcting red oak, which splits so quickly it almost snaps apart. If a riving runs off center so far that you see no possibility of correcting it, you can try to save the piece by "back

riving." Stop riving and remove the froe. Turn the piece end for end, and resume riving from the new end. If the original crack was determined to run in one direction, you may be able to compensate by starting the new riving a little off center. With luck, the two rivings will run together and the bolt will come apart. Sometimes you have to settle for only one good piece—and sometimes you lose both pieces.

Sawed Rivings

When a bolt will barely make two rivings, and the wood has been splitting predictably, go ahead and rive it. But if the wood is less predictable, it makes sense to go after these critical divisions with a band saw or rip-tooth panel saw. A saw cut will eat a kerf, and there will be a bit of jitter and wandering during the cut. But carefully done, sawing is predictable, and the quality of the parts will be as true to the grain as pure rivings.

For bolts that are to be band sawed, the facet of the riving that slides on the band-saw table must be smoothed and fairly flat. (If it's irregular, the bolt will twist during sawing, the saw blade will bind in the kerf, and you won't be able to control the cut. Jagged bits of wood fiber may even pull off the circular guard plate that the blade passes through.) For band-sawing rivings, I clamp a homemade *point fence* to the band-saw table, directly in line with the saw teeth. (The point fence is a block of wood shaped so that only the tangent of a rounded end makes contact with the wood being sawed.) Sometimes I band saw freehand, following a line drawn on the wood. For band sawing pieces that are heavy or longer than 3 feet, you'll need a buddy to catch the sawed pieces, or a stable roller stand.

CHAPTER 6

Post-and-Rung Construction:
The Country Workshops Ladder-Back

The finished ladder-back chair, before weaving the seat

The ladder-back with a hickory-bark seat

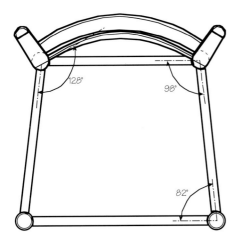

FIG. 6.1. Plan view

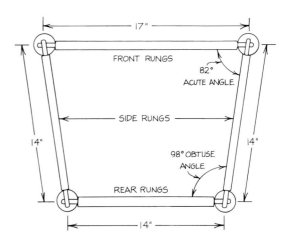

FIG. 6.4. Plan view of the ladder-back frame, with parallel front and rear rungs. Rung lengths include 1-inch tenons at both ends.

Scale: 1:8

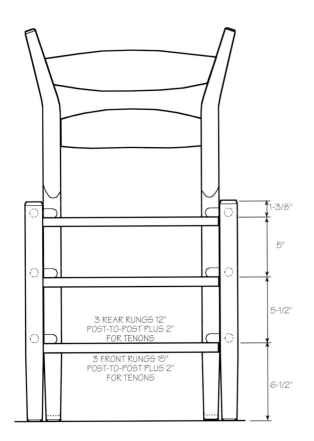

FIG. 6.2. Front view

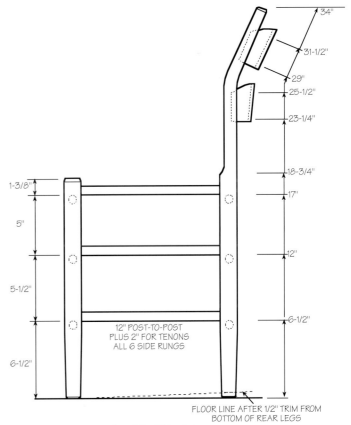

FIG. 6.3. Side view

The post-and-rung chair you will make in this chapter is an ambitious first project in green-wood chairmaking. If you are a novice chairmaker, I suggest you make the post-and-rung stool in Part 4 first. I chose the ladder-back as the first chair project because in making it you learn all the basic concepts and shop techniques you'll need for making chairs from green wood. It's a great deal to absorb: You're dealing with the essential skills and knowledge of an entire specialized trade. Think of this chapter not just as instructions for making a post-and-rung chair, but as your basic chairmaking reference.

Based on the chair described by John Alexander in *Make a Chair from a Tree*, this tutorial ladder-back takes members of a Country Workshops class six full days to make, including its Shaker-tape or hickory-bark seating. Although traditional in style, it weighs less, looks lighter, and is probably stronger than most older post-and-rung chairs.

All the chair's parts are shaved, not turned. I prefer shaving wood, unless precise roundness is required. The ring-porous woods such as oak, ash, and hickory that rive easily work exceptionally well with a drawknife and spokeshave. These species can also be turned, but they are less suitable for turning than the diffuse-porous woods, which are perfect for lathe work. If your wood source is primarily diffuse-porous species, such as maple or birch, consider using sawed stock and turned parts for your chairs.

Whether turned or shaved, however, handmade chairs offer something special, and better, than chairs made in a factory. In a culture where neat, round things are common and precision manufacturing is the norm, even for the cheapest object, we are again coming to appreciate things made by skilled hands that leave a unique mark on the work. (If you choose to use a lathe to make parts, I suggest turning green wood; the procedure is basically the same as for shaving. Turning blanks can be rived or selected sawed stock.)

BEFORE YOU BEGIN: LOOKING AT MATERIALS AND DESIGN

For a shaved chair, all the wood you need can come from one straight red or white oak, ash, or hickory log (or other ring-porous hardwood), with clear sections at least *40 inches long*. You can use a log as small as 8 inches in diameter, but a bigger log will give you more leeway in case of imperfections or hidden knots (to select a log, see Chapter 4; for riving, see Chapter 5).

The chair's frame has twelve rungs (eight remain visible after the seat is woven). The side and rear rungs are the same length, the front rungs several inches longer. The rung lengths are in even inch increments, because the tenons are an inch long, and the seating material (if it is Shaker tape) is an inch wide.

The front and rear rungs are parallel, and the side rungs are divergent, a chair plan that is a symmetrical trapezoid.

The acute angles formed by the intersections of the side and front rungs are complementary to the obtuse angles formed by the intersections of the side and rear rungs (see fig. 6.4). The front and rear rungs are located below the lower tangent of the side rungs. If the two sets of rungs intersected the posts at the same height, it would greatly weaken the joinery. For seating comfort, the front and rear rungs take the lower position so that the woven seat drops down slightly in front.

SHAPING TOOLS

While you can shave chair parts using a bench vise or other holding device, a shaving horse makes the task easier and more enjoyable. So before you start shaving rungs, I recommend you make a shaving horse (see Chapter 18).

If you're new to drawknife work, try using your drawknife bevel up and bevel down. I usually work bevel down, depending on the drawknife and how it's sharpened. (See Chapter 3 for details on blade geometry.) The drawknife is basically a pulling tool, with depth of cut controlled by tilting the handles. Think of wood fiber as fur—a smooth, controlled shaving requires that you pull the drawknife into ascending wood fiber, or in the natural direction of the fur.

Practice shaving with a drawknife on a spare riving. The first strokes will cut downward, leaving ascending fibers at the wood surface (fig. 6.5a). As long as you shave in this direction, you are "stroking the fur" and producing a controlled cut. But at some point you must turn the stick end for end, so that you can shave the other end. When you shave into descending fibers, the drawknife tends to act like a wedge instead of a cutting tool; the fibers split ahead of the drawknife cutting edge, leaving a rived surface (fig. 6.5b). You'll continue to create this rived surface until you work down to the area where you are drawknifing parallel or into ascending fibers, when you'll resume smooth cutting.

If you reverse the wood end for end quite often, you drawknife into the fiber only at a shallow angle and run little danger of splitting wood. The surface left by the drawknife will always be smooth.

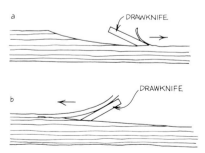

FIG. 6.5. Basic wood shaving: *a*, for a smooth cut and control, always shave into ascending fiber; *b*, shaving into descending fiber results in a wedgelike effect, with the wood tearing ahead of the cutting edge.

Making a Chair Stick

Chairmakers traditionally make post-and-rung chairs not from a plan on paper but with a chair stick like the one shown for the Country Workshops ladder-back. Each chair style has its own chair stick, which includes most of the design information. Once you use a chair stick, you'll find it much more convenient and dependable than a tape measure or folding rule (although we'll use both plans and rulers in constructing this ladder-back).

Make your chair stick from a planed wooden lath about 1/4 inch thick, 1-1/2 inches wide, and at least as long as the rear posts. On the front of the stick is a schematic for the front and rear posts. The cross lines and circles on the lower half of the stick indicate the location for boring the side rungs. Borings are located by tangent lines, not center points, as in most other construction. The circles above the tangent lines remind you to bore above the lines, not below or centered on the lines, a frequent mistake. The narrow rectangles on the upper half of the stick represent mortises for the slats. The stick also indicates the top of the front and rear posts, the diameter of the posts, where the posts begin to taper, and to what dimensions. The reverse side of the stick shows the rung lengths, only two for this chair.

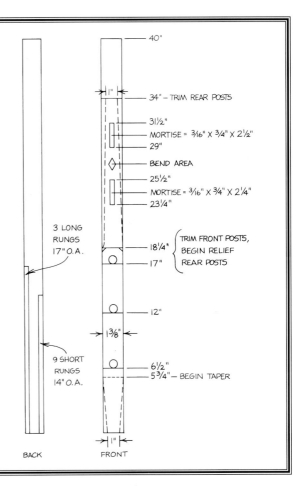

There are times when you purposely use the drawknife as a splitting tool, to quickly reduce oversized stock to close dimension. With practice, you'll learn how to split away waste wood quickly and efficiently by tilting the drawknife as you pull into the fibers.

Then you begin careful shaving, cutting into ascending grain and turning the stock end for end frequently.

SHAPING RUNG RIVINGS

Here's the drill for shaving the sixteen rungs for this chair: Shave all the rung rivings into regular, square-shaped sections, then into octagonal sections, then into nice, round cylinders. It takes some practice. (You'll use the same approach to shave the front and rear posts.)

The tools you'll need are

- Sharp drawknife
- Flat spokeshave
- Shaving horse
- Green rung gauge
- Ruler
- Water-soluble pencil

The green rung gauge is a notched piece of wood or other material you'll use to quickly determine the width of a piece of wood. A typical wooden gauge might be 2 by 5 inches and 1/4 inch thick (see fig. 6.6). Sometimes I make these gauges out of colored acrylic plastic, which shows up

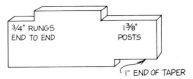

FIG. 6.6. Gauge for shaving posts and rungs from green wood

better if I drop one among the shavings on the shop floor. Since you're shaving green wood, you need a 3/4-inch-wide rung notch, a 1-3/8-inch notch for the cage section of the posts, plus a 1-inch notch for the taper at the post foot end. You'll make separate gauges for green and air-dried stock. If you don't want to make a rung gauge, you can use a standard 3/4-inch open-end mechanic's wrench.

In green-wood chairmaking the terms *ray plane* and *growth-ring plane* refer to conceptual planes roughly parallel to the rays or tangent to the growth rings (fig. 6.7). It is often

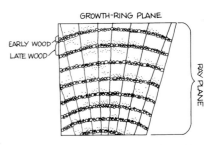

FIG. 6.7. A typical trapezoid-shaped riving

important to know which plane you're working on. (Technically, the rays are convergent, and there are no real growth-ring planes; "plane tangent to the growth rings" is a more accurate description, but too cumbersome.) In the figures, concentric arcs indicate growth rings and more-or-less straight convergent lines indicate rays.

The two planes are perpendicular. When you shave on the ray plane, the growth rings are facing up, and vice versa.

Shaving Rung Rivings into Squares

Before you start shaving a riving, examine it. Is it big enough? Is there too much curvature? Any other defects?

Select the better of the two ray planes to shave first. This orientation offers less resistance, and the work is easier than shaving the growth rings. Set the riving on the shaving-horse bridge with the growth rings running up and down (fig. 6.8a). As you shave the ray plane (fig. 6.8b), the growth-

ring plane diminishes, so you'll have less work when you shave the growth rings. Remove just enough wood so that the surface is flat, straight, and free of defects. Just kiss the surface with your drawknife. As you shave, reverse the rung end for end several times so that you won't be cutting deeply into descending fiber. Bringing the dimension to 3/4 inch will be done from the opposite side.

Look at the riving from one end, down the length of the stick, a perspective that exaggerates any curvature. A surface can be flat but twisted lengthwise. You see twist by comparing the near and far ends of the surface being flattened (fig. 6.9).

Rotate the rung 90 degrees to dress the best growth-ring plane (fig. 6.8c). Follow the line of the growth rings, which you can see on the sides of the rung. You can do some straightening on the growth-ring plane, but remember that you'll be creating descending fiber.

Drawknife Safety and Special Techniques

A drawknife with a sharp blade can be dangerous—not the apparent danger of pulling the drawknife into your torso (try it in slow motion), but cutting your fingers or legs on the end corners of the blade. You can prevent many drawknife cuts by filing or grinding a radius at these sharp, square corners.

A fairly common accident with a drawknife feels like a gut punch. The chunk of wood you're shaving pulls loose from the jaws of the shaving horse and socks you in the stomach, usually when you're shaving large, heavy, wet or frozen bolts. To prevent getting punched by a bolt of wood you can: (1) Take lighter shavings; (2) put some kind of teeth on the lower edge of part of the shaving-horse jaw—a piece of a Surform blade works nicely; or (3) wear a breast bib, a protective plate that hangs from a string looped around your neck. My bib is a piece of 1/2-by-6-by-9-inch hardwood, with a hole for the string drilled lengthwise through the upper end.

For extra control, or when you're shaving very hard or figured wood, skew or slice the drawknife. To skew, hold the drawknife at an angle to the direction of the cut, with one hand well ahead of the other hand as you pull it toward you. To slice, draw the blade sideways (for instance, from left to right) as you pull the drawknife toward you. You can also combine skewing and slicing. Experiment.

When you must shave the end of a riving that has descending fibers, you have several options. You can always use the drawknife as a push tool, although it's more difficult to control. Or you may be able to place the wood on the far side of the shaving-horse jaw, so that you can shave the end into ascending fibers with a standard pull cut. Another option is to secure the wood with a vise or dogs on a workbench.

For fine work, use a spokeshave or a block plane. Both tools have fenced blades and work well in pull or push directions.

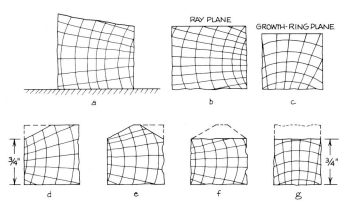

Shaving on the growth-ring plane surface before thicknessing. Note the skew angle of the drawknife.

FIG. 6.8. Shaving a rived trapezoid into a square section: a, the riving; b, shave one ray plane; c, shave one growth-ring plane; d, begin thicknessing on shaved ray plane; e, continue on opposite ray plane; f, shave straight across the top; g, rotate the piece 90 degrees and follow steps d, e, and f, ending with a square section.

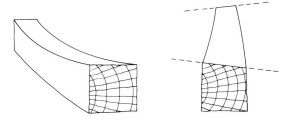

FIG. 6.9. Bowed and twisted surfaces seen from an end view of the rung

After dressing a ray plane and a growth-ring plane, you're ready to reduce the rung to specified thickness by shaving the opposite sides of the riving. Measuring from the common arris, pencil a 3/4-inch mark at the ends of both dressed sides. Then use the pencil and your hand as an improvised marking gauge. Hold the pencil between your thumb and first finger. Set your middle finger under your thumb and against the adjacent dressed side of the rung. Adjust your fingers so that the pencil is on one of the 3/4-inch marks. Slide your hand along the edge of the rung to the other end. This may seem inexact, but it's close enough for chairmaking. With a little practice, marking with a hand-held pencil becomes a very useful technique.

Place the rung on the shaving-horse bridge with the rived (unshaved) ray plane facing up. The thicknessing line is visible on only one side of the riving. In three steps, you'll shave the rung to the correct thickness. First, shave a chamfer to the marked line (fig. 6.8d). Then chamfer the opposite side to approximately 3/4 inch (fig. 6.8e), forming something like a gable roof. (An approximation is okay because the octagon and final cylinder will clip off the corners.) Finally, shave

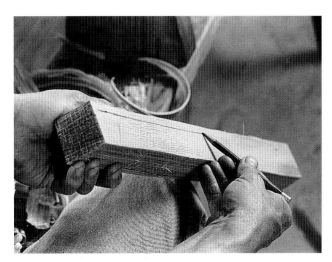

Penciling lines 3/4 inch from the common arris of a dressed plane—use your hand as a marking gauge.

away the gable peak to 3/4 inch (fig. 6.8f). Be sure to turn the wood end for end frequently in this last step.

Rotate the rung 90 degrees to the final rived surface, a growth-ring plane, and follow the same three-step process (fig. 6.8g). Use the notch gauge to check rung width on all four sides.

Shave your complete set of rung rivings into square sections before shaving any of the rungs into octagons.

Taking an angled shaving down to one of the penciled lines. The ray plane is facing up.

Flattening the gable roof. The rung blank is now very close to 3/4 inch in width across the growth ring plane.

Angling the billet onto an arris, to shave the square into an octagon. Note the small V-notch cut into the bottom of the shaving-horse jaw.

Taking an angled shaving on the side opposite the penciled line. Since the rung will eventually be round, you can guess how far to shave on this side of the riving. Note the resulting "gable roof" on the ray plane.

Using the notch gauge to check the dimensions of the shaved square rung. The growth-ring plane is still about 1/16 inch proud (oversized).

Spokeshaving the square rung billet into an octagonal section. Skewing produces a smoother surface and causes the shavings to eject to one side.

Shaving Rung Squares into Octagons

Reexamine the rungs for accurate dimensions and use a spokeshave to dress any that require sizing. You can shave regular octagons only from neat square rungs.

You don't need a measured layout for shaving the flats of the octagon. Place the square rung blank on the shaving horse at a 45-degree angle, with one arris on the bridge and the opposite arris face up for shaving. To steady the tilted square rung you can saw away a small inverted V on the underside of the shaving-horse jaw.

Spokeshave a narrow chamfer along the arris. End for end the piece to continue the chamfer. Rotate the rung 180 degrees and start another narrow chamfer. Continue by chamfering the third and fourth arrises. You should now have an octagon whose original flats are considerably wider than the new chamfers (fig. 6.10a).

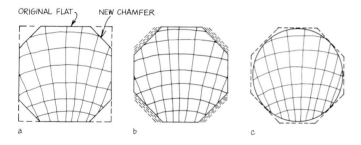

Fig. 6.10. Shaving a square into a circle: *a*, square billet with new chamfers started at the edges; *b*, continue chamfering until the new chamfers are as wide as the diminishing original flats; *c*, spokeshave the octagonal billet into a circular section.

Continue spokeshaving the new chamfers until their width matches the original flats of the square. As the chamfers widen, the original flats get narrower. Rotate and end for end the rung frequently, sneaking up on the final dimensions. Don't try to quantify how wide the chamfers should be—visually compare the width of the flats and chamfers. Stop when it becomes difficult to distinguish flats from chamfers without referring to the growth-ring pattern on the ends of the rung (fig. 6.10b). Check the dimensions with your notch gauge. Rounding the rungs (fig. 6.10c) is best done after the octagonal rungs are dry.

I usually air dry octagonal green rungs for several weeks by stacking them crisscross in a breezy shed, an ideal method. (For details on drying, see Chapter 4.) Rungs can remain in this air-drying stack until a few days before you need them, even years later.

Your rungs need to be thoroughly kiln dried (or the equivalent) before you make tenons. Make a simple kiln, as described in Chapter 20, or find a drying area around your house or shop. A rack above a furnace or woodstove works fine for drying small quantities.

Spokeshave Techniques

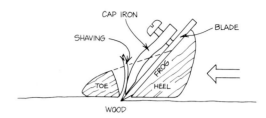

Using a spokeshave is easier than drawknifing, but for good spokeshaving, you need a properly tuned and sharpened tool (for help, see Chapter 3). Although a spokeshave is generally pulled, it also works nicely as a push tool. Its fenced blade determines depth of cut.

You can avoid two common missteps if you (1) set the depth of the blade to take a thin shaving and, (2) after sharpening, remember to replace the blade bevel down in the spokeshave body.

A spokeshave is basically an extremely short hand plane. For proper shaving, ride the tool so that the toe (the leading section of the sole) and the protruding blade are in contact with the wood, as shown in the figure. The function of the heel (the trailing section of the sole) is to support the blade. If you hold the spokeshave so that it rests on the heel, the tool will chatter, and the wood will be torn rather than shaved.

When spokeshaving ornery or figured wood, take very thin shavings and add some skewing or slicing action to your stroke. Skewing also ejects shavings to one side, so there is less chance of shavings jamming just behind the throat.

A common problem with spokeshaves is making tiny nicks on the surface of nicely finished cylindrical rungs and posts, just by setting the blade down on the wood. To avoid them, adjust the blade at a slight angle, with one end of the edge backed off above the sole (zero blade protrusion). Begin the cut by setting the spokeshave down at the "bladeless" part of the sole. Slice to one side as you pull the spokeshave. The angled blade won't nick at the beginning of the cut.

To monitor drying, weigh the same bundle of rungs on succeeding days. I use a digital postal scale that measures in tenths of an ounce and units of 2 grams. When they stop losing weight (moisture), they are as dry as they're going to get in the current environment. Kiln-dried rungs feel dry against your cheek and make a sharp sound when tapped against each other, compared to the dull sound of green rungs tapped together.

The tutorial post-and-rung chair has standard round upper rungs, but I often use a special "air-foil" rung across the front of the seat. Some post-and-rung chairs use air-foil rungs for the entire round of seating rungs. Air-foil rungs serve two purposes: First, the extra width helps support the seating material; it is less likely to sag, and there is greater supporting surface area. Second, air-foil rungs are much stiffer than conventional round rungs, which can cave in when a seat is tightly woven across them.

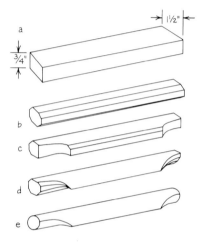

Start by riving a rectangular long rung blank, roughly 1 by 2 inches in section. Ideally, the growth rings are parallel to the 2-inch width. Shave the blank 3/4 inch deep and 1-1/2 inches wide (a). Shape the blank to an octagon section, making chamfers about the same width as if the blank was 3/4 inch square (b).

To rough out the 1-inch tenons at the ends, use a drawknife, bevel down, to scoop out the waste. Begin the scooping cut about 2-1/2 inches from each end (c). Shave the tenon part as close as possible to 3/4 inch square. Shape the scooped part and tenon to octagon sections (d).

Shave the space between the two scooped areas to the air-foil (or teardrop) section. Finish shaping the air foil with a spokeshave. Finish shaping the tenons with a rasp or tenon cutter or on a lathe (see the sidebar "Alternative Tenon-Making Tools and Methods" in this chapter).

SHAPING THE FRONT POSTS

Shaving the front posts begins with the same procedure as shaving the rungs: Shave squares from the rivings, then octagons, then cylinders. The major difference is that you'll taper the lower ends of the posts before you shave the upper ends into octagons. Post rivings that are bowed can often be straightened without sacrificing strength. You'll use the same tools as for rungs, with the possible addition of a block plane. Plan on taking a full day to shave three front and three back posts.

Rivings for finished front posts of 1-3/8 inches diameter should be about 1-3/4 to 2 inches wide on each side. You have some flexibility: Perfect rivings can be slightly under 1-1/2 inches on each side, or you could make the posts lighter, perhaps 1-1/4 inches in diameter. Rivings that are more than 2-1/4 inches across should be rived again at 1-3/4 inches to save time when it comes to drawknifing.

Although the front posts will be trimmed to 18-3/4 inches, you want rivings about 20 inches long to help prevent the post from splitting when you drive the top rungs into the mortises.

Shaving with a small block plane, very useful for straightening a curved post or dealing with wavy grain. Note the skewed angle.

Penciling a line around the post's four sides—the tapers begin about 3/4 inch below the tangent line for the lower rungs.

Shaving Front-Post Rivings into Squares

Saw a square foot at the lower end of each front post blank. This is important, since you measure with the chair stick from the foot upwards.

As with rungs, begin by shaving one rived side on the ray plane to a straight, flat surface. Then rotate the post stock 90 degrees to shave a growth-ring plane. Follow the same steps as for rungs (see fig. 6.8). Stop when the post is 1-3/8 inches square in section. Square up the remaining front posts in the same way.

Tapering the Squared Front Posts

To lay out the taper on the lower section of the front post, first examine a square post from an end view to decide which end you want to taper. If the post is fairly straight, either end can be tapered. If it curves mostly at one end, shave the taper into the curved end. If it has a uniform curve of over 1/4 inch, I recommend trying another riving.

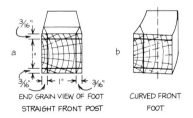

FIG. 6.11. Layout for tapering post ends: a, for a straight post, center layout on the end; b, for a curved post, the 1-inch square is in line with the rung (cage) section of the post.

Use the chair stick to mark the beginning of the taper, 3/4 inch below the lower rung tangent line on all four sides of the post. Secure the square post vertically in a bench vise. Now draw a 1-inch square centered on the rung section of the post; if the post is straight, you'll draw two sets of parallel lines 3/16 inch in from the edges of the post (fig.

6.11a). You now have a 1-inch square centered on the end of the post. If the post is bowed at one end, you will have to locate the 1-inch square in line with the mass of the cage (rung) section of the post (fig. 6.11b)—it won't be centered on the bottom of the post. Use a 1-inch-wide strip of stiff material (wood, plastic, cardboard) to determine the spacing. Move your model strip crossways until it visually aligns with the rung section. Use the model as a pencil guideline. (Save the model; you'll use it on the rear posts.)

Using a 1-inch-wide strip to center the 1-inch foot on the bottom of the post

You can do all your tapering with a drawknife, but you can also use a spokeshave or block plane.

For shaving on the ray plane, draw the tapers on the growth-ring sides. The tapers on the ray planes should be straight (fig. 6.12). Start by very lightly shaving this chamfer *(a)*—take care not to shave too deeply. Make successive shavings lower

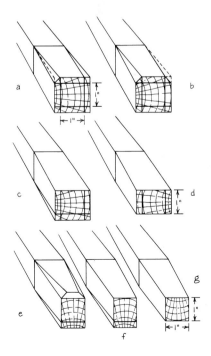

FIG. 6.12. Steps for tapering ends of posts, a combination of drawknife and spokeshave work

on the taper. Shave a similar triangular chamfer on the opposite side of the post *(b)*; the post remains in the initial orientation—shaving on the ray plane and crossing the growth rings. Shave down the length of the ray plane, creating a flat ramp from the beginning of the taper to the upper, horizontal 1-inch line at the foot of the post *(c)*.

Rotate the post 180 degrees, so that the opposite ray plane faces upwards. (To be sure the tapers are centered, you shave opposite sides, not adjacent sides as you did when squaring the rungs and posts.) Follow the steps for tapering the first ray plane. Be sure to keep the distance from ray plane to ray plane across the foot at a full inch *(d)*. Remember to keep the taper flat.

Draw the growth-ring plane taper lines on the shaved ray planes. Position the post to shave the taper of one growth-ring plane. Shave a triangular chamfer on each arris *(e)*.

Finish the taper by shaving across the growth-ring plane to the lines on each ray plane *(f)*.

Rotate the post 180 degrees. Repeat the steps used to taper the opposite growth-ring plane. Be sure to keep the foot 1 inch across *(g)*.

Beginning the taper by shaving a gradual, straight-sided wedge from one side of the post

Shaving the flat section after shaving tapered wedges from both sides of the post

You now have a symmetric, square taper centered on the lower end of a front post. Go ahead and taper the lower ends of the other front posts.

Shaving Squared Front Posts into Octagons

Shaving squared posts into octagons is much like shaving squared rungs into octagons, except that you'll use a drawknife for much of the work, and you have the tapers to deal with. (For the final passes, you can use a spokeshave or block plane.)

Begin by chamfering the straight section of the posts, the cage area from the upper end to the bottom of the lower rung. Tilt the square post onto an arris, at a 45-degree angle. As with chamfering rungs, start by shaving a narrow flat along the arris. Let the chamfer run out to nothing, beginning just past the line that designates the beginning of the tapers. (You'll chamfer the tapers after the chamfers in the cage section of the posts are finished.) Rotate and end for end the post frequently as you shave the chamfers. Be sure to let the tapers run out to nothing in the taper section. Stop shaving in the cage section when the growing width of the new chamfers equals the shrinking width of the original growth-ring and ray flats.

Chamfering the tapers connects the cage chamfers to the bottom of the post, which will become octagonal. The chamfers in the lower section must taper in width. Maintain a width of 1 inch across the foot with each pair of opposing chamfers.

Once all the front posts are shaved into octagons, set them aside for air drying.

SHAVING AND BENDING THE REAR POSTS

Rear posts are longer than front posts and have details on the upper section that form the chair's slatted backrest. Above the cage you'll make a long, gradual taper, followed by a negative relief cut that defines the plane of the slat mortises. Although shaving the rear posts repeats the steps used to shave the front posts, this is the place to outdo yourself. This section is bent—and highly visible in your finished chair. I suggest resharpening your tools, if you haven't sharpened them recently.

Unlike the front posts, you cut back posts to finished length first because they will taper at both ends. Your back-post rivings are roughly 1-3/4 inches on a side and 40 inches long. Position the chair stick at different places along the riving to see if there is any optimum position before cutting to the 34-inch trim length.

If the riving is very good, make a fresh saw cut 1 inch from an end, measure up 34 inches, and make the second saw cut. If the riving isn't perfect, which is common, consider these factors in deciding where to cut: (1) The upper

Shaping the cage (or rung) section of the post into an octagon section before tapering. (The new chamfers on the cage are allowed to run out as they enter the tapered section.)

section with the back bend needs to be the best wood; (2) since both ends of the shaved post are tapered, there can be considerable taper in the riving at either end; (3) the post riving requires only enough wood for a round section of 1-3/8 inches in the cage area that connects the rungs; (4) in checking for straightness, consider that the bend will be parallel with the growth rings. Saw the riving to length.

Shaving Rear Posts from Rivings to Octagons

To shave a rear-post riving into a square, begin by lightly shaving one side on a ray plane. Straightening and flattening on the ray plane is acceptable and usually quite easy. Rotate the post 90 degrees and shave an adjacent growth-ring plane. Pencil a hand-gauged 1-3/8-inch width from the common arris onto each dressed side. Shave the entire post to a 1-3/8-inch-square section. (Don't worry if the rived ends that will be tapered to 1 inch are less than 1-3/8 inches across.)

Now you need to do some careful layout work on the post. Decide which is the upper end. Looking down the post from the upper end provides the best view of any curvature along the growth rings. Use the chair stick to locate cross lines that indicate the beginning of the end tapers. The lower taper begins 3/4 inch below the lower rung tangent line. The upper taper begins at the beginning of the relief, which is also the trim height of the front posts.

To lay out 1-inch tapers at both ends, use your 1-inch-wide model strip from the front posts to position both back-post squares: Secure the post vertically in a vise, so that it's easy to view down the post from one end while positioning the 1-inch square at the ends. Visually center the 1-inch square on the cage (or rung) section of the post. Draw 1-inch squares at each end.

Draw taper lines on the sides, then shave the tapers. Follow the same steps as in tapering the lower part of the front posts (refer to fig. 6.12). When you shave the tapers of the back

support, be careful to begin with a very gradual cut. You may want to finish this work with a spokeshave or block plane, especially if the shaped post intersects descending wood fibers due to curvature in the original riving. Periodically, stop shaving to observe the post from an end view.

To shave the back posts into octagons, begin with the cage section. The chamfers should run out as you shave into the tapered ends. Once the cage is a nice octagon, go on to chamfering the tapers. Be sure to keep the ends 1 inch across.

Shaving the Relief

Not only is the relief one of the dramatic visual elements of this chair, you'll also use it to define the layout for the slat mortises and as a reference plane for boring rung angles (see fig. 6.13). This all means that the shaved depth of the relief is critical.

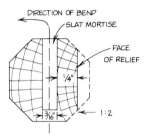

FIG. 6.13. Slat-mortise layout in upper end of the rear posts

The slat mortises are centered on the ray-plane flat on the inner side of each post. For strength, you'll need to leave about 1/4-inch thickness between the mortise and the relief. As indicated in the figure, you will shave off about two-thirds of the width of the chamfers on the relief side.

Before shaving the chamfer, look down the post from the upper end to make a final decision about which growth-ring plane to shave. If the post has a natural curvature, plan the relief on the convex side of the curve. Use the chair stick to draw a new cross line on the growth-ring plane indicating the beginning of the relief. (This should coincide with the beginning of the taper and the trim height of the front posts.)

The relief is shaved with the drawknife bevel down. You can shave a shallow practice relief above the line that indicates the beginning of the real relief. Start by shaving a scooping cut on one side of the relief area. (This is like starting to shave the tapers, except that now you cut in fairly quickly to make a concave shape.) To make this concave cut you have to rotate your wrists as you slice with the drawknife. Do this cut slowly, combining strength with control. Slicing sideways may be helpful. Shave the opposite side. Then come down the center to form a flat surface.

After practicing, shave the relief where you've marked it—be careful not to cut downwards too quickly. Shave the relief all the way to the top end of the post, taking care to keep the upper part of the relief flat. Remember to leave a third of the original width of the side chamfers.

Finish the relief with a smooth surface. You may want to finish the flat relief section with a spokeshave or block plane. If the fibers tend to tear, stop before shaving to the relief line. It will be easier to make a clean cut later, when the posts have dried.

Bending the Rear Posts

The bent back posts are largely responsible for the chair's comfort and dramatic appearance. The lightweight bent posts also have a bit of springiness, which adds to sitting comfort. The bend of this ladder-back rear post is moderate compared to bends in some other chair styles. The main factor you need to pay attention to is that the posts remain straight in the sections below and above the actual bend. (For general information on wood bending, see Chapter 4.)

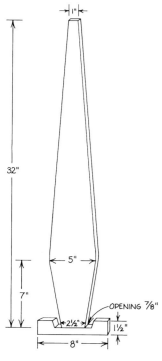

FIG. 6.14. Bending form for ladder-back rear posts

To bend the back posts, you'll need a steam box, bending form, and—optionally—a limbering jig. To make a steam box, see Chapter 4; you can heat it with an electric hot plate or, more efficiently, with a propane burner. Each bending form consists of a 32-inch 1 by 6 with an 8-inch 1 by 2 keeper nailed into one end (fig. 6.14). The upper ends of the hot steamed posts are inserted in the 7/8-inch space between the keeper and the form. Loops of twine secure the posts against the form.

A limbering jig, while not required, is easy to make and helpful—it exercises the wood in the bending area before you secure it to the bending form. (If the ladder-back posts are bent without limbering, the wood tends to bend in a long, continuous curve.) With this chair we want the bend to be located between the two slats, with straight slat-mortise sections on either side of the bend. (For directions for making a limbering jig, see figure 4.6 in Chapter 4.) Instead of using a jig, you can limber the posts using any appropriately distanced space between two fixed stations, such as the jaws of an opened bench vise. The advantage of the jig is that the interior bending surfaces are rounded; limbering with vise jaws may indent the wood.

Organize your work space so the bending operation can take place quickly and efficiently. Because you'll be dealing with piping-hot wood, everything must be ready in advance. Bending the ladder-back posts isn't difficult, although it will be impressive the first few times you do it.

Pencil the center of the location for the bend onto the relief of the back posts. Tie a piece of twine, about 18 inches long, to the foot end of each post. Have the steamer set up and boiling.

Insert the posts through both ends of the steam box, locating the sections to be bent over the pot of boiling water. The twine tails hang out under the foam plugs. Check the time, and plan to begin bending in forty-five minutes.

The limbering fixture can be secured in a workbench vise. At hand you need bending forms, two premade loops of twine, and good rubber gloves. Have several clamps handy, in case some persuasion is necessary to get the wood to bend where you want it to.

Limbering a hot rear post

Remove one post from the steamer. Replace the foam end plug. Insert the post in the limbering fixture, relief side up. The hot green wood will hold sufficient heat for several minutes. Locate the bending point over the bearing surface of the limbering fixture. Bend downwards on the foot of the post with your eyes on the bending—you can actually see the wood stretch. Bend deliberately, with a speed between slow and moderate. The arc of the post foot end during limbering is about 10-12 inches. Continue with limbering, moving the post an inch or so to either side of the bending point. Limber five or six times. Don't limber in the slat area!

Insert the top of the post into the bottom of the bending form, with the post relief facing out. Set the foot of the post against the end of the form. Snug a loop of twine over the post and bending form to hold the post in place against the form. Take a moment to see if the post fits flat against the form, especially in the area of the lower slat. If it's arched, use a clamp to pull the post against the form while the wood is still hot. To prevent denting or discoloring the post with the clamp, place a small caul (a piece of wood or leather) between the clamp jaw and the post. Force the twine loop farther down to secure the post in place.

Holding the post against the bending form with a loop of twine. The upper end of the post (pictured upside down) was slightly undersized, so a wedge was driven between the post and retainer on the floor. The first loop of twine will be removed for the second post, if there is one.

Using a clamp to pull the post against the bending form (not always necessary). Note the wood caul placed between the clamp jaw and the post.

Now limber and bend the second post. If necessary, reset the clamp. In about an hour the bends should be set well enough to remove any clamps. Leave the twine loops in place. Air dry the posts. You will know the bends are set when the posts fall loose from the bending forms, which may take several weeks, depending on environmental heat and humidity.

CHOPPING THE SLAT MORTISES AND FINISHING THE POSTS

After shaping with a drawknife, the front posts have been stacked to the side for air drying. Shaved back posts are steamed, bent, and air dried. When the post bends have case hardened, you can move on to the next stage—at this point, there is no spring back when you remove the posts from the bending forms.

Choosing Right and Left Posts

If the temperature has been moderate and not particularly humid, posts should be adequately air dried in five or six weeks. You can decrease the waiting time to two or three weeks by using some heat.

You're now ready to chop slat mortises in the rear posts. I prefer to chop mortises into octagonal section posts—or even square posts with some chairs. Securing a round, bent post in an exact position to a workbench is much harder than working with posts that have flat surfaces. Layout and the actual mortising are also easier with a flat surface.

Examine your posts to spot matching pairs. (If you're making one chair, you should have made three posts to choose from.) The main consideration is matching curves at the bend; secondarily, match for thickness. Differences in thickness at various sections can usually be adjusted with a spokeshave.

This is the time to determine right and left rear posts The side of a chair is designated from a sitting position, or looking over the back toward the front of the seat. From this point on, you must continually be aware of left and right posts, especially during boring and assembly. Set the posts bottom-end down on the floor, holding one post with each hand, and look down their lengths as if looking over the back of a finished chair. Look for peculiarities that indicate if a post would be better as a left or a right. Try switching them between your hands. When you've decided, pencil a large L or R on the appropriate post ends. Designate left and right front posts also.

Marking and Chopping the Mortises

On one post locate the flat surface where you'll chop mortises. (As seen from above, the mortises in a left post are located on the flat to the right side of the post.) Stand the post and the chair stick upright on the workbench, or butt the lower ends against a stop, such as a wall behind the workbench. Pencil two cross lines onto the post at the exact height and spacing of the lower mortise, as shown on the chair stick. To locate the upper slat mortise, roll the chair stick over the bend area of the post, so that the stick lies flat on the upper end of the post. Pencil cross lines for the upper mortise onto the post.

On the second post, again locate the correct flat—be sure you're making left and right posts, and mark as for the first. Then hold the two posts together, their feet on the bench top, and check to see that the mortise marks are across from each other, and that both mortise sets are located on the inner side of each post.

The tools you'll need are

- Mortise chisel (3/16 inch)

- Butt (or flat) chisel (about 1-1/2 inches wide)

- Hammer or mallet (14–18 oz.)

- Ruler

- Try square

- Sharp pencil (not water soluble)

- 2 bar clamps

The blade of the mortise chisel should be at least as deep as it is wide. Your goal is to make the mortise the same width as the chisel. A traditional Japanese mortise chisel is ideal. The butt chisel should be thin, so that it can extend easily into a 3/16-inch-wide mortise to a depth of 7/8 inch. Both chisels must be very sharp. I also like using a Japanese hammer designed for striking chisels.

Use two clamps to secure a post to your workbench, with the flat to be mortised facing up. Use the try square to make sure that the relief is perpendicular to the bench top. Adjust by shimming, if necessary. To minimize vibration, be sure that there is solid support under each mortise area. Pencil in the sides of the mortises, locating the leading edge 1/4 inch from the arris of the relief. Draw lightly. Mortise width is 3/16 inch; you've already transferred the length from the chair stick.

Slat mortising is one of the more challenging and time consuming tasks in making a post-and-rung chair. The best way to make these mortises, which are particularly narrow and deep, is to chop them out with a chisel. Don't hurry—with practice, you'll get both a little faster and much neater.

Begin by outlining the mortise area with the mortise and butt chisels, which prevents fibers from tearing loose at the rim of the mortise. The initial outline does not extend to the ends of the mortise. (With the mortise chisel, you'll pry against the ends of the mortise, causing an unsightly indentation. You'll chop the actual ends after you've excavated the center section of the mortise to depth.) Set the mortise chisel about 3/16 inch inside one end of the mortise, bevel facing the mortise center. Use your hammer or mallet to hit the end of the chisel just once. Be sure to hit the chisel handle square on. Repeat at the other end. Set the butt chisel on the side outline on the relief side of the mortise. The flat side of the chisel should face the relief. Relocate the chisel to finish the side outlines. An ideal mortise is an even width from rim to bottom and perpendicular to the surface (and the bench top).

Chopping a series of cuts into the outlined surface with the mortise chisel, bevel down. Hammer lightly.

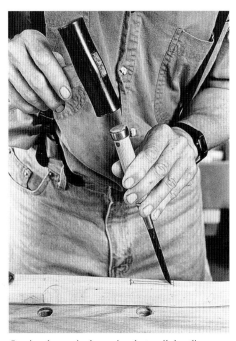

Starting the mortise by scoring the penciled outline

Cleaning the cheeks with the paring chisel. Use body pressure and a shearing (skewed) cut.

Set the mortise chisel at one end of the outlined mortise. Use the try square to be sure that the mortise chisel is perpendicular to the bench top and parallel with the relief. Hammer the end of the chisel handle fairly lightly. One hammer impact should be adequate. Two hits are okay. Carefully lift the mortise chisel out of the wood—never wiggle the chisel with a sideways action. Again place the mortise chisel into the mortise area, about 3/16 inch inside the previous chop. Hold the chisel about 40 degrees from vertical. Be sure that the chisel is perpendicular to the bench top. Hammer the chisel once or twice. Lift the chisel up and out. Repeat the process until you get to the other end. You now have a row of partially lifted chips inside the outlined mortise area. Remove the chips by levering with the mortise chisel, bevel down. Be especially careful when lifting chips while the mortise is shallow.

Re-outline the mortise, this time hammering both chisels with more force. Be sure that the butt chisel is perpendicular, in visual alignment with the try square. Take several more chopping passes with the mortise chisel. Clean the mortise cheeks (sides) using only hand pressure on the butt chisel, and slicing very thin wafers. Don't allow the mortise to widen. As you chop deeper into the mortise, increase the force of your hammer blows. These mortises must be at least 3/4 inch deep; I prefer a 7/8-inch depth if possible. Use the ruler to check depth.

To chop the ends of the mortise, after the center section is at full depth, set the mortise chisel about 1/16 inch beyond the excavation end, its bevel facing into the excavation. Hold the chisel straight up and down, and hammer it straight down to the bottom of the mortise. Tilt the chisel into the mortise to break away the chip. Repeat this process until you get to the end lines of the mortise.

Cleaning the bottom of the mortise

To finish, clean up the excavation with the butt and mortise chisels. A tidy mortise is a sign of careful crafting, but this slat mortise is not a glue joint; the slats will have their corners lopped off, so that they cannot hang up when fitted to the mortises.

Finishing the Posts

Rounding the octagonal posts is a simple operation, mostly spokeshave work. Make sure that the paired posts are relatively even in thickness, especially at the ends.

If the rim of a mortise is slightly crumpled, you can usually shave off enough wood to leave a new, clean rim. When shaving opposite the mortises, be careful not to take off too much wood; it's possible to shave through the wood into the bottom of a mortise.

FINISHING THE RUNGS AND FORMING TENONS

At this stage your rungs should be the equivalent of kiln dried (in moisture content, about 6 percent). Look over the rungs in preparation for sawing them to final length. The rungs will have changed shape somewhat during drying. Green rungs that you shaved to a uniform octagon in section are now conspicuously elongated. You can easily see that the dimension in the ray plane is greater than the dimension parallel to the growth rings. In addition to shrinkage, some rungs that you shaved straight may now have some lengthwise curvature. Toss out banana-curved rungs, but a slight amount of curvature is okay. Rungs shaved less than 3/4 inch across at the ends may now be quite close to the 5/8-inch tenon diameter, or even smaller.

Sawing the Rungs

Look through the rungs to select the best three long front rungs and nine short rungs for the side and rear panels. Choose the ends with the squarest and cleanest saw cuts. On rungs where both ends are rough, use a dovetail saw to make a square-cut new end. If the weather is humid, keep the rungs in the kiln or other dry environment (a plastic bag works), except when you're working on them.

Butt the good end of the three long front rungs as a group against something straight, such as a piece of wood or the wall behind your workbench. Use the chair stick to lightly pencil mark the front-rung length on each. Butt the set of short rungs in the same way, and mark the length on the two outside rungs. Lay a straightedge across the marks and pencil length marks across the set. Use a dovetail saw to cut all rungs to length.

Spokeshaving Tenons

Sizing the tenons accurately is a critical step in making a post-and-rung chair. You will form tenons that are actually a bit oversized and pound them into the post mortises.

Rung tenons for this ladder-back chair require no special tenon-making tools—they're made by spokeshaving and sanding. Other faster and more accurate tenon-cutting systems require special tools or a lathe (see the sidebar "Alternate Tenon-Making Tools and Methods").

Alternate Tenon-Making Tools and Methods

Some novice chairmakers enjoy making shaved and sanded tenons, but others find the technique takes too much time and lacks the accuracy they desire. Happily, there are several alternate methods to choose from.

Hollow augers are devices that form a cylindrical tenon by cutting around an oversized blank. The tenon will always be shouldered. Hollow augers made in the nineteenth century were designed for use with a bit brace. Most cut tenons of fixed diameters, with little possibility for fine-tuning the cut. Of these, A. A. Woods hollow augers, which are no longer being made, are coveted because they are infinitely adjustable, and the cutter can be fine-tuned to leave a fairly clean surface. There is also a built-in depth stop. You can find antique hollow augers at used-tool dealers and sometimes flea markets.

Plug-and-tenon cutters are contemporary devices designed for making cylindrical tenons on machine-made furniture and for plugging holes of countersunk screws and other fasteners. These devices are intended for use with a drill press, but some can be used with a brace also. Although the size is not adjustable, and they are difficult to sharpen, the best ones form a nice tenon. I used one on my English Windsor for making the tenons on the crinoline stretcher.

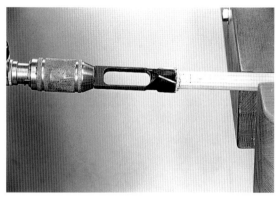

Using a plug-and-tenon cutter

One serious and common problem with plug-and-tenon cutters and the old hollow augers is aligning the two tenons at the ends of a rung with each other. Post-and-rung chairmaker Brian Boggs has designed a tenon-cutting hollow auger that spins the rung between centers. The cutter is a flat, square plate, with a 5/8-inch-diameter hole, and a slot cut from the hole to one side. The slot is ground to a cutting edge. The cutter is screwed to a simple wooden stationary puppet that in turn rests within two wooden ways (like a simple lathe bed). A second puppet with a 1/2-inch-diameter center hole located at the height of the center also rests on the ways. This puppet supports a drive rod that connects to a bit brace outboard from the ways. The inner end of the drive rod is filed to an X, which in turn fits a pair of crossed kerfs in the ends of the rung.

Turned tenons. Of course, chair rungs shaped on a lathe use turned tenons, but shaved rungs can also be chucked onto a lathe for the single purpose of turning the tenons. Almost any lathe is adequate; I've turned many tenons using the spring-pole lathe described in Chapter 21.

The major advantage of turning tenons is that you can make them any diameter or length. Also, sharp tools and good technique will produce tenons with a smooth surface, which is necessary for a really good joint. Turning is also the most efficient method for making tapered tenons, which are used for many Windsor chair joints. (For the technique for turning tenons, see the section on Windsor leg stretchers in Chapter 9.)

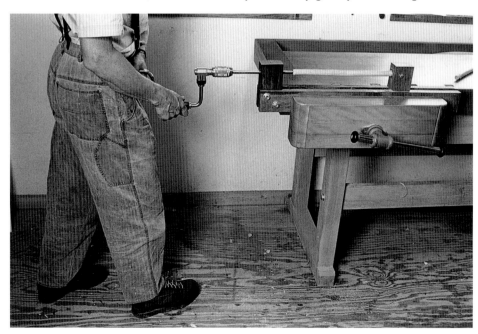

Using the Boggs tenon former

Spokeshaved tenons have no shoulder—the tenon at the end of a rung is basically an extension of the rung—a style that makes for a strong rung, as forces are evenly distributed throughout the piece. You'll be working with nine well-dried octagonal side and rear rungs that you've trimmed to 14 inches overall and three front rungs trimmed to 17 inches.

The tools you'll need are

- Sharp spokeshave

- Coarse file

- Shop-made sizing gauge

- Rat-tail rasp

- Soft pencil

- Strip of cloth-backed, 120-grit sandpaper, 1 by 8 inches

- Dial gauge calipers (optional, but highly recommended)

The sizing gauge should be about 3/8 by 2 by 6 inches; make it from any dry hardwood (see fig. 6.15). Bore three 5/8-inch-diameter holes in the gauge using the same drill and bit you'll

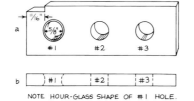

FIG. 6.15. Tenon-sizing gauge and section view. Note the hour-glass shape of #1 hole.

use for the mortises. Label the holes 1-3 on both sides of the gauge. In hole #1: Modify the hole with a chamfer around both rims; use the rat-tail rasp to shape an hourglass section, leaving the original 5/8-inch diameter in the midsection of the hole; smudge the inner surface with a soft pencil. On one corner of the gauge block, saw a notch 11/16 inch long by about 1/4 inch wide.

The tenoning process is combined with final rounding and cleanup of the octagonal rungs. You'll do all the work at a shaving horse, rounding and tenoning one rung at a time. Remember to keep the rungs you're not using in a plastic bag or in the kiln.

First, check the ends of the rung with the 11/16-inch notch gauge. Shave the rung to 11/16 inch. On the

FIG. 6.16. Typical rung end after drying. Shave shaded areas to a cross section of 11/16 inch.

growth-ring plane, rung ends that have dried very close to 5/8 inch in section are all right as long as the dimension exceeds 5/8 inch (fig. 6.16).

After checking the octagonal rung for size and reshaving dimensions as needed, you are ready to round it—all

spokeshave work. Rounding is straightforward, since you have neat, octagonal rungs. The rung dimension at this stage is about 11/16 inch from end to end.

Be careful to avoid overshaving the midsection of the rung. If anything, leave the midsection slightly larger than the ends. Also take care to avoid "pencil pointing" the ends of the rungs, the result of putting too much pressure on the spokeshave at the end of each pass. You can avoid this by skewing the spokeshave and by lifting the spokeshave just slightly toward the end of each pass. To avoid making tiny nicks on the rung surface ("dinging"), refer to the sidebar "Spokeshave Techniques" earlier in this chapter. (Dinging often isn't visible until you look at a rung in low-angle light.) Stop spokeshaving when the rung is round.

The next step is filing a chamfer on each end of the rung. To make a neat chamfer, roll the rung on your lap with one hand, while holding the file at an angle over the end of the rung. I roll the rung toward myself while simultaneously filing forward with my other hand. This makes a neat, even chamfer. The end of the chamfer should be just under 5/8 inch in diameter— 9/16 inch is perfect.

Filing a narrow chamfer around the ends of the rung. Roll the rung on your knee toward the file as you simultaneously move the file forward.

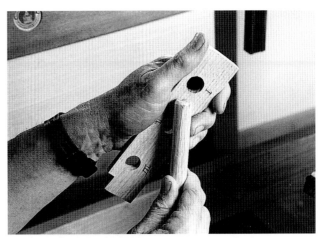

Using hole #1 on the tenon-sizing gauge. Note small smears of pencil graphite on the rung high points.

Press and rotate the end of the rung against the hourglassed #1 hole on the sizing gauge. The pencil smudges in the hole will leave traces on high points around the circumference of the rung. Continue by spokeshaving the rung in these high areas. (The smudges at the ends indicate high areas that extend partway along the length of the rung.) Periodically, repeat the smudge test at hole #1. Be careful to avoid pencil pointing the end. Stop spokeshaving just before the rung can pass through the first hole.

Sanding Tenons

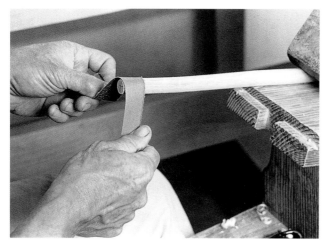

Sanding with 120-grit cloth-backed sandpaper for final tenon sizing

Final sizing is done with the sandpaper strip. Secure the rung in the shaving-horse jaw. Hold the sandpaper with thumb and first finger of each hand, with the sandpaper looped over the tenon end of the rung. Work the sandpaper up and down, exactly like polishing a shoe. Again, take care not to pencil point the rung end. Rotate the rung, so that you sand the full tenon circumference.

The critical dimension is the ray plane. The rungs will be oriented with rays vertical in the post mortise. (Bearing forces on the assembled rung are almost exclusively on the upper and lower surfaces of the tenon. Structurally it doesn't matter if the dimension in the growth-ring plane is slightly undersized.)

After sanding, try fitting the tenon into hole #2. Rotate and press the rung against the hole, but without excessive pressure. If necessary, refile the end chamfer so that the rung begins to enter the hole. You can pencil smudge the interior of #2, or look for burnish marks from the test fit. Continue to sand as necessary, until you get a snug fit into hole #2. It should not be necessary to push the tenon more than 1/2 inch into the hole—if the tenon isn't pencil pointed. Use hole #2 to finish sizing the first six rungs. Then use hole #3 for test fitting the second batch of tenons.

You can also measure tenon diameter at different points with a dial gauge. The objective is to have tenons that are .01 inch larger than the mortise, that is, .635 inch.

Checking tenon diameter with a machinist's dial gauge

Keep your finished rungs in a closed plastic bag until assembly. You don't want the carefully sized tenons to enlarge by picking up atmospheric humidity.

BORING POST MORTISES

Until now, you've been making parts. If anything went wrong, you could easily start over with another piece of wood. That's about to change, because you are now ready to begin boring mortises in the posts. Mortising requires careful work and methodical procedures. It is easy to mix up parts, so that you find you've bored a mortise at the wrong angle, or even in the wrong side of a post.

This chair requires boring twenty-four mortises. Since the posts and rungs are not perfectly straight, you can't expect to make every boring perfect—there's nothing in the chair that is really accurate or dependable to measure against. The best you can hope for is to keep errors to a minimum and hope they cancel each other out.

You greatly improve the chances for getting your chair assembled successfully if you can visualize the chair layout. From front and side views, the borings for this chair frame are all 90-degree (right) angles. From above, the chair frame is a trapezoid. The front and rear rungs are parallel. The side rungs converge symmetrically toward the rear (see fig. 6.1). A clear understanding of these trapezoid angles is your best insurance against mistakes. (In case you don't remember basic geometry, an acute angle is less than 90 degrees, and an obtuse angle is more than 90 degrees; when acute and obtuse angles add up to 180 degrees—a straight line—they are complementary to each other.) Because the front and rear rungs are parallel, the acute and obtuse angles are complementary. The junction of the front and side rungs forms an acute angle of 82 degrees. The side and rear rungs form an obtuse angle of 98 degrees.

Another design consideration, *post flare*, greatly enhances the chair's appearance and widens the slat area, which means the backrest is more comfortable (fig. 6.17). Post flare results when the rear posts are rotated; the bend in the

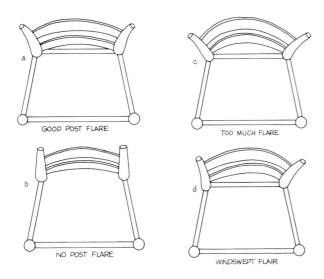

FIG. 6.17. The effects of rear-post flare

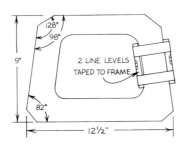

FIG. 6.18. The potty seat, used as a guide for boring front and rear posts

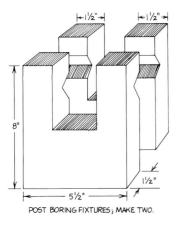

POST BORING FIXTURES; MAKE TWO.

FIG. 6.19. Horizontal post boring fixtures— make two.

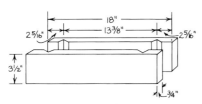

FIG. 6.20. Post-flare fixtures, used to check or determine axial rotation of rear posts—dimensions can be varied.

slat section causes the upper end of each post to swing out-wards to the left or right. While the perfect amount of flare is a subjective decision *(a)*, posts with too little flare create a very plain-looking, narrow backrest *(b)*. Too much flare forces the connecting slats to take so much curvature that the backrest has no contact with the sitter's back *(c)*. In all cases, the flare of the rear posts must be symmetrical; when it's not, the result is a "windswept" chair that looks as if a gale had twisted the back section to one side *(d)*.

You control post flare by the angles at which you bore the rung mortises, which must be correct relative to the plane formed by the slat relief. To deal with this chairmaking challenge, I designed the "potty seat," which mimics a plan view of the chair (fig. 6.18). The diagonal cut across the acute 82-degree front corner does not represent a par-ticular angle. The corner is cut away so that you can place a post in alignment with the front and side rungs. The diagonal cut at the obtuse rear corner represents the flare plane of the bent rear posts.

The tools you'll need are

- Bit brace with universal chuck

- 5/8-inch powerbore bit (or 5/8- inch forstner, or spiral auger with lead screw shortened)

- 12-inch bit extension (for the powerbore)

- 3 line levels

- Workbench with front vise (recommended, but not necessary)

- 12-inch ruler

- Combination square

- Ladder-back chair stick

- Pencil (not water soluble)

- Masking or electrical tape

- Shop-made potty seat

- Shop-made horizontal boring fixture

- Shop-made post-flare angle fixture

Make the potty seat from a 1 by 10 or a piece of plywood 1/2 to 3/4 inch thick. Tape two line levels to the left side-rung section. To locate the inner line level, a critical place-ment, rest the potty seat on edge on a leveled table; locate the inner line level along the curved inside cutout at the spot where it reads level.

Make the two units of the horizontal boring fixture from a 2 by 6 (see fig. 6.19). Dimensions are not critical.

Make the post-flare angle fixture from two 1 by 4s, 18 inches long (see fig. 6.20). The vertical notches 13-3/8 inches on center duplicate the spacing of the rear posts.

Boring the Front Posts

All rung mortises for this chair are 5/8 inch in diameter. Mortises for shaved and sanded tenons are 1 inch deep. (If you're using a different tenoning method that creates a shoulder, make the mortise 1-1/16 inch deep.) You'll start by boring side-panel rung mortises in the front posts. (You've already determined left and right for these posts.)

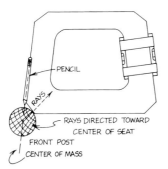

Fig. 6.21. Determining the orientation for boring rung mortises in the front posts

Set the potty seat on a low horizontal surface, such as your shaving-horse bench. Stand the right front post in the corresponding corner notch of the potty seat (see fig. 6.21). Orient the post so that the right side of the potty seat is directed toward the center of mass of the post. The post rays should be directed toward the approximate center of the seat area. (If possible, orient the growth rings so that they form a pattern that is concentric with the seat plan, although this is a secondary and purely visual consideration.) Pencil a vertical (lengthwise) line on the post in line with the right panel side of the potty seat—this will serve

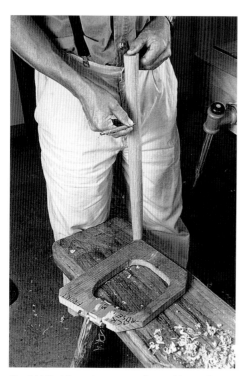

Locating the right front leg at its corresponding position on the potty seat, lining up the penciled line with the potty seat's right side

as a general orientation line when you position the post in the horizontal boring fixture.

Hold the front post vertically on the workbench, along with the chair stick. Transfer the chair-stick tangent lines to the post, crossing the vertical orientation line made with the potty seat. Draw small circles on the post just above the tangent lines. (At Country Workshops we draw smiling faces in the circles to represent chair- boring gods, reminders to bore side-rung mortises above the tangent lines.)

Set the horizontal boring fixture in the front vise of the workbench. Place the front post in the horizontal notches, with the middle circle centered in the fixture. It's not necessary to position the posts exactly horizontal; an eyeball estimate is close enough. Close the vise, but not tightly. Rotate the post so that the lengthwise orientation line is centered on the post when viewed from the boring position. Axial positioning for boring the front-post side rungs is only approximate. Tighten the vise jaws to secure the fixture and post. You may want to reposition the height of the setup to suit your height and personal boring position.

For boring mortises in this type of chair, my preferred boring rig consists of a bit brace, 12-inch spade-bit extension, and 5/8-inch powerbore bit. I tape a line level to the extension. The extension helps to make freehand boring more accurate by exaggerating any variations in alignment. For a depth gauge, I put a strip of masking tape 1 inch behind the bit's cutter.

To use the spade-bit extension, the bit brace must have universal-type jaws (see Chapter 2). The brace-turned bit is fast enough for nonproduction work, if it is sharp.

Positioning the drill bit on the horizontal post is one of the critical steps in making the chair. You'll be boring a 1-inch-deep, 5/8-inch-diameter hole in a 1-3/8-inch-diameter post—this leaves only 3/8-inch clearance on the sides and bottom of the mortise. A small error can find you boring through the post or with misaligned rungs. Because you are boring into a rounded surface, you need to position yourself so that your sighting eye is level with the post.

This step is so vital, I'm going to explain in detail the sighting procedure that I've found works best—reverse the directions if you're not right-handed. Position yourself with your left knee on the floor, your right foot flat on the floor, and your right knee in a line directly above your right foot. Your right elbow rests on your right knee. Your right forearm, which holds the bit brace, is vertical. For further stability, hold the bit brace with the crank hanging downwards.

Now, with your left hand, position the boring bit so that the bit edge lines up with the tangent line of the center circle (or chair-boring god). Lightly press the bit center point into the post. Adjust the bit brace so that the line level reads horizontal. With your right eye in line with the shaft of the bit and extension (the shaft will look level), look at the bit in relationship to the horizontal post. It

Centering the boring bit. This body position puts your sighting eye in line with the level bit shaft.

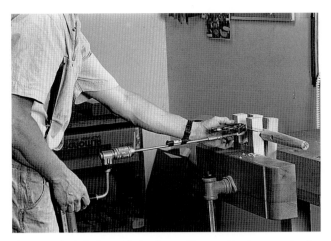

A rear post in the horizontal boring fixture. Use a combination square to align the boring rig perpendicular to the length of the post.

should be centered on the post. If it isn't, reposition the bit vertically on the post with your left hand. Be sure to stay correctly oriented with the tangent line. When the bit is centered, push the bit's center point into the wood to make a well-defined center mark. You can now remove the drill; the center mark will hold your place.

From a standing position, set the bit point into the center mark and find a comfortable place on your pelvis to hold the bit-brace knob. Hold the knob in place with your left hand. Adjust the shaft vertically so that the line level reads horizontal—you may need to change the location of the brace knob on your hip. Or you may need to reposition the boring fixture higher or lower in the vise jaws. After making any adjustments, recheck the line level.

The mortise borings for this chair are all at right angles to the length of the post. Since the post isn't really straight, we will sight off the near face of the boring fixture (see fig. 6.22). Place your combination square against both uprights of the boring fixture, with the movable right angle positioned to one side of the boring bit and extension shaft. Adjust the bit extension parallel with the right angle. (It's helpful to have an assistant to help with this alignment.) Lines on the workbench or floor running perpendicular to the front edge of the workbench are also useful alignment aids. (These lines can be strips of masking tape or you can draw them on a piece of cardboard.) Once you're in position, hold the brace knob against your hip with your left hand and turn the brace crank with your right—keep an eye on the line level as you turn, and recheck for perpendicular alignment.

When you begin boring, waste chips will be ejected by the bit. Once the hole is about 1/2 inch deep, chips may not automatically eject, since this bit does not have a spiral chip auger. When chips stop flowing out, you must remove them, or they will jam in the hole. The simplest way is to continue turning the brace clockwise, at the same time backing off pressure on the bit. When you see the back of the cutter head, push forward again to continue boring. You'll probably need to clear the hole twice for each boring.

Boring a mortise. Keep the boring rig level while boring all three mortises.

Stop boring when the tape depth gauge indicates that you are approaching a depth of one inch. Use a narrow ruler (or a stick with a 1-inch mark) to measure depth of the mortise at the point of entry. For rungs with shoulderless tenons, mortise depth is the tenon stop during assembly, that is, you will pound each rung tenon into its post mortise until the tenon end bottoms in the mortise.

Use the same procedure to bore the upper and lower mortises. Usually, I do not move the post from its position in the boring jig. If you must move the post, insert a dummy 5/8-inch-diameter rung with another line level taped to it into a finished mortise. After moving the post, make sure that the dummy rung is level before tightening the vise screw.

Repeat this process for the mortises for the other front post—be sure to consider right and left sides in the axial layout.

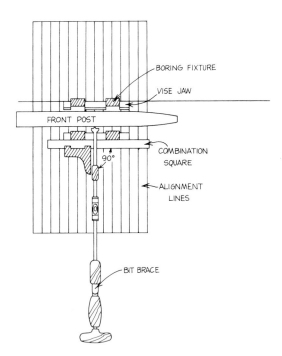

Fig. 6.22. Boring the front-post mortises: Boring-bit alignment must be perpendicular to the post. Use a combination square and optional alignment lines on the workbench or floor.

Boring the Rear Posts

Before boring the rear-post mortises, check the bend in both rear posts. First, visually inspect the relief of each post from an end-view perspective to be sure that the relief is flat and not twisted below the bend. (This is important because you use the relief as a benchmark for judging axial rotation of the post in the boring fixture.)

You'll need to be even more precise than with the front posts when you position the rear posts in the boring fixture. The rear-post side-rung mortises must be correctly oriented relative to the plane of the post relief below the bend in the upper part of the back section. Move your shaving-horse bench under the workbench vise and set both halves of the post-flare angle fixture into the front vise. Put both rear posts into the vertical grooves in the fixture. Since the posts rest on the shaving-horse workbench, they are level with each other. Left and right posts must be on their proper sides of the fixture; slat mortises are toward the center. Rotate each post so that, seen from a front view, post flare at the upper back slat appears symmetrical and visually pleasing. Also, inspect the positioned posts from a side view, looking for similar curvatures, and from above, looking for symmetry. Some variation is common and acceptable, but you don't want to assemble a chair with a readily apparent problem.

Check to be sure that you can use the standard flare angle by holding the relief cutout on the potty seat against the actual relief of a back post. Hold the potty seat somewhere near the lower slat mortise, below the area where the post begins to bend. If the posts are correctly positioned, the rear panel of the potty seat will be parallel to

Visually checking the rear posts for flare and symmetry before boring the mortises

the angle fixture and front of the workbench (fig. 6.23). You'll often need to reduce some of the post flare originally set up by eye judgment—there's a natural tendency to try for too much flare. Try adjusting both posts with the potty seat. Then take another look at them from front, side, and top views.

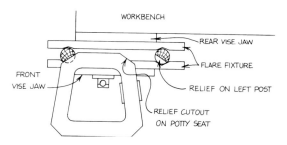

Fig. 6.23. Checking post flare with the potty seat and post-flare fixtures. The rear panel of the potty seat is parallel to the flare fixtures and the front of the workbench.

If the posts have different bends, you may find that the axial position using the potty seat results in a setting where the posts appear windswept or have too little or far too much flare. In these cases, you need to use a custom axial setting (refer to the sidebar, "Customized Flare Angles" in this chapter).

Visualizing the chair is half of the trick in getting these rear-post rung mortise borings correct. Hold both posts about 12 inches apart, with post bottoms on the floor and post flare approximated, and positioned as if you were looking over the back slats of the chair. Do slat mortises of both posts face inwards? Visualize the junction of the side rungs and the posts, noting how the rungs will look in relation to the post-flare angle.

Determining the axial orientation lines on the rear posts is similar to the same task with the front posts, except that this time you sight off the flare angle. Place the potty seat on your shaving-horse bench. Position a post so that the flat relief is parallel to the relief on the potty seat. Center the post along the appropriate side rung of the potty seat. View the post from above and behind the rear rung position.

Holding the rear posts over the potty seat before boring, to mentally picture the boring angles

Holding the post so that the relief is parallel to the corresponding relief notch on the potty seat

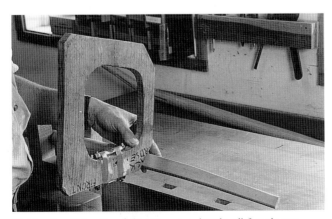

Holding the relief section of the potty seat against the relief on the post

Customized Flare Angles

When post flare needs customizing, you'll disregard the relief cutouts on the potty seat and find the new flare angles using an adjustable bevel gauge. Set the slotted base of the gauge against the relief of a post (a).

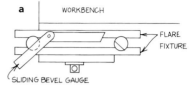

Adjust the bevel wing so that it lies parallel to the flare fixture and front of the workbench. Tighten the gauge thumbscrew. Place the base of the gauge against the rear panel of a cardboard model of the potty seat (b).

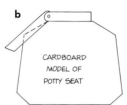

Draw a line on the cardboard potty seat following the wing of the gauge. Then reset the gauge, with the base against the side panel of the cardboard potty seat, and the wing in alignment with the new flare line (c). (You're trans-

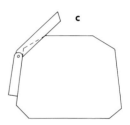

ferring the flare angle from the back rung to the flare angle at the side rung, which you need to set up for boring the mortises.) Draw this new side panel post-flare angle on the cardboard potty seat, or record the degrees using a protractor. Repeat this procedure for the other post, recording separate flare angles if necessary.

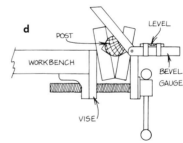

Tape a line level to the body of the bevel gauge. Set the post in the horizontal boring fixtures, as if you were using the potty seat. Adjust the axial rotation of the post with the bevel-gauge wing held against the flat relief portion of the post (d).

Draw a vertical pencil line on the post indicating the axial orientation of the right side rungs.

Use the chair stick to draw tangent lines of the side rungs crossing the axis orientation line. As with the front posts, draw small circles just above the tangent lines. Place the post in the horizontal boring fixture, with the middle circle centered. Orient the post so that the axial orientation line is approximately centered when the post is viewed from the horizontal boring position.

Fine-tune the axial orientation by holding the appropriate relief bevel of the potty seat against the lower straight section of flat relief on the post. Adjust the axial orientation of the post so that the inner level on the potty seat reads horizontal.

You'll bore the rear-post side-rung mortises the same way you bored the front-post side-rung mortises. Bore all three mortises for both rear posts.

Comparing Glues for Chairmaking

Of the perplexing types and brands of glue on the market, which work best for chairmaking? For chair assembly, I have recently converted from using ordinary white glue (polyvinyl acetate) to liquid hide glue, which has a long open time, that is, it doesn't set quickly. The main advantage of using hide glue is the ease of future repairs: You can disassemble joints secured with hide glue by inserting alcohol between the parts. I don't use yellow glue (aliphatic resin), which grabs so quickly that it may be impossible to drive a tight joint all the way home; an axial adjustment would also be impossible unless the joint is very loose. In a tight cylindrical joint, hot hide glue also grabs very quickly.

The thicker versions of instant glue (sometimes called "superglue") work fine if you're sure that joints fit perfectly and quickly—this glue can set in as little as thirty seconds. Thickened instant glue is excellent for repairs of failed parts, such as a minor tension failure of a bend or check opening in a Windsor seat.

The newest of these glues is polyurethane based. In trying it out, I've found that joints that were tight when dry are easy to adjust an hour after assembly but well set the next day. Since urethane glue reacts with moisture in the wood while curing, don't use it with joints where both components are kiln dry. Excess glue foams up around the margins of the joint but is easy to remove after curing.

The most impressive use of polyurethane glue that I've seen was in repairing several tension failures in Windsor bows immediately after steaming and bending—that is, gluing saturated, green wood. These repairs were almost miracles.

For filling gaps, the best glue is two-part epoxy—various fillers can be added, including wood dust and silica. Polyurethane glue will look as if it has filled gaps, but the filled area is not structurally a sound joint. Good waterproof glues include epoxy and polyurethane. For long setting time, try liquid hide glue or polyurethane.

ASSEMBLING THE SIDE PANELS

Clear your workbench of all tools and chair parts that you won't need for assembling the right side panel. From your six tenoned side rungs, select a set of three. (A rough but sturdy rung is okay for under the seat, where it won't be seen.) Recheck tenons with the sizing gauge or calipers. You'll be assembling the right panel first, so put the front and rear posts of the left panel away from your work area, so that you don't use them accidentally.

The tools and supplies you'll need are

- Dead-blow or iron-and-rawhide mallet
- Tape measure or folding rule
- White glue or liquid hide glue
- Acid brush
- Clean white rag
- Leather scrap, about 4 by 8 inches
- Container of water
- 36-inch bar or pipe clamp

About glue: You can put this chair together without glue if tenons are properly sized and rungs and posts are the recommended moisture content. The disadvantages of gluing are that glue squeeze-out requires careful cleanup after assembly, and in the future, you may need to disassemble the chair to repair it. Unless you use hide glue, tight glue joints will be difficult to take apart. On the plus side, glue acts as a lubricant during assembly and a moisture barrier in the finished chair. Of course, glue is necessary if joinery is not close to perfect.

Connecting the Rungs and the Right Front Post

Recheck the rung tenons before applying any glue. A common problem with shaved and sanded tenons is making their diameters too small at the end and too large at full depth. Oversized pencil-pointed tenons could split a post during assembly. Check to be sure that there is a slight chamfer on the leading edge of each tenon. Make corrections as necessary. Also, scrape or spokeshave off all pencil layout lines on the posts. Do other post cleanup now, before assembly.

Use the acid brush to apply a light coating of glue to all three mortises of the front right post, and to one tenon of each side rung. If you're working alone, place the front post horizontally into your front bench vise. If a helper is available, one person can hold the post on the leather pad on the workbench surface.

Hold the chamfered and glued tenon of a rung at the opening of a mortise. Rung tenons are oriented in the

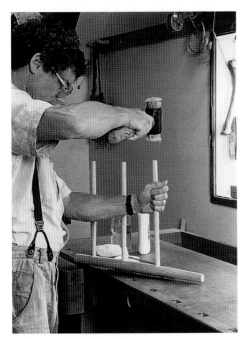

Pounding rungs into the post mortises with a rawhide-and-iron mallet

Checking across the tops of the rungs to see if they line up—it's important that the center rung is not longer than the upper and lower rungs. The misalignment to the sides will easily pull straight when the rear post is fitted.

Coping with Loose Tenons and Errors in Boring

If a rung tenon fits perfectly, it requires pounding home with a hammer or using clamps. If a tenon fit is snug but not tight, you can probably count on glue to do the job.

A common problem with shaved and sanded tenons is "pencil pointing"—the tenon is loose at the tip and tight at the base. (If the base is too tight, the tenon won't fit to full depth, and you risk splitting a post.) Don't give up. Several solutions for loose tenons exist. For example, you can locate rungs with undersized tenons in the center of the side panel, where they'll undergo the least stress. You can also use a gap-filling glue, such as epoxy.

Or you can tighten a loose tenon with an internal wedge, as the figure illustrates, a process known as *fox wedging*. Saw a narrow kerf in the tenon perpendicular to the ray plane. Saw or whittle a small wedge to fit into the kerf. Sizing the width of the wedge correctly is the tricky part of the operation: If it's too narrow, it won't do any good, and if it's too wide, the tenon will expand too much and you won't be able to drive the rung fully into place.

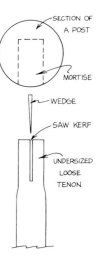

Another solution is to use a smaller diameter drill for the mortise. This requires a plug if the mortise is predrilled. You can drop down to an 11/16-inch mortise and tenon diameter. Some bits can be ground or filed to a smaller diameter.

The common cause of errors in boring is the trapezoid shape of the chair seat, and the best way to keep such errors from ever happening is to know that the front-post angle is acute and the rear-post angle is obtuse. When you have a post secured horizontally in a vise, you need to visualize that post as part of the completed chair lying on its side. When you use the potty seat, hold the appropriate angle against the post. If you find a mistake in boring before you insert the rungs, you can make plugs and rebore at the correct angle. Since most of the plug is usually bored away, only a small crescent-shaped section of plug will remain visible.

Tenon plugs should fit tightly and reach to the bottom of the mortise. The tenoned end of an extra rung will work as a plug, but it will be an end-grain plug. You can make side-grain plugs with a plug or tenon cutter designed for use with a drill press. (Cutters that make a tapered plug are not appropriate; the mortise bottoms will not get filled.)

When rungs have been inserted into mortises bored at the wrong angle, you have two choices: Saw off the rungs to save the posts, or split the posts to save the rungs. In the first case, the inserted tenons act as premade plugs.

Discovering a mistake on a project to which you've given so much loving attention is always disappointing. A natural tendency is to think that the chair is now greatly compromised. I recommend going through with the repair work. Not only is learning how to repair one's work integral to mastering any craft, but in this case you'll be surprised at how effective a good repair can be.

mortises with rays in line with the post's length. (Growth rings will be perpendicular to the post). For strength and appearance, rungs are also oriented crown up. (Any lengthwise curvature should be convex on the assembled panel.) Use the mallet to start driving the tenon into the mortise. Start all three rungs.

Remove the post from the vise. (A bench vise is not made for the heavy pounding that may be necessary for driving the tenons home.) Before doing any more pounding, look under the post to make sure there is contact directly below the rung to be pounded. You could accidentally pound the rung through the post, or cause a crack to open. If there is a gap, adjust the placement of the post and leather pad.

Continue pounding on the rung. When the rung tenon bottoms in the mortise, the sound will change from a hollow sound to a dull thud. Drive all three rungs home.

The three extended rungs should each measure 13 inches. If they measure longer, try pounding them farther into the post. You can also use a bar clamp to pull in the rungs. Then look across the rungs from an end-view perspective. The rung ends should be in a straight line. It's all right if the rungs tilt slightly sideways, but you don't want the center rung to stand proud (higher than the top and bottom rungs). If necessary, trim and rechamfer the end of any rogue rungs.

If the chair will have a natural oil finish, you can clean up glue squeezeout with a dampened rag before gluing the other ends of the rungs. If you plan to use a varnish, stain, or dye, residue from cleaning glue with a rag could alter the appearance of the finish. Allow glue squeeze-out to harden to a soft plastic consistency, then pare it off with a chisel.

Connecting the Rungs and the Right Rear Post

Apply glue to the exposed rung tenons and the mortises of the right rear leg. Put the rear leg in your bench vise or have a helper hold it steady on the workbench. Hold the front post with the three rungs in position over the rear leg. (Be sure to have the bottoms of both posts at the same end of the side panel.) If the rung ends don't line up with the mortises, pull them into position. They are surprisingly bendable.

Begin driving the rung tenons into the mortises by lightly pounding on the upper side of the front post. Alternately pound above each rung, progressing a little and then moving on to another rung, until all three tenons are about 1/2 inch into the mortises. Stop pounding.

Examine the side panel for flatness by looking down the sides of the rungs. If the side panel is warped, you can probably pull it back into a flat plane at this time: Put either post in the bench vise, grab the upper post, and twist it in the desired direction. Recheck for flatness.

Continue pounding the rungs home into the rear post. (Again, don't use the vise to hold the panel.) Put the lower post on a piece of scrap leather on the workbench. You can pound on the front or rear post; it doesn't seem to matter.

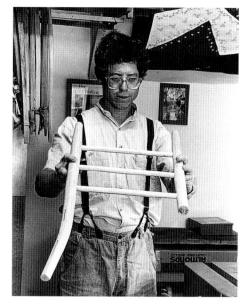

Checking across the side rungs to see if the panel is flat. You can try to correct warp by twisting in the opposite direction.

Be sure that there is direct support under the post and in line with the rung you are pounding in. Pound each rung down about 1/4 inch, then move on to pounding another rung. Stop when all rungs seem to be pounded home.

Measure the rung lengths between the posts; they should be 12 inches apart. If necessary, continue pounding, or try using clamps. Then check the panel again for flatness. Correct if necessary. The panel can take a surprising amount of twisting force.

Following the same steps, assemble the left side panel. Hold both side panels as a matched set, viewing them from above. They should now look like the sides of a chair.

COMPLETING THE CHAIR FRAME

The upper tangents of the front and rear mortises overlap the lower tangents of the side mortises by 1/16 inch—this

Cross section of the intersecting rungs within a post. The front rung tenon cuts through a narrow section of the side rung tenon to lock the side rungs in place.

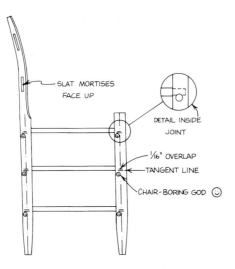

FIG. 6.24. Tangent layout for boring front- and rear-rung mortises in the posts

locks the joint in place. You can eyeball this 1/16-inch overlap, but drawing new tangent lines will help (see fig. 6.24). Lay a side panel on your workbench, slat mortises facing up. Use a straightedge and a sharp pencil to draw tangent lines based on the lower tangent of the side rungs. On the front post, draw the tangent lines in from the visual center of the post. This will indicate an acute angle for the front posts. On the back posts, draw tangent lines out from the visual center of the posts. Measure upwards 1/16 inch and draw a set of parallel lines above the first lines. Then draw circles (chair-boring gods) below the paired lines to indicate which side of the paired lines will be bored.

Always remember that the junction of the front and side mortises forms an acute angle, of the rear and side mortises, an obtuse angle.

Set a side panel in the boring fixture. You can bore the front or rear mortises first; it doesn't matter. If you bore the front posts first, angle the panel leaning forward slightly (away from the bench), so that it will form an acute angle to the horizontal boring rig. If you start with the rear posts, tilt the panel back (toward the bench) to form an obtuse angle.

Fine-tune the panel tilt using the potty seat. To bore the obtuse mortise in the rear posts, hold the obtuse angle of the potty seat against a rung on the tilted side panel. Adjust the tilt so that the inner level on the potty seat reads horizontal. To adjust the tilt angle for boring the front posts, set the front of the potty seat against the side panel rungs and adjust as necessary.

Bore the side front and rear mortises exactly like boring the side-panel mortises.

Make tenons for the front and rear posts with the same shaving and sanding technique used for the side rungs.

Before gluing, spokeshave or scrape off any pencil marks on the posts. Lay an assembled panel on your workbench.

Brush glue in all the mortises and on one tenon of each front and rear rung. Position the rungs with rays in line with the posts, and with rung crowns facing upwards (relative to the chair).

As for the side-panel rungs, pound the rungs into the mortises. The front and rear rungs will angle backwards and be parallel to each other. Measure the lengths of the rungs, then eyeball across the ends. Make any necessary adjustments.

Brush glue in the post mortises of the other side panel and on the exposed rung tenons. Hold the side panel in position above the protruding rung tenons. Start pounding rungs into the front and rear posts. Stop when rung tenons are about 1/2 inch into the post mortises.

Check the frame alignment by viewing across the front and rear rungs, which should be parallel. If they aren't, try some chiropractic work on the frame. Determine which corner of the front panel is high and place that corner post on the floor, then bear down on the opposite corner of the same panel. You can also try some correction by placing the foot of a rear post on the floor and then bearing down on the upper end of the front post on the other side of the chair. Think this out before doing it; you want any corrections to be in the proper plane.

Proceed by pounding all the rungs home into the posts. Measure the space between front posts and rear posts. Pound again or clamp if necessary. Recheck for frame alignment, again viewing across the front and rear rungs. If corrections are needed, try using your body weight to make them—the assembled frame can take an enormous amount of force on

Adjusting the angle of the side panel using the potty seat. When you bore the rear-post rung mortises, the side panel must be at an obtuse angle.

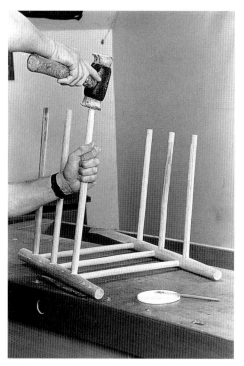

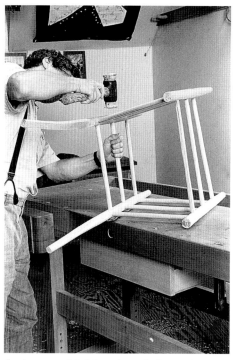

Pounding the front rungs into place. Note the acute angle.

Starting to pound the left panel onto the front and rear rung tenons

Looking across the frame of the assembled chair to see if the front and rear rungs are parallel. A side view shows if the bends in the rear posts line up.

the joints. If body weight doesn't work, use a 36-inch bar clamp. Observe the rung correction as you close down the clamp. Overcorrect to some extent, then back off the clamp to see if the correction holds. If it doesn't, reclamp and leave the clamp in place for a few hours. This often works, but if it doesn't, you can often compensate for imperfect frame geometry when you're leveling the frame.

Remedial chiropractic can sometimes pull an unaligned frame into the desired geometry. Some frame irregularities can also be corrected when the frame is leveled and trimmed.

LEVELING THE CHAIR FRAME

When first assembled, most chair frames rock when set on a flat surface—you need to level the chair frame and adjust the leg lengths before making and fitting the back slats. In addition to trimming for contact, you're going to tilt the frame toward the back, which makes the chair more comfortable by giving the seat some slope and the back some "slouch."

The tools you'll need are

- 24-inch ruler

- 3 or 4 narrow wedges, about 3/4 inch thick at the big end

- Scribing compass with pencil

- Dovetail saw

- Very sharp chisel, about 1-inch width

Place the chair frame on a flat surface (I use my table saw or a flat workbench), with a wedge under each front leg. Use the 24-inch ruler to measure the distance from the table top to the bottom tangent of the upper left and right side rungs at the front posts. Adjust the wedges until the side-to-side measurements are equal. Then measure from the table top to the bottom tangent of the top side rungs at the rear posts. Adjust the wedges so that the rear side-rung tangents are 1/2 to 5/8 inch lower than the front. This can take some fiddling. (If the assembled frame is warped in a spiral, it will be impossible to get the leveling and tilt perfect; you will have to make some compromises.)

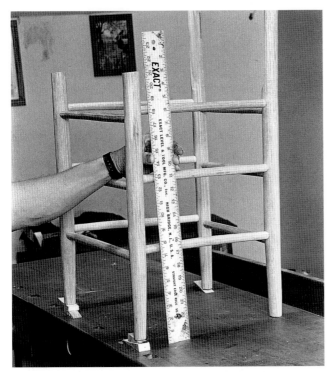

Leveling each side of the chair using a ruler and wedges. The front legs are also elevated 1/2 inch, to give some slouch to the seat and a bit of tilt to the lower section of the rear posts.

Double-checking the measurements with a visual survey. Variations in the bend of the back posts may suggest tilting the chair slightly.

With the ruler, draw lines indicating the trim height of the tops of the front posts, 5/8-3/4 inch above the side rungs. Now take a look at the chair from a straight-on front view. You may decide to tilt the chair a little to change the appearance of the bent rear posts or for some other irregularity.

(Most of what look like problems to you now will disappear when people look at the finished chair.)

Spread the legs of the scribing compass to equal the distance from the table top to the bottom of the front post that has been wedged the highest. Use the compass to scribe a line at this height around the bottom of each leg. Extend the pencil on the compass several inches beyond the length of the other compass leg. (If you don't have a compass, use a wedge or wood scrap that will support a pencil at the correct distance above the table top.)

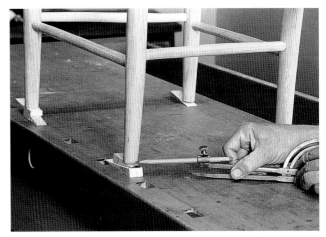

Scribing a line at a uniform height around each post using a compass. The front post with the most elevation will require very little trimming.

To saw off the bottoms of the posts, following the scribed lines, secure the posts one at a time horizontally in a bench vise. Use a dovetail saw, aligning the saw blade with the scribed lines of the other three posts.

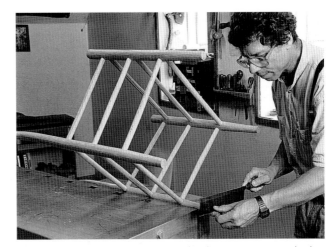

Aligning the saw with the scribed lines on the other posts to ensure cutting in the correct plane. To minimize saw vibration reposition the chair frame in the bench vise for each post.

Check the trim job by setting the chair on a flat table, not on the floor— you don't want floor grit embedded in the bottoms of the posts. If you did the trimming perfectly, the chair will sit steady on all four legs. If the chair rocks, look for the contact points that cause the rocking. To correct rocking, secure the chair frame upside down in the bench vise. Before paring the bottom of the post, chisel a chamfer around the arris of the post; this prevents tearout along the sides of the post and leaves less end-grain paring, which is more difficult. Now pare down the high points with a well-sharpened chisel, used bevel up, with a slicing action. Test for contact on the flat table, and pare again as necessary.

Once all four legs lie flat, pare an even chamfer around the arris of each post bottom. I also pare across the rear third of the bottom of the rear posts at about a 10-degree angle. This creates a small, angled pad, so that when the chair is tilted onto its rear posts, it won't dent a wood floor.

Trimming the top of a post by taking slicing cuts with a very sharp chisel. The arris has already been chamfered.

Trim the tops of the front posts and chamfer the upper arris. I pare the tops of the posts with a chisel, forming an almost imperceptibly convex surface, which I think looks better than a dead-flat surface. Use the chisel with a slicing action, working from the chamfer uphill toward the center of the post top.

Trim the upper ends of the rear posts. I leave the "ears" (the wood above the slats) tall. Chamfer the arris and pare the top of each post.

SHAVING AND FITTING SLATS

I use dummy slats precut in 1/4-inch units to determine the length of the slats (fig. 6.25). You can make the dummy slats from cardboard, vinyl flooring scraps, or thin plywood. Cut the ends at an angle to add some back tilt to the slats: The lower corner angle for the bottom slat is 95 degrees and for the upper slat, 101 degrees, to accommodate post flare and slat tilt.

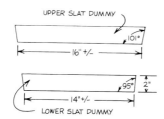

FIG. 6.25. Slat dummies, made from any semiflexible material

UPPER SLAT DUMMY

101°

16" +/-

95° 2"

14" +/-

LOWER SLAT DUMMY

Measured from the bottom of each slat mortise along the lower edge of the slat, the length of the lower slat ranges from 13-1/2 to 14-1/2 inches, of the upper slat, 14-1/2 to 16 inches.

Insert dummy slats into the mortises on the assembled chair frame—be sure that the ends fill the mortises on both posts. Now assess the curvature formed by the dummy slat—you're looking for a graceful curvature and for a fair transitional curve from one slat to another (fig. 6.26). Try slats of different lengths. Every chair will be a little different

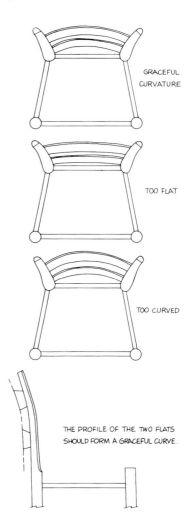

GRACEFUL CURVATURE

TOO FLAT

TOO CURVED

THE PROFILE OF THE TWO FLATS SHOULD FORM A GRACEFUL CURVE.

FIG. 6.26. Testing slat lengths and curvatures

Riving the Slats

You'll rive slat blanks from the 18- to 20-inch clear bolt of top-quality wood you set aside when you began selecting material for the chair parts. You'll be custom matching the thickness of the slats to the mortises in the rear posts, which nominally are 3/16 inch. I make the crown of the upper slat 3-1/2 inches wide; the lower slat is 3-1/4 inches wide.

Rive off the inner heartwood. Then rive the block in half radially. Continue riving until you have blanks about 5/8 inch thick. If you are using oak, and the wood is wide enough, rive off the sapwood. I try to avoid making slats that combine heartwood and sapwood.

Lightly dressing one face of each riving, the first step in shaving slats. A drawknife with a slightly bowed blade makes slat shaving easier.

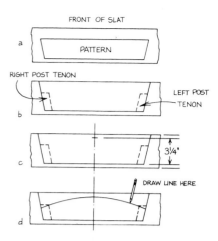

Fig. 6.27. Laying out a back slat: *a*, transfer pattern dimensions to slat blank; *b*, transfer individual post-mortise dimensions; *c*, locate center line and top of curve; *d*, draw a curve connecting mortise corners and the peak of the curve.

Begin surfacing by shaving one side of a riving with a drawknife. If you have a bowed drawknife, with a bevel on the concave side of the blade, use it. Take wide, thin shavings. Shave a smooth surface across the full width and length of the riving. If possible, this should be the finish surface of the front side of the slat. If you have a slat riving that is twisted, like a propeller, follow the twist rather than trying to flatten the riving. The twist will not affect the shape of the slat when it's fitted to the chair frame.

When you've finished cleaning up one surface, flip the slat blank over and begin shaving the other side. I generally do an initial shaving to about 3/8-inch width.

Place the dummy for the lower slat on top of the smaller dressed blank, the bottom of the dummy slat in line with a growth ring (fig. 6.27a). Trace the bottom and end outlines of the dummy. Continue the angled end lines across the width of the blank (fig. 6.27b). Measure the height and depth of each lower slat mortise on the rear posts; transfer these measurements to the slat blank (fig. 6.27c).

For slats with a simple curve, begin the layout by finding the center of the blank. Draw a cross mark 3-1/4 inches above the base (fig. 6.27d). If the blank isn't 3-1/4 inches wide, use a lower curve or different slat design. For the upper slat, draw the cross mark 3-1/2 inches above the base. Draw a fair curve by holding a flexible straightedge at the three described points (best done with a helper), or sketch the curve freehand. Continue the curve to the end of the slat.

I shape the slats with a uniform arc on the upper edge, and a straight line for the lower edge, but you can choose from a number of design variations or design your own (see fig. 6.28). The same slat dummies are used for any pattern.

Saw off the waste at both angled ends of the slat. With a drawknife, then a spokeshave, shave the straight bottom line and curved top. You now have a thick version of the slat, made to correct dimensions and overall shape.

Using slat dummies as patterns to determine the length and end angle of both slats

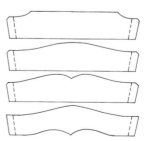

Fig. 6.28. Slat design variations

115

Arching a narrow ruler across the end and midpoints of each slat to create the curved upper edge. A helper is useful, but not necessary.

Roughing out the upper curve of a slat with a drawknife

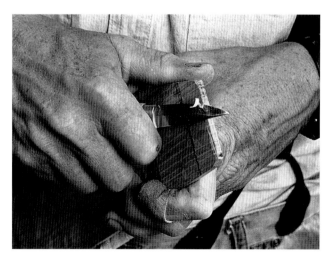

Cutting a chamfer around the ends of the slats with a sharp knife to help prevent jamming when the hot slats are fitted into their mortises. The lower slat corner has been cut off.

Slowly ladling boiling water over the slats. Rotate and end-for-end the slat to distribute the heat evenly.

Limbering a slat at a shaving horse. Limber the entire slat, but only in the bending direction.

Measure the thickness of the slat mortises on the posts, and transfer this measurement to the slat, measuring from the finished front face. It's important to make the slat's thickness as even as possible—overly thick sections resist bending, and thin sections tend to buckle. Use your thumb and first finger as calipers to check for overly thick areas—it's surprising how well this works. When you are close to the correct thickness, use a knife to carve a slight chamfer at the ends of the slat. Also, carve off the lower corners, so they won't jam as the slat is inserted in the mortises. You can finish evening the slat to exact thickness with a spokeshave or hand plane. Make sure that both slat ends fit to full depth in their mortises.

Fitting the Slats

Although you may use a steamer, the quickest way to plasticize the finished slats is to ladle boiling water over them, which works especially well with thin slats and when the wood is green. With rubber gloves on, submerge one end of the slat in a pot of boiling water, then slowly ladle water down its length. Turn and end for end the slat, so that it is thoroughly heated. One or two minutes of ladling is enough.

Before you try to insert the slat in the post mortises, limber it in the direction of the bend, using your shaving horse or a bench vise as a limbering fixture. Move the slat to different points within the jaws of the shaving horse or vise, limbering its full length.

If the slat is very flexible, you can pop it into the mortises immediately after limbering. If it still feels stiff, ladle boiling water over the slat, and limber a second time.

Insert one slat end into its mortise, then bend the slat by holding your left hand near the center of the slat, and pressing the free end into a curve with your right hand. The posture required is a bit like wrestling. I generally sit on a shaving horse and hold the chair steady by wrapping my legs around the lower frame. You can often squeeze tight-fitting slats into place by hugging across the two posts.

When you're sure the slats are fully inserted into their mortises, examine their curves and how they relate to each other. Put a piece of plywood across the top rungs so that you can try sitting in the seat. How do the slats feel against your back? You can easily modify the tilt angle of the slats while the wood is still wet. Push or twist them where you want them to be. Use a reject rung, twine, and a bit of invention to hold a repositioned slat in place while it dries out. If you have to, take the slat out of the mortises and rework or replace it.

As they dry, the slats will shrink in width and thickness. A narrow, lengthwise slit opens behind each slat mortise, and gaps appear at the top or bottom of the slat mortises. In two or three weeks, after the slats dry, you'll fill these spaces with special wedges.

Fitting the lower slat into the mortises—something of a wrestling match.

Modifying the curve of a freshly bent green slat—you can use sticks, wedges, string, or anything else that will hold the slat in the desired position for a few days.

PEGGING THE SLATS

When the slats are dry, they are ready to be pegged (not glued) permanently in place, but first you'll fill the gaps in the slat mortises. The tools you'll need for this phase are

- Knife
- Light hammer
- Drill
- 5/32- or 3/16-inch brad-point bit
- Glue

Push the slats to the upper extreme of the mortises, so that any gaps appear below the slat itself. Crosscut a few pieces of dry post or rung scrap between 1-1/2 and 2-1/2 inches long, then use knife and hammer to split wedges the approximate width of the gap, but somewhat thicker than the opening is high. Whittle the blank into a long, gradually diminishing wedge. (Steep wedges are more likely to come loose.) Use a hammer to test fit the wedges, and rewhittle if you need to. Don't glue wedges or trim off excess material yet.

With the bottom wedges in place, split out wide, thin wedges to fill the narrow gaps behind the slats. Whittle these wedges with a uniform thickness in length, and a diminishing thickness in width. Test by hammering into place. (A light, square-sided hammer is useful for this work.)

Pegs for securing the slats in place may be square, octagonal, or round in section. I generally use round pegs, two at each end of both slats. I like the subtle decorative effect of the exposed peg end on the smooth surface of the post relief. Make the pegs to fit a hole 5/32 or 3/16 inch in diameter, splitting slightly oversized squares from the same stock used to make the wedges. Don't use commercial maple dowels for

pegging slats; they're not strong enough. Whittle the pegs with a slight wedge shape to fit tightly into the holes, testing each in the hole where it will eventually stay.

To make the peg holes, I recommend using a brad-point twist bit. (An ordinary twist bit will work, but the rim of the holes will not be as clean.) For a drill stop, you can either wrap tape around the twist bit or—better—make a stop by drilling through a piece of rung scrap cut to a length, that stops the drill at the proper depth. Use a hand-powered eggbeater drill or a hand-held electric drill.

The holes are bored through the face of the relief to a depth far enough to insure the pegs will hold, but not through the post— 5/8 to 3/4 inch, depending on the thickness and position of the slats (see fig. 6.29a). Locate holes so there will be maximum slat fiber in tension behind each peg. For twin pegs, center the upper peg 1/2 inch below the top of the slat and the lower peg 1/2 inch above

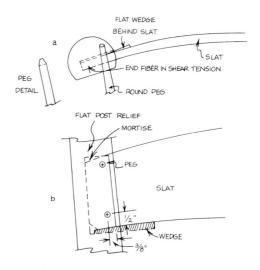

FIG. 6.29. Details for fitting pegs and wedges to secure the slats: *a*, plan view; *b*, front view

---

Another Way to Make Pegs

If you have a drill press, you can easily make a dowel plate, which offers an alternative to whittling pegs. This is a piece of flat steel at least 1/4 inch thick with various sized holes drilled in it.

With a knife, chamfer square-sectioned, rived hardwood blanks at one end, so they begin to fit one of the plate holes. Position the plate over a well or opening on your workbench, then smash the riving through the hole with a hammer.

Although some pegs will come through with a missing side or other defect, this method is quick and the sizing is exact. The pegs will not taper.

Riving out slat pegs and wedges

Slat pegs and wedges, just before trimming with a sharp knife

the bottom of the slat. Horizontally, the holes are centered 3/8 inch from the inner tangent of the post (fig. 6.29b).

After fitting all of the pegs and wedges, glue them in place. If the wedges fit tightly, you can trim off excess wood immediately after gluing. Use a sharp knife to trim the flat wedges behind the slats. Use a chisel to trim the pegs and the square wedges under the slats.

By now you're probably eager to weave a seat on your chair, this should wait until you've put a finish on the wood.

FINISHES

Wood finishing is a complex subject that I try to keep simple and safe ecologically by using materials that show off the natural color, texture, and grain pattern of the wood, and by avoiding strong solvents, stains, and toxic materials. (For details on using more complex finishes, I suggest reading a book devoted to the subject, such as Bob Flexner's *Understanding Wood Finishing*.)

With any kind of finish, surface preparation is half the job, for only a clean, smooth surface will show off the natural

beauty of the wood. You may need to scrape or sand the assembled chair frame. You can bring the surface to a smooth sheen by rubbing the wood, with the grain, using a handful of dry spokeshave shavings—before you scoff at the idea, try it.

Chairs made from wet oak sometimes get speckled or smeared blackish purple stains that are usually only superficial. When the wood is dry, you can remove these stains with a scraper or wipe them with a rag dipped in a mild solution of oxalic acid.

Oil Finishes

Oil finishes look great, but they are comparatively soft and provide very little protection against moisture. Do not use an oil finish on chairs that may be exposed to the weather, even under a covered porch. A single, windblown rain will turn a handsome oil finish into a blotchy mess. Oil finishes exposed to weather will be dull grey by the end of one summer. For exposure outdoors, I now use an exterior rated alkyd or urethane varnish, with ultraviolet inhibitors. These are available in flat, satin, and gloss surfaces.

I've always finished indoor post-and-rung chairs with mixtures based on linseed or tung oil, both too thick and slow drying to use in their pure form. You can use proprietary products, often sold as "Danish penetrating oil," or you can make your own mixture. (Sometimes shredded beeswax is melted into oil-varnish finishes to make finishing paste, which I don't recommend using.) Two kinds of linseed oil are available—raw and boiled. Raw linseed oil cures (hardens) extremely slowly. Boiled linseed oil contains metallic driers, such as salts of cobalt, manganese, and zinc. Tung oil has less color than linseed oil. Pure tung oil will harden in its storage container if air gets inside.

To make your own linseed- or tung-oil finishing mixtures, simply mix two parts oil with one part paint thinner. To make a finish with more scratch and moisture resistance, add a half portion of alkyd or urethane varnish to the mixture. If the mixture is thick, add some paint thinner to create the consistency you like. Adding paint thinner will make the mixture easier to apply, but you'll need to apply more coats to build up a protective surface.

Safety note: Rags soaked with either linseed or tung oil can oxidize and combust spontaneously. Oil-soaked rags have caused many serious fires. After use, spread oil-soaked rags out to dry, or put them into a fire-safe container. (Recently I picked up a small, oily rag that had been set aside for about two hours; it had already heated to the point where it was definitely warm.)

Oil and oil/varnish finishes are attractive and easy to apply. Wet a soft, clean, white rag with the finish and then wipe it over the wood, which generally absorbs the first application. Flood on more finish until absorption stops. Wipe off any excess. When the surface has dried, apply a second coat. Wait about fifteen minutes and wipe off any

Chairmakers and their chairs after six days' (and some evenings') work

excess. If the amount of varnish in the mixture is low, you can apply additional coats. After drying, the surface can be buffed with a dry, smooth cloth.

After finishing with an oil/varnish mixture, you can apply paste wax to create a smooth, attractive luster. A buffed wax surface will also be easier to clean. Use beeswax paste or commercial paste wax sold for floors and furniture. Don't use liquid waxes—they contain solvents that can dissolve oil finishes.

For further details on using a natural finish on chairs that combine several types of wood, see Chapter 8; for ideas and methods for painting chairs, see Chapter 9.

An Environmental Note

In recent years we've begun to see major changes in the chemistry of wood finishes. Because the petroleum base of many solvents, paints, and finishes causes serious environmental problems, new regulations require their phasing out. With this green spirit in mind, I have tested several water-based "varnishes" that might be candidates for chair finishes but have not as yet found a satisfactory substitute for an oil finish.

I continue to use the older tried and tested materials, but with a consciousness compatible with environmental awareness. I recycle solvents, for instance, many times before throwing them out. I clean brushes carefully, so that they can be used for years. I avoid using the stronger solvents and more toxic finishes, which are often offered as spray-ons.

CHAPTER 7

Post-and-Rung Seating:
Shaker Tape, Hickory Bark, and Genuine Rush

Post-and-rung chair frames have an opening at the seat which must be filled in, a process sometimes referred to as *bottoming*. Seats are usually woven across the top rungs of the chair frame, but in old chairs, solid wood panels were also used. Most post-and-rung chairs have a trapezoid-shaped seat; the front rungs are several inches longer than the rear rungs. Stools are easier to bottom because they have rectangular seat dimensions.

WOVEN AND WRAPPED SEATING

The two types of seating commonly used for post-and-rung chairs are woven and wrapped seating. In this chapter I'll explain three bottoming techniques: weaving with Shaker tape and hickory bast, and wrapping with genuine rush.

You can think of woven chair seats with a warp and weft as large-scale versions of standard weaving techniques. This seating uses flat materials, such as hickory inner bark (bast), oak or ash splints, and cotton (Shaker) tape. Seating material wound around the front and rear rungs is the *warp*, and seating material that passes from one side to the other, the *weft*. A simple under-one, over-one weave and a staggered herringbone are the most common patterns.

I usually bottom my post-and-rung chairs with hickory bast, which I find much more attractive than white oak or ash splint, or with Shaker tape. Bark is prepared in long strips, so I don't have to make the many splices necessary with oak and ash splint. Shaker tape is a good quality natural product available in a range of handsome colors, 5/8 inch or 1 inch wide.

An inexpensive material for woven seating is reed, which comes from the pithy core of the rattan palm. You can also use rawhide, either by weaving strips or as a solid sheet laced around the upper rungs that form the chair seat. (Caning, reserved for chairs with a flat frame forming the seat, uses thin strips of the vine sheath of the rattan palm woven into an octagonal pattern.)

Weaving Shaker tape on ladder-back chairs at the end of a chairmaking workshop

A new, beautifully detailed corn-husk seat on an old ladder-back chair, weaver unknown

Wrapped seating employs various cordage materials wound over the rungs beginning at the corner posts of the chair frame. Classic wrapped seating uses rush, which can be cattail (*Typha latifolia*, called *reed mace* in England) or bulrush (*Scirpus Lacastris* and *Scirpus Maritimus*). Other long grasses can also be used.

With the exception of well-kept antique chairs, genuine rush seating is rarely seen in the United States, although it is still common in Great Britain. Most wrapped seating you see today is made from a twisted paper cordage called "fiber rush." "Sea grass" and "Danish cord" are among the many other products that can be used for a wrapped chair seat. A rare but very impressive traditional material for woven seating is corn husks.

Both woven and wrapped seating use some kind of filler between the layers of the seat. Rush seats are usually stuffed with rush scraps. Several years ago Brian Boggs showed me a system for stuffing spokeshaved wood shavings into a sewn cloth envelope, the method I presently use for bark and tape woven seats.

BOTTOMING WITH SHAKER TAPE

The Shakers didn't use the 1-inch-wide cotton webbing sold today as "Shaker tape" until the late 1800s. Seating materials for their earlier chairs, especially those made for the Shaker communities, included cane, rush, splint, and occasionally leather or solid wood. Early Shaker tape was wool, woven by the Shakers; cotton tape was their commercial offering. Contemporary Shaker tape is available from chair-caning and basketry suppliers.

To bottom the double-slat Country Workshops ladder-back, you'll need 25 yards of 1-inch-wide Shaker tape, or about 37 yards of 5/8-inch-wide tape. A solid color is attractive, but you can also weave a two-colored checkered pattern, as the Shakers themselves often did on chairs sold for use outside their community.

The tools and supplies you'll need are

- Scissors
- 2-3 small spring clamps
- Flexible butter knife with smooth blade (not serrated)
- Needle and thread
- Thumbtacks
- Hemostat or needle-nose pliers (useful, but not necessary)
- Cotton fabric for envelope
- Dried green-wood spokeshave shavings

Winding the Warp

Attach the tape to the bottom right end of the front rung with a thumbtack or spring clamp, about a foot from the beginning of the tape; let the end dangle, or wrap and tack the end to the right rung.

Begin weaving by wrapping the warp around the front and rear rungs. Keep the tape in a tight roll throughout this stage of the process. Wind the coiled warp over the top of the front rung, then back and over the rear rung. Continue by winding under the seat so that you come up from under the front rung, and then go over the back of the rear rung. This winding should be fairly snug, but not so tight as to cause the rungs to cave in later when you are weaving the weft, a balance you can only be sure of with experience.

Beginning a Shaker-tape seat by winding the warp around the front and rear rungs. Hanging from the front rung is the foot-long tail, to be woven into the weft toward the end of the process.

Continue winding the warp. Be sure to keep the tape flat; it's easy to accidentally twist the warp on the bottom side of the seat. If you do, go back and untwist it. When about half of the warp is in place, secure it with a spring clamp.

Shaker tape sags with use, so I use padding between the layers. Clean spokeshave shavings from green wood are resilient, besides being a nice use of a chairmaking by-product. Stuff dry shavings into a simple, rectangular envelope made from inexpensive cotton fabric of a color similar to the color of the Shaker tape (see fig. 7.1). You need sew only two seams, one on each side of the envelope. After stuffing with shavings, fold the flap over the opening of the pocket. Press the stuffed envelope down, so that the shavings are matted and not too springy.

Insert the envelope between the upper and lower windings with the flap facing the left side rung, so that you can reach inside to redistribute the shavings if this becomes necessary.

The last round of warp passes over the top of the rear rung and against the inner side of the left rear post. Take the tape around the inside of the post and then around and over the left side rung. Secure the warp with a spring clamp at the rear rung.

As you work, you'll probably need to make one or more splices in the tape, because Shaker tape is sold in random-length strips. To splice, overlap the new length of tape about 1 inch, then sew the two tapes together. The stitching pattern doesn't matter. Of course, you want to make all splices on the bottom side of the seat.

To make a checkered pattern, change tape color at the end of winding the warp. Cut the warp tape about 1 inch past the center of the inner left rear post and make a splice with the new color.

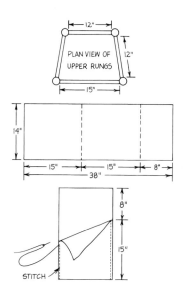

Fig. 7.1. How to figure cloth dimensions of an envelope for stuffing with spokeshave shavings

Weaving the Weft

To weave the weft you have to let the coiled tape come loose. (To keep it from getting soiled, I work on a clean floor or keep the loose tape in a cardboard box.) To ensure that the tape is not twisted, run your thumb and index finger along its length from the end of the warp to the end of the tape.

Packing spokeshave shavings into a simple cloth envelope to stuff into a Shaker-tape seat

Inserting the stuffed envelope when the warp is about half complete

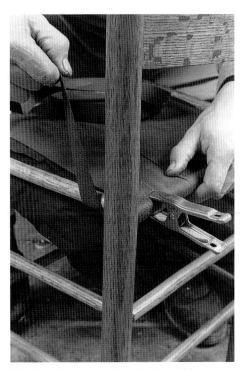

Wrapping the tape under the post and over the adjacent side rung when the warp is filled in, before weaving the weft

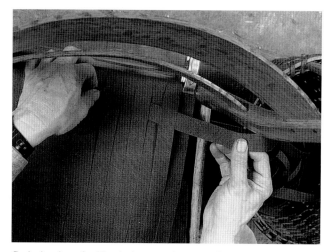

Beginning the weft with a basic over-under-over-under weave

Pulling the middle section of the weft toward the back rung to keep the weave straight

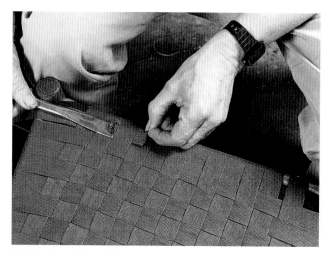

Pushing the weft through alternating winds of the warp with a butter knife when the weaving gets tight

Start the weft by passing the tape over the left side rung and over the last winding of the warp. Tuck the tape end under and then over the successive windings of the warp in a basic under-one, over-one weaving pattern. A looser weave will result in a sagging seat.

Pull the weft tape fairly snug when you get to the opposite side rung. Then pass the tape over the right rung. Continue with the over-one, under-one weave on the bottom of the seat. The weft will tend to bow outwards in the midsection of each round. Pull the tape back so that it lies in a straight line between the side rungs.

Begin weaving the next round by inserting the tape under the strand of warp at the left side rung. Continue with the over-one, under-one pattern.

As you weave the weft, the entire fabric will begin to tighten, making the last rounds something of a challenge to weave. This is where the butter knife comes in. With its blade, push downward on the warp just ahead of the strand that you need to tuck the weft tape under. Then use the knife on the other side, pressing down on the next warp to make an opening for the tape to come up through—it becomes a ramp for the emerging end of the tape. When the weaving gets really tight, use needle-nose or hemostat pliers to pull the weft from under the warp.

Finish the weft by weaving a last round underneath the seat. It's not necessary to tack or stitch the end in place. Tuck it under a few strands of the warp.

Filling in the Ears

To fill in the ears; the small triangular openings at either side of the seat, you'll weave short pieces of tape across the weft. First, take the strip left dangling at the beginning of the warp and weave it across the weft on the bottom side of the seat. Cut a strip to the estimated length above and below the seat and weave it from the front rung toward the back of the seat, as far as possible toward the back rung. Take the other end of the strip over the front rung and weave toward the rear rung. If you are using 1-inch-wide tape for the two-slat ladder-back, you'll need three strips to complete the ears, because there is a 3-inch difference in the length of the front and rear rungs.

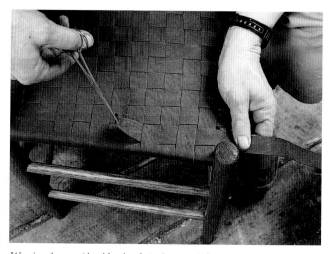

Weaving the ears (the side triangles). A surgeon's hemostat (a locking pliers) is useful here—hospitals throw them away.

Harvesting and Preparing Hickory Bark

The inner bark of hickory makes a wonderful chair seat. It's a very durable material whose looks improve with age. The major challenge in making a hickory bast seat is getting good quality material. You'll seldom find hickory bark for sale, and when you do the quality is often disappointing. The best way to get hickory bark is to collect it yourself, a task that requires careful work.

Stripping and Shaving the Bark

The best time to strip hickory bark from logs is during the first half of each year's growing season, usually late May through early July. You can use the inner bark of any hickory subspecies or of pecan, which is closely related. Stripping a sapling is less work than getting bark from a bigger tree, but bark from smaller diameter trees will cup more as it dries and is usually more likely to have knots. The smallest sapling worth stripping is about 6 inches in diameter at chest height; my preference is for 8- to 10-inch trees. Look for a straight tree free of low branches or knot scars in the bark.

After felling the tree, crosscut the log to the longest practical length that you can deal with. For weaving, the longer the strips of bark the better. Buck the log at a length where there are quite a few knots so it's not worth stripping any higher. Strip the bark on the spot in the woods, or haul the log to a shady shed or yard. (You can use the wood, but it's often of poor quality on the smaller trees.) It's better not to work in direct sun, which will dry the bark very quickly. I do the stripping work from a standing posture, with the log supported by two saw horses.

The tools you'll need are

- Sharp drawknife
- Shop knife with short, sharp blade
- Bucket of water and an old scrub brush

Start by shaving off the outer bark (see fig. 7.2). (You'll find that outer hickory bark is extremely hard stuff.) When the brittle outer bark is removed, you begin to cut into the bast—yellow, tough, and leathery. When bits of gooey bast stick to the drawknife, clean them off with water and the scrub brush. On the exposed surface of the bast, you'll

Hickory bast woven in a herringbone pattern on a sixteen-year-old seat

Shaving hickory bark with the log at comfortable work height

Shaving off the coarse outer bark and most of the heavily netted section of the bast

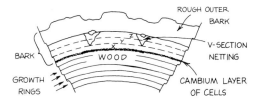

FIG. 7.2. Section of hickory bark and outer annual sapwood growth rings: *x*, premium quality bast; *y*, second-grade material; *z*, weak reject material

begin shaving into a nettinglike pattern, the beginning of splits in the bark that result from growth in diameter of the tree. As you shave deeper, the netting lines become progressively narrower and then disappear. This deepest area (zone x in the figure) makes the best quality bast seating.

125

Be very careful when shaving down to the innermost layer—the bast is stringy, and the cambium layer may have surface ripples. You can get an idea of bast thickness by stabbing the point of a knife straight in toward the wood. You don't want to shave into the wood. Shave an area 3 to 4 inches wide the full length of the log.

Peeling the Bast

When you've finished shaving, you are ready to peel the first test strip of bast. Use the knife point to cut down to the wood along the full length of the log. Try to run the cut fairly straight, with gradual curves where the log twists or changes shape. Make the second cut 5/8 to 3/4 inch to one side of the first cut. Wash gooey matter off the knife when it begins to resist cutting.

Use the knife to pry loose one end of the bast strip from the sapwood. Take hold of the loose end and remove the full strip of bark from the cambium, almost like peeling a banana. If the slicing on the sides of the strip doesn't cut fully to the cambium, recut the edges as you peel away the bast. With the first strip removed, you have a cutaway view into the remaining bast on either side. This allows you to fine-tune your shaving depth for the next strips.

The final thickness of bark strips used for seating should be about 1/16 inch. As a generalization, thick bark strips tend to be weaker than thin strips, because they are less pliable and more likely to crack around the rungs of a seat frame. The bark thickness that you strip also depends on whether the peeled bast can be split into two pieces. Some bast splits nicely, and some doesn't.

Test for splitting quality by slicing across the thickness of one end of a strip. Begin to pull the halves apart, keeping your hands close together and creating symmetrical bends in the bark at the origin of the split. Do this slowly and carefully, applying equal pressure to each half of the split. As you peel the bark into halves, reposition your fingers close to the beginning of the split. At some point, one piece of the split will begin to run out. When this happens, apply more pressure and a tighter bend to the thicker piece. If you can control the splitting process and get two good bark strips, then shave the remaining bast down to about 1/8-inch thickness. After splitting you will have a double yield. Some bast doesn't split with enough reliability to make splitting worth doing. In this case, shave down to about 1/16-inch thickness.

Do as much shaving as possible while the bast is attached to the cambium. Although you can reshave the bark at a shaving horse after peeling, it's difficult.

As you peel successive strips, you will have to deal with log taper and probably some knots. All but the smallest knots result in holes in the bark. Try to keep the strips between 5/8 and 7/8 inch wide. You can do some side trimming later, with heavy-duty scissors or tin snips. (Don't make long, tapering strips at the end of the log.) Large knots are good places to end some of the strips. You can cut strips to

Coiling the bast as it peels from the cambium

surround small knots that are less than 1/4 inch in diameter—knotholes at the side of a strip may end up on the bottom of the seat. A half strip width is more than adequate on the seat bottom.

Coil the strips as you peel the bark from the log. The natural coil will have the cambium on the outside. Tie the coils with bast scraps or string. Dry the coils in a well-ventilated area; you can store the dry coils indefinitely. (Although you can weave freshly peeled bast onto a chair frame, the bark will shrink and leave spaces between the strips; I prefer to dry the coils and then re-wet them just before weaving a seat.)

Once dry, the coils of hickory bast will keep indefinitely.

WEAVING HICKORY BARK SEATING

Soak coils of bark in warm water about half an hour before you start to weave. The seat on the Country Workshops ladder-back requires about 120 feet of good quality bast that averages 5/8 inch in width. Inspect the bark for quality after it softens. Side trim sections wider than 7/8 inch with shears or tin snips; thin heavy sections with a drawknife. (Be very careful not to slice through the bark.)

If you're working in a heated shop or during dry weather, you may have to rewet the woven bark from time to time. Try to finish weaving the seat in a single sitting.

Winding the Bark Warp

Winding the bark warp is basically the same process as winding Shaker tape. The only difference is that the warp should be considerably looser, to accommodate the stiffness and thickness of the bark when you weave the weft. For weaving, you'll orient the bark with the cambium side down, against the rungs. Padding in a hickory bast seat is optional—the bark will sag with use, but an unpadded seat can still be comfortable. If you want padding, use wood shavings in a cloth envelope, as described in the earlier section in this chapter on Shaker tape seating.

You'll splice the bark as you go along by tying a knot, always on the lower side of seat. (Once you've begun weaving the weft, you can dispense with knotting splices, instead back weaving new strips of bark into the existing weft; when the bark dries, the woven-in strips will not come loose.) A sheet-bend knot is easy to make and lies flat (see fig. 7.3). Cut the ends of the strips to be tied into thongs about 1/4 inch wide. To prevent tearing, make the cut from the full width to the thong with a gradual taper.

Fig. 7.3. Sheet-bend knot—begin by making a loop with strip A.

At the end of the warp, wrap the bark under the rear rung, past the inner portion of the leg, then up and over the left side rung. Because the bark is stiff, you'll get some buckling from winding around the rungs and post. You can make this detail neater in appearance if you cut away some of the bark width in this confined area: Wrap the corner, so that you can see where to start and end the cut, then make a scissors cut about 3 inches long to remove bark from the post side of the strip. (You don't want the narrow section of bark to show on the exposed areas of the rungs.)

Weaving the Bark Weft

With hickory bark, the weft is generally woven with a herringbone pattern, a handsome look that also represents just about the right amount of weaving tightness for this material.

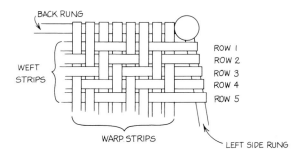

Fig. 7.4. Starting the herringbone weave. Rows of warp and weft on an actual chair would be packed together. Note stepping that occurs where weft wraps around the angled side rung.

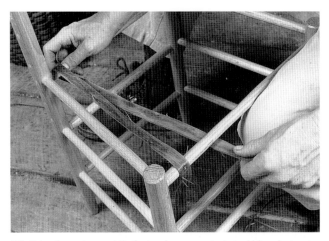

Wrapping the warp around the front and rear rungs to start a hickory-bast seat

The first row of the herringbone weft on the upper side of the seat: Pass over two rounds of warp, then under two…

The third row of weft: Pass under two rounds of warp, then over two…

For each set of weft rows, there are four different starts (see fig. 7.4):

Row 1: Beginning at the back of the chair, *cross over the first two* strands of warp and under the next two strands, then weave over-two, under-two until you get to the bottom of the seat.

Row 2: *Cross over one strand* of warp, then weave under-two, over-two.

A double-row checker pattern on the underside of the seat. The splice on the next warp row will be hidden by the weft passing over the knot.

Weaving the last row of weft, a challenge in which a flexible butter knife proves useful. Pointing the end of the bark also helps.

Row 3: *Pass under the first two strands* of warp, then weave over-two, under-two.

Row 4: *Pass under one warp strand*, then weave over-two, under-two across the seat.

Repeat the pattern every four rows.

The herringbone pattern may seem confusing when you first weave it, but take your time, follow the row directions, and you'll amaze yourself. Pull the weft taut as you work and keep each row straight, from one side rung to the other. Pull the center of each row in toward the rear rung.

Weave the seat bottom in double row checkers of over-two, under-two. For the bottom weft:

Row 1: Starting at the back, pass the strip over the first two strands of warp, then weave under-two, over-two.

Row 2: Repeat Row 1.

Row 3: Pass under the first two strands of warp, then weave over-two, under-two.

Row 4: Repeat Row 3.

Repeat the pattern every four rows.

As you weave toward the front of the seat and the warp gets tighter and tighter, thin the lead end of the weaving strip to about 3/8 inch wide, and then point the end. Use the butter knife to help guide the bark under and then back over the warp strips.

Weave in as many rows of weft as possible. To make weaving easier, trim the weft on the bottom of the seat to a narrower width. Persist, although it's difficult at the end.

Finish by weaving across the bottom for a final row. The bark will stay in place once it dries out.

Fill in the ears on either side of the chair frame with short pieces of bark, weaving them as far as possible on both the upper and lower side of the seat.

When it dries, your new bark seat will have a dull brown appearance. Don't be tempted to wax it or apply a finish. With use, the upper surface will develop a beautiful, natural sheen.

A new hickory-bast seat, woven in a diamond pattern by Dave Sawyer

DOING GENUINE RUSH SEATING

Rush is a generic term for several long-stemmed plants that grow in shallow lakes and along the banks of slow-moving rivers. Although I have never been attracted to the twisted paper product known as "fiber rush," I rank genuine rush along with hickory bast as the premier materials for seating a post-and-rung chair. Most rush work in the United States traditionally used cattails; English and European chair seats use both cattails and bulrush. Finding either product for sale is not easy, but you can try the specialty caning and basketry suppliers. Bulrush consists of round, hollow stems, tapering toward the tips. Cattail leaves form a pulpy

Natural rush seating materials: left, *common cattails harvested in North Carolina;* right, *bulrush from Portugal*

half-circle section at the butts, tapering to flat leaves at the tips. Cattails grow throughout most of the United States, so you can probably harvest your own supply.

The information on using natural rush in this chapter comes from Thomas Donahey and Carl Swensson, two chairmakers who work with rush seating. I learned about collecting cattails from Nevil Neal, a chairmaker who works with his son, Lawrence, in Warwickshire, England. (For further details on the many variations possible in rush seating, I recommend *Chair Seating,* by Kay Johnson, Olivia Barratt, and Mary Butcher.)

The weaving pattern used for rush seating is considerably more complex than the checkerboard weaves used with Shaker tape, hickory bark, and other flat materials. Dealing with the "ears" of a trapezoid-shaped chair seat can be confusing. You should practice twisting the rush material into a rope before tackling a finished seat. Allow most of two days for your first rush seats. (After many years in the business, Nevil and Lawrence Neal still allow four hours to complete one seat.) You can expect to do several rush seats before achieving quality results.

Harvesting Cattails

The Neals make an annual trip to harvest a year's supply of bulrush for their chairs. Nevil says that the best quality grows in slow-moving rivers, not still lakes. The Neals plan

their rush-gathering trip at summer's end, when the rushes are at full height and still bright green. (As the tips begin to brown, the plant fiber becomes weak and less pliable.) The rushes are cut just above the mud.

Once you have a supply of fresh rushes, you must dry the leaves carefully. Divide the leaves and throw away any central cattail stalks with a seed head. Spread the leaves on improvised racks in a drafty shed. If necessary, rearrange them every few days. Good air circulation is important. You want to avoid mold, which will discolor and weaken the rush.

When the leaves are thoroughly dry, tie them into loose bundles. You'll need almost three pounds to bottom a typical side chair. A dark storage area will help to preserve the beautiful, bright color.

Preparing the Rush

Although in the photographs, Tom Donahey is working with purchased cattails on a chair with a flat front frame, weaving on the standard ladder-back frame is no different. If you use bulrush, your procedures will be slightly different than those illustrated for cattails.

To check for quality, sort through the pile of cattails or bulrush, grabbing each tip about 8 inches from the end between your thumb and index finger and pulling vigorously. If it breaks, repeat the process about 4 inches from the new end. You need sound material. Use scissors to cut each butt end at a long, acute angle. Trim off any roundish sections near the base of the butts. The base of each trimmed butt should be no more than a shy half circle in section. Keep the rush trimmings and broken leaves for stuffing into the seat.

Both cattails and bulrush require rehydrating before use. Sprinkle and then wrap the rush in a damp blanket to "mellow" for eight to twelve hours. (Rush absorbs too much water if it is simply soaked and will shrink a great deal on the wrapped chair, resulting in a sagging seat; soaked rush is also less pliable than carefully dampened rush.) After mellowing, squeeze excess water and air from the leaves: Grab the thin end of a leaf with your thumb and index finger, then slide your clutched fingers to the base of the leaf. With some rush, you'll actually burst internal air bubbles with a sharp pop. Squeezing also seems to limber the fiber, making it easier to work with. If the leaves are dirty, you can clean them by squeezing with a rag between your fingers and the rush.

Making the Rush Cord

The tools you'll need are

- Spring clamp
- Several clothespins
- Sharp scissors
- Tamping block
- Stiff wire hook
- Ruler
- Table knife

There's more than one way to make the twisted rush cord. With cattails, the cord consists of three twisted leaves, while a bulrush cord may use just two strands if the material is particularly bulky. The important factor is the thickness of the cord, which should be uniform and appropriate for the chair being bottomed. Heavy cord suits rustic chairs; more refined chairs should be wrapped with uniform, fairly narrow cord.

With bulrush, the cord is twisted only in the visible sections—the seating surface and the rung edges. New leaves are inserted into the twisted cord only at the corners, where they are held in place by friction. You begin each insert with the butt. Bulrush strands can also be tied together, using an ordinary half-hitch knot. The knots must be located in a nonvisible area of the seat.

Using cattails, Tom Donahey prefers to make a continual twist, always in one direction. New leaves are added into the twist on any section of cord that will not be visible on the finished seat. All leaves are added with the trimmed butts leading into the twist.

Before you twist the cord for your first seat, twist several yards of practice cord. At hand you have mellowed leaves you've prepared, snapped at the tips, and trimmed at the butts. Hold three leaves together, all butts to one side and spaced 6 to 10 inches apart. Use a spring clamp to secure the first butt to something stable, such as a table edge. Use clothespins to secure the second and third leaves in place. Start twisting slightly behind the third butt. Always twist clockwise, with the thumbs and index fingers of both hands, maintaining constant tension on the cord as you twist it.

When the twisted cord begins to get thin, introduce a new leaf. Inserted leaves are always staggered, so that the cord does not become too bulky. Position the leaf with its outside curvature toward the outside of the cord—you want the cupped shape of the cattail leaves to nest together. You can also add an extra leaf by tying it in place—against the existing cordage—with soft cotton string. Maintain your tension as you continue twisting. Always pay attention to the thickness of the cord and the pattern on the surface of the twist. As you twist, tuck the tip ends into the cord, so they can't unravel. Snip off any extra bits that stick out of the cord. For the practice cord, you'll have to step backwards as you increase the length. Save the material in the practice cord for stuffing.

After some practice, start twisting the cord that you intend to use on a chair. Once you've twisted about 2 feet of real cord, snip off the lead end just in front of the third butt.

Beginning to Wrap the Rush

Of the many possible ways to start wrapping the seat, Tom Donahey begins by tying a loose loop—about 12 inches in circumference—around the left end of the front rung (see fig. 7.5). Use a bowline knot, which won't slip, and place the loop against the left front post (fig. 7.6).

Keep tension on the cord by pushing against the chair frame with your knee. When this isn't possible, use a spring clamp to secure the cord to a chair rung. Rotate the chair, so that the back faces you. Twist a little more than a foot of cord. You're now ready to begin the basic wrapping pattern (see fig. 7.7):

(1) Pass the cord over the back rung; I call this the "approach rung."

(2) Wrap the cord under the back rung and up through the center of the seat.

(3) Make a perpendicular turn to the left, passing over the original strand and over the left ("departure") rung.

(4) Pass the cord under the departure rung and under the original strand tied to the front rung.

Repeat Steps 1-4, next wrapping the cord around the rungs at the right rear post.

Twisting three strands of cattail leaves—new strands are added butt end first.

Chairmaker Tom Donahey's rush technique begins by wrapping a loop of twisted cord around the left end of the front rung. The knot is a bowline.

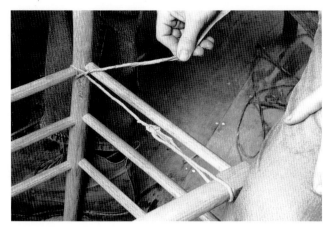

Observing the path of a single strand makes the rush pattern simple to understand.

Holding the cord in tension and simultaneously weaving the seat and twisting the leaves

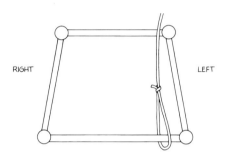

FIG. 7.5. Starting rush with a bowline around the front rung

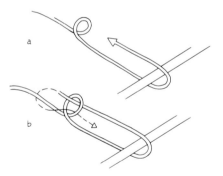

FIG. 7.6. Tying the bowline: *a*, make a loop; *b*, pass rope around the front rung, up through the loop, around the rope, and back down through the loop.

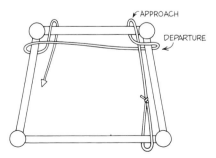

FIG. 7.7. Diagram of pattern for basic corner wrap. Pull the wrap tight and against the corner posts.

You may need to reposition the chair as you wrap the cord. As you work, you must pull the cord tight and push the wraps toward the corners (against the posts). Continue repeating the four steps for one full trip around the chair frame before dealing with the ears. You'll be continually adding leaves as you work.

Squaring the Trapezoid

With bark, splint, and cotton-tape seats, you deal with the trapezoid seat shape at the end of the weaving job. With a rush seat, you square the hole shortly after beginning the weave. There are several ways to square the trapezoid. The basic idea is to weave extra strips of cord along the sides and front of the seat, without adding to the back.

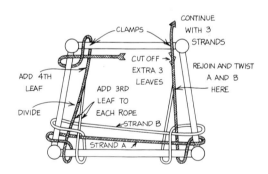

FIG. 7.8. Filling in the trapezoid corners by splitting the rope into two strands, woven at the side and front rungs (figure omits the first round, pictured in fig. 7.7).

You can use the approach shown in figure 7.8 with real rush or any material that is twisted into a cord as the wrap progresses (this won't work with paper rush):

(1) After completing one and a half rounds of the basic pattern (Steps 1-4, just explained), bring the cord under the right side of the rear rung and clamp it to the rear rung so that it can't unravel.

(2) Add a fourth leaf into the cord, twist a few inches, then divide the cord into two strands (A and B in the figure), each with two leaves.

Dividing the cord to create the extra material for filling in the corners of the seat

(3) Clamp Strand B so that it can't unravel.

(4) Add a third leaf to Strand A. Wrap Strand A around both front posts using the basic wrapping pattern. Clamp the end of Strand A to the left end of the rear rung.

(5) Add a third leaf to Strand B. Wrap Strand B around both front posts.

(6) Twist Strands A and B together into a single cord, twist for a few inches, then snip off three leaves. You now have a standard cord consisting of three twisted leaves.

After crossing the front of the seat, the two cords are reunited along the opposite side rung.

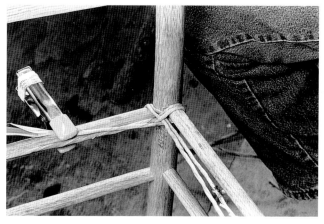

The wrap pattern after two rounds

(7) Wrap the cord around the chair using the basic pattern for one full round.

Repeat Steps 2-7. As you work, take measurements across the openings at the rear and front rungs. Discontinue using the split weave when the center openings at the front and rear rungs are equal. Continue weaving the seat using the basic wrapping pattern.

Cords are divided and reunited until the gap is equal at the front and rear rungs. The seat's three layers are evident: upper wrap, travelers, and lower wrap.

As you twist the rush and wrap the seat, remember to

- Keep the diameter of the twisted cord consistent.

- Maintain tension on the twisted cord at all times. If you can't hold the end, secure it with a spring clamp or clothespin. Pushing the chair away from yourself with your knee maintains tension.

- Be sure that the cord passes straight across the chair from left to right sides, and from front to back.

- Keep the wraps around the rungs pressed toward the posts at the corners. Use a block of wood to compact the rush against the posts.

- Keep the diagonal woven lines that originate at the corners straight.

Stuffing the Seat

Begin to stuff the seat with padding when the corner wraps are about 3 inches wide. As the wrap progresses, you will notice that the pattern forms a middle layer of cord between the top and bottom surfaces of the seat. This middle layer is hidden when the seat fills in.

You'll start with dry material, beginning at the corners by stuffing pockets that develop above and below the middle layer of cord. First, stuff the short snippings of rush you saved when you sorted and trimmed the leaves. Use a blunt-ended stick to shove the stuffing into the corners.

Filling the pockets at the corners with short lengths of scrap rush to begin the stuffing.. Tom Donahey stuffs the top and bottom layers; other chair "bottomers" stuff only the bottom.

When the center hole is about 4 to 6 inches across, you can stuff longer pieces of rush scrap across the gaps. Fold the rush so that you have clumps about 8 inches long. Stuff the ends into opposite corner pockets. Add stuffing as the center hole fills in. It is impossible to do a good stuffing job when the wrap is close to filling in the center of the seat.

Spreading larger scraps of stuffing across pairs of corner pockets as the gap closes in

It is unlikely that you will wrap an entire seat in one session. When you take a break, clamp the cord to a rung so that it can't unravel. For a short break, you can wrap the wet end in plastic to keep it pliable. For an overnight stop, wrap the seat in a damp towel. If the weather is humid,

the rush will stay damp overnight. If the break will be longer than a day, allow the seat and any dampened rush to dry— rush kept damp for several days may begin to mold or decompose. An advantage of taking a long enough break to allow the rush to partially dry (and shrink) is that you can tighten the wrapped rush before starting your final work session. Wet and wrap the dry rush end in a damp cloth to make it pliable for the final wrapping session.

Figure-Eight Weaving and Finishing

As the seat fills in you will usually create a rectangular center hole that can't be filled with the basic wrapping pattern; the side rungs are completely filled in, but there is still a central space to wrap on the front and rear rungs. Fill in this final section using a figure-eight weave (see fig. 7.9). You can work from left to right or right to left. Be sure to keep the figure-eight weaving tensioned and packed against the previous cord loops on the rungs.

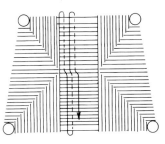

FIG. 7.9. Completing a rush seat using a figure-eight wrap

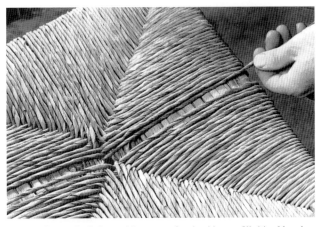

Using a front-to-back figure-eight weave after the sides are filled in. Note the stuffing.

To make a figure-eight weave:

(1) Pass the cord over the top of either the front or rear rung.

(2) Bring the cord end under the seat and then up through the center of the remaining hole. (You will have to part the center strands in the middle layer to do this.)

(3) Continue by passing the cord over the top of the opposite rung.

Repeat Steps 2 and 3 until the center is filled in. Then

Wrapping a loop or two of cord around the center of the seat bottom to finish. This photo shows the butts of new leaves added into the rope at the diagonal lines.

squeeze in two or three additional figure eights to compensate for shrinkage when the rush dries. For the final passes, you may need to use a table knife or screwdriver to make an opening in the center. Use a piece of stiff wire with a hook bent in one end to pull the cord through the center.

Complete the weave on the underside of the seat by winding the end of the cord several times around the central figure-eight strands.

How a rush seat should be finished or whether it should be left alone is a matter of personal preference. After the seat is thoroughly dry, a traditional finish consists of one or two brushed-on coats of linseed oil thinned with mineral spirits. Tom Donahey uses water-based satin urethane varnish cut with about one-third water. A rush seat without any finish will be harder to keep clean than one with a light oil or varnish coating.

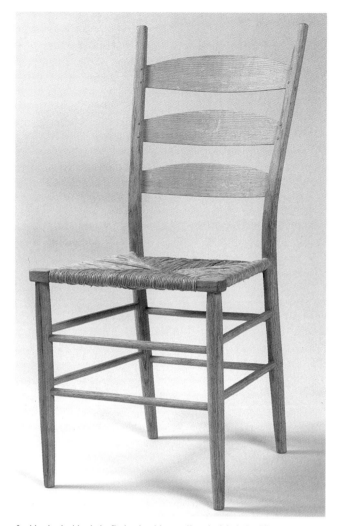

Ladder-back side chair. Red oak with cattail rush. Made by Thomas Donahey, Marshall, North Carolina.

The finished cattail seat, by Tom Donahey

134

Historic Chairs from Britain

Post-and-rung spindle-back armchair, c 1920. Ash with rush seat. North West Dales.

Post-and-rung wavey ladder-back armchair, c 1780. Ash with rush seat.

Double-bow Windsor.
Yew with elm seat.
Made by John Amos
(fl. 1814-42).

Post-and-rung pass armchair, late nineteenth century. Rush seat. Probably from Sussex. The "pass" arm support was a French innovation. Chairs with this design are sometimes called Morris chairs.

Bergere smoking Windsor, c 1870. Wycombe. Fruitwood with elm seat.

Continuous-arm Windsor, with double bobbin turnings, c 1815. West Country, probably Yealmton. Ash with elm seat.

High-back Windsor with cabriole legs, c 1740-70. Thames Valley. Yew with elm seat.

High-back stick Windsor, c 1760. West Country. Ash with elm seat.

Part Three:
Windsor Chairs

CHAPTER 8

Stick Windsors

The tutorial stick Windsor, a pieced-arm high-back combining an elm seat, birch bow and comb, and red oak legs, made by the author

Low-back version of a stick Windsor, made by the author

MATERIALS LIST: STICK WINDSOR

Number of Pieces	Description	Rived Green Dimensions	Shaved Green Dimensions	Finish Dimensions
6	Arm sticks	1" sq x 12"	3/4" oct x 12"	11/16" dia x custom length
6	Back sticks	1" sq x 24"	3/4" oct x 25"	11/16" dia x custom length
4	Legs	2" sq x 20"-22"	1-3/4" > 1-1/4" x 20"	Same, with 2" tenons

Seat	1-1/2"–2" thick; 15"-20" deep; 17"-24" wide. Planed on top.
Arm bow and crest	Options: sawed to pattern from 1"–1-1/4"-thick curved planks; or bent from 1-1/4" sq x 50"-60" riving or straight-grained, sawed stock
Comb	1-1/4" thick, 3" wide x 12"-15" long. Sawed from 3"-4"-thick sawed plank. Can also be bent.

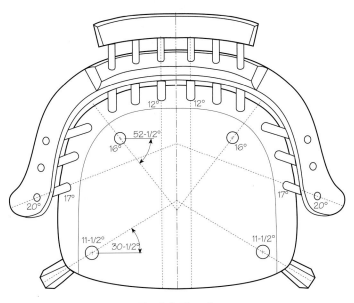

Fig. 8.1. Plan view

Scale: 1:8

Fig. 8.2. Front view

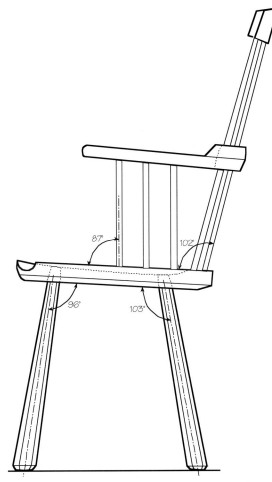

Fig. 8.3. Side view

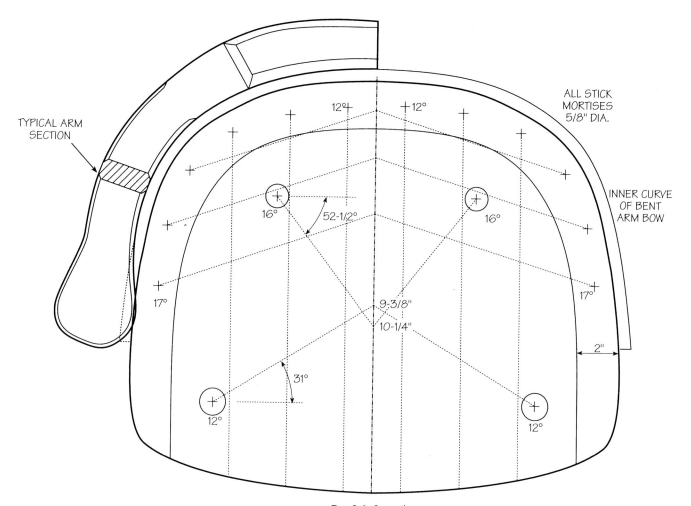

TYPICAL ARM SECTION

12° +   +12°

ALL STICK MORTISES 5/8" DIA.

16°   52-1/2°   16°

INNER CURVE OF BENT ARM BOW

17°   17°

9-3/8"
10-1/4"

2"

31°

12°   12°

FIG. 8.4. Seat plan

Detail of a low-back stick Windsor by the author. The steam-bent arm has an added crest rail and hand pieces at the ends of the bow. Red oak, with tulip poplar seat.

Like their fancier Windsor relatives, a stick Windsor is designed around a solid plank seat. Legs are tenoned into the bottom of the plank, and a back bow supported by an array of sticks is tenoned into the upper surface of the seat. Cylindrical mortise-and-tenon construction is used almost exclusively. The style serves as an excellent introduction to making any type of Windsor chair.

Country-made stick Windsors and Appalachian ladder-backs are sometimes called "primitive" chairs. I prefer to call them "folk" chairs. Compared to more sophisticated furniture, their construction and design are simple and straightforward. It is true that some vernacular chairs have poor joinery, and they are not always comfortable. But folk chairs can also suggest fresh and inspiring directions, especially if you're interested in exploring new ways to make and design handcrafted furniture.

Two themes that run through the making of a stick Windsor are improvisation and individuality in design. These chairs have personality. Although characteristically simple and useful, they can include decorative elements. Stick Windsors have never been made in factories or in sets of identical units. And they are never pretentious. Old stick Windsors were home-made, handmade, do-it-yourself furniture.

Welsh chairmaker John Brown, the most prominent practitioner of the craft, inspired me to try this style. His stick

Windsors, like John Alexander's American post-and-rung chairs, are inspired by vernacular chairs, rather than by the refined and elaborate chairs more commonly considered examples of fine furniture. John Brown has demonstrated that the style easily incorporates elegant lines, comfort, and a fine finish.

Before You Begin: Looking at Styles and Materials

In a sense, these stick chairs are Windsors made with post-and-rung chairmaking methods. This is an opportunity to make a Windsor chair that looks handmade, because it is. These chairs appeal to those who appreciate good woodworking and functional furniture.

Styles

Stick Windsors are generally made in two basic styles, low-back and high-back. The low-back version has a single, horizontal bow for both arm and back support (see fig. 8.5). In old examples, the bow is often hewn from two or more sections of naturally curved tree limbs or saplings that are then connected with a simple lap joint. Bows were also made in sections from planks. Some were steam bent. John Brown calls his low-back a "library chair." In England, this may be called a "smoker's chair," and it is also related to the American "captain's chair."

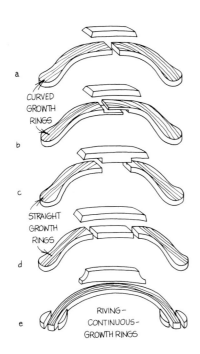

Fig. 8.5. Variations for making pieced arm bows

The high-back version is similar in construction to an American comb-back Windsor. This style has a horizontal arm bow, like the low-back. The vertical sticks at the back of the chair pass through the horizontal bow and terminate at a horizontal comb.

Legs for these chairs are usually sawed out and planed smooth, or draw shaved, but they can also be turned. Most legs on the old chairs were cylindrical, although some were shaped in an octagonal section. Leg stretchers are optional. Some chairs have a single rear leg. Chairs with three legs were suitable for uneven dirt or stone floors in the old peasant cottages.

Old country-made stick Windsors were often made with short legs and low seats. The legs of surviving old chairs have worn down, and the average adult was shorter. But another reason for the low seat is that poor country folk often didn't have a table—they set things on the floor when they sat down after a hard day's work.

The old folk chairs were made without patterns. A plank was found for the seat, often with the original waney edge just inside the bark. Bows were made from something growing in a hedgerow or local woods. Inspiration, intuition, and experience guided the design. In many cases, poaching the wood was integral to the tradition.

The stick Windsor in the plans includes an arm bow and crest laminated from 1-inch-thick planks. The plans are for a high back, but a novice would find making a low-back version easier. The only differences are that all the sticks are short, and there is no comb. The chair has no leg stretchers, which are unnecessary if the leg joints are well fitted and assembled with parts at appropriate moisture contents and optimum growth-ring orientation. (Directions for making and fitting stretchers appear in Chapter 9 on the American bow-back Windsor.) The seat plank must be a solid wood, no softer than tulip poplar; the chair in this chapter has a two-piece elm seat.

Don't be timid about making stylistic changes, such as detailing of the hands at the ends of the bow. Feel free to change the shape, length, and width of the seat to suit your taste or available wood.

Parts and Materials

Instead of using a chair stick, most Windsor chairmakers use seat and bow patterns. I use patterns and drawings, in addition to notes on three-by-five cards. I've found that most novices are more comfortable if they have specifications to go by when they start out.

Still, measured plans and materials lists for making a stick Windsor contradict the native spirit of the chairs, for improvisation plays an important role in the chairs' design and construction. I encourage you to use the plans in this chapter as a starting point, if you care to, and, if you are a novice chairmaker, you can follow the dimensions and various angles. But I urge you to pursue your own design ideas and to use what tools and materials are available.

Seat plank • Seats of the old stick Windsors were generally elm, ash, or oak. (You can make them from softer woods, such as white pine, if you use leg stretchers.) I like a fairly large seat, but you may prefer a seat that is wider or narrower, deeper or shallower than the one in the plans.

The seat for that stick Windsor is 17 inches deep and 20 inches wide, with the grain running from front to back.

John Brown generally glues his elm seats from three separate boards, with the grain running front to back. He says that gluing the seat down the center using only two planks divides the chair into two distinct halves, which will look good only if the boards are well matched. Using three planks also means that narrower boards can be used.

Legs • Leg blanks are 1-3/4 to 2 inches square, and 20 to 22 inches long. Any straight- grained hardwood will do. Ash and elm were traditionally used in Wales. For shaved legs, oak and hickory are appropriate; for turned legs you can use maple, birch, cherry, and beech. I prefer shaving or turning legs from green wood; air-dried wood is also suitable.

Bow • For bows made from naturally curved stock, you can use any fairly hard species that is available. The bow for the tutorial chair was made from a 1-inch-thick plank sawed from a naturally curved birch. Hewed and pieced bows are usually about 1 inch thick and 2 inches wide, with optional swellings at the hand ends.

Make bent bows from any good riving species, such as ash, oak, or hickory. As long as you saw the blank from clear, straight-grained stock, you may also use elm, cherry, and walnut. Yew wood is highly prized throughout Britain for bows and other chair parts. A typical bent bow is shaved or planed 1 inch square, and 50 inches long. Compared to an American Windsor, the chair bow is very heavy in section.

John Brown makes bent bows from clear ash that is carefully sawed through and through into 1-1/4-inch slab planks, which he then saws into straight-grained, square-sectioned bending blanks.

A *crest rail* is often attached above the center of the back bow to reinforce spliced bow joints. A crest rail also thickens the bow, making the back rest more comfortable, in addition to adding a visually attractive element.

Sticks • The backrests of Welsh chairs are supported by four to twenty sticks. On an American or English Windsor, the armrest and back-support uprights are generally referred to as *spindles*. Sticks for Welsh chairs are usually shaved but occasionally turned. Some old chairs utilized splats (narrow boards) instead of round sticks. Unlike American Windsors, the front sticks at the hand positions of the Welsh bow are usually identical to the others in the set.

Comb • The comb is generally sawed from stock 3 to 4 inches thick. Typically, it has no ornamentation, but some combs have ears, scallops, or other curvatures along the top.

MAKING SEAT BLANKS

Seats for old Welsh stick chairs and other Windsors were made from a single plank. While attractive, making a single-plank seat presents a number of problems in terms of procuring and drying the wood.

Selecting Seat Planks

It takes a large tree to get out the 16- to 20-inch-wide boards a single-plank seat requires. Conventional sawing begins by slabbing the sides of a log, forming a square central bolt considerably narrower than the original log. The square bolt is sawed into boards of uniform width. You can often get wider boards from a mill that does through-and-through sawing, easy to do with a horizontal band mill. This yields planks with waney bark edges and random widths. Although planks toward the center of the log are widest, the plank that contains the pith will check during drying and should therefore be disqualified for making chair seats—although you could rip the pith section out of the plank, and then glue the sides back together.

Full-width green planks 12 feet long are heavy. Also, many hardwoods, including elm and tulip poplar, often warp and check during drying, problems harder to control when drying wide planks.

Another factor to consider is growth-ring orientation (see fig. 8.6). *Quarter-sawed wood* (also called *edge grain* and *vertical grain*) has growth rings that cross the plank at angles ranging from 90 to 45 degrees. All other saw cuts are labeled *flat sawed* or *side grain*. (Sometimes boards with 35- to 60-degree growth rings are called *rift sawed*.) Quarter-sawed planks are not particularly desirable for seat blanks—they are more likely to split from stresses of wedges, tapered tenons, or incipient wind shakes. Flat-sawed stock has a more interesting grain pattern, a consideration in chairs with a natural finish.

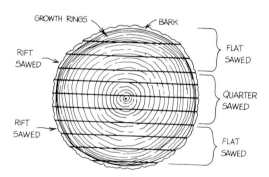

FIG. 8.6. A 26-inch diameter log sawed through and through into 2-inch-thick flitches. The quarter-sawed plank in the center should be ripped into two planks; the pith will cause cracking.

I buy custom-sawed planks for Windsor seats directly from a local sawyer. I try to be at the mill when the logs are sawed. I have 10- or 12-foot tulip poplar and white pine logs sawed into planks 2-1/4 inches thick and 10 inches wide. Elm planks can be sawed 1-3/4 to 2 inches thick. Planks 10 inches wide can be glued into seat blanks having the grain running front to back or side to side.

Look for logs that are straight and appear to be free of knots. With white pine, which is seldom clear inside the log, look for logs with knots spaced far enough apart to get seats in between. Disqualify any log with a wind shake or pine with heavy resin pockets. Avoid center-cut planks that contain the pith.

Crosscut the freshly sawed planks into lengths of 40 to 60 inches, a convenient size for handling and drying, in addition to being wide enough to make up two or three seat blanks. A paraffin end-grain sealer or two coats of ordinary latex paint reduces checking and warping. Brush on the sealer; dipping the sealer will trap air pockets and not seal well.

If possible, stack the green planks in a breezy shed or loft to air dry, with 1 by 1 stickers between each layer and heavy weights on top of the stack to reduce warping. (I use pieces of railroad track and cinder blocks.) Tulip poplar and white pine planks 2 inches thick will air dry in four to six months of moderate weather. Elm seat planks need a year or longer.

After drying, pick through the planks to find pairs for seat blanks that match in grain pattern and color. Surface plane and edge joint the air-dry planks. If you don't have the machinery, joint the common edges with a hand plane..

Gluing the Planks

Several types of glue are suitable for edge gluing planks into chair seat blanks. I usually use ordinary yellow glue (aliphatic resin), which is inexpensive and has a quick clamping time and some moisture resistance. I've also used epoxy and polyurethane glue. These edge-to-edge glue joints form a bond stronger than sound wood. I don't use dowels or other inserts in this type of joint.

For gluing, you need three to five heavy-duty bar or pipe clamps 2 to 3 feet long and a pair of short clamps for pinching the ends of the joined boards into alignment. My glue-up work station is simply a pair of sawhorses set in the middle of the shop floor so that I can work all around the long seat blanks. The top rails of the sawhorses must be in plane with each other; check for plane by viewing across the rails from about 6 feet away. If they aren't parallel, find appropriate wedges to put underneath the sawhorse feet to correct the difference.

Before gluing, check carefully to make sure that the planks are well jointed—the common edges must be in contact from end to end. Orient the planks so that the growth rings form side-by-side arches. If possible, match the direction of rising grain in the joint.

Stack the paired planks onto one edge, so that you can easily see both sides of the joint. The face of the planks should form a flat plane. A slight gap in the center of the stacked planks is acceptable. If you tilt the upper plank, and then set it down on the lower one, you should feel solid uniform contact across the joint. Any tendency to rock indicates that the edges are not properly jointed. If

the jointed edges fit well, pencil a large V across the joint. Aligning the V assures that the same orientation will be used during the glue up.

Set the planks crossing the sawhorse rails with glue surfaces facing up. Brush a priming coat of yellow glue on both glue surfaces. Wait for about ten minutes, while some of the glue penetrates the surface of the wood. Then apply another coat of glue to one surface. Fit the planks together and clamp them, beginning with the center section. Use the short clamps to hold the ends of the planks in alignment.

With yellow glue, you can remove the clamps in forty minutes. Then use a scraper or chisel to remove any semihard glue squeezeout along the joint. Don't stress the joint until the next day. If you use polyurethane glue, which has very little tack, keep glued seats clamped overnight.

SADDLING

Although saddling can make the seat more comfortable and is aesthetically pleasing, many old chairs in this tradition had flat seats. On country-made Welsh chairs, saddling is generally shallow.

The plan view of the seat (fig. 8.4) shows the locations for boring the leg and stick mortises. The straight lines connecting the centers of the leg mortises to the seat centerline are *sight lines* for boring the leg mortises. The plan also shows centers and sight lines for the sticks. Using sight lines, along with *resultant angles* (the number in degrees at the mortise centers), is explained in the later section on boring the leg mortises; a typical country craftsperson would not use this conceptual approach, but it proves a useful tool for many contemporary chairmakers.

The plan view also includes a U-shaped line in front of the stick mortises. The U-shaped area behind the line, which I call the deck, and one point at the front center of the seat are left at the original thickness of the plank. The remaining surface area of the top of the seat is contoured.

Positioning the Seat on the Plank

Before tracing the plan outline to the seat blank, you need to decide on orientation of the growth-rings (seen on the end grain) and direction of the grain. When I'm making a painted chair, I prefer to work with the growth rings arching upwards, like a lowercase *m*. Hollowing the saddle in the center of the seat is easier when you're carving across the growth rings, and there is less chance of splitting caused by tenons inserted into the top of the chair seat (fig. 8.7a). If the seat will have a natural finish, orientation with the growth rings pointed downwards reveals a more interesting grain pattern (fig. 8.7b).

Whether the grain runs front to back or sideways depends on several factors, among them the width of available planks and dimensions of the seat. Wide, shallow seats—such as the American comb-back and sack-back

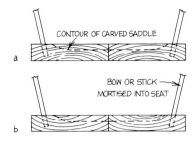

FIG. 8.7. Orientation of cathedrals in a joined double-plank seat as seen from the end grain: *a*, structurally superior and easy to carve; *b*, more attractive grain pattern for chairs with a natural finish

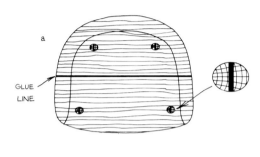

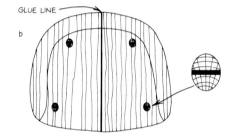

FIG. 8.8. Differences in grain direction and wedging for side-to-side and front-to-back glued plank seats: *a*, preferred for seats that are wider than they are deep; *b*, somewhat stronger and easier to saddle

Windsors—are almost always made with side-running grain (refer to fig. 8.8a). Seats with extended tail braces are logically oriented with grain running front to back.

When a seat is roughly equal in width and depth, I generally orient the grain running front to back (fig. 8.8b). The best reason for this orientation is that leg joints are stronger and more stable when stress is concentrated on the end grain, and this stress, called *racking*, is basically fore and aft. Saddling the seat is also somewhat easier.

Trace the seat pattern onto a piece of poster stock. Cutting out the seat pattern with a razor knife will produce a window the exact shape and size of the seat plan. Very often, seat blanks are not perfect. There may be knots or other defects that one hopes to avoid or minimize. This seat window is useful in determining where to locate the seat on the blank stock. If your seat plank is undersized, or you find defects that you want to avoid near the edge of a plank, you can fudge the seat dimensions in width or depth by as much as 1 inch, a time-honored practice among traditional chairmakers.

Whenever possible, position two-piece seats having front-to-back grain orientation with the centerline on the glue joint. You then have a permanent centerline for taking measurements during saddling and assembly. If you must choose between centerline placement and avoiding defects, it's more important to position the seat where defects can be avoided. Most of the upper surface will be carved away.

After deciding on orientation and position, trace the plan outline onto the blank. Draw the centerline and the outline for the deck. Do not mark centers for the legs or other sticks at this time.

Saddling Tools and Adze Work

The tools you'll need for saddling the seat are

- Turning bow saw (or band saw or contractor's saber saw)
- Hollowing adze (short, medium, or long handle)
- Inshave
- Travisher (optional, but very useful)
- Round-bottom plane (optional)
- Flat spokeshave
- Drawknife
- Bench vise
- 2 clamps, with plastic or leather pads
- 24-inch ruler
- 12-inch ruler
- 1 or 2 plank scraps the thickness of the seat blank (optional)
- Scraper (curved)
- 80- and 120-grit sandpaper
- Random-orbit sander (optional)

The saddling for this chair usually descends from a central front pommel, forming a gentle, sloping ridge from front to back. Saddling begins with roughing out a cavity with a hollowing adze. (If you don't have an adze, start the excavation with an inshave or a heavy, hooped gouge and mallet. The work will be slower, but it will be easier to control the contours of the cavity.)

An option before adzing is to bore two depth-gauge holes in the area of the deepest excavation. Then you'll know how far to adze, without having to take measurements. If the chair will be painted, you can use an ordinary auger bit to bore the holes. For chairs with a natural finish, bore holes with a spoon bit or a standard twist bit.

For a Welsh-style stick chair, adze to a depth of 1/2 to 5/8 inch. Draw a conservative outline of the area you plan to work with the adze, about 2 inches in from the flat deck

An adze is one of the few woodworking hand tools that uses the momentum of a swing to power a cut. You can adze by cutting across the grain or in line with it. Cross-grain adzing leaves a rougher surface, but there is less chance of a dig into descending fiber. When adzing in line with the grain, you cut downwards from opposing directions, so that you're always cutting into ascending fibers (fig. 8.10). Determine a midline crossing the excavation area. Adze from both sides, cutting toward the midline. Deepen the adze zone gradually, as you expand the perimeter.

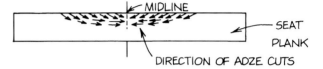

FIG. 8.10. Adze into ascending fiber by cutting from the perimeter toward the center line, widening the area as the excavation deepens.

If you're using a long-handled adze, stand on the margins of the seat blank so that you straddle the adze zone. Use scrap seat-blank stock to support your heels. Hold the end of the adze handle with your left hand, steadied by placing the forearm against your hip or thigh. Support your right hand, which does most of the lifting and chopping, by placing the elbow against your right thigh. This position also helps to support your back. Start by taking light, gentle swings that

John Brown hewing an elm seat at Country Workshops with a short-handled adze made by his son, Matt Sears

area (see fig. 8.9). You don't want to adze into the deck. The wave shape at the front of the adze zone leaves wood for the pommel ridge. If you do a good job with the adze, you can enlarge the area and adze it again before going on to inshave work.

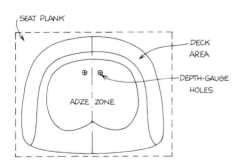

FIG. 8.9. Seat outline on plank, with a conservative adze zone

The length of your adze handle will partly determine how to position the seat blank for adzing. John Brown uses a short-handled adze, with his seat blank secured vertically in a machinist's bench vise. Dave Sawyer also uses a short-handled adze, but with the blank clamped flat on his workbench. I prefer using a heavier, long-handled adze, with the seat blank on the floor. You can use a hollowing adze with a mid-length handle (about 20 inches long) with the blank on the floor or secured to a low bench.

Hewing an elm seat with a chairmaker's adze designed by the author

don't actually cut into the seat plank. Begin adzing after you have a feeling for swinging the adze and a good idea of where it will start cutting. Be sure to work from both directions toward the midline of the adze zone. I believe this method is safe, but you must be very careful whenever using this tool.

With a short-handled adze, you'll still use a two-hand grasp to increase the power and control of your swing. Your right hand has the primary grip on the handle, with your left hand bunched around the right—or use your left hand to reinforce your right wrist. You must be careful to avoid wrist strain when using a short-handled adze.

If you clamp the seat blank flat on the workbench, you may find the adzing position uncomfortably high. Use a platform, such as a forklift pallet, to stand on. This is my least favored adzing position. If I'm using a short-handled adze, I clamp or wedge the blank horizontally on a bench about 20 inches from the floor, about the height of a shaving-horse bench.

Adzing is one of the most strenuous woodworking workouts, especially in hardwoods. Pay attention to your body's messages and take breaks when you need them.

Try to create a smooth surface as you chop into the adze zone, with a gradual slope around the perimeter. Don't let the adze dig in steeply, creating a choppy or channeled excavation. When the adze leaves a smooth surface, the follow-up passes with the inshave will also be smooth. The slope from the front of the excavation should be shallow (fig. 8.11). The slope at the rear can be a little steeper, and it should be concave, so that the bottom of the excavation is almost flat. The sides of the excavation should be cut with a gentle slope. Don't dig in at a steep angle, leaving a V-groove at the bottom or a distinct junction between the downward slopes from the front and back of the excavation.

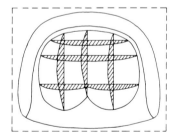

FIG. 8.11. Section views of enlarged adze zone at finish of adze work. The depth depends on chair style: stick Windsors, 5/8 inch; English Windsors, 5/8 to 3/4 inch; American Windsors, 3/4 to 7/8 inch.

If you're pleased with the results and the accuracy of your swing, you can enlarge the adze zone. Stretch it out as far as you dare to go. Using an adze is high-energy work, but it's also much faster than the other saddling tools.

Measure the depth of the excavation by placing the 2-foot ruler on edge across the seat blank and using the shorter ruler to measure downwards. The deepest area on the bottom of the excavation should be contoured like a shallow pond . Doing a good job is more important than the actual depth. Do not adze so deep that the integrity of the leg

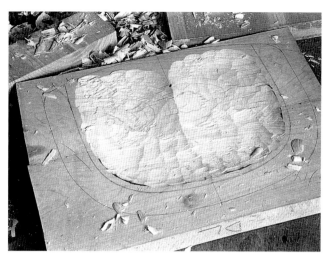

The finished adze work. Note the gradual slope on all sides of the excavation and the rather flat bottom area.

mortises will be compromised. A straight-sided, 1-inch-diameter tenon will need a mortise 1-1/2 inches deep. When leg tenons are tapered, the corresponding mortises can be shallower.

Sawing the Front Seat Outline and Inshaving

When you've completed the adze work, saw the seat outline of the front of the seat plank with a turning bow saw, a band saw, or a contractor's saber saw. (For now, leave the rear section of the rectangular plank intact.) If you're using a bow saw, secure the plank vertically in a vise or flat on the bench top. I prefer to have the plank vertical, so that I'm holding the saw more or less level. Quick, light pressure strokes are more efficient than bearing down on the saw, which tends to buckle the blade. Unlike Western panel saws, bow saws are designed to cut with a pull stroke. However, since some people have better success with a bow saw when cutting on a push stroke, try both ways.

Sawing the front edge of the seat with a shop-made bow saw. The knobs at the bottom of the handles can be rotated to change the angle of the blade in order to saw the seat outline.

Draw lines on the sawed front edge of the seat that indicate a new, lower arris between the pommel and the deck corner, 3/8 inch below the upper surface of the seat plank (fig. 8.12). Note the gradual curves leading to the high points at the center of the saddling and the corners of the deck. This arris will be lowered another 1/4 inch after most of the inshave work is complete.

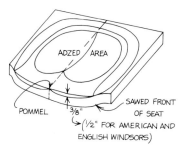

FIG. 8.12. Sawed front of the seat, with layout lines for inshave work

You'll do most of the remaining excavation with an inshave, a tool that requires practice, partly because the inshave's upswept handles throw it off balance. A sharp inshave edge and properly shaped bevel are essential.

Use two clamps to secure the seat over a corner of your workbench. Start inshaving by removing wood along the front edge of the seat. The inshave forms a contour that runs straight into the seat, at the height of the drawn lines. (Easing the front edge of the seat comes later.) Gradually work in toward the adze excavation. Inshave to the lines defining the deck and the arris at the front of the chair.

A major consideration when using an inshave is reading the fiber direction of the wood. In saddling, wood fiber comes into the excavation from all directions. You also have to work with a continually changing grain pattern and with the joint line of glued-up seats, which adds to the mix of shifting fiber direction.

Using an inshave, which requires constant reading of the seat's grain combined with skewing and slicing cuts. Most of the remaining saddling will be accomplished with this tool.

Taking many smooth, shallow cuts is better than digging in and leaving a rough or deeply gouged surface. Skewing and slicing will allow you to cut anywhere in the excavation. Try a different cutting direction whenever the inshave chatters or digs.

Blend the inshaved area into the adze zone. Taper the ridge line from the pommel downwards. Gradually enlarge the excavation at the back of the adze zone to the line defining the deck. Extreme skewing is often necessary. As you work, try to create a smoother and smoother surface. Figure 8.13 shows section views of the excavation at the completion of this stage.

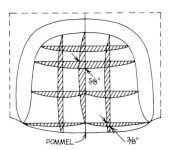

FIG. 8.13. Section view of finished inshave work

Draw lines that indicate the rolled edge at the front of the seat (fig. 8.14). The saddling-depth line drops down another 1/4 inch. All the lines begin and end at zero points—the peak of the pommel and the corners of the deck. You can remove wood in this area with an inshave, drawknife, or flat-bottomed spokeshave. Do not connect the edge and plan lines with a straight cut. The front edge should be slightly convex, to create a comfortable roll where a seated person's legs leave the seat. The back portion is blended into the previous excavation work.

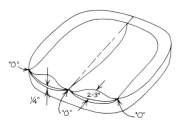

FIG. 8.14. Dimensions for easing the leading edge of the seat

Smoothing and Finishing

Smooth the saddle area using a combination of tools—a spokeshave for the rolled front edges, a travisher (also called a bottom shave or chairmaker's shave) on either side of the saddle ridge, an inshave for the most difficult area to finish, the concave slope below the stick deck. Round-bottom planes also work nicely here, if the plane sole matches the curvature of the excavation, or you can scrape and sand.

Using a spokeshave to shape the front edge of the seat and blend the convex rolled front into the concave inshaved area

Finishing the center area of the seat with a travisher made by the author

Smoothing the concave slope below the flat deck with a small plane whose sole curves lengthwise and crosswise. A travisher can also work this area.

Scraping the difficult concave slope area is also useful.

Using a travisher requires a light, sensitive touch. Because the nose is curved front to back and sideways, you have to find just the right tilt angle to get the tool to cut. Shallow-sweep travishers are easier to use than ones with a tighter curvature. By using a sideways, slicing cut, you can tighten the effective sweep, making it possible to take shavings in the deep curve below the deck area. Slicing also reduces the effective included angle of the bevel, especially helpful when you need to work tricky grain patterns.

To increase the travisher blade setting, tap lightly on the protruding tangs. Alternate tapping from one tang to the other will keep the tangs from jamming. To retract the blade, tap the upper side of the handle against something solid, such as the surface of the workbench.

As you finish saddling, check the contours by running your hands over the seat. You want smooth transitions, with no redundant bumps or hollows. A low-angled, raking light will also help reveal areas that require attention.

When you've completed the saddle work, saw out the back half of the seat blank.

SHAPING THE SEAT BOTTOM

Draw a continuous line on the sawed seat edge, 5/8 inch above the plank bottom. On the plank bottom, draw a loop around the perimeter (fig. 8.15). The distance from the arris is a subjective choice. For a seat like this I come in 2 inches at the front of the seat and about 1 inch around the sides and back.

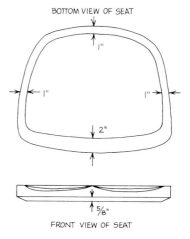

BOTTOM VIEW OF SEAT

FRONT VIEW OF SEAT

FIG. 8.15. Dimensions for shaping the bottom of the seat

Secure the seat vertically in a bench vise. The vise jaws must contact only the seat deck; do not clamp onto the carved section.

You'll use a sharp drawknife for chamfering on the bottom. To start, position the seat with the grain horizontal—parallel with the workbench—and the area to be chamfered facing out into the room (toward you). Shaving downhill from the high point and with the drawknife bevel up, take a few careful cuts across the arris at the widest point of the seat plank. After you've read the grain, begin

Dealing with Seat-Plank Defects

Saddling a perfect seat plank is one of the joys of making a chair. But perfect wood is rare stuff. Often you must deal with the challenges of defects—an important part of learning a craft.

Warpage and cupping occur during drying. Trying to build a chair with a warped or cupped plank will throw off all your measurements and boring angles, ruining the chair's symmetry. Seat planks must be close to flat, with no more than 1/10-inch deviation. Use a plane at a 45-degree angle to the plank.

To deal with small knots, locate them on the bottom of the chair seat or position the seat so that a small knot lies spaced between the spindles. Knots are much harder than the clear sections of the blank; perhaps the biggest problem is dealing with the reversing grain patterns in the wood that surrounds a knot. When a knot is in the saddling area, you have to be extra careful during adzing and inshaving. It's extremely easy to cut accidental catches in descending grain in knotty areas. Use a very sharp, shallow-sweep gouge or chisel to pare around and across knots. Hard knots in conifers can also cause chips in the edges of sharp tools. Some knots may require sanding, a slow process.

If you're working with white pine or another conifer, you're working with resin, a never-drying, gooey substance that can saturate entire areas of a plank. You can tolerate resin flecks and light streaking, but a large quantity of resin weakens the wood to the point that you should not use it for seating—how much is too much is a judgment call.

Resin also clogs sandpaper and bleeds through oil-based finishes. Before you apply an oil-based natural or painted finish, seal resinous seats by removing surface resin with a clean rag and naptha and applying a coat of shellac.

You can prevent the visible and incipient checks that may develop in the end grain during drying by using an end-grain sealant and by keeping temperatures moderate during early stages of drying. Sometimes checks open up during the saddling process, especially if you bring an air-dried seat plank into a dry, heated shop area. You can fill small checks with white or yellow glue: Apply glue over the crack, then rub it in with your finger or a flexible spatula. Fill larger checks (with gaps no more than 1/25 inch) with epoxy.

If a seat begins to split during construction, you can reinforce the repair by inlaying a butterfly patch on the underside of the seat. In fact, butterfly inlays can add a distinctive feature to the finished chair. The inlay should be about 3/8 inch thick, 1 inch wide, and 2 inches long, cut from a piece of sound, close-grain hardwood. Chop out a shallow, flat-bottomed mortise to fit the butterfly, and secure it with a gap-filling glue. If possible, clamp the split closed while chopping the mortise.

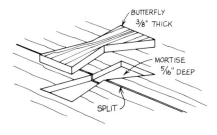

Wind shakes, those circular checks that follow the growth rings, are a particularly nasty surprise, for they often remain invisible until you've invested considerable time in saddling a seat, and they can run the full length of a board. I recommend trashing any seat plank with a wind shake.

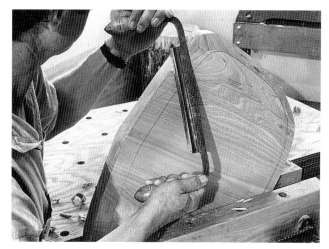

Working with the drawknife on the seat bottom, using extreme slicing and skewing action cutting into the endgrain at the front of the seat

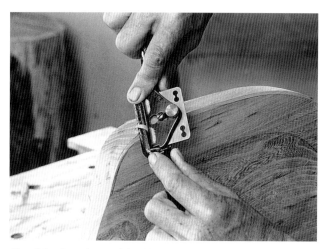

Chamfering the arris around the sides and back of the upper part of the seat with a spokeshave

taking bold, deep cuts into the wood along this side-grain area. Skew and slice as you approach the end grain. Do the easy shaving parallel to the grain on both sides of the seat before attempting to cut directly into the end grain.

Reposition the seat so that you can reach the end grain with the drawknife. Sneak into the end grain gradually, removing fine, smooth shavings. Extreme skewing and slicing will allow you to cut directly across the end grain, leaving a glassy, smooth surface. Finish the bottom chamfer by spokeshaving. Again, make use of skewing and slicing.

Spokeshave the vertical sides around the perimeter of the seat. If you choose to, angle the sides inwards by a few degrees. I like to leave a distinct arris defining the sides and the chamfer on the bottom. Another option is spokeshaving a narrow 45-degree chamfer along the arris at the back of the deck: Shave in and down about 3/16 inch, making a chamfer a little more than 1/4 inch wide.

Finish the seat by scraping and sanding. I do most rough sanding with 80-grit paper working across the grain. This will raise the surface fiber somewhat, but it doesn't create ridges caused by hardness differences of late and early

wood in the growth rings as sanding with the grain does. Do your finish sanding with 150- to 220-grit paper parallel to the grain. I've found that a random-orbit sander works effectively on the saddled contours of any Windsor seat.

As your last step in saddling the seat, sign and date the chair. Some chairmakers burn their name or a logo into the bottom of the seat. I chip carve my initials and the last two digits of the year.

MAKING THE BOW

Several ways for making the horizontal bow on stick Windsors are open to you: Hewing it from one piece of wood, assembling it from two or more pieces, or bending it.

Single-Piece Bows

The most direct (and ambitious) method for making a bow is hewing it from a single C-shaped piece of wood. Finding a tree stem or limb with enough curvature is not easy; the ones I find often require felling a tree. Cull trees and leftovers from a logging operation are an excellent resource for crooks and bends. The pieces you want have no commercial value, but it's wise to get permission before scavenging a logging operation.

Assembled Bows

You can use material with less curvature than the arc a chair bow requires by assembling the bow from two or more pieces (refer to fig. 8.5). (Old Welsh chairs were often made with pieced-together bows.) Bow sections can include some cross grain; 30-degree cross grain at the ends of the pieces is acceptable. A butt joint will usually involve less cross grain than a half-lap joint, which requires longer pieces. You can make a bow with three sections, with a fourth piece used as an overlapping crest, from lumber with no curvature.

The bow on the tutorial stick Windsor consists of three pieces. To make the bow I first made pasteboard patterns

Sawing the joint between two halves of a pieced armbow. The single cut will pass through both boards.

A low-back stick Windsor, made by John Brown, Newport, Wales

Bent Bows

If straight-grained, ring-porous wood is available, you can bend the bow. Bent bows are much narrower than pieced bows and do not lend themselves to the heavier pieced bows' sculptural shapes and details. For a bent bow, rive or saw bending blanks from straight-grained, clear stock 45 to 60 inches long. Most bows will be trimmed to less than 50 inches, but the longer length makes bending considerably easier.

Bent bows are square in section or somewhat wider than deep. John Brown's sawed bending stock is 1-1/4 inches square. For my bent bow low-back pictured at the opening of this chapter, the shaved section was 1-1/8 inch wide and 7/8 inch deep. (Rivings are considerably heavier.) At each end of the bow, I glued two rectangular pieces that were shaped into hand pieces, an innovation borrowed from American Windsor chairmaking.

Bent bows require a bending form, which I make from plywood. The form extensions should be at least 1 inch thick, so that you can use hefty dowels to pin the bow in place. Dowels smaller than 3/4 inch in diameter will not hold up for bending these rather stout bows. Make the form from scrap lumber or plywood, using the bow curve in figure 8.4 as a pattern. Steam bows made from green wood forty-five minutes to an hour. For air-dried bows, which will bend just as well, double the steaming time. If you have bending failures, try using a bending strap, explained in the section on bending in Chapter 4.

You can remove a steam-bent bow from its form one or two hours after bending, holding the bend in place with twine or a board and two clamps to insure that the arms won't twist out of plane during drying. A steamed bow is ready to use when it rattles loose in the bending form, or when there is only a little springback when you untie or unclamp it. You can speed up case hardening by putting bows into a low-heat kiln (90 to 100 degrees).

RIVING AND SHAVING THE STICKS

The low-back version of the stick Windsor uses up to fourteen short sticks; the high-back uses six to eight short sticks and four to nine long sticks. The rough length of the short sticks is about 12 inches, of long sticks, 20 to 30 inches. The long sticks in my high-back stick Windsor chair in the photos are 24 inches long.

Rive the stick blanks 1 inch across (see figs. 8.16 and 8.17). Shave the blanks into 3/4-inch squares. For the high-back, shave a gradual taper after shaving the squares, beginning 12 inches above the bottom of the sticks; taper the upper end to 5/8 inch in section. Shave the squared sticks into octagons.

Dry the sticks in a kiln and round them when they are thoroughly dry. Spokeshave the sticks 11/16 inch in diameter from end to end. Keep the sticks dry (in a kiln or plastic bag) until tenoning and fitting to the other chair parts—you can't shave the tenons until you know the exact height of the bow or comb.

for the horizontal bow (the arm and backrest) and the crest. These were sawed from a curved plank milled 1 inch thick, then planed flat. I sawed out the half laps, then carefully pared and scraped them until I had an acceptable fit. I glued the half-lap sections to make the full bow before gluing on the crest. Contouring the surface to create a comfortable shape and pleasing visual effect was drawknife, spokeshave, rasp, and sanding work. The curved stock that I used has a wavy figure, which is visually attractive but difficult to work.

John Brown sometimes makes pieced-together arms using a single 2-inch-thick plank sawed to the shape of a half bow, then ripped in half to form matching pieces. He uses a plain butt joint instead of the half laps. The overlapping crest holds the joined halves of the bow together.

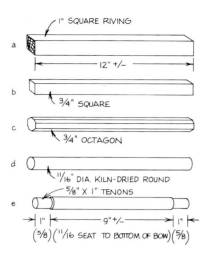

FIG. 8.16. Steps in making the short sticks

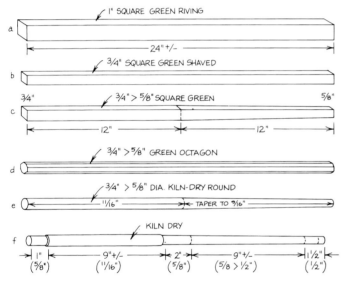

FIG. 8.17. Steps in making the long sticks

Many old stick Windsors were made with shaved, round legs, possibly finished with some hand planing. Turned legs were also used. Tapered legs shaved in an octagonal section were rare, but I feel this design is aesthetically compatible with the overall feeling of these chairs.

Make legs from either rived stock or straight-grained, sawed planks about 1-3/4 inch thick. Shave the legs to 1-3/4 inches square. Taper the squares to 1-1/4 inches at one end. Shave or plane the tapered squares into octagons. Before tenoning, put the legs into a kiln or other warm place to dry thoroughly.

The leg tenons can be tapered or cylindrical. A round tapered tenon is especially strong if it fits properly; however, discrepancies result in poor contact and compromise strength. Tapered joints must be made with a uniform included angle. The sides of the mortise and the tenon

Tapering the octagonal legs with a hand plane

must be straight. Grabbing power greatly diminishes as the included angle increases. Round tapered chair joints work best with an included angle of 8 to 10 degrees, although 12 degrees is common and acceptable (see fig. 8.18). The proportions for a tapered tenon depend on the available mortise reamer and matching taper cutter.

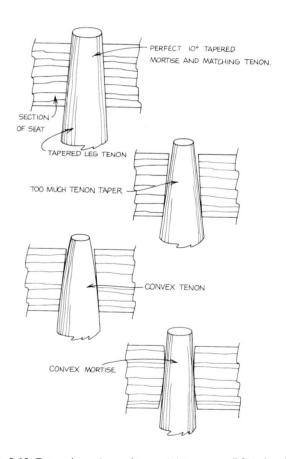

FIG. 8.18. Tapered mortise-and-tenon joints: *a*, a well fitted and extremely strong joint; *b*, *c*, and *d*, poorly matched components, very poor joints—fortunately, wood compression tightens these joints considerably.

If you opt for cylindrical tenons, remember that the shoulders are their weakest point: If the tenon is shouldered, it should be beveled. Typical cylindrical tenons are 1 inch in diameter and 2 inches long. The mortise for a 1-inch-diameter tenon should be at least 1-1/2 inches deep.

The easiest way to make conical or cylindrical tenons is to turn them on a lathe. To turn tenons, find centers at each end of the leg. Use a center punch to indent the center marks. Chuck the preshaped leg on a lathe. After rounding the tenon end of the leg, use calipers and a narrow parting tool to define the tenon diameter at the shoulder and tenon end. Then use a roughing gouge or skew chisel to turn the tenon to size.

You can also make cylindrical tenons with a hand-turned hollow auger or a tenon former. Secure the leg in the front vise of a workbench. Be careful aligning the cutter with the leg; it's easy to make the tenon off center.

Finally, you may choose to shave tapered tenons with a tapering (or rounding) plane, made by following the plans in Chapter 2. For other methods, refer to Chapter 6.

BORING MORTISES AND FITTING THE LEGS

Boring the leg mortises in the seat is one of the more challenging procedures in making any Windsor chair. In old handmade Windsors, you'll often see legs at irregular or peculiar angles. Developing a system for dealing with these angles is very useful.

Measuring Angles

Locations for the leg mortises usually form a trapezoid pattern on the seat, so that the rear legs are closer together than the front legs. The leg mortises are bored at compound angles. Leg angle forward and aft is called *rake*. Leg tilt to the sides is known as *splay*. When compound angles are depicted in front- and side-view drawings, splay angles show up in the front view, rake angles in the side view (see fig. 8.19).

Using a parting tool and outside calipers to size the base and end of a tapered tenon that will be shaped on a lathe

Shaping the taper with a 1-inch roughing gouge, a safe, easy tool to use

protractor). A rake angle of 102 degrees from a rear leg to the bottom of a seat can also be specified as 12 degrees (see fig. 8.20).

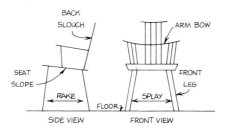

FIG. 8.19. Seat-geometry language

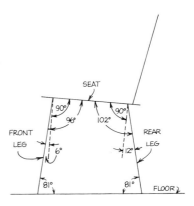

FIG. 8.20. Leg angles are always measured from the seat, not the floor line

Leg angles are measured from the bottom of the seat, not from the floor. Chairmakers often designate leg, stick, and spindle angles in degrees from perpendicular (past 90 degrees on a

The general method for boring compound angles is to set two bevel gauges to the rake and splay angles. Place the bevel gauges on the seat plank or workbench so that the base of the rake bevel gauge lines up with the front-to-back centerline and the splay bevel gauge is parallel to both front or both back legs.

Place the center of the drill over the center of the mortise, then tilt the drill so that the bit is parallel to the rake or splay angle as set on a bevel gauge. This first angle is maintained while the drill is tilted parallel to the other angle of the second bevel gauge. Hold the first angle and then tilt the drill at a crosswise angle to line the bit up with the second bevel gauge. (Viewed from the front, the bit is parallel to the splay bevel gauge; viewed from the side, it is parallel to the rake bevel gauge.) Because of the combined views, this is called a compound angle. Recheck and make adjustments for parallel compared to the first bevel gauge. Having an assistant to help in sightings while you position the drill is very useful.

For hand-held borings, this method is cumbersome (though workable) and difficult to do consistently even though the concept is very basic.

Another method that I generally prefer combines the rake and splay into a sighting angle and a resultant angle (see fig. 8.21). Once you have established a sighting line, you no longer need to look at a compound angle from front and side views. Instead, you line up the drill so that it tilts directly over the sighting line (or toward a sighting point). You are still dealing with two angles, but one of these is always a 90-degree angle perpendicular to the sighting line. The amount of drill tilt is the resultant angle. (See the Appendix for a chart that shows all rake and splay angle combinations between 0 and 30 degrees, the result of a collaboration between Dave Sawyer and Rusty Ault.) If you don't like this math-based approach, determine approximate sighting and resultant angles using the wire-leg chair models that I also describe in the Appendix.

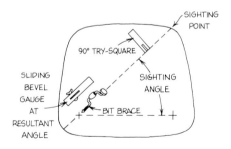

FIG. 8.21. Layout for boring compound angles using a try square and one sliding bevel gauge. The bit brace and leg of the sliding bevel gauge are tilted at the resultant angle.

Leg Angles (in degrees from 90) for the Stick Windsor				
	Rake	**Splay**	**Sighting**	**Resultant**
Front	6	10	30.8	11.6
Rear	13	10	52.6	16.2

John Brown boring cylindrical leg mortises at Country Workshops, with his brace positioned at a compound angle aligned with the legs of both bevel gauges

You can also take sighting lines and resultant angles directly from an existing chair. Use a plumb bob to find the two opposite points where a leg (or stick) appears to be straight up-and-down. Sight straight across the chair seat while the plumb string is in line with the leg. This is the sighting line. Any location along the line can be called a sighting point. The sighting angle is the angular relationship of the sighting line to a second line that connects both front legs or both rear legs. You need the sighting angle in order to draw the sighting line when you're not copying angles from an existing chair.

Use a sliding bevel gauge and a protractor to find the resultant angle on an existing chair. (For directions on making a bevel gauge, see Chapter 2.) Place the bevel gauge next to the angled chair part, with the base parallel with the sighting line. Adjust the bevel-gauge leg to line up with the center of the chair part. Read the angle on a protractor. Or don't use a bevel gauge—simply place the protractor beside the leg, with the base of the protractor parallel with the sighting line. Then eyeball down the center of the leg and read the protractor directly.

Boring Leg Mortises

The tools you'll need to bore leg mortises are

- 11/16-inch auger bit

- Bit brace

- Sliding bevel gauge

- Try square

- Protractor (cheap plastic)

- 2 "C" or bar clamps with clamp pads

Use the chair pattern to locate the leg mortise centers on the saddled top of the chair seat. Prick centers with an awl. Write the appropriate resultant angle beside all four drilling centers. Make pencil marks on the seat's center line indicating the sighting points for front and rear legs. If the chair will be painted, you can also pencil sighting lines from the mortise centers to the sighting point. For chairs that will have a natural finish, you can pencil lines and other specs over strips of masking tape.

Boring a compound-angle leg mortise using the sighting line and resultant angle method. The brace is aligned with a bevel gauge set parallel to the sighting line and a try square set perpendicular to the sighting line. Masking tape on seat areas allows lines or other notations to be penciled in.

Clamp the seat to the workbench with the front or rear leg boring centers overhanging the workbench. You can work from the front of the bench, but you will get better support if you clamp the chair seat over a corner of the bench. Set the bevel gauge for the specified resultant sighting angle (12 degrees from 90 for the front legs; 16 degrees for the rear legs). You can set the arm of the sliding bevel on either side of perpendicular, forming either an acute angle or an obtuse angle. I generally use an acute angle, because the bevel gauge is more stable with the arm placed over the base.

Place the bevel gauge on the nearby area of the flat deck, with the base of the gauge eyeballed parallel to the sighting line. The bevel-gauge leg must point outward when a line is projected through the bottom of the seat.

Place the try square on the far side of the deck. Position the base at an eyeballed right angle to the sighting line.

Set the lead screw of the auger bit on the pricked center hole for the leg mortise. Position yourself so that your body is in line with the sighting line on the chair seat.

Start by boring straight in, perpendicular to the surface of the seat. This scoring prevents tearout from the auger when it begins to enter the wood. Look across the seat toward the try square and adjust the shaft of the auger so that it is parallel to the arm of the try square.

Begin tilting the brace when the side nicker of the auger has scored the perimeter of the hole. Simultaneously turn and tilt the brace until the shaft of the auger is parallel to the angled leg of the bevel gauge. The knob of the brace will be toward the center of the chair seat.

Take a few more turns with the tilted brace, then stop with the brace crank centered over the auger. Let go of the brace—it will balance in this position, allowing you to step back to check alignment with the sliding bevel and the try square. Step to the side to compare the angle of the auger shaft with the sliding bevel leg. They should be parallel. If not, note if the brace needs to be lifted or dropped lower, and about how much. Then compare the auger shaft with the try square. Make a mental note if the auger needs to be tilted to the right or left.

Stepping back to check the brace alignment with the angled bevel gauge and the try square (if you're using a standard auger bit, you can let go of the brace after taking a few turns into the wood).

Return to your boring position. Tilt the brace forward or aft, left or right, as you've noted was necessary. Turn the brace slowly as you adjust the angle. Take several turns, and then stop again, with the brace positioned with the crank over the auger. Again compare angles.

When the boring angle is in line with the sliding bevel and try square, you can continue boring dead on—*but do not bore straight through the seat.* This would cause fiber tearout when the auger nicker comes through the plank. Stop boring when the lead screw begins to emerge through the bottom.

Continue by boring the other three leg mortises. Be sure to change the arm of the sliding bevel gauge when switching from front to rear posts.

The next step is back boring into the holes you started on the top side of the seat. Turn the plank over when the four holes are bored. Transfer the sighting lines from the top of the seat. Begin back boring by drilling straight down at one of the holes where the lead screw came through the plank. When you've scored the mortise circumference, begin angling the drill outward, at the appropriate angle of the leg angle.

Fitting the Legs

You'll do the fitting work from the bottom of the seat and on the kiln-dry leg tenons. It's important to be organized and methodical; it's surprisingly easy to set the legs into the wrong sockets during assembly. Penciling sighting points, labels, and arrows on the seat bottom and the legs will serve you well.

Transferring sighting points from the upper side of the chair seat to the bottom

Labeling

When the seat is turned over with the bottom facing up, the left side of the seat is on your left *when the front of the seat faces you*. When you're working on the mortises for the rear legs, with the rear of the seat facing you, left becomes right and vice versa. To avoid confusion, label the left and right sides as well as each mortise (see fig. 8.22).

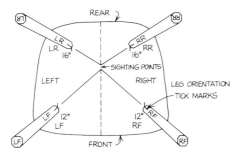

FIG. 8.22. To prevent errors, label the four legs and resultant angles and make tick marks for axial rotation.

Identifying each leg and its mortise by penciling tick marks on matching parts so that alignment will be consistent during trial fitting and final glue up

Next, label the legs and their growth-ring orientation relative to the seat plank. If the front and back legs are different lengths, separate them. Hold a leg in place over its respective mortise. Rotate the leg so that the rays are in line with the direction of the seat grain. Pencil a tick mark on the base of the tenon and the corresponding location at the perimeter of the mortise. Label the leg on its side and on its foot. Pencil the resultant sighting angle beside each mortise.

Reaming the Mortises

Reaming the mortises and fine tuning the tapered tenons are among the more challenging tasks in making the chair. The included angle of the reamer must match the included angle of the tenons. If the tenons were turned or shaved from green wood, they will now be oval in section; you'll modify them with a rasp or coarse file.

The tools you'll need are

- Reamer
- Rasp and/or coarse file
- Soft lead pencil
- Sliding bevel gauge

- Try square
- Protractor
- 2 clamps

Reaming a tapered mortise

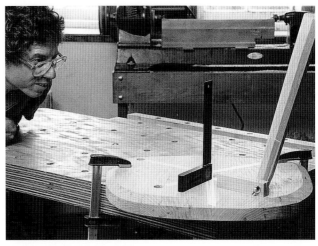

Checking the fit of the tapered mortise and the reaming angle with the leg that will go in this hole

Clamp the chair bottom to a corner of the workbench with the mortise to be reamed extending out from the table top. Adjust the sliding bevel gauge to the resultant angle. Place the sliding bevel parallel to the sighting line. Set the try square perpendicular to the sighting line.

Use caution when reaming. The action of the reamer changes as it cuts through quadrants that alternate between ascending and descending fiber (fig. 8.23). Reamers cut easily into ascending fiber, but in unskilled hands a reamer tends to catch and sometimes causes tearouts as it cuts into descending fiber. The problem is particularly acute when reaming a soft wood, such as white pine. Reaming tulip poplar is much easier. Because of the alternating fiber-direction quadrants, the reamed hole will be off round to some extent. The reamer also tends to suck itself into the hole too quickly. Ease into reaming, so that you have control of the direction and resultant angle and can make corrections as needed. Hold the reamer back a little as you rotate it through the quadrants.

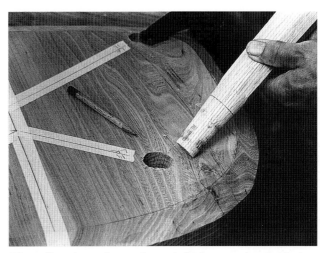

The pencil smudges on the tapered tenon, indicating areas where the joint is too tight. Use a rasp or file to remove these high spots.

tenon into the mortise. When doing a test fit, always position the leg so that the tick marks on the tenon and seat bottom line up. Rotate the leg in alternating directions to seat it into the hole. When the leg seats, compare its angle to the sliding bevel and the try square. If your bevel gauge doesn't have a translucent arm, the most useful view is from the bottom of the leg looking down toward the seat plank.

Check and correct the angle as you continue reaming. Test the tenon fit and leg angle often.

When the leg is about three-quarters seated, begin fine-tuning the tenon. To check for contact, mark the inside of the mortise with the soft pencil. Seat the tenon and wiggle it left and right a little. (Be sure that the tick marks line up.) When you remove the leg, pencil smudges on the tenon indicate high points on the tenon or mortise. Use the rasp or file to remove wood at the smudged areas. When the fit is good, continue with reaming.

Be sure to keep the reamer flat against the sides of the reamed mortise. Novices often overream the small end of the mortise (on the upper side of the seat), a result of allowing the reamer to wobble.

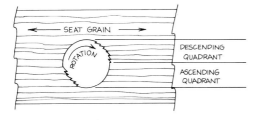

FIG. 8.23. Changing reamer action. The cutter of a tapered reamer passes through four quadrants, cutting ascending and descending fiber alternately. The resulting imperfect mortise must be matched when fitting the corresponding tenon.

Hold the reamer tilted at the resultant angle and pointed directly over the sighting line. Begin rotation clockwise. At first the reamer will cut only a chamfer along the rim of the hole; it won't hold any particular angle.

As you ream into the hole, the angle begins to set. You can now take the appropriate leg and try fitting the tapered

Checking the resultant-angle reamer in the second rear mortise. Leave the first rear leg in place to check for lateral symmetry and alignment when viewed from one side.

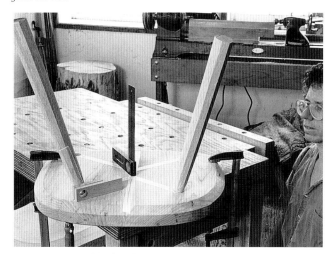

Checking the second leg for alignment with the try square

Stop reaming and tuning the tenon when a predetermined depth is reached. On turned legs, I use a scored line 2 inches from the upper end of the leg. A similar line could be penciled onto tenons that are shaved or made with a rounding plane.

The final fit includes seating the joint by striking the bottom of the leg with a mallet.

When you've fitted the first leg, leave it in place as a sighting aid in getting the angles matched while you work on the opposing leg.

Pounding the legs home during glue up of the stool

Assembling the Windsor "Stool"

For chairs without stretchers, like the project chair, assembly is a straightforward procedure. (See Chapter 9 for leg assemblies that include cross stretchers.) Saw a slot for the wedges in the ends of the tenons (see fig. 8.8)—orient the wedges perpendicular to the grain of the chair seat. (Wedges in line with the grain could split the seat.) Make four wedges roughly 3/16 inch thick, 11/16 inch wide, and 1-1/2 inches long (refer to the sidebar "Making the Wedges").

Set all four legs loosely in their mortises. Align the tick marks. Double-check to be sure each leg is in the correct mortise.

If any tenons protrude past the deck level, saw off excess waste, so that the assembled stool can be set upside down on

Option: Cylindrical Mortise-and-Tenon Joints

If you don't have a reamer and a method for making tapered tenons, you can use plain cylindrical mortises for the leg joints. I suspect this was the technique most makers of the old stick Windsors used, for they often had only a few tools to work with.

Fitting cylindrical tenons in straight-bored mortises is much easier than working with angled mortises. You'll make the tenon to fit the mortise as exactly as possible, or taper it slightly. A well-shaped wedge driven into the top of the leg will spread out the tenon so that it fits the mortise. If the tenon is shouldered, cut or shave a chamfer around the base.

the workbench. About 1/4 to 1/2 inch of the tenon end should still protrude through the top surface of the seat.

Remove one leg only. Smear white or liquid hide glue in the mortise and on the sides of the tenon. Rub some glue into the sides of the wedge kerf. Insert the leg back into the mortise. Check for tick-mark alignment. Use a mallet to drive the leg home. Finish gluing the set, one leg at a time.

Turn the stool over, so the legs are on the floor or workbench. Smear a little glue on a wedge. Tight tenons use thin wedges; loose tenons require thicker wedges. Use a hammer to tap the wedge tightly in place. Be sure that the leg getting wedged contacts the floor. You could knock it out with the hammer.

To level the stool, see the leveling instructions in the section on assembling the ladder-back in Chapter 6. Adjust the tilt of the seat to your personal preference and the intended use of the chair. Be sure to chamfer the arris at the bottom of the legs.

Once you've leveled the stool, you need to trim the protruding tenons and wedges flush to the seat before proceeding with the sticks and bows. Use a fine-toothed saw to trim the front leg tenons, taking care to saw slightly above the surface of the seat. Trim the rear leg tenons with a wide, shallow gouge driven with a hammer or mallet. Set the gouge bevel down on the seat, up against a protruding tenon. Tap the gouge into the tenon. Repeat around the perimeter of the tenon. Use a chisel to split off segments of the tenon, placing the chisel edge about 1/2 inch above the seat and driving in the chisel at about a 20-degree angle. Pieces of the tenon will split loose. When the last bit of

tenon resembles a thin-stemmed mushroom, be very careful—it can easily break, tearing fibers below the surface of the seat. Finish each tenon end by paring with a shallow-sweep gouge. Take slicing cuts at a shallow angle.

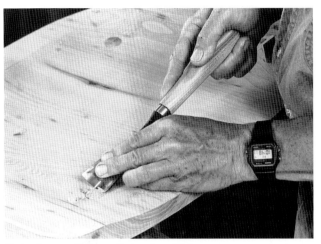

Paring the protruding tenon flush to the saddled seat

BORING STICK MORTISES IN BOW AND SEAT

The challenge in boring mortises for the sticks is finding and boring at the proper angles for supporting the horizontal arm/back bow. All borings in the seat and bow for this chair are 5/8 inch in diameter. Bow borings for the low-back version run through the bow, but not through the crest in the center. Borings for the high-back continue through the crest.

Spindles should be thoroughly dry. Tenons can be made using any of the methods discussed in Chapter 6.

Boring Fixtures

My preferred method for dealing with angled borings is to anchor the horizontal bow above the seat with boring

Using the set of three bow fixtures to position the bow for boring mortises

fixtures, exactly where it will be in the assembled chair. (I use these same boring fixtures for the horizontal bows of American and English Windsors.) With the bow in place, you can experiment with the spacing of the sticks and with the stick angles, then bore the mortises with the bow secured in place. For boring the seat mortises, you use a drill extension that passes through the bow mortises. With this method, you don't need to deal with sighting lines and specified resultant angles, and you can modify the number of sticks and angles for individual chairs without drawing plans or making trig calculations. (If you prefer to, however, you can bore seat and arm mortises without using the horizontal fixtures; the seat plan shows sighting lines and resultant sighting angles for boring the seat mortises.)

Saw the boring fixtures from 2-by-6 lumber (see fig. 8.24). The left and right end fixtures mirror each other, because the arm bow drops slightly toward the back of the chair. The back fixture is 7/16 inch lower than the end fixtures and has a notch cut out of the post to make room for a clamp.

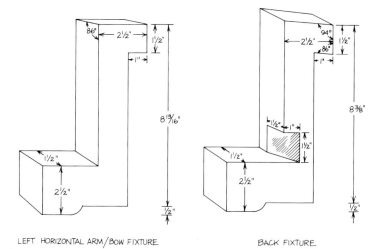

LEFT HORIZONTAL ARM/BOW FIXTURE.   BACK FIXTURE.

FIG. 8.24. Fixtures for boring horizontal Windsor bows. Make a mirrored pair of side fixtures and one or two center fixtures.

Making the Wedges

Windsor chairs often employ wedges to secure leg tenons in their seat mortises and spindle tenons to arm bows.

Make the wedges from any hard, straight-grained, dry wood. To be effective, wedges should be shaped with a fairly narrow included angle. A wedge 1 inch long should be no more than 3/16 inch in thickness. The sides of wedges must be flat, neither convex nor concave. The width should equal the diameter of the mortises.

You can produce multiple wedges quickly with a band saw. Saw a block at least 6 inches long to the approximate width of the wedges. Growth rings run up and down, so that the wedges are basically flat sawn. Pencil a line across the blank to indicate the length of the wedges. Draw zig-zag lines representing the sides of the wedges. Due to the saw kerf, the actual wedges will not follow the lines. The lines indicate the angle the wedges are sawed at. Saw the full set of wedges across the block—be careful to leave a little connective fiber at the ends of the wedges inside the block. When you've finished ripsawing, saw across the block to release the full set of wedges.

You can also shape wedges by riving out stock and then shaving or whittling the convergent sides. It's much easier to shape a series of wedges from the end of a long blank than to whittle short wedges individually. Rive out a blank that is the width of the mortises. Shave the blank to about 3/16-inch thickness. Shave a wedge on the end of the blank, saw it loose, then shave another wedge.

When you need wedges later to secure the sticks into the bow, you'll make them by splitting the larger leg-tenon wedges.

Clamp the back fixture at the center rear of the seat. The foot and base of the fixture should contact the seat. Clamp the left and right side fixtures beside the boring locations for the end sticks. Set the bow across the top of the fixtures. Use a sliding bevel gauge set at 102 degrees to locate the placement for the back of the bow. This determines the back slouch angle. It's also important that the bow is symmetrical as viewed from above, and that the arms are in alignment when inspected from a side view. Check the bow from a front view to be sure that the arm splay to each side is equal. Use clamps to secure the bow to the fixtures. So you can replicate the setup if it has to be taken apart, pencil sets of tick marks locating the position of the bow on the fixtures and of the fixtures on the seat.

Arranging the Sticks

Before boring any mortises, arrange all the sticks in place around the inside of the bow to see how they look. If they roll off position, secure them with masking tape. Pencil small Xs on the seat and bow indicating the boring centers. Use your eye and personal judgment—as a starting point, the long back spindles on the stick Windsor here are spaced 2-1/4 inches on center, beginning 1-1/8 inches from the seat centerline. Since the long spindles are parallel, the spacing on the bow is the same. The armrest spindles are spaced 2-1/2 inches on center. The arm spindles rake forward at 87 degrees from the seat plank.

View the arrangement of the sticks from front, side, and plan perspectives. From the front and plan view you're looking for symmetry. From the side view, check to see if corresponding sticks on the two halves are in alignment. Look too at the general appearance of the arrangement from random perspectives. Small spacing variations can make a great difference in the chair's overall appearance.

When the stick placement is right, use an awl to indent the center of each mortise on the seat and bow.

Taping sticks against the bow to check their placement before boring mortises. Make corresponding center marks in the bow and seat deck.

Boring the Mortises

You can choose from several types of drills to bore the mortises. You must be able to match the mortise diameter to the tenons. In the photos I'm using a bit brace and powerbore bit, mainly because it accepts a standard spade-bit extension. Other bits work fine, but finding an extension may be a problem. Remember that many auger bits are 1/64 inch larger than their nominal size. A hand-held electric drill with variable speed control can be used with bits that won't fit a bit brace.

Begin boring the arm mortises with the bit perpendicular to the arm surface. After you've scored the perimeter, tilt the bit so that it aims directly at the center for the corresponding mortise on the seat. Check the angle by sighting the shaft of the bit from front and side perspectives and correct it if necessary. Stop boring when the lead point begins to emerge through the bottom of the bow.

Bore the remaining bow mortises. Remove the bow from the fixtures, and then back bore the mortises from the bottom of the bow.

To bore the seat mortises, add an extension to the boring bit. Use tape to make a depth gauge on the shaft. Mortise depth for 1-inch shouldered tenons is 1-1/8 inches. For straight spindles without shouldered tenons, set the depth gauge at 1 inch.

Low-Back Bent Bow • The procedures differ for boring bent bows and for pieced bows for the low-back and high-back versions.

With a bent bow, use the boring fixtures to find the placement for the sticks, crest, and optional hand pieces. Plane the common surfaces of the crest and add-on hand pieces. The hands are rectangular blocks of matching hardwood and are sawed to shape after they are glued to the bent bow. (The crest will be glued and/or screwed to the bow after you've fitted the spindles.)

Using the boring fixture on a bent-bow low-back

Boring stick mortises with the bow secured in place on the boring fixtures

When the hands are in place, refit the bow to the boring fixture to bore mortises through the bow and into the seat.

Low-Back Pieced Bow • On a low-back with a pieced bow, the simplest method calls for a butt joint in the middle of the bow (refer to fig. 8.5). Saw out the bow sections and crest. Glue the crest above the bow overlap. Do not contour the bow and crest until after a dry fitting of the assembly.

Use boring fixtures to support the bow. Bore and fit the sticks in the arm section of the bow and seat. (Don't glue yet.) Mortises in the crest section are blind; they don't come through the crest. Arrange stick spacing in the crest area. Draw vertical center lines on the face of the crest. Use a bevel gauge to determine boring angles from the bottom of the bow to the seat mortises. Also gauge angles for mortises into the seat while the bow is held in place by the boring fixture.

Remove bow and fixtures from the seat. Bore the seat mortises. The sighting direction for the back mortises is parallel to the seat centerline.

Clamp the bow upside down to your workbench. Bore mortises in the crest area 1 inch deep. Contour the bow with a spokeshave, rasp, and sandpaper.

Using an extension that passes through the bow mortise for boring the seat, which eliminates any fussing with stick angles

High-Back Pieced Bow • Saw out bow parts and crest from 1-inch-thick stock. Glue the crest to the bow. Use the boring fixtures to locate the bow unit. Bore 5/8-inch-diameter mortises through the bow/crest unit and into the seat. Contour the bow.

TENONING THE STICKS

With the bow clamped to the boring fixture, measure the distance from the seat deck to the bottom of the arm for each stick. Add 1 inch for the bottom tenon. For short sticks, add 1/4 inch to the bow thickness for the upper tenons.

You can either shave and sand the 5/8-inch tenons or cut them with a hollow auger. On the long, high-back sticks, you need to make 5/8-inch-diameter intermediate tenons in the area where the sticks pass through the arm bow (see fig. 8.17f). Determine the tenon area for each stick. Taper the upper section of the sticks to 9/16 inch. Form the 5/8-inch midstick tenon by careful shaving and sanding. (You can also use the Boggs tenon former, as shown in the photo.) Hold off on forming the 1/2-inch tenon at the upper end of these sticks until you've determined the exact placement of the comb.

Test fit the full assembly. Correct discrepancies in mortise borings in the bow with a rat-tail rasp. You can also modify the tenons, using a file or sandpaper. When the full assembly fits together, pencil tick marks on the sticks, seat, and arm. Pencil a number on each stick and its corresponding mortise.

You can glue the upper assembly without the comb, or you can make and fit the comb first.

Cutting the intermediate 5/8-inch-diameter tenons on the long sticks with Brian Boggs's tenon former. The extended end will taper to a 1/2-inch-diameter tenon, which will be made with a plug cutter.

THE COMB

Sawed from a solid timber or bent from a riving, the comb on most stick Windsors is quite plain, although some have a decorative outline. For this chair I make a comb that is basically an elongated rectangle with a slight arch on the top.

Sizing and Positioning the Comb

The comb for the chair in the plans is designed so that the sticks remain straight. On some stick Windsors, the comb is shorter than the natural splay of the extended sticks and the sticks are pulled inward, forming a "balloon-back." The placement for mortises in the comb can also be farther apart than the natural direction of the extended sticks, which are then pulled apart to form a fan-back.

Positioning the comb. Experiment with different heights and spreads for the sticks.

You can saw the comb from any air-dried stock of appropriate thickness. The curvature of the comb in plan view is usually straighter (less curved) than the curvature of the bow, but this is a matter of preference. Draw an outline of the curvature on the comb stock using an arced ruler or an evenly cut thin piece of wood for a batten.

The comb for the stick Windsor in the plans was sawed from a 3-inch-thick curved slab of sweet birch. (The same wood was used for the pieced arm-bow.) The sawed comb is 1-1/4 inches thick and 13-1/2 inches end to end. Size the comb to fit the sticks on your chair or your design ideas.

The front of the comb is shaped with a smooth roll toward the upper arris. Resist shaping the comb until the stick end tenons are mortised into the base of the comb. The sawed-out square section of the comb is useful for laying out and boring the stick mortises. Penciling the finished outline of

the comb will give you an idea of how it will look. Draw a vertical centerline around the middle of the bow.

Try moving the comb up and down on the assembled sticks before settling on the final height. Experiment with the spacing of the sticks, too. Clamp the comb in place against the sticks. When you are satisfied with the arrangement of the sticks and height of the bow, pencil centers for the mortises and base lines for the tenons.

Draw lines across the front of the comb that indicate centers for the bored mortises, which should be parallel to the back side of the comb. Bore the mortises horizontally or vertically, with the comb secured in a bench vise. Be careful with drill alignment. A drill with an extension is useful.

Begin shaping the comb with a drawknife, and follow up with a spokeshave. You can also use a rasp and sandpaper. The comb diminishes in thickness from the base upwards. This is the time to do any final shaping on the arm bow.

Disassemble the bow/stick assembly. Saw the sticks to length. For strength, the end sticks have tenons 1-1/2 inches long. Tenons for the middle sticks are 1 inch long. Tenon the end of the sticks 1/2 inch in diameter. These tenons are shoulderless. You can shave and sand them to size or make them with a tenon former and then shave them to eliminate the shoulders.

Boring 1/2-inch-diameter mortises in the comb

Test assemble the entire upper section of the chair. When everything fits, saw wedge kerfs in the upper tenons of the short sticks. Prepare six wedges 5/8 inch wide and about 1 inch long. Every joint should have corresponding tick marks on both pieces. Sticks should also be numbered.

Assembling the Back Structure

You can choose from ordinary white glue, liquid hide glue, or urethane glue. Brush glue into all the arm-bow mortises and onto the upper tenons of the short sticks. (Don't apply glue to the midsection tenons on the long sticks.) Fit all the sticks to the arm bow.

Brush glue into all the seat mortises and the bottom ends of all the sticks. Insert the sticks (with attached bow) into the seat mortises. If the fit is tight, tap the ends with a hammer.

Be sure that the bow is level as viewed from in front, and that it's not twisted when viewed from a side. You may have to tap the bow with a mallet.

Hammer wedges into the protruding tenons of the short arm sticks. Trim flush by sawing and careful chiseling.

Brush glue on the end tenons of the long sticks and in the mortises in the comb. Set the comb. Check the comb for level from a front view before taking a work break.

Gluing all the sticks to the bow, the first step in assembling the chair

Making sure the arm bow is properly positioned, after the sticks are in place. Check from front and side views.

Seating the sticks into their mortises with a mallet

Driving wedges into the kerfs of protruding tenons

FINAL DETAILS AND FINISHING

Do some serious test sitting in your new chair before proceeding with a finish. You may want to change the height or modify the seat slope by lowering the back legs.

Sanding an assembled stick chair is time consuming, due to all the intersections and parts that you need to work on and around. John Brown prefinishes parts before assembly, an excellent technique but one that requires you to be very careful with all the parts during assembly.

Finishing begins with careful preparation of the wood surface—sanding and filling gaps and dents. Fill small dings and gaps at joints with wood putty. Patch large gaps (at poorly fitted joints) or wedge them with glued inserts. On a painted chair, you can use auto-body filler in any large spaces.

Welsh stick chairs and English Windsors are usually stained and varnished, although some are painted, as were most early American Windsors. For oil and varnish finishes, see Chapter 6; for painting a chair, see Chapter 9.

How I Finished the High-Back Stick Windsor

Day 1. The chair in the plans combined an elm seat, birch arm/bow and comb with red oak sticks and legs. Before applying any finish materials, I sanded the entire chair with 180-grit followed by 280-grit paper and filled a few small gaps around the joints with color-matching wood putty, which I sanded when dry.

Because the beautiful figuring in the birch was extremely light and difficult to see, I used brown aniline dye in a naptha base to darken the wood, which gave it an interesting mottled brown appearance. With that change, the reddish cast of the oak didn't look right, so I went over the oak with the same brown dye, highly diluted. I used a throw-away acid brush to apply the dye, which I then went over using a rag moistened with naptha.

To deal with the elm's high porosity, I gave the seat a coat of paste filler. When the surface clouded, I scraped off any excess paste filler. (I did the dye work and paste filling wearing rubber gloves in a well-ventilated room.)

Day 2. Waited for the paste filler to dry.

Day 3. I sanded the seat and gave the entire chair a first coat of a natural 'Danish oil' finish with a fairly high proportion of varnish, wiping it on with a rag (brushing tends to lay down too much material, leading to drips and streaks).

Day 4. The chair looked good from a distance, but the surface was matted and uneven. I sanded the entire chair again, this time using 320-grit paper. Then I wiped another coat of Danish oil over the entire chair.

Day 5. Instead of sanding, I used 0000 steel wool. This helps to even out the sheen, which tends to be different on the various woods and around hard-to-reach areas like the base of the sticks at the bow and seat. I used compressed air to blow off the steel-wool dust. (Lacking a compressor, you can use a wax-coated tack cloth to clean off any surface debris.) I wiped on a third thin coat of Danish oil.

Day 6. I steel wooled again, then applied a thick coat of ordinary paste wax for floors. When the surface of the paste wax glazed (after about ten minutes), I went over the chair with a soft clean cloth, buffing the surface to a slight shine. Future maintenance will mainly be dusting. A few times a year I'll clean the chair with an oil-based furniture cleaner, followed by a coat of paste wax.

Marvin and Jan Mastin, with their finished chairs at the end of a class at Country Workshops. Note the unique character of each chair.

A Classic
Bow-Back Side Chair

Two versions of a bow-back Windsor. The chair on the left has a tail brace, eleven spindles, and a turning style that combines a tapered foot with a single vase. The chair on the right is the version made at Country Workshops, with bamboo turnings and seven spindles. Both chairs are typical of American bow-backs made about 1800.

FIG. 9.1. Plan view

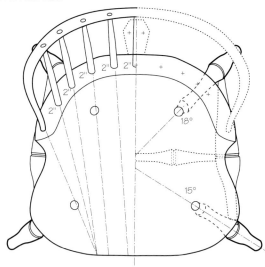

Scale: 1:8

FIG. 9.2. Front view

FIG. 9.3. Side view

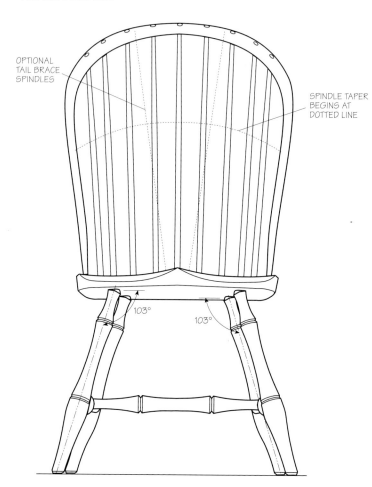

OPTIONAL
TAIL BRACE
SPINDLES

SPINDLE TAPER
BEGINS AT
DOTTED LINE

103°

103°

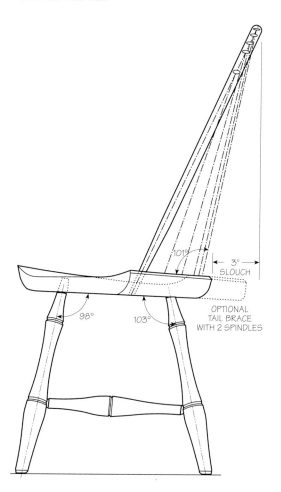

101°

3"
SLOUCH

98°

103°

OPTIONAL
TAIL BRACE
WITH 2 SPINDLES

Fig. 9.4. Seat plan and bending form

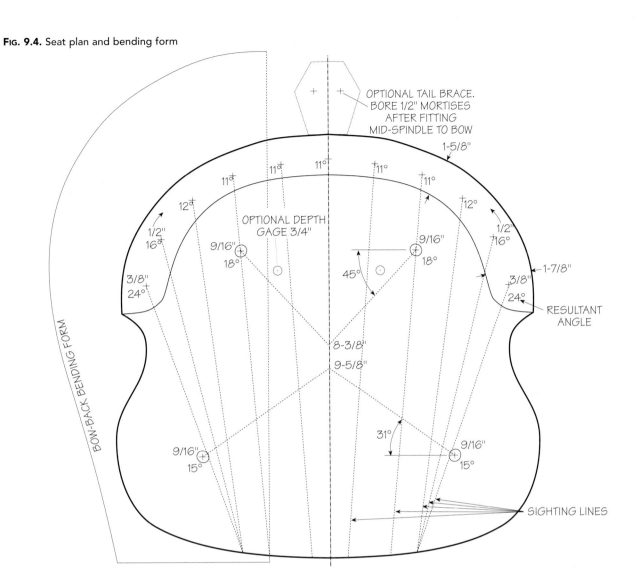

Scale: 1:4

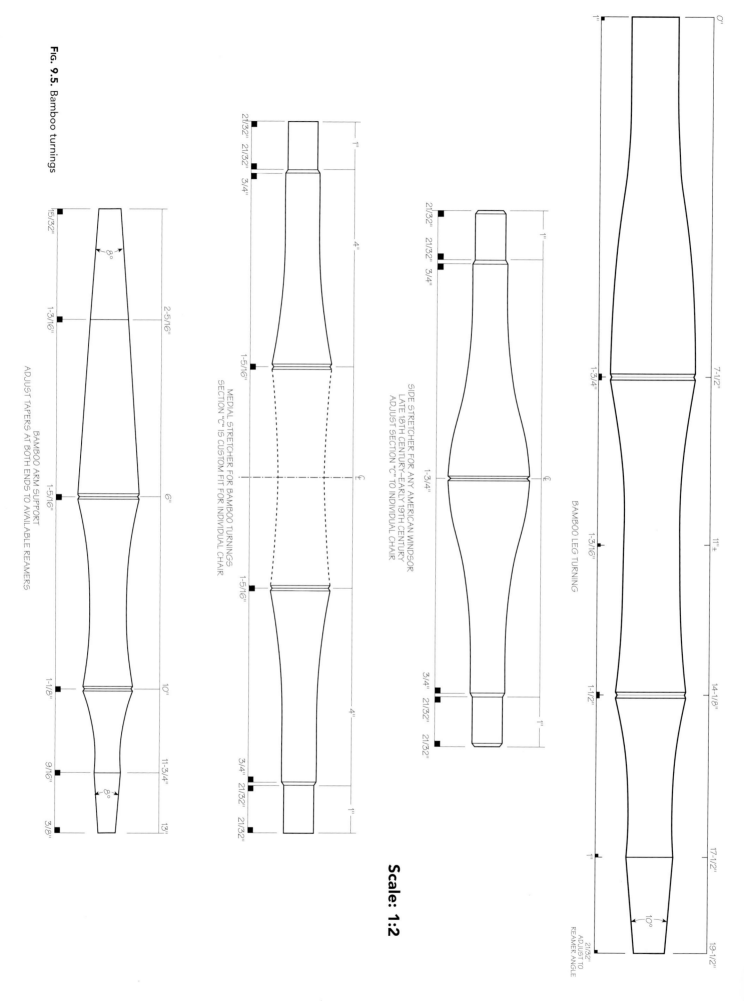

Fig. 9.5. Bamboo turnings

Scale: 1:2

BAMBOO LEG TURNING

0"
1"
7-1/2"
1-3/4"
11"+
1-3/16"
14-1/8"
1-1/2"
1"
17-1/2"
21/32"
19-1/2"
10°
ADJUST TO
REAMER ANGLE

SIDE STRETCHER FOR ANY AMERICAN WINDSOR
LATE 18TH CENTURY–EARLY 19TH CENTURY
ADJUST SECTION "C" TO INDIVIDUAL CHAIR

21/32"
21/32"
3/4"
1"
1-3/4"
₵
1"
3/4"
21/32"
21/32"

MEDIAL STRETCHER FOR BAMBOO TURNINGS
SECTION "C" IS CUSTOM FIT FOR INDIVIDUAL CHAIR

21/32" 21/32"
3/4"
1"
4"
1-5/16"
1-5/16"
₵
1-5/16"
4"
3/4" 21/32" 21/32"
1"

BAMBOO ARM SUPPORT
ADJUST TAPERS AT BOTH ENDS TO AVAILABLE REAMERS

15/32"
8°
1-3/16"
2-5/16"
1-5/16"
6"
1-1/8"
10"
11-3/4"
9/16"
8°
13"
3/8"

172

Materials List: Bow-Back Side Chair

Number of Pieces	Description	Rived Green Dimensions	Shaved Green Dimensions	Finish Dimensions
1	Seat plank	(Sawed)	2-1/4" x 18" x 18"+	1-7/8" x 17-1/4" deep x 17-3/4" wide
1	Bow riving	1-1/4" sq x 62+"	13/16" dia x 60"	3/4" dia x 60"
4	Leg blanks (rived or sawed)	2-1/2" sq x 22" rived or 2" sq x 22" sawed	1-3/4" dia x 21"	Refer to turning specs on plans
2	Left and right side stretchers (rived or sawed)*	2-1/2" sq x 16-1/2" rived or 2" sq x 16-1/2" sawed	1-3/4" dia x custom fit	Refer to turning specs
1	Medial stretcher (rived or sawed)*	2" sq x 18" rived or 1-5/8" sq x 18" sawed	1-5/16" dia x custom fit	Refer to turning specs
5	Spindles	3/4" sq x 23"	9/16" > 3/8" dia	33/64" > 21/64"
2	Spindles	3/4" sq x 22"	9/16" > 3/8" dia	33/64" > 21/64"
2	Spindles	3/4" sq x 21"	9/16" > 3/8" dia	33/64" > 21/64"
2	Spindles	3/4" sq x 20"	9/16" > 3/8" dia	33/64" > 21/64"
13	Wedges			As required

*Approximation only. Detailed measurements are made during assembly.

Leg Angles (in degrees from 90) for the Bow-Back Side Chair

	Rake	Splay	Sighting	Resultant
Front	8	13	31.3	15.1
Rear	13	13	45	18.1

Making a traditional American Windsor chair with hand tools requires a wide range of craft skills and presents ample challenges for any woodworker. The model chair for this tutorial, a bow-back side chair that could have been produced about 1800, is made with a fully saddled seat with a sculpted, pinched waist.

BEFORE YOU BEGIN: A LOOK AT HISTORIC STYLES AND MATERIALS

This Windsor chair formally introduces lathe work to the chairmaker's workshop. A major challenge for many novices will be the turnings. The tutorial bow-back uses a much simpler turning style than the classical double-baluster turnings, which are not realistic for a beginning turner whose main goal is to make a Windsor chair. In any case, I find that the baluster turnings often overpower the graceful lines of the Windsor's seat and backrest. I like the turning style used in the tutorial chair, known as "bamboo" or "double bobbin," which was introduced in the early 1790s, although it was not commonly produced until later in the 1800s.

Windsor Spindles

The spokes that support the bows of American Windsors are known as "spindles," not "sticks." I always shave Windsor spindles, but you can learn to turn them with the aid of a lathe steady rest. Traditional American bow-backs were made with five to nine back spindles, more often with an odd number like our tutorial chair with nine. English bow-backs commonly have six or eight spindles and a fret-worked splat mortised to the center of the bow, which adds considerable comfort. American bow-backs with eight spindles are less common but possibly more comfortable than versions with a spindle centered on the back bow. For your first Windsor, I recommend shaving plain, straight spindles with no bulge.

Materials

Gathering the materials for this chair can be a challenge. While contemporary, factory-produced Windsors are often made from just one kind of wood, such as ash or red oak, classic American Windsors combined a variety of materials chosen for specific reasons such as bendability, strength, and weight. Because these chairs were generally painted, no particular attention was paid to the visual blend of the different wood species. Chairs with a natural or stained finish can be made from a single species or a mix that is visually compatible.

Although you may resist the idea of painting something that you've made from wood, I recommend that before you get started with this project you decide in favor of painting your first Windsor. Most early American Windsors were painted, either black or green. The traditional mix of various woods makes constructing the chair much easier than using any single wood species. Paint ties the chair together visually and allows you to hide mistakes and areas of imperfect craft work that would be difficult to disguise on a chair with a natural finish.

Seat Planks • Lightweight and easy to carve, white pine is the most common choice for Windsors made in the traditional American style. Carving tulip poplar, another good and traditional choice, is more challenging, but tulip poplar is also considerably stronger than pine. For the seat of a painted chair, another possibility is basswood (also know as linden, and "lime" in England). These and other species are discussed in Chapter 4.

The seat must be made from dry wood (air or kiln dried). Pine and poplar seat planks must be at least 1-7/8 inches thick, and 2 inches is better, especially for pine. The pattern for the tutorial bow-back is 17-1/4 inches deep and 17-3/4 inches wide. It can be a single piece of wood or joined, as discussed in Chapter 8 on the stick Windsor.

Fudging on the width or depth of the seat by as much as 1 inch is acceptable and common in antique Windsors. The pattern is for a large seat.

Bow Riving • Wood for the 60-inch bow may be the most difficult material to obtain. Commonly used species are red and white oak, hickory, and ash. Bows for Windsors that will not be painted can be made from several other wood species, including cherry, walnut, and elm. The bow stock must be clear and straight grained. I prefer to make and bend Windsor bows from rived, green wood, but you can also bend them by resawing a blank from a perfect, air-dried board.

Turning Blanks • Short-fiber, dense wood species such as hard (sugar) maple, birch, and beech are best; red maple is acceptable. Turnings for chairs with a natural finish can be made from oak, ash, walnut, and cherry. Elm and yew are used for all parts of some English Windsors. If you choose to shave the legs and stretchers, use oak, ash, or hickory.

Turning blanks can be rived or sawed. Turning green wood is a great pleasure, but remember that tenons on turned stock must be thoroughly dry before final sizing and assembly. Keeping green blanks for turning presents several challenges, while air-dried stock keeps indefinitely.

Spindles • Red and white oak, ash, and hickory are the preferred woods. Straight-grained elm and fruitwood blanks (which must be sawed) are also suitable.

Wedges • This chair uses fifteen wedges, sawed or rived from any straight-grained hardwood.

PREPARING THE SEAT BLANK

I prefer to begin making a Windsor by working on the seat, the foundation for the chair. Work begins by tracing the seat pattern, then boring mortises in the flat seat blank for the bow ends and spindle mortises, using sight lines and resultant angles. (These terms are explained in Chapter 8.) You can instead bore the spindle mortises after saddling and getting the back bow secured in place, as you did with the stick Windsor.

Prepare the seat blank as explained in Chapter 8 on the stick Windsor. For the American bow-back Windsor, the grain runs front to back. Orient the end-grain like arches, so that most saddling will be crossing the growth rings.

Trace the outline of the seat pattern on the seat blank (refer to fig. 9.4). Draw the deck and the centerline. The deck is 1-7/8 inches wide directly across from the bow mortises and 1-5/8 inches wide from the second spindle to the center.

With an awl, mark boring centers for the bow ends, spindles, and depth gauges. Mortises on the deck are 2 inches on center. Spindle mortises are 7/8 inch from the rear edge of the seat. Bow mortises are 15/16 inch from the edge.

Use a straightedge to draw sighting lines from the mortise centers to the sighting points at the front edge of the seat.

Transfering the outline from the seat plan in figure 9.4, then drawing the spindle deck on the seat plank

Copy the mortise diameter and resultant angles from the plan to each boring center on the seat blank.

Boring the Bow Mortises

The tools you'll need are

- 2 bar clamps
- Protractor (cheap plastic)
- Sliding bevel gauge
- Try square
- Bit brace
- 3/8-inch auger bit
- 1/2-inch auger bit
- Pencil
- 24-inch ruler

Clamp the seat plank over a corner of the workbench, with the deck section directed out. You'll bore the bow mortises first, 3/8 inch in diameter, later to be reamed to 3/4 inch at the deck.

Boring the bow and spindle mortises is exactly like boring leg mortises in the stick Windsor. Use the 3/8-inch auger bit to bore the two 3/4-inch-deep depth gauges toward the rear of the seat, and bore the spindle mortises with a standard 1/2-inch-diameter auger bit to a depth of 1 inch.

SADDLING THE SEAT

Saddling this classic American Windsor seat is a major production. At Country Workshops' Windsor chairmaking classes we devote a full day to this task. Although the

Preboring the spindle mortises in the deck—one option. You can also bore these mortises after the bow is fitted to the seat.

process is similar to that for a stick Windsor, the saddling is deeper and the contours more complex. (The depth gauges are 3/4 inch, but you can saddle deeper, especially with poplar or the harder woods.) The configuration of a classic American Windsor seat may be described as a shallow, triangular hollow originating at the peak of the pommel, with no center ridge. (The center-ridge pattern from the stick Windsor can also be used, but it is less common on early American Windsors.) The pinched waist at the sides of the seat, traditional but not required, adds visual punch to the chair. On old chairs, the shape and degree of this cutout vary.

Adze Work and Inshaving

The tools you'll need are

- Hollowing adze
- Inshave
- Travisher
- 24-inch ruler
- 12-inch ruler
- Round-bottom plane (optional)
- Scraper (optional)
- Sandpaper

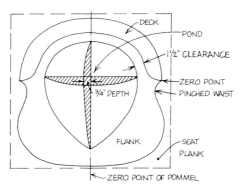

FIG. 9.6. Layout of the bow-back Windsor seat, with adze zone in center. Shaded area indicates depth at different points.

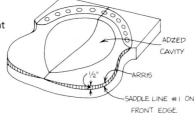

FIG. 9.7. Layout for front and flanks of the seat

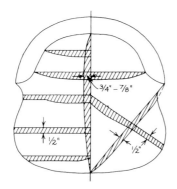

FIG. 9.8. Shaded areas indicate depth of saddling.

Adzing the seat is basically the same as doing the stick Windsor seat, although the outline of the adze zone differs slightly.

The adze zone for this seat resembles an avocado pit (see fig. 9.6). Adze toward a medial centerline across the seat. The front of the adze zone is at a very shallow slope. The concave slope from the nine o'clock to three o'clock positions blends into the bottom of the "pond" — the center area of the avocado pit. If you have adequate control, you can enlarge the adze zone to within 1/2 inch of the deck.

When adzing is finished, saw the outline for the front half of the seat. Do not saw the outline behind the spindle deck at this time.

Saddling continues with an inshave. Referring to figure 9.7, pencil saddle line #1 on the sawed outline around the front half of the seat. The slope approaching the peak of the pommel and the deck corners should be very gradual. The rest of saddle line #1 is 1/2 inch below the plank surface.

Use an inshave to hollow the entire saddle area, except the peak of the pommel (fig. 9.8). The flanks along the front of the seat are inshaved straight in from saddle line #1. The center area of each flank is 1/2 inch deep. Blend the flanks into the adzed cavity. Enlarge the back of the adzed cavity to the line defining the spindle deck. There should

Drawing saddle line #1 a half inch below the arris around the front flanks of the seat

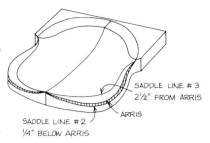

FIG. 9.9. Details for blending the flanks into the saddled cavity

SADDLE LINE # 3
2½" FROM ARRIS

ARRIS

SADDLE LINE # 2
¼" BELOW ARRIS

Lowering the seat flanks in two stages: First, draw saddle line #3 (fig. 9.9) 2-1/2 inches in from the arris, then gently blend this area into the inner part of the seat with a spokeshave.

be a distinct, but subtle, concave dish dropping from the peak of the pommel.

Referring to figure 9.9, draw saddle line #2 on the sawed outline around the front of the seat, dropping down an additional 1/4 inch from saddle line #1 (3/4 inch from the original seat plank surface). Maintain zero points at the pommel peak and corners of the spindle deck. Draw saddle line #3 on the upper surface along the flanks of the seat front. The maximum width is 2-1/2 inches from the arris.

As you now remove wood between saddle lines #2 and #3, do not cut straight across from the lines. This area is slightly convex in section. Blend the area along line #3 into the general cavity with a drawknife or flat spokeshave.

Smooth out the concave dish behind the pommel with a travisher (hollowing shave). You can also use the travisher at the much steeper concave drop below the spindle deck. A slicing action allows the travisher to take a tighter cut

With practice, you can learn to use an inshave to quickly finish most of the seat surface. To take cuts into ascending fiber, you will need to read the grain continually.

Continue by finishing the contours of the entire upper surface. Do as much as possible with the inshave. Don't cut too deeply into the seat surface—you must maintain adequate thickness for the leg mortises. Lots of slicing and skewing action is required for this process. Check for high points and lumps with a low raking light and your fingers.

Smoothing the pond area with a travisher, a tool you can also use in the steep concave area below the deck. Take extreme slicing cuts; this tightens the effective sweep of the blade.

than the sweep of the blade. Some Windsor chairmakers also use a round-bottom plane in this area below the spindle deck. The arris separating the spindle deck and the concave drop-off into the saddle area should be crisp and well defined (see fig. 9.10). If necessary, clean up this edge by sanding the saddle drop-off. The drop-off angle should be about 45 degrees (if it's too steep, the edge of the gutter will be extremely fragile).

FIG. 9.10. Section view of spindle deck, gutter, and concave drop-off into the saddled area

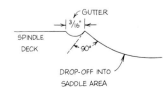

GUTTER

3/16"

SPINDLE DECK

90°

DROP-OFF INTO SADDLE AREA

Once the cavity is down to specs, leave it. You can fill in accidents later, before you paint the chair.

Finish saddling the cavity with a curved scraper and sandpaper.

Carving the gutter, continually wiggling the gouge left and right while advancing in small increments

Carving the Gutter

The gutter between the spindle deck and saddled seat area is an option. (A poorly carved gutter is very visible on an otherwise nicely saddled seat.) Begin by penciling a series of marks 3/16 inch in from the spindle-deck arris. Connect the pencil marks with a light, fine line.

To carve the gutter, you'll use a very sharp, deeply fluted 1/4- to 5/16-inch gouge—a number 11 sweep straight gouge is about right. Instead of pushing the gouge straight into the cut, wiggle it from side to side, moving forward about 1/16 inch for each wiggle. (This prevents grain tearout, which can be a disaster.)

Cut the gutter in three stages (fig. 9.11). First, cut down the center of the channel, without contacting either side outline *(a)* . Next, cut to one of the side outlines, always being

careful to proceed into ascending wood fiber *(b)*. Last, cut the other edge, working in the opposite direction *(c)*.

After gouging, touch up the gutter with a rolled edge of sandpaper, using a very light touch. Be careful to maintain a crisp arris at the saddle drop-off.

Sawing and Shaping the Seat Bottom

The tools you'll need are a turning-bow saw, electric saber saw or band saw, a drawknife, and a spokeshave.

You'll shape the bottom side of the seat with a drawknife and spokeshave. The pinched waist and zero points at the spindle deck corners require an extra bit of attention.

Saw the outline of the seat behind the spindle deck. (If you're adding a tail brace, this is the time to saw that as well; see the sidebar "Bow-Back Style Options" later in this chapter.) If you're using a band saw, tilt the table 8 to 10 degrees. If you're sawing by hand, cut perpendicular to the flat bottom surface of the seat.

Referring to figure 9.12a, draw bottom line #1 along the front of the seat 1 inch in from the arris, closing in to zero at the spindle-deck corners. Draw line #2 around the back of the seat 1/2 inch in from the arris, fairing the line to 1/4 inch from the arris at the deck center corners. Referring to figure 9.12b, draw edge line #3 around the edge of the seat 7/8 inch above the arris at the bottom of the plank, curving up to zero at the corners of the spindle deck. Draw edge line #4 around the back of the seat at an even 7/8 inch above the bottom arris.

FIG. 9.11. Carving the optional gutter: *a,* gouge the center section of the outline; *b,* gouge into ascending grain on the saddled side of the gutter; *c,* gouge ascending grain on the deck side of the gutter.

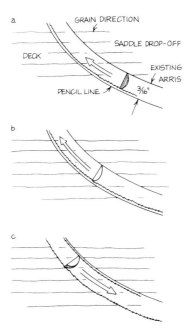

FIG. 9.12. Layout for initial drawknife work on the bottom of the seat

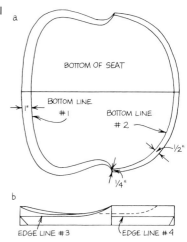

Set the seat on edge in a bench vise, with the long grain in line with the bench. Basically, you will be connecting edge lines #3 and #4 on the sides of the seat with lines #1 and #2 on the bottom. With the drawknife bevel up, start by shaving the high point of the seat flanks at the front half of the chair. Take special care at the beginning not to split off a chunk of wood with descending grain. Test the grain direction by taking light cuts before getting aggressive.

Extreme slicing and skewing to shave the end grain on the bottom of the seat, with the drawknife bevel facing up

Drawknifing the pinched waist by taking a slicing cut while rotating the blade into the curve, with the drawknife bevel down. Make several downhill passes into ascending fiber, cutting from opposing high points of the curve.

Gradually shave into the end grain at the front of the seat. Use exaggerated skewing and slicing. I pull the drawknife downward with more sideways slicing than forward cutting with each stroke.

Use the drawknife bevel down when shaving into the concave curve of the pinched waist, cutting downhill from the flank and from the deck corner. Alternate cuts meet at the bottom of the curve. Here you combine a hingelike wrist action with slicing—there is no room to skew. Some Windsor chairmakers consider this rasp work, but you can learn to cut this curve with a drawknife.

Reposition the seat in the vise as necessary. The vise jaws should contact only the flat deck and bottom of the seat. Shaping the area around the back of the seat is straightforward slice and skew drawknife work, bevel up again.

Shaving the second chamfer, the next stage in shaping the bottom, is optional. It gives the seat a light, graceful appearance. If you choose to do this, referring to figure 9.13, draw line #5 on the front half of the bottom 1 inch in from bottom line #1. Draw line #6 on the back half of the bottom 1/2 inch in from line #2. Draw lines #7 and #8 on the side of the seat 1/2 inch above the bottom arris. Line #7 comes to a new zero point at the bottom of the pinched waist. This second chamfer around the bottom is drawknifed exactly like the first chamfer. Remember to work from easy-shaving long grain into the challenging end grain. Slice and skew as always.

FIG. 9.13. The second stage of drawknifing the seat bottom

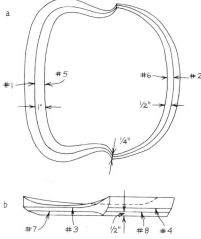

Smooth the drawknifed chamfers with a spokeshave. You can blend the chamfers together into a continuous curve or leave a distinct arris between them.

Completing the Seat

At this stage the upper half of the front edge of the seat is still perpendicular to the original plank. The front edge and pommel are now canted inwards at a pleasing angle. This area is all end grain. Use a spokeshave, taking rather long, skewing strokes from either side of the pommel. Leave a narrow band of unshaved wood on the edge between the upper seat and the shaped bottom.

Bow-Back Style Options

One fascinating aspect of traditional Windsors is that there are so many variations. For the tutorial bow-back, some possibilities include adding a tail brace, shaping the bow in a D-section, changing the spindle profile, and adding armrests.

A tail brace at the back of the seat stiffens the back support system and adds two extra spindles. In my opinion, a tail brace does not necessarily add to the chair's life, for the stiffer back support has considerably less give than a standard bow-back's; stress on the back is transferred to the joinery, rather than being distributed throughout the spindles. A tail-braced bow-back may also prove less comfortable than the standard chair, which has a bit of spring when you lean into the back. On the plus side, tail braces are fun to make and add an attractive element to the chair. An antique Windsor with a tail brace is always more valuable than the plainer version.

Making a tail brace is not difficult. Saw the tail-brace outline when you cut out the back of the seat (refer to the figure). Shape the tail with a drawknife and a sharp paring chisel. Determine the lengths of the two extra spindles after you make and fit the spindle array across the back. Bore the 5/16-inch bow mortises and the 1/2-inch seat mortises with the spindle/bow assembly in place.

Some bow-back Windsors have bows shaped with a D-section—the bow presents a flat face against the sitter's back. The flat of the "D," modestly decorated with two continuous beads made from a simple scratch stock, adds some comfort to the chair and enlarges the boring area for the upper ends of the spindles. To make the D-section, you leave the two front corners of the shaved bow square, instead of chamfering them to form an octagon.

Scratch the decorative beads before gluing the bow/spindle assembly. (To make a scratch-beading tool, see the sidebar in Chapter 2.) I locate both beads 5/32 inch from the edges of the bow face. Cut the bead in several passes, making sure to maintain contact between the center of the fence and the bow . Fiber runout on the surface of the bow will tend to push the fence away from the bow, especially when scratch beading a coarse wood like oak.

The spindles on fancy bow-backs are often made with a row of decorative bamboo nodes or with a bulge in the center. This bulge can be a gradual swelling or almost bulbous, and as much as 3/4 inch in diameter. Spindles with a bulge are much harder to make than the plain-vanilla straight spindles of the tutorial chair. You must take care to make the swellings consistent in diameter and in vertical placement on the set of spindles.

Spindle specifications for the bow-back in the plans are quite thin. You can enlarge the base of the spindles to 9/16 inch in diameter and the tip ends to 3/8 inch. However, since boring 3/8-inch mortises in a 3/4-inch bow is risky, if you decide to enlarge the spindle ends, I suggest you also enlarge the diameter of the bow from 3/4 inch to 7/8 inch. With the heavier bow, the chair will appear a little heavier, and there will be more chance of a bending failure.

Though rare, bow-backs with armrests can be quite handsome. The armrests are usually carved with a graceful curve and a scroll at the handholds, their extended ends supported by a turned arm support similar to the ones used for other Windsor armchairs, with one or two short spindles added to each side. The back end of the armrest terminates in a tenon, fitted to a mortise in the back bow (not a particularly strong joint).

SPINDLE DECK

SPINDLE MORTISE CENTER

PLAN VIEW

3/16" CHAMFER

SIDE VIEW

3/8"

BOTTOM VIEW

Take the seat out of the bench vise and examine its front edge. The narrow band of unshaved wood provides an opportunity to do some final shaping on the upper front edge of the seat. First, check the two halves of the seat for symmetry. Make corrections as necessary with a spokeshave. You can also make variations on the seat style at this point. For example, you can modify the saddle curves from the pommel, lower the flanks on either side of the pommel, and roll the front edge or shape it with a distinct, jazzy arris.

The final step is spokeshaving a 1/4-inch-wide chamfer across the back arris of the deck. A fancy option is gouging a rear-deck gutter into this chamfer.

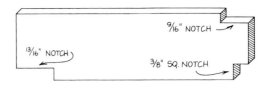

FIG. 9.14. Gauge for shaping green bows and spindles

Make a bow-and-spindle gauge (see fig. 9.14). Cut 9/16-inch and 3/8-inch spindle notches from the corners of a hardwood scrap about 6 inches long. Cut a 13/16 inch-notch for the bow from a third corner. Mechanic's open-end wrenches can also be used for sizing gauges.

Shave green spindles into square sections, 9/16 inch on each side. Saw the square-section spindles to the lengths in the materials list. Taper the upper third of each spindle to 3/8-inch square section. Use a spokeshave to shave the spindles into octagons. Put the spindle blanks in a kiln or other warm place for thorough drying. (You can weigh the entire set, and then track the descending weight until it stabilizes.)

Trim the bow blank to 60 inches. Shave, saw, and/or plane the bow blank to a 13/16-inch square section. While the bow is square, taper the ends from 13/16 to 3/8 inch. The length of the taper depends on the included angle of your reamer: With an 8-degree reamer, the taper begins 3-3/16 inches from end; with a 10-degree reamer, 2-7/8 inches from the end; with a 12-degree reamer, 2-1/16 inches from the end. I prefer a reamer with an 8-degree included angle, but use what you can get. Careful fitting is more important than the actual angle.

Shape the entire bow to an octagon, taking care to maintain an even thickness from end to end. Use a sharp spokeshave, and try to avoid fiber tearout. A small amount of grain runout along the length is acceptable. You can steam the bow as an octagonal or round section. Octagons are less likely to have tension failures since stress on the outside of the bend is spread over a greater area. But rounding an octagon after it is bent is more time consuming than rounding a bow when it is a straight blank.

Chamfering the back edge of the deck with a spokeshave

Making the Bow and Spindles

The spindles are the easiest part of the chair to make, but crafting a fine set of spindles requires care and attention. Make several extras, in case some curl during kiln drying and so that you can reject poorly shaped spindles.

Riving, Sawing, and Shaving

Rive blanks for the bow and spindles from clear, straight-grained white or red oak, ash, or hickory, in exactly the way parts were rived for the ladder-back (see Chapter 5).

You may also saw bows and spindle blanks from clear, air-dry lumber, a useful alternative if appropriate riving species aren't native to your area. An all-elm Windsor will also require using sawed parts—a handsome, underused ring-porous hardwood with excellent bendability, elm is known for resisting attempts at riving.

Grain runout for sawed blanks should be less than 1 lateral inch to 24 lineal inches. Bow and spindle blanks can be sawed at an angle to the edge of the board. Follow the fiber direction, not the milled edge of the board. Determining grain runout on the side of a board is difficult. Test sawed blanks by trying to break them before proceeding with shaping, bending, and other details.

Making the Bending Form

Copy the bow bending pattern from figure 9.4 onto a piece of 3/4-inch plywood (or several pieces, if necessary). Note the reverse curves at the bottom of the form. Bow-backs with this detail are sometimes called "loop-backs." Use a bow saw, saber saw, or band saw to cut out the form.

Screw hardwood extension boards onto the back side of the plywood form. One extension board is screwed to the base of the plywood form. The extension boards should extend past the plywood form by 4 to 5 inches. In order to secure the steamed, bent bow to the extension boards with pegs and wedges, bore peg holes 2 inches on center from the curved bending form. Make hardwood pegs and wedges as determined by the width of the bow and distance to the peg holes.

Bending this bow does not usually require use of bending straps. The wedges at the bottom of the form are driven in from below. The pegs and wedges at three and nine o'clock can be removed immediately after bending if there is no spring-back from the form.

Bending the Bow

Before putting your bow in the steamer, pencil a centerline arrow indicating the direction of bend. The bend is usually with the growth rings, but it can be changed if the bow blank has a natural curve in another plane. Tie a string tail to one end of the bow. Steam bows made from green wood for about forty-five minutes. Double the time for air-dry bows made from rivings or lumber.

Bending the American Windsor bow is exactly the same as bending a stick Windsor bow, explained in Chapter 8.

A Note to Novice Turners

Learning to use a wood lathe is a specialized skill. If you're a novice at turning, you'll save yourself a lot of time and effort by getting some instruction from an accomplished turner rather than trying to learn on your own. The Bibliography also lists several excellent books for novice and intermediate turners. Here I introduce only the basics of spindle turning and explain details that relate to Windsor turnings.

INTRODUCTION TO LATHE WORK

Although you can fit the bow and spindles to the seat at this point, I prefer to turn the legs and stretchers and assemble the stool section first. I like to see the bow in place on the stool when I fit the tapered bow ends to the seat mortises. I turn and fit the leg tenons to the seat before turning the leg stretchers, because a slight error in boring and reaming the angles of the tapered leg mortises will cause a significant variation in the stretchers' required lengths.

For legs and stretchers, I use uniform specifications for green or dry stock, which are never combined in one set of turnings. Slight differences in dimension of dry and green wood are insignificant. (All assembly will be with dry wood.) You also may use rived or sawed blanks. Sawed turning blanks are fine if fiber runout is within conservative limits. When turnings are not especially thin, you can use sawed blanks with up to 1-inch lateral fiber runout over 19 to 20 inches, the approximate length of the legs. Rived or sawed turning blanks must be made from sound, good-quality wood. Reject blanks with cracks or decay. Nothing larger than pin knots is acceptable.

Dimensions for the turning blanks are on the materials list at the beginning of the chapter. Sawed turning blanks for legs and side stretchers should be 2 inches square. Rived turning blanks must be large enough to turn a 1-3/4-inch cylinder at the major diameter, 12 inches below the tenon end of the legs.

Turning Tools and Equipment

For Windsor turnings you need only a few tools (see fig. 9.15) and a basic lathe—you can use a spring-pole lathe (see Chapter 21) as well as one driven by an electric motor. You may also opt to shave the legs and stretchers with a drawknife.

The tools you'll need are

- Full-face shield
- Turning pattern (transferred to a flat stick or card)
- 1 or 2 roughing gouges (3/4 to 2 inch)
- Parting tool (1/8 to 1/4 inch)
- Skew chisel (3/4 to 1-1/4 inch)

- Sandpaper (80, 120, 180 grits)
- Awl
- Hammer
- 1 to 5 outside calipers (3 to 5 inches)
- Ruler
- Pencil
- Shaving horse and drawknife
- Dust mask (for sanding)

Optional tools and equipment include

- Diamond-point scraper
- 24-inch tool rest
- Live center on lathe tail stock
- Spindle gouge (1/2 inch)
- Safety glasses

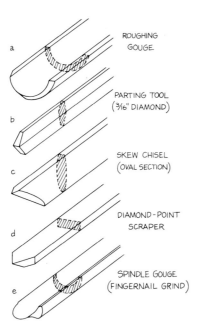

FIG. 9.15. Basic tools for Windsor turnings, with section view of each shaded: a, 3/4- to 2-inch roughing gouge; b, 1/8- to 3/16- inch diamond-section parting tool; c, 3/4- to1-inch oval-section skew chisel; d, 1/2- to 3/4-inch diamond-point scraper; e, 1/2-inch spindle gouge with fingernail grind

You'll need the full-face shield for the initial turning from shaved octagonal stock to a cylinder. This is the roughest part of a turning operation, when a spinning blank might fly off the centers, or when you could lose control of a cutting tool. When the blank is a cylinder, most turners substitute safety glasses for the full- face shield, which tends to collect dust and reflect light with a bothersome glare.

The safest and easiest to use of all lathe tools, roughing gouges are long, square-nosed gouges for turning rived or octagonal blanks into cylinders, and for doing simple _shaping work. A roughing gouge won't produce a glassy smooth surface, but you can use it for all of the contours of the bamboo turnings used on this bow-back Windsor. Ideally, you should have two of these tools, the larger 1-1/2 to 2 inches wide and a smaller 3/4- to 1-inch version. You can look forward to achieving good results with your roughing gouge after only a little practice.

Parting tools cut a narrow groove in a turning to a predetermined diameter, which is gauged with outside calipers. These grooves are used as location and diameter benchmarks for shaping contours. A standard parting tool has opposing symmetrical bevels ground straight across the width of the blade that converge at its center. A 3/16- or 1/8-inch diamond-section parting tool is my choice for parting to dimensions on chair parts.

I recommend an oval-section skew chisel with a 1-inch blade for cutting V-shaped bamboo nodes in the turnings. Capable of leaving a glassy smooth surface and highly adaptable, skew chisels are also the most challenging of all spindle-turning tools. In unskilled hands, they will unexpectedly catch and dig into a turning, ruining the surface.

Skews have opposing symmetrical bevels ground at an angle across the width of the blade. Those with oval-section blades are much easier to use than the traditional, flat-sectioned blades, although sharpening is a bit tricky.

If you're a novice, you may choose to use a diamond-point scraper (sometimes called a beading and parting tool) instead of a skew chisel for cutting the bamboo nodes. This is a "cheater technique" for making acceptable bamboo nodes without having to wrestle with a skew chisel.

A spindle gouge with a fingernail grind can be used for finish cuts of bamboo turnings. It's the preferred tool for cutting the beads and coves of more complex patterns, such as the American Windsor double baluster, and the traditional English bead, cove, and ring turnings.

Standard tool rests for spindle turning are 7 to 10 inches long. A 24-inch tool rest, available for some lathes, allows you to work along the full length of a turned leg or stretcher. As they're expensive to buy, you may choose to make one from hardwood and a steel strip (see fig. 9.16).

FIG. 9.16. Section view of a shop-made tool rest used for Windsor turnings. It should be 22 to 24 inches long; adjust dimensions to your lathe.

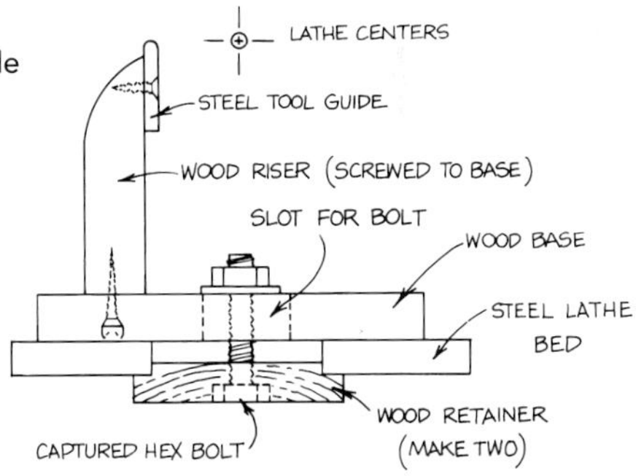

Turning tools made from "high-speed steel" hold an edge much longer than the older carbon-steel tools. Turning tools must be kept sharp. You should resharpen at least once in a half-day session at the lathe. Edge geometry is more important than the included angle of the bevels (see Chapter 3).

Sawing and Shaving the Turning Blanks into Octagons

Saw four leg blanks 1 to 2 inches longer than their trim length. You need some extra bobbin wood at the drive, or spur, center at the lathe head stock. A bobbin at the tail end isn't necessary, if the tail stock has a pointed, live center. The length of front and back turned legs is 19-1/2 inches. After the chair is assembled, the foot end of the legs will be trimmed off, so you needn't be concerned about indentions from center points and spur drives.

Draw an X connecting opposite corners on both ends of the blanks. Use an awl and hammer to punch an indention at each X intersection.

Use a drawknife to shave the blanks into octagons. On sawed turning blanks with moderate grain runout you will usually be able to drawknife in one direction only. Perfect octagons aren't required.

183

Lathe Work: Shaping Cylinders

If your lathe tail stock has a dead center (a center without bearings), squirt some motor oil on the tail-stock end of each blank. Secure the blank between the drive and tail-stock centers. Tighten the tail stock enough to prevent loosening and vibration, but not so tight as to cause undue friction. The spurs of the drive center will enter the wood as you tighten the tail stock.

Adjust the tool rest so that the turning blank barely clears it when you rotate the stock by hand (see fig. 9.17). Although this is a matter of personal preference, I choose to position the tool rest slightly higher than the lathe centers, with both ends extending past the segment to be turned. (It's critical that turning tools contact the tool rest whenever you're making any kind of cut.)

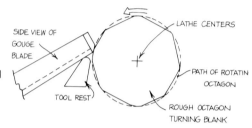

FIG. 9.17. How a roughing gouge cuts. The hollow-ground bevel should rub against the turning wood.

Adjust a pair of outside calipers to 1-3/4 inches, the major diameter of the bamboo leg turnings. For a test run to make sure that the blank clears the tool rest, and that the centers are properly engaged, set the lathe speed at a low rpm, put on a full-face shield, stand to the side of the lathe, and turn on the lathe switch. Allow the blank to spin for a few moments, then turn off the motor.

Stand directly in front of the lathe, with legs spread slightly in a secure stance. Set the roughing gouge on the tool rest, perpendicular to the turning blank and 1 inch inboard from its end. With your left hand, rotate the turning blank toward the cutting edge of the gouge. Lower the handle end of the roughing gouge to an angle where the beveled edge cannot possibly cut into the wood. Then slowly raise the handle, so that the edge lowers into the rotating wood. Observe the relationship of the gouge bevel and its edge to the rotating blank. For effective cutting you should use the steepest possible handle angle where the edge can cut. At this angle, a properly sharpened gouge will make a shearing cut. If the tool is positioned closer to horizontal, you will make scraping cuts, which require less skill than shearing but result in much rougher surfaces. If the tool position is correct, you will take some light cuts while turning the blank by hand.

Retract the gouge and turn on the motor. Hold the gouge at a steep angle, where it can't cut into the blank. Your right hand holds the handle end of the roughing gouge. Your left hand secures the gouge against the tool rest using an underhand grip, with your thumb on top of the gouge. Gradually lower the gouge by raising the end of the

handle. The gouge bevel will begin to bump into the uneven rotating blank. Find the steepest gouge angle where cutting begins. Besides finding the angle, you will also need to adjust the fore and aft placement of the gouge.

As you work, watch the far side of the blank, not your turning tool. The rough blank will appear as a ghost image until you have turned a cylinder. From then on, the far side of the turning is where you see the profile that you're cutting.

Use very gentle tool pressure until the blank is turned fully round. Continually move the roughing gouge left and right along the tool rest, so that a large section of the blank is turned into a cylindrical shape. Be sure to keep the gouge perpendicular to the turning stock.

Stop the lathe when the blank has been turned into a cylinder. If you have a short tool rest, reposition it to round the next section of the blank. If you have a 24-inch tool rest, move it closer to the newly turned cylinder.

Detailing the Bamboo Turning

As the blank is turning, pencil a ring at the major diameter of the leg (see fig. 9.5). This is the lower bamboo node. Use a pencil directly off the pattern. Be sure to leave at least 1 inch of extra bobbin wood at the drive end of the turning.

Adjust the outside calipers to 1-3/4 inch. To cut a sizing groove at the major diameter, hold the parting tool in your right hand and the calipers in your left at the far side of the revolving blank. Gradually move the parting tool straight into the revolving cylinder. It's important to hold both the parting tool and the calipers perpendicular to the turning blank. Stop parting when you can ease the calipers across the parted groove.

You can part one or two additional sizing grooves to the major diameter, or simply eyeball the diameter from the first groove. The turning descends in size on both sides of the major diameter.

Reset the calipers to 1-1/2 inches, the diameter at the upper bamboo node. If you have several calipers, set them to the other dimensions of the turning. (I have a row of nails on the wall above my lathe where I hang calipers for a turning pattern in a sequence.)

Pencil a ring for the upper bamboo node. Part a sizing groove 1-1/2 inches in diameter. Turn the tenon end of the leg to this diameter.

Use the roughing gouge (and other turning tools) by cutting downhill from the major diameter. When you cut toward a small diameter, the gouge cuts into ascending fiber; you won't get tearouts. If you cut uphill into a larger diameter, the result tends to be rough, and you risk an unexpected dig in the descending fiber.

The bamboo turning pattern appears simple and in fact requires less turning skill than concentration on the shapes coming off the lathe. The profile of the center section

Detail of the finished seat and bamboo turnings on the tutorial chair

between the major diameter and upper bamboo node resembles a heavy cable that is given a little slack. The section immediately above the upper bamboo node mimics the profile of a nuclear cooling tower. The sides of the tapered tenon must be straight. The most difficult part of the turning is the section below the major diameter, which is shaped in a subtle S-curve.

You're now ready to shape the center section of the leg. Position the tool rest as close as possible to the turning. If you have a short tool rest, locate it to work this full area.

You can part a 1-3/16-inch sizing groove in the middle of the center section, or simply check with calipers as the shape takes form. Use the roughing gouge to cut downhill from the major diameter and from the upper bamboo nodes. The middle area of the center section has a very shallow curvature.

Part a 1-inch-diameter groove at the base of the tapered tenon. Part the small end of the taper to match the reamer that you'll use for the leg mortises in the seat. To determine the correct size, mark the point on your reamer where it is 1 inch wide; measure 2 inches toward the small end of the reamer, and measure the width of the reamer at this location. If the included angle of the reamer is 10 degrees, the small end of the tapered tenon is 21/32 inch in diameter.

Turn the cooling tower and tapered tenon at the upper end of the leg with the roughing gouge. If you're an experienced turner, finish these cuts with a skew chisel. Novice turners should finish by sanding.

Dealing with Lathe Chatter

The major technical problem that you're likely to have while turning the legs is called harmonic vibration, also known as lathe chatter. The result is a ripple pattern on the surface of your turnings. You can take several steps to eliminate this problem.

- Try changing the turning speed. Many lathes produce excessive vibration at particular speeds. Fine-tuning a lathe to minimize vibration is discussed in the turning books listed in the Bibliography.

- Be sure to grind your turning tools with proper bevel geometry and keep them very sharp. Roughing and spindle gouges should have hollow-ground bevels.

- Until you're an expert, take your time and turn with a light touch. The bevel should ride against the rotating wood as you cut.

- Keep roughing and spindle gouges perpendicular to the turning stock. If you hold the gouge at an angle, the heel of the bevel contacts stock of a slightly different diameter than the area actually being cut. This can start the chatter pattern, which is difficult to stop. Vibration begets more vibration.

- Turn thick sections first, and work from the center to the ends of the turning.

- Try using your left hand as a damper. This may seem dangerous, but it is an accepted turners' practice. Be sure your arm or clothing can't contact an exposed drive belt or pulley—if you're wearing a long-sleeved shirt, button the cuff. Your right hand grasps the tool handle in the usual manner. Position your left hand over the turning, with your fingers just brushing the far side of the spinning blank. Extend your left thumb over the turning and onto the top of the tool being used. (Your left thumb should be directly above the tool rest.)

- You can often eliminate harmonic vibration problems with very thin turnings by using a steady rest. *The Lathe Book*, by Ernie Conover, includes plans and a detailed text on making an excellent version.

The upper end of the turning requires a bamboo node at the minor diameter and a scored line at the base of the tapered tenon. If you have the turning skills, do these now, without moving the tool rest. If you're a novice, relocate the tool rest to the lower end of the turning. You can practice cutting bamboo nodes using a skew near the bottom of the leg before cutting the S-curve below the major diameter.

To cut the nodes with the skew chisel, hold the tool upright, on its flat edge, so that the long point leads into the turning. Push forward directly into the turning. This will make a scoring ring. Reposition the point about 3/32 inch to the right of the scored ring. Swing the handle of the skew to the right, until the right bevel is directed toward the scored ring. Push the point of the skew into the wood, keeping the right bevel in a consistent line toward the scored ring. Reposition the skew to the left and repeat the previous cut in a mirror image.

You should now have a cleanly cut bamboo node, ideally about 3/16 inch wide. If the node is too narrow, repeat the full procedure, beginning with the scoring cut aimed directly at the center of the V. When you're satisfied with your practice bamboo nodes, shape the S-curve on the lower leg.

When the S-curve is finished, cut both bamboo nodes. In addition, cut a light scored ring at the base of the tapered tenon. Don't score a ring in the center of the middle section.

If you're not comfortable with the skew chisel, you can use a diamond-point scraper to form the bamboo nodes. Position the scraper with the bevel side down, directly across from the location of a bamboo node. Simply slide the diamond point directly into the turning.

The front and rear leg turnings are identical; they will be cut to length after you've assembled the Windsor "stool." The critical dimensions in this turning are the major diameter (at the lower bamboo node) and the dimensions of the tapered tenon. All other specifications are open to interpretation.

If you're turning air-dried stock, you can finish up by sanding the legs while they are spinning on the lathe. For safety, remove the tool rest. Fold a sheet of sandpaper into quarters and hold it on the far side of the turning, across from the tool rest. Move the sandpaper from left to right as you sand. If your turnings are rough, start with 80-grit paper, then graduate to 120 and then to 180 or 220 grit.

Saw or part the turnings free from their bobbins.

Drying the Turnings

The moisture content of the turnings at the time of assembly is important. The mortise area for the side stretchers (at the major diameter) should be air dried (15 to 25 percent m.c.). Moisture content at the tapered tenons should be the equivalent of kiln dried (6 to 8 percent m.c.)

If you made your turnings from air-dried stock, you can leave them on a shelf until about twelve hours before assembly. If your shop is heated, store them in a tight plastic bag, so that they don't continue drying. Green turnings should be air dried for several weeks.

Drying legs and stretcher tenons in warm sand (120 to 140 degrees). Check the temperature at the bottom of the sand. The sand pot is on a wood stove; an electric hot plate also works fine.

When you're ready to begin assembly (and not sooner), you can "kiln dry" the tenon ends of the air-dried turnings in hot sand or in a small kiln. Hot sand works faster, but it is quite tricky to regulate the temperature of the sand, which tends to heat in layers. The maximum temperature of the sand or kiln should be 140 degrees—if the sand is too hot, you'll find charcoal at the ends of your turned legs.

Heat sand in a bucket for a few hours beforehand. A small electric hot plate works fine for this. Stir frequently, and use a dial thermometer to check the temperature. When it stabilizes between 120 and 140 degrees, stick the tenon ends of the turnings into the sand. Remove the legs frequently to inspect the tenons. When they have become oval, you're ready for assembly. Any tanning on the tenons indicates that the sand is too hot.

Drying tenons in a kiln is slower but less risky. To prevent the mortise areas from drying, wrap the midsections of the turnings in aluminum foil. Put the air-dried turnings into the kiln about twelve hours before you're ready to begin assembly. The tenon ends will dry much faster than the mortise area at the lower bamboo node.

Assembling the Stool and Turning the Stretchers

At this stage you have finished leg turnings with dried tenons at the ends. Boring and fitting the leg tenons duplicates the procedure explained in Chapter 8 on the stick Windsors. All leg tenons must be fitted to a uniform depth, in this case 2 inches. The scored ring on the base of the turned tenons indicates the correct depth.

Taking Measurements for the Stretchers

When all four leg tenons are fitted to their tapered mortises, you can take measurements for the stretcher lengths. Set the stool upside down on your workbench. To avoid confusion, fill in the measurements for each stretcher on a chart like the one shown here.

1/8 inch to the node-to-node measurement.) This is the shoulder-to-shoulder length for the side stretcher. Add 2 inches for the 1-inch-long tenons at each end of the stretcher. Then add 1 inch for some extra bobbin length at the ends of the turnings.

Fill in all the measurements on the chart for both side stretchers. Unless you're very good—or lucky—each side stretcher will have a different length.

To determine the length of the medial stretcher, measure the node-to-node distance across the two front legs and between the two back legs. Add these number sets and divide by two. This is the shoulder-to-shoulder length for the medial stretcher. Again, add 1/16 to 1/8 inch for stiffness, then 2 inches for tenons, then 1 inch plus for the extra turning bobbins.

The final figures on the right end of the chart are the overall lengths of the three turning blanks. Blanks for the side

Part	Shoulder to shoulder =	Plus 1/16" to 1/8" =	Plus two 1-inch tenons =	Plus bobbins 1"+ =
Left stretcher				
Right stretcher				
Medial stretcher				

Determining the shoulder-to-shoulder length of the side stretchers with a folding rule and extension. Add 1/16 to 1/8 inch, depending on the tightness of the prefitted tapered leg joints in the seat.

Use a folding carpenter's ruler with a sliding extension to measure the distance between the front and rear legs at the lower bamboo nodes. (If you don't have an extension ruler, use two thin sticks that are about three-fourths the length of the distance between the measuring points on the legs. Hold the two sticks together, and then extend a stick until one end of each stick contacts a bamboo node of each leg. Transfer the overlap of the sticks to a ruler.) Record the measurement.

To stiffen the understructure, add 1/16 inch to the node-to-node measurement. (If the legs do not fit tightly, push them apart while making the measurement, and then add

stretchers need to be 2 inches square. With the major diameter of the medial stretcher at only 1-5/16 inches, this blank should be about 1-1/2 inches square. *The major diameter of the stretchers is the same as the major diameter of the legs.* If it isn't, you must account for the difference in figuring the length of the medial stretcher.

Vermont Windsor-maker Dave Sawyer, turning leg stretchers

Turning the Stretchers

Trim the blanks to length, with square saw cuts at both ends. Draw an X on each end and indent the intersection with an awl. Drawknife the blanks into octagons.

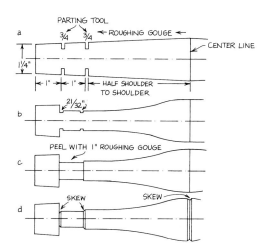

Fig. 9.18. Steps in turning side stretchers

PARTING TOOL
3/4 3/4 ← ROUGHING GOUGE ←
a
← CENTER LINE
1-1/4"
1" | 1" | HALF SHOULDER TO SHOULDER
21/32"
b
PEEL WITH 1" ROUGHING GOUGE
c
SKEW   SKEW
d

Be sure to label the left and right stretchers. Use a roughing gouge to turn one side stretcher blank to the major diameter, 1-3/4 inches. To locate the center of the side stretcher on the turning cylindrical blank, measure from the left: The center is located by adding half of the shoulder-to-shoulder distance plus 2 inches (1 inch for the drive-end bobbin and 1 inch for a tenon).

Use the roughing gouge to turn a descending contour on both sides of the centerline. When the ends of the turning are about 1-1/4 inches in diameter, measure from the centerline and pencil in marks indicating the tenon ends and tenon shoulders (fig. 9.18a). With a parting tool and calipers, cut a 3/4-inch-diameter groove at the shoulders and the end of the tenons. Turn the stretcher to the shoulder grooves (fig. 9.18b). The profile for these stretchers is slightly bulbous in the center, with thin ends that taper very gradually. This requires a distinct S-curve beginning at the centerline. Then use the parting tool to outline the tenons at 21/32-inch diameter. Turn both ends of both side stretchers with a similar profile.

Turn the tenons to 21/32 inch (fig. 9.18c). You can adjust this dimension, considering moisture content of the wood (eventual shrinkage), the exact diameter of the boring tool for the mortises, and your ability to be accurate in turning tenons of a precise diameter. I suggest turning all tenons oversize, with the expectation of filing or sanding them to size after the tenon ends are kiln dried. Use the 1-inch roughing gouge rolled on its side to peel tenons to the correct diameter. Then use the skew to cut small chamfers at the tenon ends and tenon shoulders (fig, 9.18d). Turn a bamboo node at the centerline. A diamond-point scraper can also be used to make these chamfers and V-cuts. If the stretcher is dry, sand it smooth on the lathe.

Before turning the medial stretcher you must determine the length of the center section. The tapering ends on either side of the section are a constant 4 inches. Take your shoulder-to-shoulder length and subtract 8 inches. The remainder is the length of the center section.

Turning the medial stretcher follows the same basic sequence as the side stretchers. There are two major swellings 1-5/16 inches in diameter. The curves forming

the ends and center section are all concave, similar to the line formed by a slightly loosened cable strung between two horizontal points.

Saw the turning bobbins off the stretchers. Dry the tenons until they turn into an oval section.

Boring the Side-Stretcher Mortises

While the side-stretcher tenons are drying, you'll bore stretcher mortises in the legs 5/8 inch in diameter and 1-3/16 inch deep by one of two methods I'll describe. The first method is easiest, but don't use it if the tapered leg joints are not fairly tight.

Firmly secure the legs in their seat mortises. Be sure that the location and growth-ring orientation are correct for each leg. Set the stool top side down on the workbench. Saw off excess tenon ends if they contact the workbench.

The mortises are centered on the lower bamboo nodes (the major diameter) of the legs. To locate the center of the right front leg, position your nose on the right rear leg and look straight across to the front leg. Eyeball the center, then mark the spot with a pencil. Find and mark stretcher centers for the other legs.

View straight across the legs to mark the center points on the bamboo nodes.

Direct Mortise Boring (Method #1) • This method bypasses numeric angles and special boring setups. Although you can do this with a bit brace, it works best with a hand-held, variable-speed electric drill. Outfit the drill with a 5/8-inch bit such as a Stanley powerbore and a 12-inch spade-bit extension. Tape a depth marker on the bit 1-3/16 inches from the cutter.

Rotate the right front leg a few degrees, so that the pencil mark at the bamboo node appears centered when you look at the leg by sighting from a side of the right rear leg. Place the lead of the bit on the center mark. Use your left hand to steady the right front leg. Hold the drill in your right hand, with the extension crossing the bamboo node of the right rear leg. Using a gentle trigger action, start by boring perpendicular to the leg at a very slow speed.

When the drill seats, lower the shaft to the correct alignment. Bore to the tape depth mark. You may need to clear boring chips about halfway into the mortise. Bore the other three mortises.

Shooting the angle by aligning the base of a protractor with bamboo nodes of paired legs—mortise method #2. Note the sighting pin on the front leg.

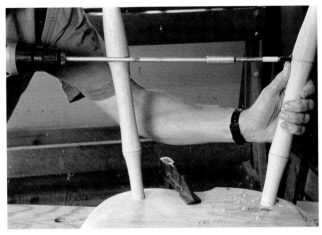

The easiest way to bore mortises for the side stretchers is with the legs fitted to the seat, here with a powerbore bit and a standard paddle-bit extension. Start by boring perpendicular to the axis; then lower the drill so that it aligns with the bamboo node on the opposite leg.

Indirect Mortise Boring (Method #2) • This method requires a flat plastic protractor with a small hole at the center point. Find the mortise centers on the lower bamboo nodes of each leg. Rotate a "designated leg" (the leg getting mortises) and a "sighting leg" so that the center marks are 90 degrees to the original location.

Use a push pin at the center mark to locate the protractor on the side of the designated leg. Hold a sharp pencil or awl point on the center mark of the sighting leg. Rotate the protractor so that the straight base is in line with the center mark on the sighting leg. Hold the protractor in this position. Take a reading by looking down the center of the designated leg. For the chair in this example, the angle was 79 degrees. (This may differ by several degrees in the chair you're making.) Pencil the reading on the designated leg. Repeat this sighting and labeling procedure for the remaining leg stretcher mortises.

Replicating the angle by tilting the leg in a bench vise. Leather padding in the vise jaws prevents marring the turning.

Replicate the sighting angles in a horizontal boring setup at the front vise of a workbench. You can use a sliding bevel gauge, but I prefer to gauge directly off the transparent plastic protractor. To prevent marring, wrap a leather pad between the leg and vise jaws. The boring bit should have an extension, with a line level taped to the shaft. I prefer the slow speed of a bit brace for this boring. Start by boring perpendicular to the axis at the angled leg. Shift to a horizontal position after the side nicker scores the outline at the mortise. You must be careful to keep the bit level and directed through the center of mass of the leg. (You'll bore the mortises for the medial stretcher after you've fitted the side stretchers in place.)

Boring the mortise using a level attached to the bit extension

Fitting the Side Stretchers

Fit the side-stretcher tenons in the leg mortises when the stretcher tenons have dried into an oval section. Orient the side stretchers with the growth rings perpendicular to the legs (fig. 9.19). In this position, the growth rings form onion rings (mirrored cathedrals) when you view the stretchers from the bottom of the stool. Pencil front and rear designations on both side stretchers and orientation tick marks on the paired parts to help assure correct positioning during fitting and glue up.

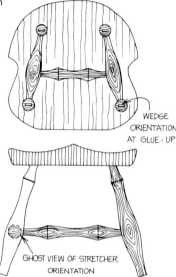

FIG. 9.19. Grain orientation for the bow-back seat, legs, and stretchers

Bring oversize tenons to size with a file or strip of sandpaper, taking care to avoid "pencil pointing" — making the lead of the tenon too small while you concentrate on getting the shoulder to fit. Stretcher tenons should be snug, but not very tight. As you fit each tenon to its designated leg mortise, pay attention to correct growth-ring orientation. (Undersized tenons are discussed in Chapter 6 on post-and-rung construction.)

Boring the Medial Stretcher Mortises and Fitting the Medial Stretcher

When you've fitted the side stretchers, bore mortises for the medial stretcher tenons. Locate and mark the centers for the mortises by eyeballing from one side stretcher to the other.

For direct mortising (method #1), twist one side stretcher slightly, so that you can bore through the center of mass using a boring bit with an extension. Hold the electric drill over the center of the opposite side stretcher. Mortises for the medial stretcher are also 5/8 inch in diameter and 1-3/16 inches deep.

For indirect mortising (method #2), place the seat with fitted legs and side stretchers top side down on the workbench. Set a ruler across the nodes of both side stretchers.

The direct method for boring the medial stretcher mortises in the side stretchers. Rotate the target stretcher slightly, so that the center mark aligns with the upper tangent of the sighting stretcher.

Finding the angles for boring medial stretcher mortises using method #2. Take angles from both side stretchers; they could differ.

Position a plastic protractor against the ruler and eyeball the center line of the side stretchers. Take separate measurements for each side stretcher. Record the angle on each stretcher.

Replicate the boring setup you used for the side stretchers. Custom fit medial-stretcher tenons to the side-stretcher mortises.

Test Assembly of the Stool

You're now ready to test fit the entire assembled stool. For your own information, check the leg and stretcher angles against the specifications in the side- and front-view projections for the chair (figs. 9.2 and 9.3). Don't be alarmed if you find differences—variations are common in handmade chairs of this complexity. You're looking for a "sore thumb"— a leg that sticks out badly, a component in the wrong location, a wrong axial rotation. When the chair is assembled and finished, most irregularities will disappear or be discernible only by another chairmaker.

When everything fits and looks good, go over every joint to be sure that there are labels and tick marks indicating the exact position of each piece. Draw a ring around the base of each exposed leg tenon on the top side of the seat. Draw lines across the ends of the leg tenons to indicate the orientation of the saw kerfs for the leg-tenon wedges (fig. 9.19).

Disassemble the undercarriage. Saw kerfs for the wedges in the leg tenons, extending them about 1 inch below the rings drawn at the base of the extended tenons.

Reassemble the undercarriage.

Gluing Up

Clear your workbench and your mind before beginning glue up of the Windsor stool. Each part must be in the right place, with proper orientation.

The tools and supplies you'll need are

- White glue (or liquid hide glue)
- Glue brush (old toothbrush or acid brush)
- Water in container
- Clean white rag
- Mallet
- Hammer (6 to 13 oz.)
- Wedges
- Shop knife (a Swedish sloyd knife is perfect)

Following my step-by-step Windsor glue-up procedure may seem tedious, but your prudence will pay off. You'll start with the dry-assembled stool set top side down on the workbench, then break down and glue one joint at a time. This way you maintain complete control of the process. When only one joint is apart there is almost no chance that you'll put something together in the wrong place or position.

Gluing up the Windsor stool by disassembling, gluing, and reassembling one joint at a time cuts your chances of accidentally getting a component in the wrong place or position.

Start by removing the entire leg/stretcher assembly as a single unit from the bottom of the seat. To loosen the assembly, you may have to hammer on the exposed leg tenons on the upper side of the seat. Pull apart one medial/side-stretcher joint. Apply glue to the mortise and tenon for this joint, then reassemble it. The glue will make the joint feel looser. Refit the entire leg/stretcher assembly to the chair seat. Tap the bottoms of the legs with a hammer, making sure that everything is back in place. Use a damp rag to clean up any glue squeezeout around the joint.

Now remove the entire leg/stretcher assembly again. Pull apart the other medial/side stretcher joint. Glue and reassemble the entire undercarriage assembly. Be sure to clean up glue on the surface before continuing.

Continue by individually disassembling, gluing, and reassembling the four side-stretcher/leg joints. Fitting the entire undercarriage home into the seat mortises assures that the many compound-angle joints are at their correct orientation. Glue squeezeout is cleaned up as it happens. You can leave the job at any stage in the process. If the phone rings, no problem.

When all six stretcher joints are glued, remove the leg/stretcher unit for the last time. Brush glue into the chair-seat mortises and onto the leg tenons. Use a finger or a glue brush to get glue into the sides of the tenon-wedge kerfs. Reassemble. Drive the leg joints tight with a mallet or hammer.

Turn the stool right side up to drive wedges into the leg tenons. Apply a little glue to the sides of a wedge. Be sure that each leg contacts the floor when you hammer in its wedge.

Adjust the plane of the seat and trim the bottoms of the legs. The height and slope of the seat will affect how you slouch the bow. The plans show a typical bow slouch. For a work or dining chair, you may want very minimal seat slope (1/4 inch) and a rather straight back, perhaps 98 degrees. Bow slouch can be increased up to 105 degrees for a loafing chair, or if you like to lean back when socializing; then give the seat more slope, 1/2 to 3/4 inch. The seat slope is measured at the peak of the pommel and the back of the spindle deck. Trim the protruding tenons and wedges. (I discuss these steps in Chapter 8 on the stick Windsor.)

FITTING THE BOW AND ASSEMBLING THE BACK SUPPORT

Fitting the bow is an exacting procedure. You must ream the mortises following the sighting line and the resultant angle, custom fit the bow tenons to each mortise, and make final decisions on back slouch and symmetry of the bow (from a front or top view).

At this stage, bow tenons are rough and octagonal in section. Round the bow with a spokeshave and sandpaper.

Use a spokeshave to shape the tapered bow tenons, matching the taper to the enclosed angle of your reamer.

Reaming the Bow Mortises

It's very useful to have a dummy bow end for test fitting and during initial reaming of the mortises. At your lathe, turn a straight 3/4-inch cylinder 8 to 10 inches long. Then taper one end, matching the enclosed angle of your reamer.

Transfer the bow sighting line from the chair plan to the chair seat. If the chair will be painted, you can draw this line right across the seat. (Otherwise, lay a strip of masking tape on the seat and draw the line on the tape.) For 102-degree bow slouch at the center spindle, adjust a sliding bevel gauge to 24 degrees from vertical. Place the try square at a right angle to the sighting line somewhere on the spindle deck.

Begin reaming with a light, careful touch, following the directions for reaming tapered leg joints. Use the dummy bow end to check the reaming against the sighting line and resultant angle. Switch to testing with the actual bow tenons when the reamed mortises are about 5/8 inch in diameter. You'll need to customize the tenon and the mortise. Mark up the inside of the mortises with pencil lead. Test fit individual bow tenons and the pair of tenons together. Wiggle the bow to get pencil marks on the tenons when you're testing a joint.

While fitting the bow tenons, also monitor the front and top perspectives of the bow, which should be symmetrical from either view. Always fit the bow tenons in their proper mortises. (Don't flip the bow, reversing front and back positions.)

Use a carpenter's framing square to check the bow slouch angle —the overhang distance from the back of the seat to the back of the bow (fig. 9.20). If the back spindle slouches at 101 degrees, the overhang should measure 3 inches, assuming the top of the bow is 21-1/2 inches above the center spindle mortise. (On a chair of this back height, 2-1/2 to 3-1/2 inches slouch is common.) You're finished when the small end of the bow tenons begin to protrude through the bottom of the seat mortises.

FIG. 9.20. Back slouch measured with a carpenter's framing square

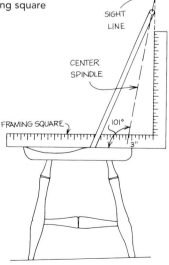

Boring Spindle Mortises in the Bow

With the bow in place, you are ready to bore bow mortises for the small ends of the spindles. These are through mortises, 5/16 inch in diameter, bored with the bow in place. This is the last really challenging step in making this chair.

The tools you'll need are

- Bit brace
- 5/16-inch auger bit
- 12-inch ruler
- Hand-held electric drill (optional)
- Twist bits (1/8, 3/16, 1/4, 5/16 inch; optional)

If the deck mortises still require boring, you'll also need a 1/2-inch powerbore bit and an 18-inch paddle-bit extension—use the seat plan to locate the centers of these mortises but don't bore them yet.

To bore the bow mortises, start by locating the bow's center. Place a carpenter's framing square across the back of

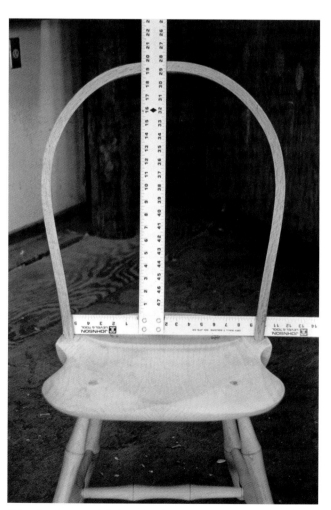

Relocating the center of the bow after fitting the bow tenons to their seat mortises. You can use a framing square placed at the back of the spindle deck, but this wallboard square, which spans the seat at the bows, is probably better.

the spindle deck, with the corner of the square over the center spindle mortise. Eyeball from the square arm up to the bow, and pencil mark this alignment. Then flip the square around and do the same with the square in a mirror position. The eyeballed centerlines should fall at or very near the same place—you may have to compromise between two marks. Place a spindle at this location and examine the bow from a front view.

Your immediate objective is to bore the center mortise in the bow and, if necessary, the seat deck, in order to fit the center spindle to the chair seat and the bow. This will stabilize the bow while you bore the remaining mortises. To temporarily stabilize the bow, you'll prop it up with a narrow stick. The assembly is secured by pulling the bow downward with twine. Saw a stick that's about 1/4 inch shorter than the distance from the deck to the bottom of the bow. Fit the stick slightly to the side of the center seat mortise and center of the bow. If the stick is too short, hold

Boring the 5/16-inch mortise for the center spindle. Hold the bow steady by wedging a stick between the seat and bow and by twine that pulls the bow downward against the stick. The cinder block prevents the chair from moving.

it in place with a narrow wedge. Tie one end of the twine to a side stretcher, loop it twice around the top of the bow, and tie the end tightly to the opposite side stretcher.

Pencil a vertical line from the center point across the top of the bow. Look down onto the top of the bow, bringing the bow centerline into visual alignment with the center spindle mortise on the seat. From this viewpoint, pencil a line on the top of the bow that crosses the vertical centerline. This cross line is visually centered on the width of the bow. Indent the intersection with an awl.

Bore the bow mortises with a bit brace and an ordinary 5/16-inch auger bit. You can also use a hand-held electric drill, my choice for the outer spindles, which are bored at a steep angle almost into end grain. Secure the chair in place with a heavy weight on top of a blanket or board set on the chair seat—a cinder block works nicely. It's useful to have some help while boring the spindle mortises in the bow.

Stand directly behind the bow. With the auger point on the boring center, look straight down the auger shaft to the center mortise. Adjust alignment left and right. Your helper stands to the side and uses a straightedge to visually align the brace bit with the correct spindle mortise on the seat. Lacking a helper, you judge fore and aft alignment by shifting your viewpoint perpendicular to the left and right alignment.

Start boring the center bow mortise. Pause several times to check alignment in both planes. With an auger bit, you can let go of the brace and check alignment once the lead screw is anchored in the bow. Stop when the bit-brace handle is centered above the boring. Make alignment adjustments, and continue boring until the auger lead begins to protrude through the bottom of the bow.

Remove the bow from the seat and secure it upside down in a vise; back bore the center mortise. Remember that the angle for back boring is offset from the plane of the bent bow. (Estimating the angle is adequate.)

Replace the bow in the seat to check the aim of the spindle boring. Look straight through the mortise to the chair seat. Observe the alignment of the bored hole in relationship to the center spindle mortise location on the seat. Ideally, you will see three concentric rings: The top of the bow mortise, the bottom of the bow mortise, and the center seat mortise. If the rings are not concentric, locate the point on the seat where the bow rings are directed. Use a rat-tail rasp to reshape the bottom of the bow mortise until you can see the three rings in a concentric arrangement. Avoid enlarging the top of the bow mortise.

If you haven't yet bored the spindle mortises in the deck, do the center deck mortise now. Slip the paddle-bit extension up through the bow mortise. Then attach the 1/2-inch powerbore bit to the lower end of the extension, and your drill to the chuck end. Bore the mortise 1 inch deep. Use this procedure for the other deck mortises, once you've finished the remaining bow mortises.

Placing the Spindles

It's time to look through your collection of dry spindles. Select the nine best, assign each a place on the back bow, and label them 1 through 9. Pencil corresponding numbers beside the spindle mortises on the seat. Some spindles may have become slightly curved during drying. You can correct the curvature by bending the spindle into an opposite curve using your thigh as a bending form. Then straighten the spindle by making any other adjustments. The corrected spindle will stay straight when it's fitted to the chair.

Hold the middle spindle (#5) at the center position on the chair. Pencil a cross mark 1/4 inch above the top of the bow to mark the approximate bottom of the 5/16-inch-diameter tenon after you've fitted the spindle to the 1-inch-deep deck mortise. Pencil another cross mark 1-1/2 inches above the first. Saw off any extra wood above this second mark. At this point, the spindle should be about 1 inch over its final length.

Make a sizing gauge for sizing the dry spindles (see fig. 9.21). The spindles are spokeshaved 17/32 inch in diameter from the base to the beginning of the taper. Shave the end of the taper 11/32 inch in diameter. Don't be intimidated by these dimensions. Since standard auger bits are made 1/64 inch larger than their nominal size, a 1/2-inch (#8) auger bit is actually 33/64 inch in diameter. These spindles are quite thin; take care not to undersize them. It's fine to shape them with a slight bulge at their midlength. Finish spindles with a spokeshave and sandpaper, or the specially designed spindle scraper described in Chapter 2.

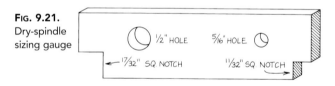

FIG. 9.21. Dry-spindle sizing gauge

File or sand the spindle tenons to fit the test gauge. Smear pencil graphite inside the test holes to find out where the tenons are too tight. File or whittle small chamfers on both tenon ends.

Remove the bow from the chair. Fit the center spindle to the deck mortise, then lower the bow over the spindle tenon. If everything fits correctly, you will get both bow tenons fully into their mortises. Be firm, but not forceful. If the bow tenons do not seat fully, you need to locate the points of resistance on the tenons. Disassemble, file or sand the tenons as required, then retest. You may have to run through several test fittings before getting the spindle and bow tenons fully seated. Be patient, especially fitting this central spindle. You want a snug fit here. When you're dealing with close tolerances, a few strokes with a file can transform an oversize tenon to one that has a sloppy fit in its mortise.

Assemble the bow and spindle. (If the bow still wobbles—it shouldn't—refit the compression stick and the twine pull-down to the side stretchers.) Pencil spacing lines for the

remaining spindles using the spindle spacing in figure 9.22. Carefully eyeball and pencil cross lines on the top of the bow. You want to bore through the center of mass of the bow straight down to the center of the spindle-deck mortises. Indent each boring center with an awl.

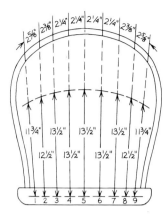

FIG. 9.22. Upper spindle mortise spacing

Boring the Remaining Bow Mortises

Bore the remaining bow mortises in pairs, beginning with the spindles nearest to the center. The next four borings (mortises #3, #4, #6, #7) are made exactly like the center

Beginning the mortises on the sloped part of the bow by boring perpendicular to the tangent. The bow is now held steady with the fitted center spindle in position. Note the antique Spofford brace.

After scoring the surface, rotate the brace so that the bit aligns with the target mortise on the seat. Turn the brace continually while you shift the angle.

Using a standard auger bit, you can let go of the brace to check alignment from a side view. Placing a flat washer over the target mortise eliminates the possibility of aiming at the wrong point.

Boring the steep mortises at the extreme flanks of the bow with an electric drill and the chicken method

spindle mortise. Be sure to stop boring when the auger lead pokes through the bottom of the bow. Don't back bore until you've bored the full set.

At bow mortises #2 and #8, the mortise enters at a pronounced curve. Start boring these mortises with the bit perpendicular to the surface of the bow. Swing the bit into alignment after the side nickers of the auger bit score the perimeter of the mortise.

Mortises #1 and #9 are the most difficult. At this steep bow angle you are boring into end grain at about 45 degrees. In this situation you must take special care to keep the auger bit from wandering and from busting out fiber on the bottom of the bow, as the side nicker may come through the underside before the lead point. You can use an auger bit, following the starting technique for mortises #2 and #8. On a chair with a tail brace, you could bore mortises #1 and #9 from below, making blind mortises that don't come through the top of the bow.

For boring mortises #1 and #9, I recommend using an alternative technique that I call the "chicken method." Start boring with a hand-held electric drill and a standard 1/8-inch twist bit. The drill must have a sensitive variable-speed trigger, so you can bore very carefully. As with the

previous mortises, begin by boring perpendicular to the bow. Rotate the drill into alignment when you have drilled a shallow seat in the surface of the bow. Aim for the mortise on the seat and carefully bore straight through the bow. Run the drill up and down in the hole a few times to clear out any wood frass. Peer through the hole to see where it points to. You're hoping that the hole is in line with the bottom spindle mortise. (Be sure that you are looking at the correct mortise on the spindle deck.) Put a 3/16-inch twist bit in the drill. If the first hole is out of alignment, do some correction as you bore through with this larger bit. Run the drill up and down (with the motor on) to grind the sides of the hole closer into alignment. Next use a 1/4-inch twist bit. If necessary, grind the sides of the hole again. You should be able to peer straight through the bow mortise to the spindle-deck mortise. The final boring, with a 5/16-inch twist bit, will be an easy one, with close to perfect alignment.

Remove the bow from the seat. Back bore the mortises where you used an auger bit. Replace the bow in the seat and check alignment of the spindle mortises through the bow. Use a rat-tail rasp to correct mortise alignment as necessary. (If you haven't done so, bore the remaining spindle mortises in the deck.)

Boring spindle mortises in the seat using the direct method, piggy-backing two paddle-bit extensions on top of a 1/2-inch powerbore bit. Use a brace or electric drill.

Fitting the bow and spindle assembly to the seat often requires some fiddling and wrestling.

Test Fitting and Gluing Up

Arrange all the spindles in position, the center spindle in its seat and bow mortises and the other spindles upside down in the deck mortises. Above the bow, pencil the cutoff heights for the set of spindles, allowing for about 1/2 inch extra spindle above the bow. Transfer the cutoff increments from the base to the tip of each spindle. Saw to length.

Refine the spindle tenons by fitting the spindles to their respective mortises in the seat deck and the bow.

Follow with a full test fitting of the entire assembly. Begin by fitting the small ends of all spindles into the bow. Then lower the bow/spindle unit onto the seat. You will have to push and pull spindles up, down, and sideways until they are all in their seat mortises. To get the full assembly in place, you may need to hammer on the bow (with a rawhide mallet) or spindle tenons (with an ordinary hammer). Fitting the bow/spindle unit may require several test assemblies.

When everything fits, you're ready for the glue up. Recheck the numbers and tick marks at the base of the spindles and spindle deck, so that everything goes back exactly as it should. Pencil lines on the fronts of the

extended spindle tips that indicate saw kerfs for the spindle wedges. It's important that the spindle wedges are oriented crossing the bow.

Disassemble the bow/spindle unit for the last time. In the bottom of the bow tenons, saw wedge kerfs in line with the plane of the bent bow. Then saw 3/4-inch wedge kerfs in the upper tenons of the spindles. Use a rasp to rechamfer both ends of the spindles.

Brush glue on the upper spindle tenons, then insert the full set of spindles into the bow mortises. Brush glue on the lower spindle tenons, on the bow tenons, and in the seat mortises. Lower the bow/spindle unit into place.

Flip the chair upside down to drive wedges in the bow tenons. Then wedge the spindles. Carefully saw off any tenon/wedge waste above the bow. Use a sharp chisel to pare the sawed-off tenons flush with the bow.

WINDSOR CHAIR FINISHES

Finishing a Windsor with anything but penetrating oil is a time-consuming process. A good paint job requires careful surface preparation and scuffing with an abrasive between each coat. (I discuss oil finishes in Chapter 6 on the ladder-back.)

The dark forest green paint commonly associated with Windsor chairs was not popular until the late nineteenth century. Eighteenth-century American Windsors were finished with lead-based oil paints, or stained and varnished. The most popular pigment, verdigris, derived from scrapings of oxidized copper, varies widely in its chromatic hue, from bright turquoise blues through blue greens to green with a hint of blue gray. There is no specific Windsor green on the color spectrum. Also, early chairmakers often modified their colors with other pigments, such as Prussian blue.

Here is an entry from an unidentified Connecticut recipe book, dated 1794-1800 (following the recipe would not only be impractical but involve using lead):

> For green chairs with Verdigrifs grind 1/4 lb verdigris on a stone…as much oil as will enable you to grind it even in a very thick paste then remove it aside and repeat the same till the whole be ground then add & stir in 1 pint of common varnish in half an hour it will be ready for use—1 pint of this will give one coat to 8 chairs after they have been primed with the following (viz) white lead and lamp Black dry them in the Sun & Day and then they will be fit for laying the above paint of which you will lay two coats & they will both Dry in one day.

I paint most of my American Windsors with a three-to-one mixture of alkyd enamel and varnish. The varnish thins the pigment and produces a hard surface when the mixture dries. Several translucent coats give the finished color a depth not found in modern, heavily pigmented paints. I buy premium quality semigloss brushing enamel and semigloss varnish. (Alkyd and urethane varnish achieve equal results.)

First, carefully sand the entire chair. Begin painting with a flat, light-gray coat of interior enamel primer, which dries quickly and can be sanded. You can fill in scratches or other voids with various woodworking fillers, such as wood putty, or with products available from auto-body paint suppliers. For instance, try filling superficial scratches and dents with lacquer putty, which dries rapidly and sands easily, and larger voids with a hardening resin commonly referred to as "bondo." Sand the filled areas, then give the chair another coat of primer.

Keeping the next paint coats free of dust is always a concern. One way to avoid the problem is to wet sand between each coat. The solvent picks up any dust from the finish, filler, or wood. Use a folded piece of 380- to 500-grit wet-dry sandpaper dipped in mineral spirits several times a minute. The chair surface will be covered with a

A Secret Weapon

If spindle mortises in your bow are far out of alignment relative to their respective seat mortises, you can use a homemade power rasp. Put a 5/16-inch rat-tail rasp in a bench vise, with about 4 inches extending above the vise jaws. Wearing safety glasses, grab the rasp with a pair of locking pliers and begin bending, or hit the rasp with a hammer. It should snap off. Chuck the short rasp piece in an electric drill set to run in reverse (anticlockwise). In normal rotation, the rasp grooves will pull the drill into the bow. Use the power rasp with respect.

This "power rasp" is a broken section of a rat-tail file. Grind a blunt point at the lead; operate the drill in reverse.

messy slurry; wipe it off with a clean rag. A single piece of wet-dry sandpaper will last many times longer than sandpaper used for dry sanding. You can buy wet-dry sandpaper, which usually has a black paper backing, at good paint suppliers. If you try this, wear rubber gloves, and work in a well-ventilated area. Wet sanding works best on the comparatively heavy primer coats. Even 500-grit sandpaper combined with solvent may be too aggressive to use on the finish coats.

If you don't wet-dry sand, you can use inexpensive tack cloths (wax-impregnated cheesecloth) to pick up dust. Cleaning around the joints of the spindles and stretchers requires special care; blasting the chair with compressed air is more effective.

When I'm satisfied with the primed surface of the chair I apply four to five coats of the enamel/varnish mixture. The idea is to build up several translucent coats, so that light won't bounce off the surface. The first coat will look like a watercolor wash. With the second coat, you'll begin to see the color that you're building up, but the paint won't look promising. After each coat is dry, I haze the entire surface with a 3M finishing pad, which also smooths over other irregularities.

Lighting is a concern during finish work, especially when you're applying the last coats of paint. It's surprisingly easy to miss parts of the chair when you use the same color for successive coats. Using a systematic approach will help, that is, follow the same sequence of painting parts as you apply each coat. Paint on spindles must be carefully brushed out; thick paint imperceptibly slumps to the base of the spindles causing blobs at the spindle deck.

You can also use water-based acrylic paints. (Acrylic is commonly known as latex paint in stores that sell house paints.) I've used a three-to-one mixture of semigloss acrylic and semigloss acrylic medium. One advantage: You can build up multiple coats of acrylic without sanding or using steel wool. This type of paint appears to dry quickly, but it does not really harden until several weeks after the last coat of paint is applied. Until then, the painted surface is more fragile than a similar paint job using alkyd paint. Use a synthetic bristle brush with any water-based paint or finish.

Several friends who make excellent Windsor chairs use powered-milk paint, topped with a coat of linseed oil. The results can be attractive and long wearing. An advantage of using milk paint is that it is nontoxic. However, the earliest historic references that I know of for the use of milk-based paint begin in the mid-1800s. If some early Windsors were finished with milk paint, they would have been exceptions.

Classic American Chairs

Shaker rocking chair, c 1840. Maple with cornshuck seating. Made at the Shaker community at Pleasant Hill, Kentucky.

Fan-back Windsor,
c 1790-1800.
Rhode Island.

Braced bow-back Windsor,
c 1790-95. Rhode Island.

Sack-back Windsor with double-baluster turnings, c 1780-90. Rhode Island.

Continuous-arm Windsor with double-bobbin (bamboo) turnings, c 1800-1803. Made by Thomas Cotton Hayward. Charlestown, Massachusetts.

High-back (comb-back) Windsor with arrow-point turnings, c 1765. Philadelphia.

Part Four:
More Chairs

CHAPTER 10

Post-and-Rung:
A Useful Stool

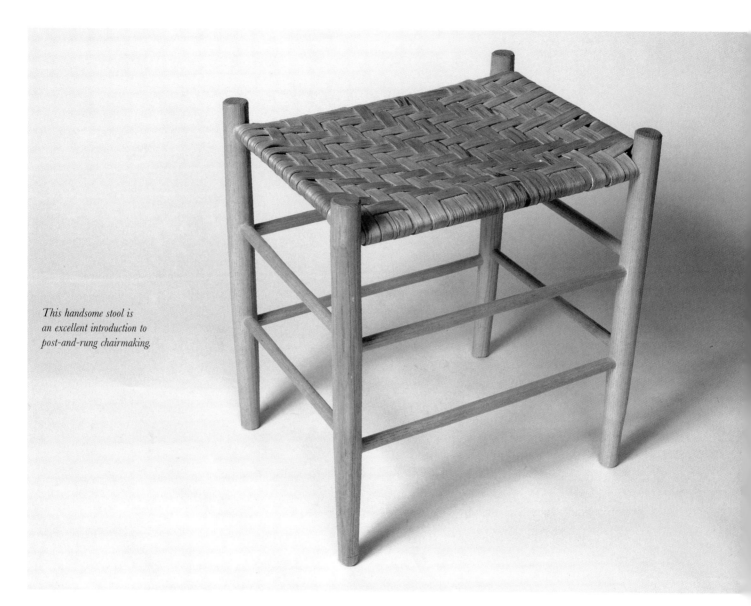

This handsome stool is an excellent introduction to post-and-rung chairmaking.

MATERIALS LIST: POST-AND-RUNG STOOL

Number of Pieces	Description	Rived Green Dimensions	Shaved Green Dimensions	Finish Dimensions
4	Posts (or legs)	1-3/4" sq x 20"	1-3/8" dia x 18-3/4"	1-7/16" dia x 18-3/4"
6	Long (front) rungs	1" sq x 17-1/2"+	3/4" dia x 17"	11/16" dia x 17"
6	Short (side) rungs	1" sq x 13-1/4"+	3/4" dia x 12-3/4"	11/16" dia x 12-3/4"

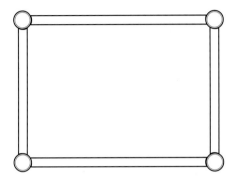

Fɪɢ. 10.1. Plan view

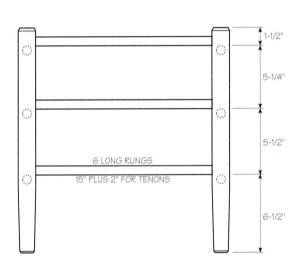

Fɪɢ. 10.2. Front view

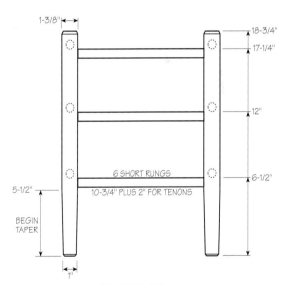

Fɪɢ. 10.3. Side view

Scale: 1:8

If you're intimidated by the complexity of the ladder-back chair in Chapter 6, I suggest you start out by making a post-and-rung stool. You'll have an opportunity to practice riving and shaving billets, working with cylindrical mortise-and-tenon joinery, and weaving a seat—and you'll end up with an attractive and useful piece of furniture.

I have also used this stool as a green-woodworking project for kids. My daughter, Ami, made a stool with eight rungs when she was eleven, and in a class where I teach parents and youngsters together, we've made stools with kids as young as eight.

Another advantage of starting with a stool is that the materials are easier to obtain—there are no long rear posts or back slats—and weaving the seat is simpler.

Before You Begin: A Look at Style and Materials

You can easily modify the stool plan to suit your own requirements. For instance, you can extend the legs to make an excellent shop or counter stool, or shorten them to make a fine footstool or seating for a young child. Locate the rungs at any position on the posts, and modify their length to suit your fancy or the materials at hand. I make stools with twelve rungs, but you can build a similar stool with eight or ten. For a stool with eight or ten rungs, locate the lower set of rungs somewhere between the position for the bottom and middle rungs of a stool with three rungs on each side. You do not have to use a common tangent line for the short and long lower rungs.

Refer to Chapters 4 through 7 for information on selecting wood, riving blanks, shaving rungs and posts, and weaving the seat. Making the stool calls for the same basic toolkit required for the ladder-back chair discussed in Chapter 6.

Before proceeding, make a pattern stick based on figure 10.4.

For this stool, use green, ring-porous hardwoods, such as red and white oak, ash, and hickory—almost any sub-species will do, if the wood is straight and relatively free of knots. This same plan can be used to make a turned stool with straight-grained, diffuse-porous woods such as maple or cherry.

You can make this stool from several 20-inch-long bolts cut from a sapling as small as 6 inches in diameter. However, with a small sapling you may have to combine sapwood and heartwood in the rivings for the posts. Larger trees will usually yield straighter rivings. Crooked rungs can add a nice rustic touch to the stool, although wavy or crooked wood is more difficult to work than straight-grained stock.

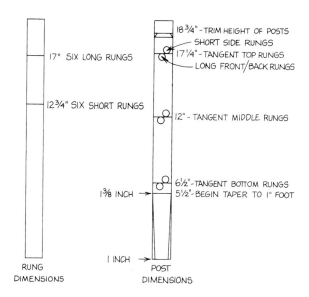

Fig. 10.4. A pattern stick for the rectangular stool. The small circles above and below the tangent lines represent side and front/back mortise locations.

Riving and Shaping Billets

Crosscut your green log into several 20-inch bolts. Rive out billets as explained in Chapter 5. Rive posts about 1-3/4 inches across, rungs about 1 inch across. Be sure to rive extra parts, for practice and to cover attrition during construction. Figure 10.5 shows how to rive parts from a small sapling.

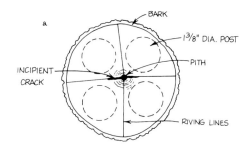

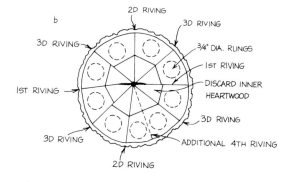

Fig. 10.5. Sequence for riving billets from a very small sapling: *a,* post billets; *b,* rung billets

Saw the rung blanks about 1/2 inch longer than their trim lengths of 12-3/4 and 17 inches. Keep the posts a full 20 inches long until trimming them, after the joinery is complete.

Referring to the steps in Chapter 6, drawknife all the rung billets into square sections 3/4 inch wide. Then spokeshave the full set of rungs into octagonal sections, followed by rounding. Air dry the rungs for a few days, then put them into a heated environment to dry. Stack the drying rungs in a crisscross pile so that there is good air circulation around each part.

Drawknife the posts as explained for shaving the front chair posts in Chapter 6. Begin by shaving the posts to a square section 1-3/8 inches wide. Shave the tapers on the bottom of the square-section posts before shaping them to an octagonal section. When shaving the tapered bottom section, be sure to shape the feet into a regular octagon 1 inch across. Air dry the posts before beginning assembly.

Saw the rungs to their trim lengths after they are thoroughly dry. As with the chair, the rung tenons are 5/8 inch in diameter and 1 inch long. If you don't have a lathe or a tenon former, shape the tenons following the tenoning procedure in Chapter 6 using a spokeshave, file, and sandpaper. The tenons should fit the sizing gauge (see Chapter 6) with a squeaky tight fit. Be sure to chamfer the ends of the tenons, but just slightly. Keep the tenoned rungs dry until assembly.

BORING THE POST MORTISES

You're now ready to bore mortises in the posts. Transfer the tangent lines for the rungs from the pattern stick. You can assemble both short (side) panels or both long (front/back) panels first. The borings above the tangent lines are for the short side rungs. For comfort, the long front/back rungs must be below the side rungs.

Growth-ring orientation of the posts in relation to the rungs will have little effect on the strength of the stool, which is subjected to almost no racking stress. I suggest orienting the rays of the posts at a rough 45-degree angle, directed toward the center of the seat—a small detail that enhances the appearance of the finished stool.

The easiest way to get all the mortises in alignment and at the same angle is boring horizontally, which you can do with a vise attached to a workbench, or with a peg-and-wedge holding system set up at a comfortable height (fig. 10.6).

For the peg-and-wedge system, bore the peg holes in the top of a workbench or a heavy plank attached to a post or wall. You can also set up a peg-and-wedge system on a low bench or the seat of a shaving horse, in which case you will do all borings vertically. From hardwood rivings about 1 inch in diameter, shave the pegs with a slight swelling at one end and a chamfer at the other. The holding wedge is about 8 inches long, tapering from 3/4 to 1-1/4 inch in width.

I recommend boring the mortises with a bit brace and one of the auger bits discussed in Chapter 6. Power drills bore very quickly; you need to be careful getting alignment, angles, and depth correct for the stool mortises. If you have a workbench with a vise, you can use a pair of boring fixtures (see Chapter 6).

Draw a line down the length of one leg oriented about 45 degrees from the rays as seen from an end view. Use the stool pattern stick to transfer tangent lines crossing the lengthwise line on the leg. If you're boring mortises for side panels first, draw small circles just above the tangent lines (see fig. 10.4). For boring front and rear mortises, draw the circles just below the tangent lines.

Secure one post in the vise boring fixture or the peg-and-wedge holding system. Set and aim the auger bit to bore into the center of mass of the post. To do this, your eye must be level with the post when you position the auger. Remember that the mortises are bored tangent to the cross lines on the post. A line level taped to the auger-bit extension makes it possible to hold the drill at a consistent, horizontal position. Bore the mortises 1 inch deep. Use tape or paint as a depth gauge on the auger. Using the boring fixture or the peg-and-wedge system, you can bore all three mortises without repositioning the piece.

You'll bore all mortises on the stool with a level auger positioned 90 degrees to the posts. Use a combination square to position the auger at a right angle to the post being bored. You'll appreciate having a helper the first few times that you do this.

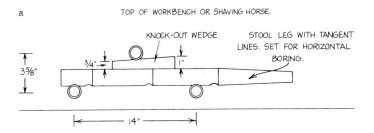

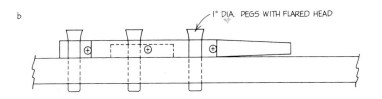

FIG. 10.6. Diagram of a peg-and-wedge holding system: *a*, plan view; *b*, side view

INITIAL GLUING UP

You can begin glue up when you've put tenons on three rungs and bored mortises in two posts. You'll need ordinary white glue, a clean white rag, a glue brush (cheap acid brushes work well), and some water.

Brush glue into the mortises of one post and on one end of the first set of rungs. Orient the rays of the rungs parallel to the length of the posts, to minimize joint loosening when the tenons shrink and expand due to changes in humidity. For appearance and strength, any curvature on the rungs should be oriented crown up. If they are strong, unsightly rungs can be used at the top of the posts, where they are hidden by the woven seat.

The joints should be a hammer-tight fit. I use a 2-1/2-pound rawhide-and-iron mallet. Put a leather scrap or other padding between the post and assembly bench top. Hammer the rung tenons into the post mortises; the sound distinctly changes when the tenons are fully home. Measure the protruding rungs to make sure that the seated tenons are at the correct depth. Look across the tops of the rungs; they should be the same height. If the middle rung is taller than the end rungs, try driving it deeper into the mortise. If this doesn't work, trim the end of the middle rung so that it lines up with the upper and lower rungs.

After rungs are in one post, brush glue on the remaining tenons and into the mortises of the matching post. Hammer the joints together.

Look across the rungs at a low angle to see if the assembled panel forms a flat plane. The rungs should appear parallel with each other. If the panel is warped, you can straighten it by putting one leg in a bench vise, and then twisting the other leg in the proper direction. Use a damp rag to clean up any glue squeezeout around the joints before assembling the opposite panel.

BORING PERPENDICULAR POST MORTISES AND FINAL GLUING UP

Mortises bored perpendicular to the assembled panels are done the same way. Set an assembled panel in the boring fixture or peg-and-wedge holding system. Use a combination square with an integral bubble level to position the panel at a right angle to the horizontal boring direction. Align the boring bit on the opposite side of the tangent lines used to bore the original panels. Be sure to bore through the center of mass, level and at a right angle to the posts. Bore mortises in both of the previously assembled panels at this time.

Brush glue in the mortises of one panel and on one tenon end of the next set of rungs. Determine rung ray orientation before driving the rungs into the posts. Drive the rungs

Stools made at a workshop by youngsters ages eight to thirteen

into this first panel. Check rungs for height (length) and clean up any glue excess.

Brush glue in the remaining mortises (on the other panel) and on the tenons of the protruding rungs. Hammer the second side panel onto the upright rungs.

Check alignment of the stool by viewing across the panels—rungs should appear parallel with each other. If the stool is out of alignment you may be able to make a correction by using a pipe or bar clamp to reshape the proportions of one or more panels. Connect the clamp jaws to opposing ends of the legs on a single panel. Observe changes in alignment as you close the clamp screw. You may need to overclamp. Experiment with this type of correction, as there are numerous causes for non-alignment during assembly. Be sure to clean up all glue squeezeout before excess glue dries.

FINISHING AND WEAVING THE SEAT

The stool frame is trimmed and leveled much like the ladder-back chair in Chapter 5. Use wedges to level the stool on a flat, horizontal surface. Use a compass to scribe a pencil line set at the base of the highest wedged leg. Saw off the bottoms of the legs at the scribed lines. Pare a chamfer around the bottom of each leg with a chisel.

Saw off post nubbins 5/8 to 3/4 inch above the top rungs. Chamfer the upper end of the trimmed legs. Chisel the flat cut made by the saw into a very slight convex surface.

Clean up the stool frame with a scraper or fine sandpaper. I use several coatings of a thin, penetrating linseed oil–based finish wiped on with a rag.

You can weave the stool seat with any of the materials discussed in Chapter 7. The only difference is that weaving the stool seat goes considerably faster than a chair seat, since the plan is a simple rectangle.

Post-and-Rung: Ami's Youth Chair

CHAPTER 11

Youth chair, designed by the author

T he main requirement for a youth chair, in addition to the necessary height, is that it be almost impossible to tip over. I made this chair for my daughter, Ami, in 1984, when she was four years old. Its inspiration came one evening while I was looking at one of our old ladder-backs. To make a youth chair, I realized, I could splay the standard ladder-back rear posts to the side and rake them back. The front legs would also have side splay but no forward rake. I drew up plans that evening and made the chair the next week. On the prototype, the front legs bow out a bit because my original drawing was not particularly accurate. Using the rung lengths in the plans will result in a chair with a slightly smaller seat.

BEFORE YOU BEGIN: DESIGN AND PREPARATION

Making Ami's chair is more complex than the ladder-back in Chapter 6, mainly because of the leg splay and rake, but the acute and obtuse angles of the plan view are the same. I like the design as it is, but you could make the chair a little fancier by shaving a relief on the back posts, like the ladder-back's.

Make a chair stick following the plans in figure 11.4. The circles indicating the rung mortises are below the tangent lines, because the front and rear panels of this chair are assembled before the sides.

You can make a special potty seat, with front (acute) angles at 82 degrees and rear (obtuse) angles at 98 degrees. The slat mortise is oriented 122 degrees from the side rungs (fig. 11.5). There is no back post relief; you will adjust angles for axial rotation by placing a short dummy slat in the slat mortises.

The rear posts of Ami's chair are bent on the same bending jig as the ladder-back's. You may need two bending jigs. I had to modify my jigs, cutting away most of one side, so that I could pull the rear posts to the form with clamps. Without the relief, the posts are surprisingly stiff.

CONSTRUCTION NOTES

Rive and shave posts and rungs following the dimensions on the materials chart. On the assembled chair, there are nine different rung lengths. Be sure to make several extra rungs.

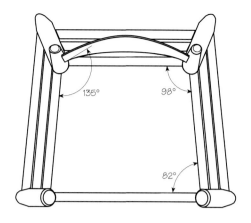

FIG. 11.1. Plan view

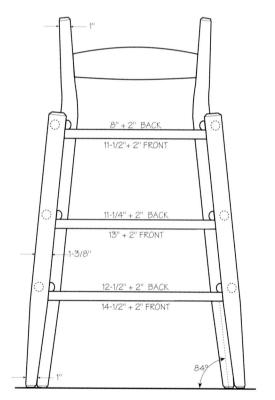

FIG. 11.2. Front view

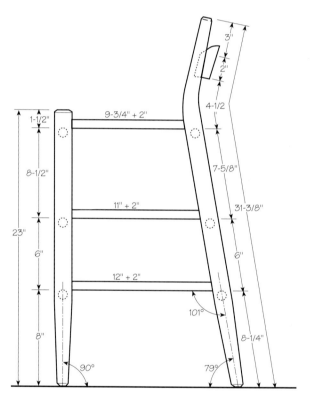

FIG. 11.3. Side view

Scale: 1:8

MATERIALS LIST: POST-AND-RUNG YOUTH CHAIR

Number of Pieces	Description	Rived Green Dimensions	Shaved Green Dimensions	Finish Dimensions
2	Front posts	1-3/4" sq x 24+"	1-3/8" oct x 24+"	1-7/16" dia x 23"
2	Back posts	1-3/4" sq x 32+"	1-3/8" sq x 32"	1-7/17" dia x 31-3/8"
1	Front rung	1" sq x 17"	3/4" oct x 17"	11/16" dia x 13-1/2"
1	Front rung	1" sq x 17"	3/4" oct x 17"	11/16" dia x 15"
1	Front rung	1" sq x 17"	3/4" oct x 17"	11/16" dia x 16-1/4"
2	Side rungs	1" sq x 17"	3/4" oct x 17"	11/16" dia x 14"
2	Side rungs	1" sq x 17"	3/4" oct x 17"	11/16" dia x 13"
2	Side rungs	1" sq x 13"	3/4" oct x 13"	11/16" dia x 11-3/4"
1	Back rung	1" sq x 13"	3/4" oct x 13"	11/16" dia x 10"
1	Back rung	1" sq x 13"	3/4" oct x 13"	11/16" dia x 11-1/4"
1	Back rung	1" sq x 13"	3/4" oct x 13"	11/16" dia x 12-1/2"
1	Back slat	1/2" x 11" x 3-1/2+"	3/16+" x 3" x distance	Same

FIG. 11.4. Youth chair stick; overall size, 1/4" by 1-1/2" by 31" at top of rear posts

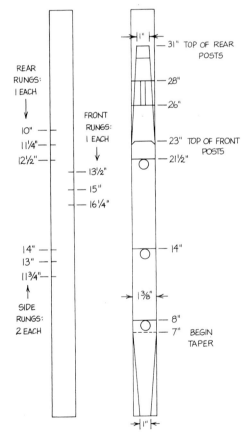

FIG. 11.5. Youth chair potty seat. The slat angle differs from the ladder-back potty seat.

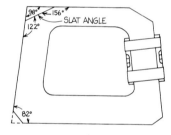

Steam and bend the rear posts. Kiln dry the rungs (or an equivalent process) and air dry the posts.

Trim the kiln-dried rungs to final lengths. The rung tenons are 5/8 inch in diameter and 1 inch deep. Use any tenoning method. Separate the rungs into groups of three based on their panels.

Assembly begins with the front panel. Determine left and right front posts. Place one front post at its respective corner of the potty seat, rotated so that its rays are directed toward the center of the seat. Draw a lengthwise orientation line on the post to indicate the axial placement of the front rungs.

Transfer tangent lines from the chair stick to the front post. Draw circles for the mortises below the tangent lines. Set the front post in the standard ladder-back boring fixture, rotated so the lengthwise line appears centered when your eye is level with the post.

If your tenons have shoulders, set the depth tape on the 5/8-inch boring bit to 1-1/16 inches. For straight tenons without shoulders, set the depth to an even inch.

Visualize the splay of the front legs. Front rung mortises are bored at an angle of 84 degrees leaning toward the top of the front posts. The complementary angle is 96 degrees leaning outwards from the base. The boring bit and extension are held level (just like boring for the ladder-back.) But instead of boring square into the post, you come in at an angle. Set a sliding bevel gauge at 96 degrees. Hold the bevel gauge against the boring fixture. Position your boring rig parallel to the extended wing of the bevel gauge (fig. 11.6). All three mortises are parallel. When boring mortises for the other front post, be sure that the splay angle mirrors the angle of the original front post.

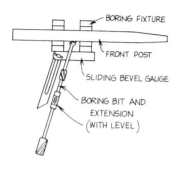

FIG. 11.6. Plan view of the setup for boring side-rung mortises on the youth chair

Assemble the front panel.

In the rear posts, chop slat mortises 90 degrees from the plane formed by the bend.

Make a 2- by 4-inch dummy slat that fits snugly into the back slat mortises. Fit the dummy slat into one of the rear posts. Position the rear post over the appropriate corner of the potty seat, with the dummy slat parallel to the relief angle at the rear corner. Draw a lengthwise orientation line on the post. Transfer tangent lines from the chair stick.

Place the rear post in the boring fixture. Adjust axial rotation by holding the slat angle of the potty seat against the dummy slat (fig. 11.7). Bore horizontal mortises leaning 96 degrees from the foot of the leg.

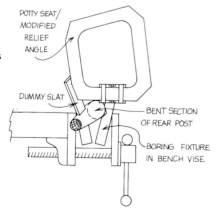

FIG. 11.7. Adjusting the axial rotation for boring rung mortises in the rear posts

Assemble the rear panel.

On this chair, there is no need to overlap the tangents of the front and rear mortises by 1/16 inch. Lay the assembled front panel on your workbench, with the inner side of the panel facing up. Pencil tangent lines and mortises for the side rungs on the posts of the back panel. Draw tangent lines on the front posts in line with the upper tangents of the front rungs. Pencil tangent lines and mortises for the side rungs on the posts of the back panel. Draw circles for the mortises above the tangent lines.

Place the front panel into the boring fixture at the bench vise. Since the front and side rungs form an acute angle, tip the front panel slightly forwards (away from the bench). Use the potty seat to adjust the axial rotation of the panel by holding the edge of the potty seat that represents the front rungs against the rungs of the front panel.

Bore the side-rung mortises at a right angle to the front posts, using a combination square to determine a 90-degree angle. Bore level, as usual.

Set the back panel in the boring fixture. Side rungs intersect the back panel at an obtuse angle, so tilt the panel toward the back of the workbench. (The panel leans away from your boring position.) Adjust axial rotation by holding the edge of the potty seat that represents the rear rungs against the rungs of the back panel.

Set the sliding bevel gauge to 101 degrees, the intersecting angle of the side rungs and rear legs. Bore horizontally, leaning 101 degrees away from the base of the legs.

FINAL DETAILS

Assemble the frame.

Level the chair so that the legs don't rock. Don't shorten the rear legs to lean the chair backwards. Trim the top of the front posts 3/4 inch above the side rungs. Trim the top of the rear posts—the "ears"—to your own visual taste. (I trim them 2-1/2 to 3 inches above the top of the slat mortises.) Chamfer both ends of the front and rear posts.

Rive a blank for the single slat. Experiment with a cardboard pattern to determine slat length, curvature, and height. Make the slat, being careful to shave uniform thickness from end to end. Installing the slat is the same as for the ladder-back.

Sand or scrape the frame smooth and finish to your requirements. Weave the seat.

CHAPTER 12

Post-and-Rung:
Dan's Rocker

This comfortable rocker is a challenging project in post-and-rung chairmaking.

Scale: 1:8

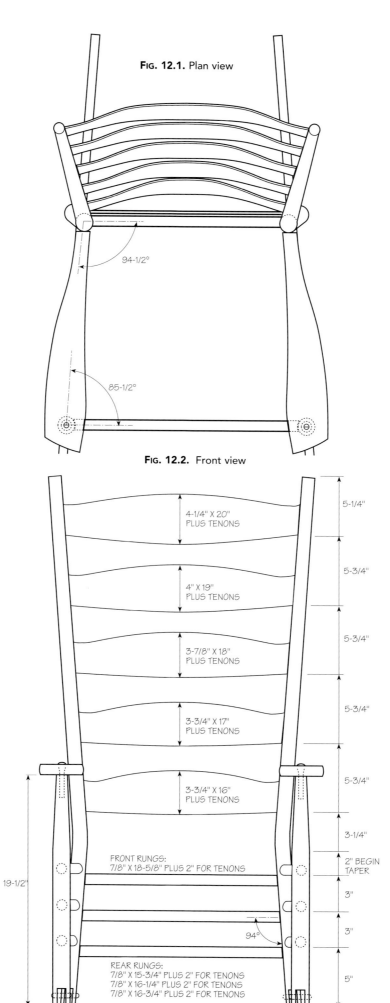

Fɪɢ. 12.1. Plan view

94-1/2°

85-1/2°

Fɪɢ. 12.2. Front view

4-1/4" X 20"
PLUS TENONS

5-1/4"

4" X 19"
PLUS TENONS

5-3/4"

3-7/8" X 18"
PLUS TENONS

5-3/4"

3-3/4" X 17"
PLUS TENONS

5-3/4"

3-3/4" X 16"
PLUS TENONS

5-3/4"

3-1/4"

FRONT RUNGS:
7/8" X 18-5/8" PLUS 2" FOR TENONS

2" BEGIN
TAPER

3"

3"

94°

19-1/2"

REAR RUNGS:
7/8" X 15-3/4" PLUS 2" FOR TENONS
7/8" X 16-1/4" PLUS 2" FOR TENONS
7/8" X 16-3/4" PLUS 2" FOR TENONS

5"

MATERIALS LIST: POST-AND-RUNG ROCKER

Number of Pieces	Description	Rived Green Dimensions	Shaved Green Dimensions/Trim Size
2	Front posts	1-3/4" x 20"	1-3/8" x 19-1/4"
2	Rear posts	1-3/4" x 48"	1-3/8" x 45-1/2"
2	Front rungs	1-1/2" x 21"+	15/16" x 20-5/8"
2	Upper side rungs	1-1/8" x 18"+	15/16" x 17-5/8"
2	Middle side rungs	1-1/8" x 18-1/2"+	15/16" x 18"
2	Lower side rungs	1-1/8" x 19"+	15/16" x 18-3/8"
1	Upper rear rung	1-1/8" x 18-1/4"+	15/16" x 17-3/4"
1	Middle rear rung	1-1/8" x 19"+	15/16" x 18-1/4"
1	Lower rear rung	1-1/8" x 19-1/4"+	15/16" x 18-3/4"
5	Slats	1/2" x 4" to 5" x 24"	1/4" x 3-3/4" to 4-1/4" x 17-1/2" to 21-1/2"
2	Armrests	1-1/4" x 4" x 20"	7/8" x 3-1/2" x 19-3/4"
2	Rockers, sawed		3/4" x 5-1/2" x 36-3/4"
or 1	Rocker blank rived	2-1/2" x 2-1/2" x 48"	Resaw and plane to 3/4" thick.
2	Front arm pins		5/8" dia x 2-1/4"
4	Rocker pins		3/8" dia x 1-1/2"
10+	Slat pins		5/32" dia x 3/4"+
2	Rear arm pins (optional)		5/8" dia x 2-1/4"

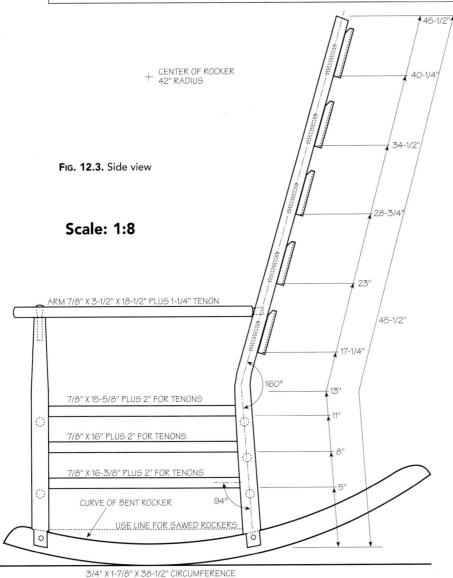

+ CENTER OF ROCKER
42" RADIUS

FIG. 12.3. Side view

Scale: 1:8

45-1/2"
40-1/4"
34-1/2"
28-3/4"
23"
45-1/2"
17-1/4"
160°
13"
11"
8"
5"
94°

ARM 7/8" X 3-1/2" X 18-1/2" PLUS 1-1/4" TENON
7/8" X 15-5/8" PLUS 2" FOR TENONS
7/8" X 16" PLUS 2" FOR TENONS
7/8" X 16-3/8" PLUS 2" FOR TENONS
CURVE OF BENT ROCKER
USE LINE FOR SAWED ROCKERS
3/4" X 1-7/8" X 38-1/2" CIRCUMFERENCE

Dan Mayner designed and made this post-and-rung rocking chair. Dan has taught ladder-back chairmaking at Country Workshops and is a professional woodworker in Columbus, Ohio. The chair in the measured drawings has rockers made from quarter-sawed oak lumber. Dan's chair in the photos was made with rived and bent rockers, which are more graceful but considerably more difficult to make.

BEFORE YOU BEGIN: A LOOK AT TECHNIQUES AND STYLE

This handsome chair combines elements of a traditional rocker with a clean, contemporary feeling. It's also very comfortable, thanks to its generous size and the ladder-back slouch of 103 degrees from the plane of the seat.

Making this rocker is an ambitious but do-able project for anyone who has completed the bent-back, double-slat post-and-rung chair detailed in Chapter 6 or a similar chair. The design calls for side rungs of three different lengths and for three different rear rungs. Also, the side panels are slightly twisted; the front legs are parallel, whereas the lower section of the rear legs diverges slightly. You can put Dan's rocker together without using glue if you assemble all the parts at optimum rela-

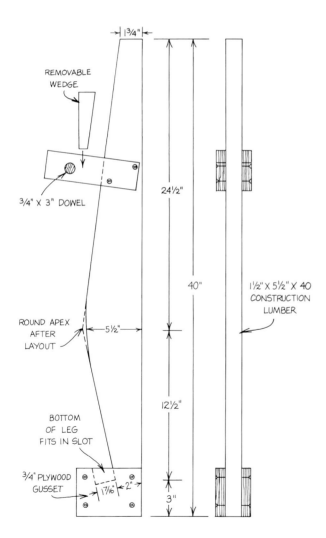

FIG. 12.4. Chair stick for Dan's ladder-back rocker

ALL SLAT
MORTISES
ARE
¼" X ¾" X 2½"

1"

6⁵⁄₃₂"

5¾"

5¾"

5¾"

45½"

ARMREST
MORTISE

5¾"

3¼"

BEGIN TAPER

1"

6¼"

2"

2"

19¼"

MIDDLE SIDE
RUNG TANGENT

3"

6"

3"

5"

5"

FRONT POST

BACK POST

1¾"

REMOVABLE
WEDGE

¾" X 3" DOWEL

24½"

40"

1½" X 5½" X 40
CONSTRUCTION
LUMBER

ROUND APEX
AFTER
LAYOUT

5½"

12½"

BOTTOM
OF LEG
FITS IN SLOT

¾" PLYWOOD
GUSSET

1⁷⁄₁₆" 2"

3"

FIG. 12.5. Bending form for rocker rear posts—make two from nominal 2 by 6 lumber.

tive moisture contents, and if they fit together tightly. If you're not sure about the details and quality of wet/dry joinery, use liquid hide glue, which has a slow set time.

You can also make several design modifications without affecting the balance or strength of the chair. For appearance, you might lengthen the back posts by 1 to 2 inches above the upper slat. If you shortened the backrest to three or four slats, the chair would be just as comfortable but less imposing, especially in a small room. You could increase the number of front rungs to three, or reduce the rear rungs to two. (Be sure to leave three rungs on each side.) The plan converts easily to a knitting rocker by eliminating the armrests.

Don't modify the radius of the rockers or the relationship of the rockers to the seat and back, unless you are ready to experiment. This chair has excellent balance.

Making the Posts, Rungs, and Rockers

Make a chair stick, following figure 12.4. One side of the chair stick shows the back rung and slat mortises in the rear posts. The other side represents the front-rung mortises in the front posts.

Start by riving and shaving posts and rungs following the procedures outlined in Chapter 5, with these few differences. The shaved rungs are 7/8 inch in diameter when dry. If you're shaving green wood, make the rungs 15/16 inch in diameter. As a design option, the ends of the rungs can taper slightly toward the tenons. After thorough drying, the rungs use standard 5/8-by-1-inch tenons.

The lower section of the front and rear posts is a straight cylinder (with no taper). A very slight taper begins 13 inches from the bottom of each post. The upper ends of the front and back posts are 1 inch in diameter. Use a hand plane to shape the tapers of the rear posts. The transition from cylinder to taper should be imperceptible.

Do not saw the slots for the rockers in the post bottoms until you've assembled the chair frame.

Steam and bend the rear posts when they are square or octagonal in section. (Don't round the rear posts until after the slat mortises are chopped.) Refer to figure 12.5 to make two post-bending forms. Steam green posts for one hour, posts made from air-dried stock for an hour and a half.

Shave the slats to a thickness just over 1/4 inch. Steam the slats. After limbering, put the slats into a bending form such as the one shown in the photos. Make the inner edges of the sides that restrain the slats 22 inches apart. At this stage, all the slats have the same length and curvature, but they can be graduated in width. You'll customize the slats when you assemble the rear panel.

Dan's bent rockers are made from a single 48-inch riving that is shaved and planed 2 inches wide by 2 inches deep. The bending form is longer than the 38-1/2-inch rockers in order to get a uniform curve from one end to the other. It uses convex and concave sections that are pulled together with clamps. The radius for the concave section is 42 inches, for the convex section, 40 inches. This allows 2 inches for the thickness of the rocker (fig. 12.6). Steam the rocker blank for two hours.

After the bend has set, ripsaw the piece into two rockers. Dress each rocker to 3/4 inch thick. Clamp the rockers together until they are thoroughly dry—they must have identical curvatures.

For rockers sawed from lumber, follow figure 12.7 for a pattern. The wood should be well dried and quarter sawed. Oak is a good choice.

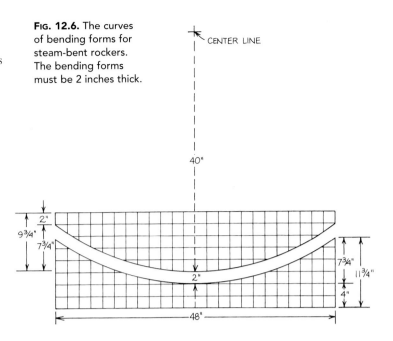

FIG. 12.6. The curves of bending forms for steam-bent rockers. The bending forms must be 2 inches thick.

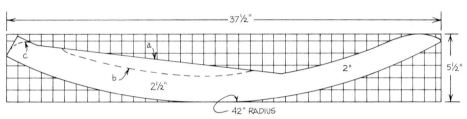

FIG. 12.7. Pattern for sawed rockers. Dashed lines *b* and *c* are sawed after the rockers are fitted to the assembled frame.

ASSEMBLING FRONT AND BACK PANELS

Use a spokeshave to round the front posts. Assembly of the front panel is straightforward. All front mortises are 90 degrees to the posts. Make the panel square and flat.

Chop mortises in the rear posts for the back slats after the bends are well set. All slat mortises are 1/4 by 3/4 by 2-1/2 inches. Round the rear posts. Bored mortises for the rear rungs are offset by 4 degrees from perpendicular on the length of the lower, cylindrical section of the posts.

Trim the slats to length. The chord at the base of the bottom slat is 16 inches, plus 1-1/2 inches for the two 3/4-inch-deep slat tenons. Each higher slat is 1 inch longer. The slat ends are angled 95 degrees from the flat base line. All slat-end tenons are 2-1/2 inches high. The slat pattern and maximum width of each slat is a matter of personal taste. (See figure 6.27 for a variety of slat styles.)

Do a dry assembly of the slat section of the back panel before the glue up. Be sure that the slats form a continuous plane. Curvature of the preformed slats can be modified somewhat. To flatten a slat, put it on the floor and press down on the center. To increase curvature, put a bar clamp on the slat ends, then overtighten with the clamp screw.

Begin assembling the rear panel by fitting the rear rungs and slats to one rear post. (Be sure to have the rungs and slats in proper sequence.) Glue the rungs, but don't glue the slats. Fit the second rear post to the rungs and back slats. You may have to pull the assembly together with bar or band clamps. Check the assembled back panel for dimensions and configuration. The two halves should be symmetrical. The lower rung section should form a flat panel. Make any necessary corrections. Pin the slats in place. Use one or two pins on each end of each slat.

Lay out tangent lines for boring mortises for the side rungs. Draw tangent lines above the front- and rear-panel rungs. The tangent for the center side rung on the front post is 3 inches above the tangent for the lower side rung.

The slight twist of the side panels requires you to bore each side-rung mortise at a slightly different angle. Take the obtuse and acute angles for the center rung off the plan view in the measured drawing; then adjust the upper and lower mortises plus or minus 1 degree, an estimate that works well enough.

Side-rung mortises in the front panel are all bored 90 degrees to the length of the front posts. Set the panel in a vertical boring fixture. Then tip the panel forward to 5-1/2 degrees off vertical. This will form the acute angle when you bore horizontally. Bore the center mortise using the standard horizontal boring procedure. For the upper mortise, tip the panel forward at 6-1/2 degrees from vertical. Then readjust the panel to 4-1/2 degrees off vertical for boring the lower mortise.

Side-rung mortises in the rear panel are bored 94 degrees from the line of the lower section of the back posts. (Refer to the side view on the scale drawing.) Place the back panel in the vertical boring fixture and tip it toward the workbench to 5-1/2 degrees from vertical. Bore the center mortise. Then readjust the tilt to 6-1/2 degrees for boring the upper mortise, and 4-1/2 degrees for the lower mortise. (The variances for boring the front and back mortises are the same, since the front and back panels are parallel to each other.)

Assemble the side rungs in the conventional manner.

MAKING THE ARMRESTS AND FINISHING THE FRAME

Make the armrests from rivings or sawed stock. After sawing the outline, sculpt the shape with a drawknife and spokeshave. The tenons that connect the armrests to the back posts can be either an integral part of the armrest or hardwood dowels mortised into the ends. To make an integral tenon, rough the tenon shape with a rasp, finished by rounding with a hollow auger.

There are several good ways to attach the armrests to the top of the front posts. One option is to use a hollow auger (or lathe) to make integral 5/8-inch-diameter tenons at the upper ends of the front posts. Kerf the ends of the tenons perpendicular to the length of the chair side panels. If you do this, make the original front post stock 20-1/4 inches long (trim length), instead of 19-1/4 inches as specified in the materials list.

A second option is to square the tops of the front posts before assembly. Bore 5/8-inch-diameter by 1-inch-deep mortises into the end grain at the top of the front posts. Glue 2-inch dry, hardwood dowels into the mortises. Kerf the ends of the dowels, oriented perpendicular to the chair side panels.

A third option employs dowel inserts. Clamp the entire armrest assembly into position. Insert the tenons at the rear section of the armrests into the rear post mortises, with the forward sections located over the tops of the front posts. Bore 5/8-inch-diameter by 2-inch-deep mortises through the armrests and into the end grain of the front posts. Saw wedge kerfs into the 5/8- by 2-1/2-inch dowels, which are oriented perpendicular to the length of the armrests. Glue the dowels in place.

At this point, you can finish the chair frame, without the rockers. Use a penetrating oil or oil/varnish finish, with an optional top coat of hard wax. If you'll be leaving the chair on a porch, use alkyd or urethane spar varnish, preferably with ultraviolet inhibitors. I like a satin varnish, but you can also use flat or gloss finishes.

Since the chair will be quite cumbersome after you've attached the rockers, I suggest you weave the seat at this point.

ATTACHING THE ROCKERS

Clamp the chair upside down to your workbench, with the back post ears flat on the floor. (The chair must be straight up and down.) Use a straightedge to draw rocker center lines from the front to back posts on the bottoms of the posts. The rocker center line crosses the bottom of the rear post about 1/16 inch off true center to compensate for the angled lower portions of the rear posts (refer to the front view, fig. 12.2). Extend the center lines down the posts for the depth of the mortises. To make these lines plumb, use a framing square set across the bottoms of the left and right posts. (The center lines are parallel to the front posts, but they are slanted in relation to the canted rear posts.) Then draw left and right layout lines for the dressed thickness of the rockers.

The depth of the rocker mortises in the posts will vary, depending on the style of the rockers. For sawed rockers that are shaped with a straight landing for the front and back posts, the depth is uniform relative to the distance from the bottom of the side rungs. (After fitting, you can trim the bottoms of the posts parallel to the curve of the rockers.) With bent rockers, you must allow for the curvature of the bend. The left and right mortises must be parallel to each other and perpendicular to the floor.

Saw the vertical cuts of the rocker mortises with a back saw sharpened with rip teeth. Be sure to saw inside the layout lines. Use a coping saw to cut the bottoms of the mortises. Adjust the slots to the rockers by paring with a sharp chisel.

Fit both rockers to their post mortises. Before attaching the rockers, check their alignment. If the rockers are not perfectly parallel when viewed from the side, the chair will wander sideways when it's rocked back and forth. Place a pair of parallel winding sticks on a flat surface. Set the chair on the winding sticks, with the rear rungs parallel to the rear winding stick. Check for rocker contact with the sticks at all four legs. If one rocker is high, make an adjustment by pushing the rocker forward or backward in the leg mortises. The curve of the rockers allows infinitely variable adjustments. Mark the fitting location when the rocker contacts the winding sticks at all four points.

For sawed rockers (fig. 12.7), cut the curved line, *b*, on the upper portion of the rockers after fitting the rockers to the post mortises. Line *c* in front of the front posts is an option.

Trim the bottoms of the legs so that they are parallel to the curve of the rockers. Chamfer the external bottom arris with a chisel.

Bore 3/8-inch-diameter pin holes through the legs and rockers. Make the pins from straight-grained, dry hardwood. Apply finish to the rockers.

CHAPTER 13

American Windsor:
Sack-Back Armchair

The project sack-back Windsor is very similar to chairs made in Rhode Island in the late eighteenth century.

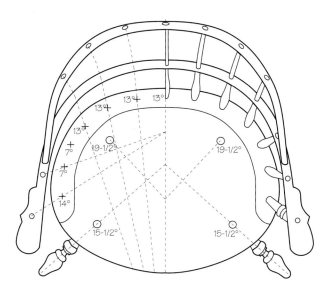

Fig. 13.1. Plan view

Scale: 1:8

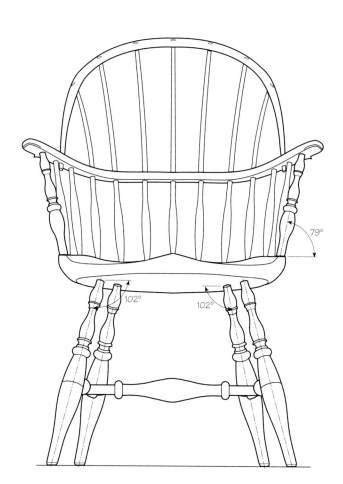

Fig. 13.2. Front view

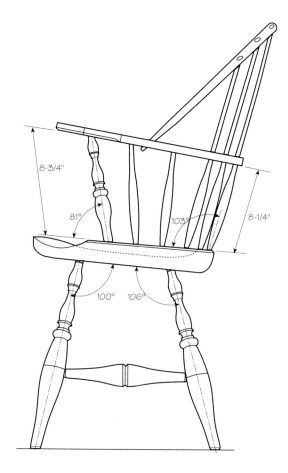

Fig. 13.3. Side view

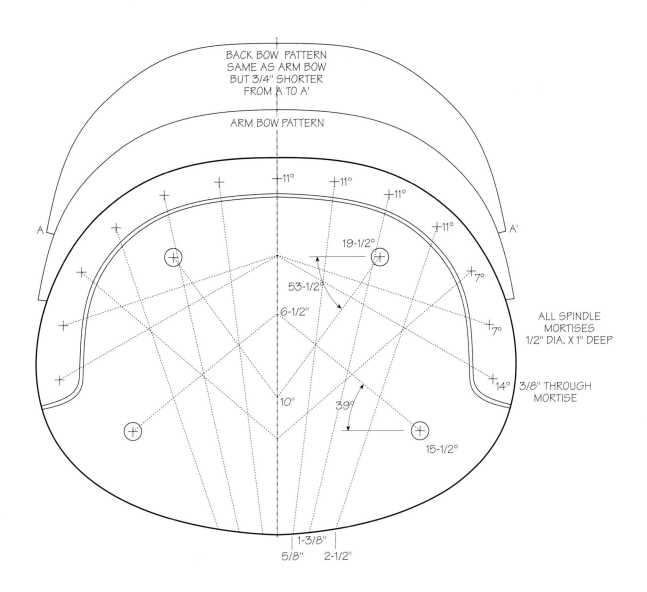

BACK BOW PATTERN
SAME AS ARM BOW
BUT 3/4" SHORTER
FROM A TO A'

ARM BOW PATTERN

A

A'

+11°

+11°

+11°

+11°

19-1/2°

53-1/2°

6-1/2"

+7°

+7°

ALL SPINDLE
MORTISES
1/2" DIA. X 1" DEEP

+14°

3/8" THROUGH
MORTISE

39°

10"

15-1/2°

1-3/8"

5/8"   2-1/2"

Fig. 13.4. Seat plan

Scale: 1:4

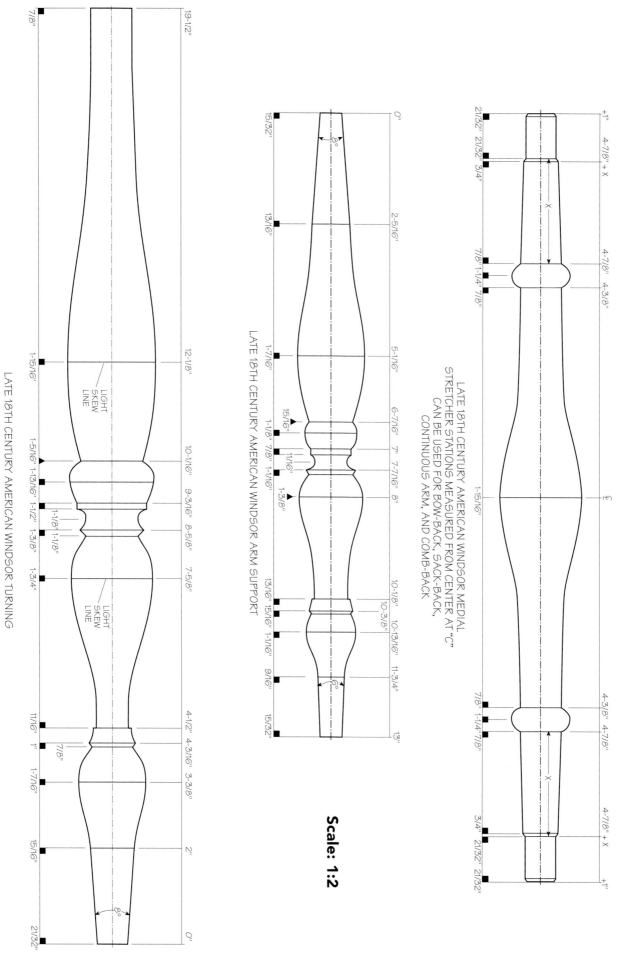

Fig. 13.5. Patterns for double-baluster turnings

LATE 18TH CENTURY AMERICAN WINDSOR MEDIAL
STRETCHER STATIONS MEASURED FROM CENTER AT "C".
CAN BE USED FOR BOW-BACK, SACK-BACK,
CONTINUOUS ARM, AND COMB-BACK.

LATE 18TH CENTURY AMERICAN WINDSOR ARM SUPPORT

LATE 18TH CENTURY AMERICAN WINDSOR TURNING

LIGHT SKEW LINE

LIGHT SKEW LINE

Scale: 1:2

MATERIALS LIST: SACK-BACK ARMCHAIR

Number of Pieces	Description	Rived Size	Green Size	Dry Size
1	Seat plank	(sawed)	2-1/4" x 16-1/2"+ x 21"+	1-7/8" x 15-3/4"+ x 20-1/4"
1	Arm bow	1" x 1-1/4" x 48"+	11/16" x 15/16"	5/8" x 7/8"
1	Back bow	1" x 1" x 45"+	7/8" dia	13/16" dia
4	Leg blanks	2-1/2" sq x 22" rived or 2-1/4" sq x 22" sawed	1-15/16" dia (double-basluster pattern)	Can be same as green
2	Side stretchers	2-1/2" sq x 16" rived or 2-1/4" sq x 16" sawed	1-15/16" (major diameter)	Can be same as green
1	Medial stretcher	2-1/2" sq x 18" rived or 2-1/4" sq x 18" sawed	1-15/16" (major diameter)	Can be same as green
2	Arm supports	1-3/4" sq x 14"	1-7/16" (major diameter)	Can be same as green
4	Spindles	1" sq x 12"	7/8" dia	3/4" dia
2	Spindles	1" sq x 18-1/2"	7/8" dia	3/4" dia
2	Spindles	1" sq x 20-1/2"	7/8" dia	3/4" dia
3	Spindles	1" sq x 21-1/2"	7/8" dia	3/4" dia
2	Hand blocks	(sawed)		3/4" x 2" x 6"
21	Wedges			As required

The sack-back Windsor is characterized by its two bent bows—a horizontal arm bow, with hand pieces at the ends, and a back bow. The back bow intercepts the arm bow at an angle between 45 and 60 degrees. The sack-back and the American comb-back Windsor both have a shallow but wide oval seat. The style is closely related to its English cousin, which is sometimes called a double hoop-back Windsor. The sack-back is not as spectacular as the American continuous-arm Windsor, but I find the design to have interesting and complex visual relationships.

Leg Angles (in degrees from 90) for the Sack-Back Armchair

	Rake	Splay	Sighting	Resultant
Front	10	12	39.7	15.4
Rear	16	12	53.5	19.6

BEFORE YOU BEGIN: A LOOK AT STYLE AND TECHNIQUE

The sack-back is certainly the sturdiest of all the high-backed Windsor armchairs. The long spindles are supported at midpoint by the horizontal arm bow. The hoop-shaped back bow forms an array of triangles with the upper portion of the spindles. The extended arm bows are supported by arm supports and short spindles that form a triangulated frame.

The handsome but shallow seat is not suited to everyone. For comfort, the back needs a generous slouch angle of 12 to 15 degrees. With a straighter backrest, a sitter tends to slide forward on the seat. Happily, deepening the seat is not difficult; you can increase the depth by an inch or two without detracting from the classic good looks of the design. The easiest approach is to extend the front of the seat, retaining the spindle and bow spacing. If you extend the seat front, relocate the boring centers and sight point for the front legs. Leave the rear legs as shown in the plans. The only other change is extending the length of the side stretchers, a measurement determined after you've fitted the legs to the seat.

This is not a simple chair to build. I strongly recommend making a bow-back Windsor before attempting the sack-back or the other Windsors in the following chapters. Making a sack-back involves several challenges. The back-bow tenons are carefully fitted at a difficult angle to tapered mortises in the rather narrow arm bow. The spindles bulge in the lower section between the seat and the horizontal arm bow. Shaving a uniform set of these spindles requires some real care. The spindles are also fitted to tapered mortises in the arm bow.

Although the sack-back in the plans has fancy double-baluster turnings, a pattern common in the late 1700s, the much simpler double-bobbin (or bamboo) pattern is also appropriate and historically correct. Another alternative is the cone and vase turning pattern shown on the plans for the comb-back Windsor. In this hybrid, simplified version of the fancier turning styles, the turned arm supports are essentially scaled-down versions of the legs.

MAKING THE SEAT

The seat for the sack-back (and the comb-back in the next chapter) is wider than it is deep. The planking runs from side to side instead of front to back, as in most other American Windsors. Draw the seat outline on the plank, along with the border of the spindle deck and the centers for all the spindles (fig. 13.4).

If you choose to, you can bore the arm support and the spindle holes in the seat deck before you saddle the seat, using the sight lines and resultant boring angles on the seat plan. My preference is to bore the arm support and spindle mortises with the bent arm bow held in place by boring fixtures. You bore through the arm bow and then continue with borings into the seat. With this method you don't deal with numeric angles, and you have more options for customizing spindle spacing and angles. Another possibility is boring and reaming the arm-support mortises only. There is less chance of splitting the seat plank if you ream the arm-support mortises before sawing the outline of the seat.

Saddle the seat following the steps in the chapter on the bow-back Windsor.

MAKING THE BOW AND SPINDLES

Before riving the blank for the arm bow, you must make a decision about the hand sections. While you can make the arm bow from one piece, with integral hands, separate blocks for the hand pieces are commonly glued in place after bending and drying the arm bow. This not only saves wood but is also easier than forming and bending the arms from a single piece of wood.

Rive out the bow and spindle blanks. The materials chart lists dimensions for an arm bow with the hand pieces glued to the sides of the steam-bent bow after drying. If you choose to make the arm bow from one piece, the riving is 1 by 2-3/4 by 48+ inches (fig. 13.6). The 2-3/4-inch width usually crosses the growth rings but can be parallel to them. Don't saw the actual hand shape until you have fitted the arm bow to the arm supports and spindles.

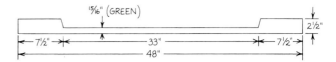

FIG. 13.6. Pattern for a single-piece sack-back arm bow. You can also glue the hand pieces to a narrower bow blank.

Shave the arm bow and the back bow to the green dimensions in the materials chart. You can shave the back bow round or as an octagon in section and do the rounding later. Don't taper the ends of the back bow until you're ready to fit it to the arm bow. Steam green bow blanks for about forty-five minutes. Double the steaming time for air-dried bow blanks.

You can use the same bending form for both bows, but fitting the back bow is easier if you make a separate bending form 3/4 inch narrower from side to side than the form used for the arm bow. Mark the bow centers and direction of the bend on the bows before putting them in the steamer.

Making the sack-back spindles requires special attention to details. Rive and trim the blanks to length, preparing several extra blanks in each length. Shave the blanks to 7/8 inches square. These can taper to a narrower dimension at one end; the bulge in the finished shaped spindles is 5-1/4 inches from the base, including the 1-inch seat tenon.

Draw a line around each square spindle 5 -1/4 inches from the base (see fig. 13.7). Taper the lower ends to a square 9/16 inches across. Taper the upper ends of the long spindles to 3/8 inch square and of the short spindles to 1/2 inch square. Then shape the spindle blanks into octagons. Kiln dry the spindles. For this chair (and the comb-back) I fit the arm bow before I continue detailing the spindles. Since the height of the arm bow drops slightly from the arm supports, the distance from the spindle deck on the seat to the bottom of the arm bow is regulated for each spindle.

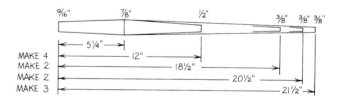

FIG. 13.7. Dimensions for shaving green spindles

TURNING THE LEGS AND ARM SUPPORTS AND ASSEMBLING THE STOOL

Turn the legs and the arm supports. A common variation of the turning pattern in the plans uses a straight taper (an elongated cone) for the lower section, which appears as a double curve in the plans and on my chair in the photos (see figs. 13.5 and 13.8). If you use a straight taper, you must

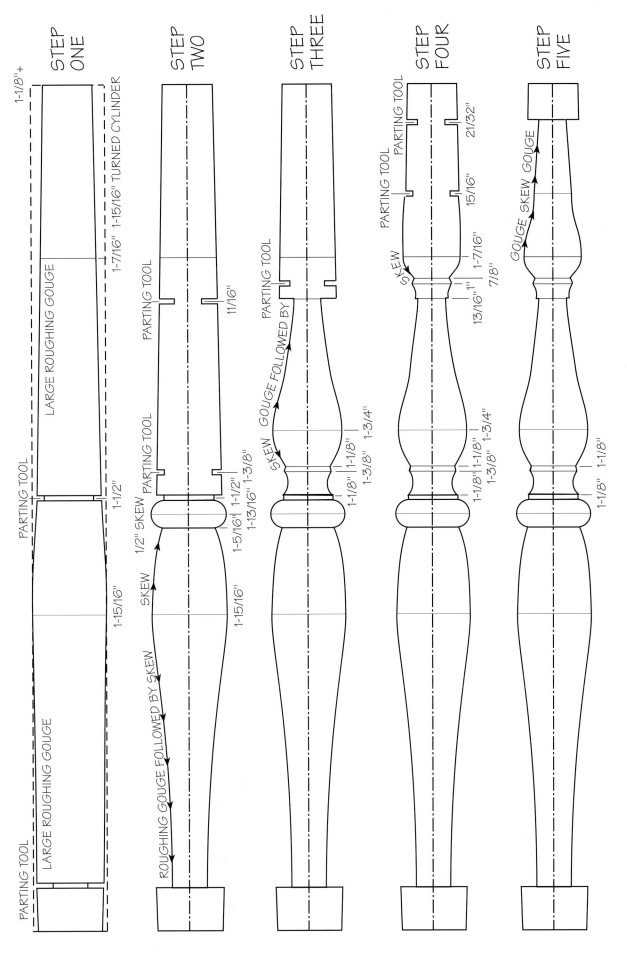

Fig. 13.8. Steps for turning double-baluster legs

Comparing sets of leg angles as the seat mortises are reamed. The plank runs side to side on this wide, oval-shaped seat.

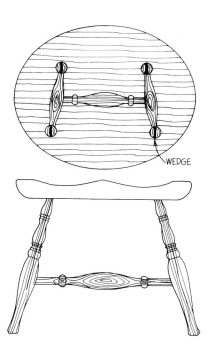

FIG. 13.9. Growth-ring orientation for sack-back seat, legs, stretchers, and wedges. Follow the orientation for the comb-back Windsor.

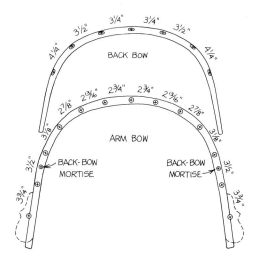

FIG. 13.10. Typical spindle spacing for the sack-back Windsor. Adjust to the bows on your chair.

adjust the major diameter of the side stretchers to match the diameter of the cone at the intersection line where the stretcher mortises are bored. The taper for the tenons on the leg and arm-support turnings should match your reamer. This may require modifying the dimensions in the plans.

Assemble the stool section of the chair following the directions in Chapter 8. Because the wide seat has grain running from side to side, growth-ring orientation for the legs is from front to back (fig. 13.9). Growth-ring orientation for the side and medial stretchers is the same as for the bow-back Windsor. Wedges for the leg tenons must be perpendicular to the seat grain. Trim the tenon protrusions on the seat and the bottoms of the legs. On my sack-back the seat drops 1/2 inch from front to back.

FITTING THE ARM BOW

The arm bow will be sufficiently dry in two or three days if it has been kept in a suitable drying environment. If the bend is springy, clamp the bow to a 1 by 3 board. Use the arm-bow holding fixtures described in Chapter 8 to support the arm bow above the seat. Be careful in selecting the exact placement. The back section of the arm bow is offset from the center spindle location by 13 degrees from vertical. The bow should also be symmetrical, viewed from above. Clamp the bow securely to the holding fixtures.

With the bow in place, you can begin to space the borings for the arm supports and spindles. Since every bow is slightly different, use the suggested arm-bow spacing in figure 13.10 as a starting guide. For a visual check on the spacing, tape straight wires or thin dowels against the inner edge of the arm bow. Use the spacing for mortises in the seat as shown in the plan. You also need to consider the location for the add-on hand pieces as you work out the spindle and arm-support spacing. The mortise in the hand piece is approximately centered in the wide section opposite the peaked triangle on the outer side. Remember that the arm bow has not been cut to length. Pencil Xs at the mortise centers.

Once you've determined spacing for the arm support and

spindles, you're ready to glue the hand blocks to the arm bow. Before removing the bow from the fixtures, pencil positioning tick marks on the arm and fixtures. The hand blocks should be about 1/16 inch thicker than the arm bow. Secure one hand block and one end of the arm bow side by side in a bench vise with both surfaces to be joined facing up. Use a sharp block plane to joint the common faces. Take very thin shavings. Stop planing when the surfaces of both pieces form a flat, common plane. Check the joint by pivoting the hand piece 180 degrees. (The inner arris of the hand block and arm bow during planing remain together as the two pieces are positioned side by side.)

Check the joint for a tight fit. The planing does not have to be absolutely square, but the two pieces must fit together perfectly. Plane again if the joint is not acceptable. This glue joint is subjected to considerable pressure during reaming, fitting, and the useful life of the chair. This is a long grain to long grain glue joint, which will be as strong as a solid piece of wood if it is done correctly.

After jointing, glue and clamp the square hand blocks to the arms. If you use yellow glue, prime both surfaces with a thin coat of glue, wait five to ten minutes, then apply another coat of glue to one of the surfaces. If you use epoxy, slightly roughen both surfaces with sandpaper.

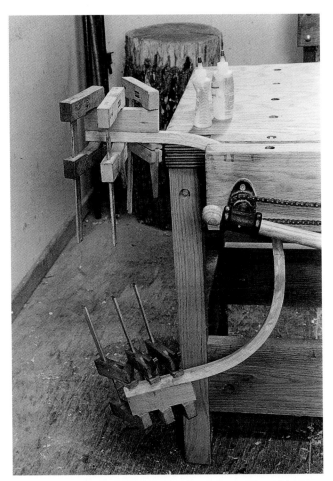

Gluing hand pieces to the arm bow

Polyurethane glue is also a good choice, especially if the wood is still slightly wet. After clamping, check to be sure that the left and right hand blocks are in the same plane.

Clamp the arm bow back onto the holding fixtures. Match up the tick marks.

BORING THE ARM-SUPPORT AND SPINDLE MORTISES

The spindle and arm-support mortises in the arm bow are 7/16 inch in diameter. (Do not bore the angled back-bow mortises until you've dry fitted the arm bow in place.) Use a bit brace with a standard auger bit, or a hand-held electric drill with a bit such as a powerbore or a forstner. Stop boring when the lead begins to break through the bottom of the bow. Remove the bow and back bore into the mortises. You can prevent tearout with an electric drill by temporarily clamping a piece of scrap wood to the bottom of the bow. Aim the drill at the corresponding mortise locations on the seat. (You'll appreciate assistance in aiming the drill.)

If you didn't bore the mortises in the seat before you assembled the stool, you have two choices for boring them now. The spindle mortises in the seat are 1/2 inch in diameter and 1 inch deep. The arm-support mortises are bored 3/8 inch in diameter, and then reamed to fit the tapered end of the arm supports. Your choices are to: (1) Use arm-bow mortises paired with corresponding seat mortise centers to determine sighting lines on the seat and resultant boring angles; remove the arm bow from the holding fixtures and bore the seat mortises using a bevel gauge and try square as guides; or (2) bore through the arm-bow mortises with the bow secured in place by the holding fixtures. For this method, you need extra-long drills or a drill extension. (A standard spade-bit extension will mate to a powerbore bit.) You will need to remove the drill from the drill chuck for each mortise in order to thread the drill shank up through the arm bow. (This is necessary because the 1/2-inch seat mortises are larger than the 7/16-inch arm-bow mortises.) The beauty of this method is that you aim straight through the positioned arm-bow mortises to the seat mortises. It's all done by eye—no boring to numeric angles or alignment with bevel gauges.

To bore and ream mortises in the seat and arm bow for the arm supports, first determine boring sight lines by aligning a plumb bob with the centers of the arm-support mortises in the seat and bow. Use a bevel gauge and protractor to record the resultant boring angles.

Remove the arm bow from the holding fixtures, and unclamp the fixtures from the seat.

Ream the seat and arm-bow mortises, using the appropriate tenons of the arm supports to check for fit and direction. (Designate left and right arm supports, and make tick marks for orientation.)

TEST FITTING THE ARM BOW AND FINISHING THE HANDS

Test fit the arm supports to the mortises in the seat and arm bow. Make sure that the hands are at the same height and in alignment with each other. The back of the bow should be 1/2 inch lower than the arm bow at the hands. Also check to see if the arm supports line up with each other viewed from the side, and if they are symmetrical viewed from the front of the chair.

This is a good time to finish the hands (see fig. 13.11). Plane the faces of the hand blocks flush with the upper and lower surfaces of the arm bow. Locate the hands so that the arm-support mortise is in line with the peak of the V-shape at the side. Flip the pattern over for drawing the curve on the inside straight section of the arm bow. Cut the outline with a coping saw or band saw. Clean up the sawed outline with a spokeshave, chisel, and fine-cut rasp.

Chamfer the arris around the upper surface of the hands, using a chisel and a half-round file. Remove no more than 1/16 inch from the upper face and sides. On the bottom arris, chamfer about 1/4 inch into the face, and 1/8 inch up the sides of the hands.

FINISHING THE SPINDLES

You're now almost ready to bore and fit the back bow to the arm bow. Finish and dry fit the central back spindle first. Having it in place helps to support and locate the back bow.

You'll finish the spindles in several steps. They must be thoroughly dry, so that they will not shrink after the chair is assembled. Finish only the center spindle now. Finish the others when the back bow is fitted to the arm bow.

You can shave, file, and sand the 1/2-inch diameter by 1-inch tenon at the spindle base to shape or you can use a tenon former of some sort. Possibilities include a hollow auger, rounding plane, or a dowel/tenon cutter designed for use with a drill press. For the sack-back in the photos I used a drill press–style tenon cutter, chucked to a standard bit brace. Be sure that the tenon cutter matches the hole made by your boring tool. (Remember that standard auger bits are 1/64 inch oversized.)

With most of these tenon cutters you need to preform a chamfer at the tenon end, so that the spindle can enter the cutting part of the tool. Make it with a cone-shaped dowel pointer or a coarse file. Put the spindle flat in your workbench vise, so that it is level, and use a line level to check for level with the bit brace. Cutting the tenon this way takes just a few seconds.

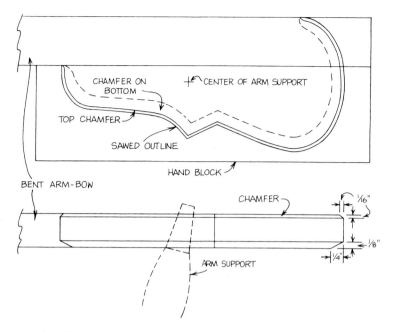

FIG. 13.11. Drawing at 1:2 scale for shaping the hand pieces

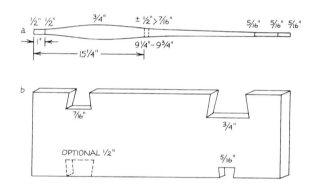

FIG. 13.12. Finishing the dry spindles: *a*, dimensions for the long, back spindles; *b*, a go/no-go dry-spindle gauge

To finish the spindles, make a go/no-go sizing gauge from a thin piece of dry hardwood with 5/16-inch, 7/16-inch, 1/2-inch, and 3/4-inch openings (see fig. 13.12). Use it to test the dimensioned sections of the spindles for correct size.

Put the arm bow in place, using the turned and fitted arm supports and the rear (center) bow-holding fixture. Take measurements for each spindle from the seat plank to the bottom of the arm bow. If everything fits correctly, there will be 1/2-inch variation. The lengths range from 8-3/4 inches for the end spindles to 8-1/4 inches for the center back spindles. Add 1 inch for the depth of the mortises in the seat.

Most of the remaining spindle work involves spokeshaving and sanding. The major diameter of the bulge is 5-1/4 inches above the end of the spindles. Spokeshave the octagonal spindles to 3/4 inch in section at the bulge. Then shave the middle area to 1/2 inch in section. This should be 10-1/4 inches from the spindle base for the middle spindle—

Fitting the long spindles into slightly tapered mortises in the arm bow

but adjust this measurement to fit your chair. Then shave the tip of the spindle to 5/16 inch in section. (At this stage, the spindles are still longer than their trim lengths.)

Round the entire spindle. Take fine shavings, then sand with 80- and 120-grit paper. (You can leave spokeshave flats as an option.) Pencil a ring around the center spindle 10-1/4 inches above the bottom end; adjust the measurement as necessary for your arm bow.

Use a 7/16- or 1/2-inch-diameter rat-tail rasp to ream the bottom of the center spindle mortise in the arm bow. The opening for the mortise should approach 1/2 inch in diameter, while the upper end of the mortise remains at the bored diameter, 7/16 inch. Smear some pencil lead into the reamed hole. Try fitting the upper end of the spindle up through the bow. Rotate the spindle to transfer pencil lead to the heavy sections of the spindle. Remove the spindle. Spokeshave or sand the spindle at the heavy sections. You can also do more reaming with the rat-tail rasp. Look for shiny places in the hole that require more work. Test fit again. Repeat the fitting procedure until the spindle fits up to the 10-1/4-inch pencil ring.

Fit the center spindle into the seat plank. If necessary, rotate the spindle so that it appears plumb when viewed from the front of the chair. (You can take some curvature out of the spindle by bending it across your thigh.) Lower the arm bow over the spindle and onto the arm supports. Check to be sure that the arm bow fits the spindle at the correct height.

You can finish the lower half of the other spindles now or later on, after fitting the back bow to the arm bow.

BORING AND FITTING THE BACK BOW

Boring and fitting the tapered back bow tenons to the arm-bow mortises on a sack-back is one of the most challenging tasks in making any Windsor chair. I'll tell you

how I do this, along with a few specifications. However, the bows of every chair are different; you'll have to think this through for the chair that you are making.

Begin by holding the center of the back bow against the tip of the center spindle, which is fitted to the seat and arm bow. The bow height can vary. I like the space between the arm bow and back bow to be slightly longer than the space between the arm bow and the seat plank. Use a spring clamp to secure the back bow against the center spindle.

The ends of the back bow intersect the arm bow between the first and second short spindles. Mark the location on the arm bow. Set the angle and height of the bow to your preference. Pencil the boring sight line on the arm bow and record the resultant boring angle. (On my sack-back in the photos, the back bow is 50 degrees from the arm bow.) Check the measurement across the arm bow and back bow. During fitting, the back bow will protrude about 3/4 inch through the arm bow. Pencil cutoffs for the ends of the back bow.

Remove the back bow. Bore 3/8-inch holes in the arm bow with the bow in place, or clamp the arm bow to your workbench—whichever makes you less nervous. Use a reamer or rat-tail rasp to taper the mortise.

Cut the back bow to the trim length. Taper the back bow ends with a drawknife and spokeshave. You can modify the effective distance across the bow ends by locating the tips of the tapers to either side of the original bow center (fig. 13.13). You have a rough inch of slack for making adjustments in the distance across the bow tips. The included taper angle should match the angle of your reamer. The fitted section of the bow tenons should have straight sides.

Use the smeared pencil-lead technique to test fit the back-bow ends to the tapered mortises in the arm bow. Adjust the tenons or mortises in gradual increments.

FIG. 13.13. How shaping the ends of the back bow can also modify the distance across the bow ends

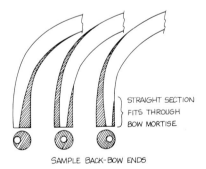

STRAIGHT SECTION FITS THROUGH BOW MORTISE

SAMPLE BACK-BOW ENDS

SPACING THE SPINDLES

Locating the spindle spacing through the back bow is partially a matter of personal taste. From a front view, you can choose to make the spindles look straight or flare to the sides. If the back bow is not very closely aligned with the arm bow, the spindles may require bending. (Bent spindles are part of the American sack-back tradition, but they are not found on English double hoop-back Windsors.)

Preparing to bore spindle mortises in the back and arm bows. The board clamped across the arm bow prevents the hand pieces from twisting out of alignment.

To space straight spindles, locate centers on the back bow that line up with the spindle holes in the seat and arm bow. If you want to try other spacing, place the spindles upside down in their respective seat mortises. Use masking tape to secure the spindles against the arm and back bows. You can also use thin commercial dowels or pieces of stiff straight wire, which allow you to experiment with the visual effect of curved spindles, in addition to being useful for aligning boring points on the upper surface of the back bow.

From a front view, the arrangement should look symmetrical. (Sometimes the spacing must be jiggled off perfect symmetry for appearance. This can be the case if the bows or arm supports are not perfectly aligned. Careful fudging can hide mistakes.) When viewed from the side, corresponding spindles on both sides of the chair should appear parallel.

Pencil centers for boring spindle mortises through the back bow. Bore these 5/16 inch in diameter. I suggest using the "chicken method" for boring the outside spindle mortises (see Chapter 9).

Finish the full set of spindles. Individually fit all spindles to their correct marks on the arm bow. Then do a partial assembly, with the spindles set through the arm-bow mortises and into the seat mortises. Fit the back-bow tenons into the arm-bow mortises, but insert only the center (previously fitted) spindle to the back bow. (For now, the other spindles will extend above the back bow.) Use a pencil to mark the assembly length at the tips of all the spindles, about 1/2 inch above the back bow.

Break down the arm/back assembly. Trim the spindles to length. Chamfer the spindle ends. Fit all the spindles to their mortises in the back bow.

ASSEMBLY AND FINISHING

To try a full test assembly, leave the arm supports in place in the seat mortises. Fit the back-bow tenons into the arm bow. Insert the full set of spindles through the bottom of the arm bow. Then wiggle and twist the tips of the spindles up into the back bow. With the exception of the arm supports, you have the complete back assembly in one unit.

Set the hand mortises of the arm bow over the arm supports. Then begin pulling the bottom of the spindles down into their respective mortises in the seat. Some will require vigorous twisting. (I have found this procedure to be easier than beginning by inserting the spindles into the seat, which also works.)

When everything fits, make alignment and depth tick marks for all the parts. Number the spindles and their mortises if you haven't done this already. Pencil the tips of the spindles and ends of the back bow indicating kerfs for the wedges. Pencil similar notations on both ends of the arm supports. The spindle kerfs must be perpendicular to the fiber direction on the back bow.

Disassemble everything. Saw wedge kerfs in both tenons of the arm supports, the back-bow tenons, and spindle tips.

Begin the final assembly by gluing the arm supports into the seat mortises. Brush glue into all the mortises in the arm bow, and onto the tenons and into the kerfs in the ends of the back bow. Fit the back bow to the arm bow. Put glue on the tip ends of the short (side) spindles and fit these to the arm bow, aligning tick marks. Fit the long spindles through the arm bow. Brush glue on their tip ends and fit the long spindles' ends to the back bow. Brush glue in all the seat spindle mortises and on the tenons at the base of all the spindles. Fit the entire arm/back assembly to the seat.

When everything is in place, examine the assembly to make sure that the arm bow is properly seated to the spindles (at the correct height and slope) and that it's symmetrical when viewed from the front of the chair. Then check the side view to see if the ends of the arm bow are in line with each other.

The final test assembly. Put the spindle/bow unit together; then fit the base of the spindles into the seat mortises.

Begin wedging by securing both ends of the arm supports. Next, wedge the center spindle and the tenons of the back bow. Then wedge the ends of the other spindles.

To finish the chair, follow the procedure used for the bow-back Windsor. One small detail that I like is leaving about 1/2 inch of back bow tenon protruding on the bottom of the arm bow.

CHAPTER 14

American Windsor:
Comb-Back Armchair

The American comb-back Windsor, an elegant and regal armchair

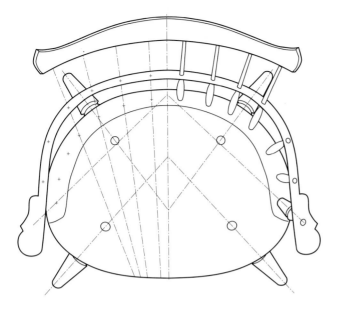

FIG. 14.1. Plan view

Leg Angles (in degrees from 90) for the Comb-Back Armchair				
	Rake	**Splay**	**Sighting**	**Resultant**
Front	14	13	47.2	18
Rear	17	13	52.9	21

Scale: 1:8

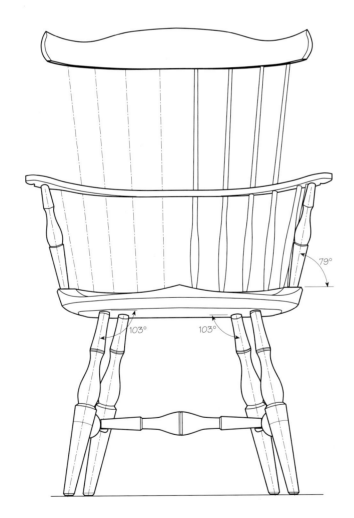

FIG. 14.2. Front view

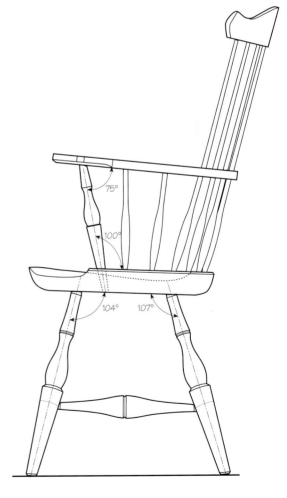

FIG. 14.3. Side view

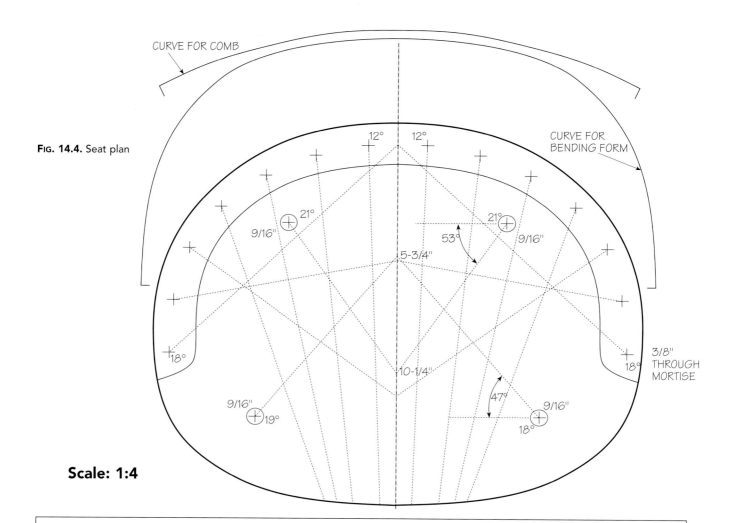

FIG. 14.4. Seat plan

CURVE FOR COMB

CURVE FOR BENDING FORM

3/8" THROUGH MORTISE

Scale: 1:4

Materials List: Comb-Back Armchair

Number of Pieces	Description	Rived Dimensions	Shaved Green Dimensions	Finish Dimensions
1	Seat plank	(sawed)	2-1/4" x 16-1/2" x 21-1/2"+	1-7/8" x 16" x 21-1/4"
1	Arm bow	1-1/4" x 1-1/2" x 50"+	3/4" x 1"	11/16" x 15/16"
4	Legs	2-1/2" sq x 22" rived or 2-1/4" sq x 22" sawed	2" dia (cone and vase pattern)	Natural shrinkage
2	Side stretchers	2-1/2" sq x 16" rived or 2-1/4" sq x 16" sawed	1-7/8" (major diameter)	Natural shrinkage
1	Medial stretcher	2-1/2" sq x 18" rived or 2-1/4" sq x 18" sawed	2" (major diameter)	Natural shrinkage
2	Arm supports	1-3/4" sq x 14"	1-1/2" (major diameter)	Natural shrinkage
1	Comb*	1-1/4" x 4" x 30"	1" x 3-1/2" x 22"	Natural shrinkage
4	Side spindles	1-1/4" sq x 12"	1" dia	7/8" dia
8	Back spindles**	1-1/4" sq x 22" +	1" dia	7/8" dia
2	Hand blocks	(sawed)		3/4" x 2" x 6"
12	Wedges			As required

* For a sawed comb, use a piece of air-dried hardwood 3-1/2 inches thick, 4 inches wide, and 22 inches long.

** The long back spindles can be extended to 28 inches in length.

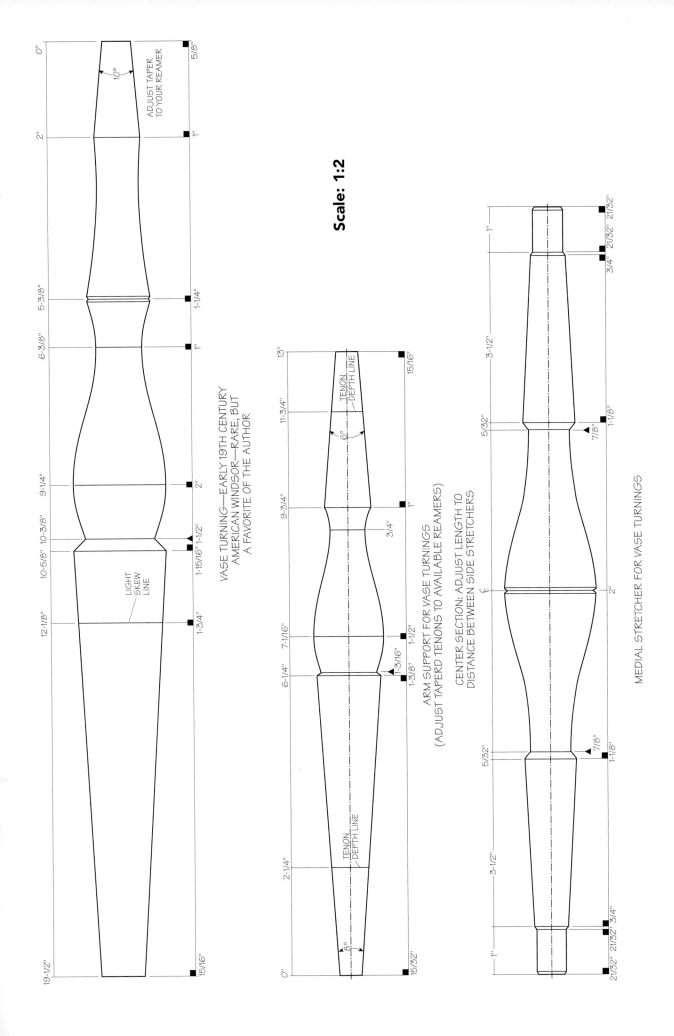

Scale: 1:2

VASE TURNING—EARLY 19TH CENTURY
AMERICAN WINDSOR—RARE, BUT
A FAVORITE OF THE AUTHOR

ARM SUPPORT FOR VASE TURNINGS
(ADJUST TAPERD TENONS TO AVAILABLE REAMERS)

CENTER SECTION: ADJUST LENGTH TO
DISTANCE BETWEEN SIDE STRETCHERS

MEDIAL STRETCHER FOR VASE TURNINGS

Fig. 14.5. Patterns for vase turnings

235

The most regal of all Windsors, American or English, the comb-back armchair is almost a throne. The wide, oval seat, similar to the sack-back's, is even wider and somewhat deeper. The English variation of the comb-back is known as a high-back.

BEFORE YOU BEGIN: A LOOK AT STYLE AND CONSTRUCTION

The comb-back Windsor shown in the plans and photos has a rather low backrest and comb. You can easily extend the backrest height simply by lengthening the center spindles. With only a slight amount of spindle flare, my comb-back is a conservative interpretation of the style. You can easily spread the spindles for a more dramatic appearance; you would of course also lengthen the comb to accommodate the increased flare. But if you do this, be sure to maintain a nice-looking overhang at the ends of the comb. You also may choose to deepen the seat farther, following the suggestions in Chapter 13 on the sack-back.

Construction is basically the same as the sack-back. The back spindles are longer and therefore a bit heavier in my version of this chair. This comb-back has the hybrid cone-and-vase turning pattern, but you could instead use the fancy double-baluster pattern (as seen on the sack-back), or the simpler double-bobbin (bamboo) pattern.

Detail of the oval seat and vase turning pattern used by the author

CONSTRUCTION NOTES

You can bend the comb from a riving or saw it from a single piece of air-dried timber. I made the chair in the photo with a bent comb. A sawed comb will have a more interesting grain pattern and can be made from figured wood, or less perfect wood than that required for bending. I suggest sawing the comb if you plan on using a natural finish. A bent comb requires less wood and is considerably stronger. You can make a special bending jig using multiple layers of 3/4-inch plywood laminated together, with a radius chosen to suit your chair (see fig. 14.6).

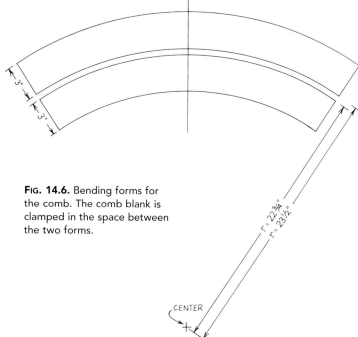

FIG. 14.6. Bending forms for the comb. The comb blank is clamped in the space between the two forms.

To make a bent comb, rive the blank considerably longer than the trim length to make bending easier and more symmetrical. Shave the comb to square dimensions. Steam the comb blank for a full hour. Bending the comparatively short, wide comb blank is challenging. Try to have help and a good selection of heavy-duty clamps on hand.

Details for shaping the comb ends appear in figure 14.7. Shape the outline with a saw or drawknife. The design for

FIG. 14.7. Details for finishing the comb

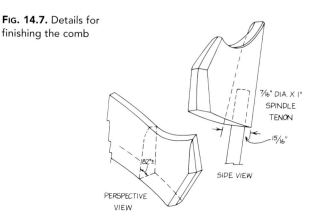

236

the flared comb ears is a matter of personal taste. Chamfer the face of the comb, so that it slopes from the base. Round the upper part of the face, leaving a 3/8-inch flat along the crest. Shave a 1/16-inch-wide chamfer on the back arris of the crest. The center of the comb is shaped with an unobtrusive convex curvature. The bottom of the comb is flat and straight.

The long upper back spindles and comb make this chair structurally weaker than the sack-back Windsor. Necessary strength comes from making thicker spindles (fig. 14.8), which in turn require a slightly heavier bow. (Some Windsor comb-backs have thin, bendable spindles; I believe that a

chair should give an impression of adequate strength, combined with graceful lines.) The spindle tenons in the seat can be enlarged to 9/16 or 5/8 inch in diameter.

Construction procedures for the comb-back stool and the arm-bow section of the back are identical to those for the sack-back. Spacing for spindle mortises in the arm bow appear in figure 14.9. Fitting the comb to the ends of the extended spindles is explained in Chapter 8 on the stick Windsor.

Be sure to leave an adequate comb overhang past the end spindles. (This chair looks bad with a short, chintzy comb.)

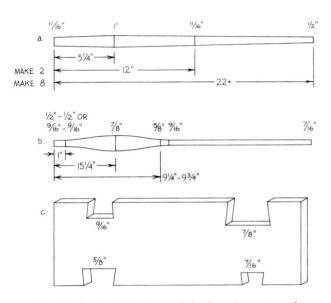

FIG. 14.8. Spindle details for the comb-back: *a*, dimensions of spindles shaved green; *b*, dimensions of finished, dry spindles; *c*, go/no-go gauge for sizing dry spindles

Detail of the arm supports, bow, spindles, and comb. Note the spindle swellings below the arm bow.

FIG. 14.9. Suggested spacing for spindle mortises in the comb-back arm bow

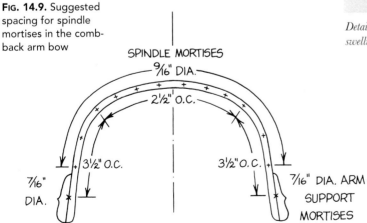

CHAPTER 15

American Windsor:
Continuous-Arm Chair

The continuous-arm Windsor, at home in period and contemporary furniture settings

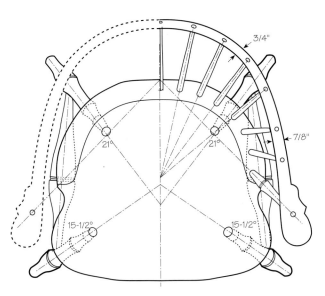

FIG. 15.1. Plan view

Scale: 1:8

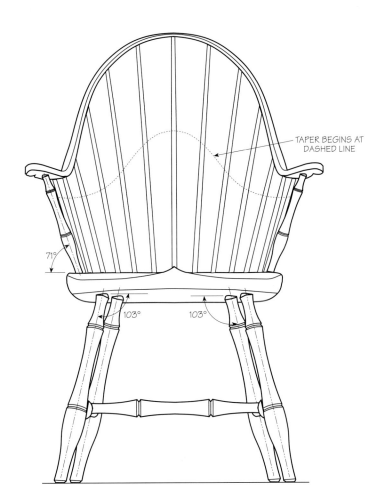

TAPER BEGINS AT
DASHED LINE

FIG. 15.2. Front view

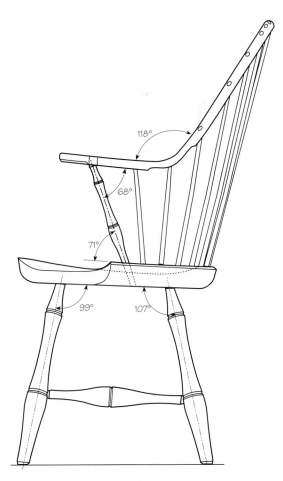

FIG. 15.3. Side view

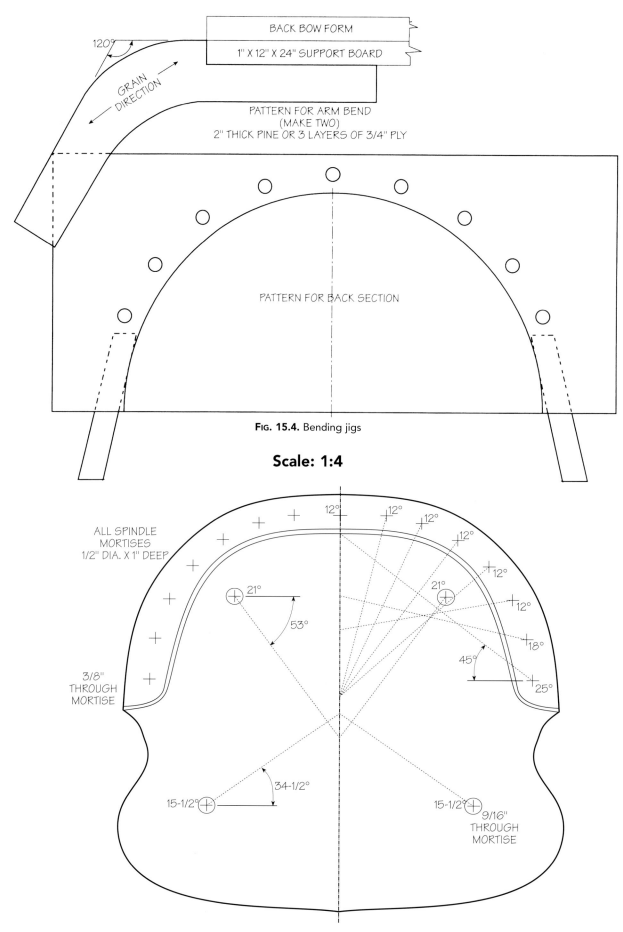

BACK BOW FORM

1" X 12" X 24" SUPPORT BOARD

120°

GRAIN DIRECTION

PATTERN FOR ARM BEND
(MAKE TWO)
2" THICK PINE OR 3 LAYERS OF 3/4" PLY

PATTERN FOR BACK SECTION

Fig. 15.4. Bending jigs

Scale: 1:4

ALL SPINDLE
MORTISES
1/2" DIA. X 1" DEEP

3/8"
THROUGH
MORTISE

12° 12° 12° 12° 12° 12° 18°

21° 21°

53°

45° 25°

34-1/2°

15-1/2° 15-1/2° 9/16"
THROUGH
MORTISE

Fig. 15.5. Seat plan

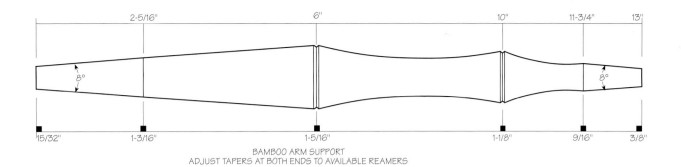

BAMBOO ARM SUPPORT
ADJUST TAPERS AT BOTH ENDS TO AVAILABLE REAMERS

Fig. 15.6. Pattern for optional arm support. This turning is not used on the bow-back Windsor side chair. It is included here because it is the appropriate design if you make a Windsor armchair using bamboo turnings.

Scale: 1:2

Materials List: Continuous-Arm Chair

Number of Pieces	Description	Rived Dimensions	Green Dimensions	Dry Size
1	Seat plank	(sawed)	2-1/4" x 19-3/4" wide x 18" deep	1-7/8" x 19-1/4" wide x 17-1/2" deep
1	Bow	1-1/4" x 1-1/2" x 62"+	13/16" sq x 62"	(Refer to fig. 15.6.)
4	Leg blanks	2-1/2" sq x 22" rived or 2" sq x 22" sawed	1-3/4" (major diameter)	Can be same
2	Side stretchers	2-1/2" sq x 17-1/2" rived or 2" sq x 17-1/2" sawed	1-3/4" (major diameter)	Can be same
1	Medial stretcher	2" sq x 18" rived or 1-5/8" sq x 14-1/2" sawed	1-5/16" (major diameter)	Can be same
2	Arm supports	2" sq x 14-1/2" rived or 1-5/8" sq x 14-1/2" sawed	1-5/16" (major diameter)	Can be same
2	Spindles	3/4" sq x 13"	9/16" > 7/16" dia	1/2" > 3/8"
2	Spindles	3/4" sq x 14"	9/16" > 7/16" dia	1/2" > 3/8"
2	Spindles	3/4" sq x 18"	9/16" > 3/8"	1/2" > 5/16"
2	Spindles	3/4" sq x 22"	9/16" > 3/8"	1/2" > 5/16"
2	Spindles	3/4" sq x 23"	9/16" > 3/8"	1/2" > 5/16"
3	Spindles	3/4" sq x 24"	9/16" > 3/8"	1/2" > 5/16"
2	Hand blocks			3/4" x 2" x 6"
21	Wedges			As required

Leg Angles (in degrees from 90) for the Continuous-Arm Chair

	Rake	Splay	Sighting	Resultant
Front	9	13	34.5	15.6
Rear	17	13	52.9	21

The most dramatic of all Windsors, yet a classic that harmonizes with period or contemporary furnishings, the continuous-arm chair represents a high point in the development of the American Windsor style. Almost certainly an American original, the style was also made in the village of Yealmpton on the southwest coast of England as early as 1820.

BEFORE YOU BEGIN: A LOOK AT STYLE AND STRATEGY

In my opinion, the clean stylistic elements of the continuous arm's back support seem most compatible with simple but carefully proportioned turnings. The plans show my version of this chair with bamboo turnings. Of course, a continuous-arm Windsor with double-baluster turnings and other fancy details can be very impressive.

Constructing a continuous-arm Windsor is basically the same as making the tutorial bow-back. The chair offers three special challenges: Bending the bow, setting the bow at comfortable and good-looking angles for the backrest and arm supports, and boring the bow mortises for the steep spindle angles at the shoulder sections of the backrest.

Not surprisingly, all three challenges deal with the spectacular continuous-arm bow. I'll explain how to shape, bend, and set the bow. (I've already discussed boring steep bow mortises in Chapter 9 on making a bow-back Windsor.) I won't withhold any secrets about the bow, but I cannot assure your success. Results with the continuous-arm bow depend more on wood-bending quality than on any other factor.

This Windsor offers a chairmaker a variety of traditional design options to consider. The chair in the plans has an unusually large seat. If your seat plank is undersized, you could still make the chair with a seat up to 2 inches narrower and 1 inch shallower. You can also add a tail brace, although it's not necessary for strength with this design. I show the chair with a simple round bow, but you can also make a D-section bow that creates a comfort-enhancing flat surface in plane with the back support. You can shape the spindles with an attractive midsection bulge, and the styling of the hand pieces is always up for interpretation.

MAKING THE BOW

Refer to the drawings in figure 15.4 for details of the special bending form you'll need. Attach the arm sections of the bending form to the back section with wood screws. The arm sections are divergent from one another. (The dramatic welcoming appearance of the chair is seriously compromised if the arms are at right angles to the front of the seat.)

The continuous-arm bow is commonly made with straight ends, with hand pieces glued on after the bent arm has dried. Directions for making a one-piece bow are included in Chapter 13 on the sack-back Windsor. This bow requires wood that bends extremely well. A perfectly crafted and correctly steamed bow can fail during bending if the wood is not the best quality. Even wood that looks perfect may not hold up from the stresses of bending. I've successfully made continuous-arm bows with hickory, red and white oak, and ash, both green and air-dried. Hackberry has a reputation for being a very reliable bending species; I've not used it.

Bending the arms

The bow's triple curve creates a twist in the orientation of the bow surfaces: The upper plane across the back of the bow becomes the outer side of the bow at the armrests, and the face of the bow at the backrest turns into the upper planes of the armrests. Think this through carefully; the multiple bends can be confusing.

I usually orient the growth rings to bend with the elbow sections, since this is the area where the bend is the most

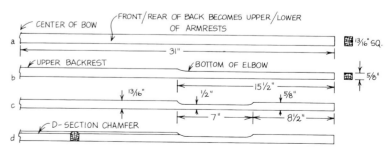

FIG. 15.7 Steps in shaping the continuous-arm bow. The hand pieces will be glued on after the bow is steamed, bent, and dried.

radical. But I've also bent continuous-arm bows with the growth rings parallel to the back curve. A flat-grain back section is appropriate if you add scratch-beaded decorative channels on the flat front of a D-section backrest. On a chair with a natural finish, I prefer to see the parallel growth rings and intercepted ray flecks on the back. (These are visual considerations that have nothing to do with bending performance.)

After riving the bow, trim the blank to 62 inches (see fig. 15.7). Do all shaping for thickness of the elbow and armrests on the bottom surface of the bow, beginning under the elbows. Shave the blank to 13/16 inches square *(a)*. Pencil a line around the midsection of the bow. Starting with a scooping cut that begins 15-1/2 inches from each end, shave the outside of the elbow and armrest to a thickness of 5/8 inch *(b)*. Then shave the elbow section to 1/2 inch thick, spaced from 15-1/2 inches to 8-1/2 inches from the ends *(c)*. For a D-section bow, leave the front surface of the bow flat. Shave chamfers 1/4 to 5/16 inch wide on the back arris of the bow, running them into the relieved elbow sections *(d)*. If you want a round-section backrest, chamfer the front arris of the bow beginning 15 inches from each end. Blend the beginning of the front chamfers into the original flats. Leave chamfers on the "D" or octagonal back section until after bending.

Re-mark the pencil line around the center of the bow, and mark bending arrows at the center to indicate the direction of the bend.

Clamp the bending form to your workbench. The extended arms overhang the front of the bench. You will need two to four bar clamps and several wooden cauls to secure the armrest sections of the bow to the bending form. Steam the bow blank for forty-five to sixty minutes. To bend the bow, you'll work with the back and bottom of the bow facing upward—the bend is made upside down. The relieved sections at the elbows face up when you set the bow into the bending form.

Wedge the center of the hot, steamed bow at the back of the form. Carefully pull one end of the bow around the large curve of the shoulder section of the bending form. Dowel and wedge the bow in place. (Help from an assistant is useful!) Secure the bow at the lower dowel and wedge on one side of the bending form. Use one hand to slowly push the arm section down and onto the armrest extension of the bending form. To help relieve stress on the outer surface of the bend, press your other hand against the outside of the bow at the bending area. Clamp the bow end in place against the arm extension. Be sure to insert a wooden caul between the bow and the swivel pad of the clamp.

Immediately begin bending the other end of the bow. Check to make sure that the entire bow is flat against the form, and in proper alignment on the armrest extensions. With green wood, you have several minutes to complete the operation. If you use air-dried wood, you must complete the bend within seconds.

Probably half of all attempted bends of continuous-arm Windsor bows result in some tension failure, that is, splintering on the outer surfaces of the bends. These failures usually occur at the outsides of the elbows, although they can occur on the shoulders. (When I'm teaching an advanced Windsor student, I'm always relieved to get past this hurdle!)

Minor tension failures are routinely repaired, even on chairs that get a natural finish. You have two choices with these repairs. You can immediately clamp or tape shallow tension splinters in place against the bow, then glue them with yellow glue after several days of drying. Or you can make a wet-wood repair with polyurethane glue, which is formulated to cure using wood moisture and appears to work as well as conventional repairs on dry wood.

CONSTRUCTION NOTES

The standard arm-bow holding fixtures (explained in Chapter 8) can't be used with the looping continuous-arm bow. Instead, bore and fit the arm supports and central back spindle while the seat blank is flat. The sighting line for the arm supports (which is 45 degrees) conveniently terminates at the gutter on the seat center line. The resultant boring angle is 25 degrees. The mortise diameter should be determined by the taper of your reamer. This is a through mortise; be sure to back bore to prevent tearout on the bottom side of the seat. Ream these mortises now, before the stool is assembled.

The center spindle mortise is 1/2 inch in diameter and 1 inch deep. It's bored at a resultant angle of 12 degrees.

Constructing the stool for the continuous-arm Windsor is exactly like making the bow-back in Chapter 9. Riving and shaping the spindles also follow the standard procedure. These are plain, straight spindles that taper to 3/8 inch (green) toward the tip. Make several extra spindles.

The turnings for the arm supports may require modifications at the tapered ends to match the included angle of your reamer.

FITTING THE BOW

You can begin fitting the bow two or three days after bending, but I prefer to wait until the bow turns loose from the bending form. If you have a green bow that's still springy, clamp the ends to a flat board, and then tie a loop of twine from the board to the center of the back bend. Use a stick to twist the twine loop tight enough to maintain the correct bend at the elbows. The clamped board securing the ends of the bow also prevents the hand sections from twisting out of plane during drying or storage.

Insert the arm supports and center spindle to their mortises in the seat. Use a spring clamp to hold the back of the bow in place against the center spindle. Adjust the height where the bow crosses the spindle so that the armrests slope downward several degrees relative to the plane of the seat. (You will have to secure the bow armrests to the sides of the arm supports.)

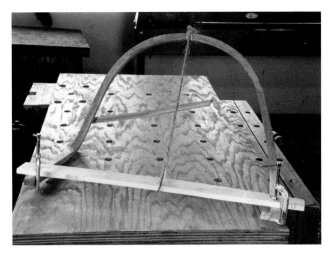

The dried arm bow, stored with a stick clamped across both ends to stop the hand areas from twisting out of plane, and to provide a tie-in for a toggle rope that holds the elbow bends in place

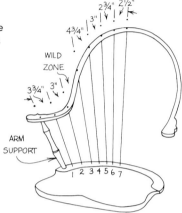

FIG. 15.8. Sighting lines and resultant angles for boring armrest mortises in the bow

FIG. 15.9. Suggested spindle spacing for the continuous-arm bow. Tape spindles (or straight wires or dowels) in position before settling on the arrangement.

Examine the chair from front and top views to see if the bow is centered. Check the placement from a side view to see if the armrests are parallel. Make adjustments as necessary.

Mark the spindle location on the bow when it's centered and at the right height. Use a bevel gauge to record the angle of the back section of the bow relative to the middle spindle. Bore a 5/16-inch hole in the bow for the center spindle. Finish the upper end of the center spindle, fitting the tip through the bow to the selected height. Set the bow and spindle in place on the chair seat.

Determine the position for the glue-on hand pieces. The arm-support tenons should come through the hand pieces across from the apex of the triangle on the sides. Glue the hand pieces to the sides of the bow ends. Plane the upper and lower surfaces flat.

Bore mortises for the arm support through the hand pieces. According to the plans, the sight line is 49.6 degrees from a connecting line between the left and right hand pieces (see fig. 15.8). The sighting angle for the arm-support mortises through the bow differs from the seat sighting angle because the armrests are not parallel to the surface of the seat. The resultant angle for boring is 28 degrees. Your angles may be different if your hand-piece centers are not 22-3/4 inches apart, or if your bow is at a different angle. The numbers in the plans are guidelines only. Ream and fit the hand-piece mortises to the arm supports. Saw out and shape the hand pieces.

Fit the bow to the arm supports and middle spindle. You now have a fairly rigid structure. If necessary, use twine to pull the armrest sections of the bow down onto the arm supports.

Lay out the spacing for the spindles, using figure 15.9 as a starting point. Tape spindles to the bow at the proposed spacing. (For more accuracy, use stiff straight wires or dowels instead of the real spindles.) Spacing for the third spin-

dle, at the steepest section of the bow, is treated variously. Some Windsor chairmakers leave a gap there; I prefer to bore a conventional through mortise, using a progression of twist bits that begins with a 1/8-inch hole, a process I described as the "chicken method" in Chapter 8. Another alternative is to bore a shallow pocket mortise from the bottom of the bow, just deep enough to hold the spindle in place; the joint is not structural.

Mortises for the two short spindles at the armrests are 3/8 inch in diameter, for the longer spindles, 5/16 inch. I prefer to bore the bow and seat mortises with the bow in place, using an extension for boring the 1/2-inch seat mortises. If you don't have a bit extension, you can record the sighting lines and resultant angles, then remove the bow for boring the seat mortises. The procedure for fitting the spindles is explained in Chapter 9.

Test assemble the entire bow/spindle unit. Observe the bow to make sure that the armrest sections are parallel and at the same height. Tick mark and number all the parts. Trim spindles to length, and saw kerfs for wedges in the arm supports and spindle tips.

During glue up, be sure to check the armrests from a side view. Twisted and out-of-plane armrests are the most common slipup in assembling a Windsor chair with arms.

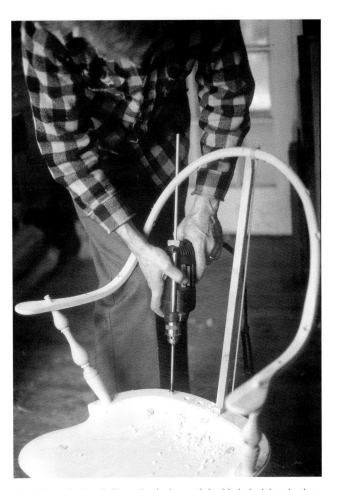

Dave Sawyer setting up to bore mortises for the arm supports

Dave Sawyer boring spindle mortises in the seat deck with the back bow in place

Dave Sawyer's continuous-arm Windsors during the final stages of test fitting

CHAPTER 16

American Windsor:
Sack-Back Settee

A Windsor settee—always an eye-catcher

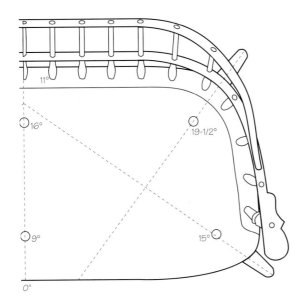

FIG. 16.1. 1/2 Plan view

Because of the width of the settee, this set of projections uses half plans for the top and front views.

Scale: 1:8

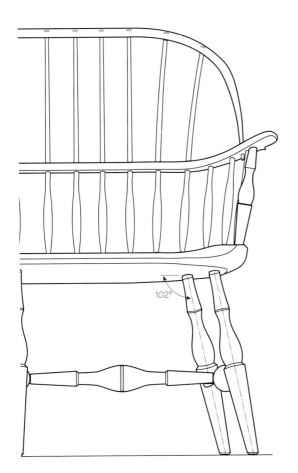

FIG. 16.2. 1/2 Front view

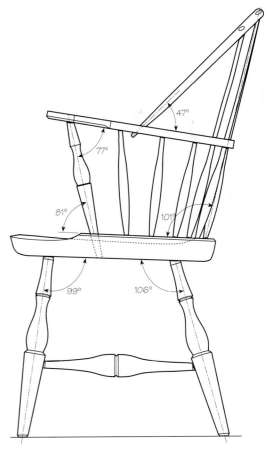

FIG. 16.3. Normal side view

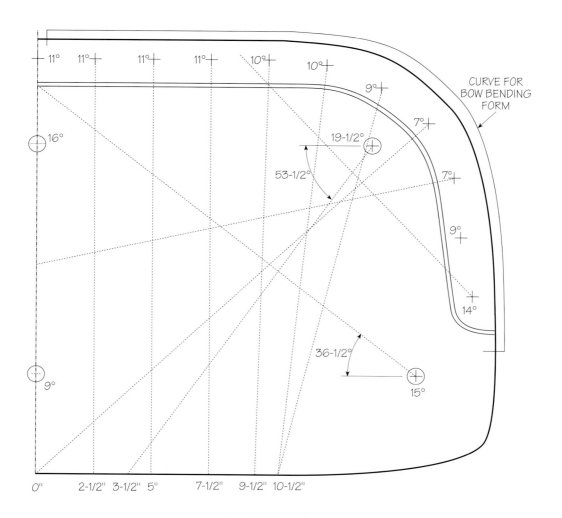

FIG. 16.4. Seat plan

Scale: 1:4

Materials List: Sack-Back Settee

Number of Pieces	Description	Rived Green Dimensions	Shaved/Turned/ Sawed Dimensions	Dry Dimensions
1	Seat plank	(sawed)	2-1/8" x 18-1/2" x 41"+	1-7/8" x 18" x 40-1/2"
1	Arm bow	1" x 1-1/4" x 67"+	11/16" x 15/16" x 67"	5/8" x 7/8" x 67"
1	Back bow	1" x 1" x 65"+	7/8" dia	13/16" dia
6	Leg blanks	2-1/2" sq x 22" rived or 2-/4" sq x 22"	1-15/16" dia	Natural shrinkage
2	Side stretchers (ends)	2-1/4" sq x 17" rived or 2" sq x 17" sawed	1-3/4" dia	Natural shrinkage
1	Center stretcher	2-1/2" sq x 17" rived or 2-1/4" sq x 17 sawed	2" dia	Natural shrinkage
2	Medial stretchers	2-1/2" sq x 18" rived or 2-1/4" sq sawed	2" dia	Natural shrinkage
2	Arm supports	1-3/4" sq x 14"	1-1/2" dia	Natural shrinkage
6	Spindles	1" sq x 12"	7/8" dia	3/4" dia
2	Spindles	1" sq x 21"	7/8" dia	3/4" dia
11	Spindles	1" sq x 22	7/8" dia	3/4" dia
2	Hand blanks			3/4" x 2" x 6"
29	Wedges			As required

Leg Angles (in degrees from 90) for the Sack-Back Settee

	Rake	Splay	Sighting	Resultant
Front corners	9	12	36.7	14.8
Rear corners	16	12	53.5	19.6
Front middle	9	0	90	9
Rear middle	16	0	90	16

Arm-Support Angles in the Seat (in degrees from 90) for the Sack-Back Settee

Rake	Splay	Sighting	Resultant
9	9	45	12.6

Size is the main difference between a settee, sometimes called a love seat, and any other Windsor—they're built in much the same way but take twice the time. Saddling a settee bench is time consuming; this might explain why many old settees were made with very shallow saddling.

The size or style of the settee is easy to modify. At 40-1/2 inches, this version is a comfortable length for two people, but the seat could be extended to 50 inches without adding another set of legs. Figure 20 inches of length per person seating capacity. Usually, each additional seating space requires an extra set of legs. Windsor settees have been made in lengths exceeding eight feet.

Most old settees were low-backs, but versions of the popular sack-back and continuous-arm Windsor styles were also made into settees. Although I'm partial to this sack-back version, continuous-arm settees are quite spectacular.

Making the sack-back settee is similar to making a sack-back armchair. Here are some tips and differences that you need to be aware of.

The long settee bows are a good place to start. These are usually made from extra-long rivings, but I see no reason why a settee bow shouldn't be spliced, especially on a painted chair—a low-angle scarf joint is just as strong as a single piece of wood. (This type of joint is commonly done on structural parts of wooden boats.) Use epoxy, polyurethane, or yellow glue. The joint should be in the straight part of the bow, but not close to the center.

The bows for this sack-back settee are about 6 inches longer than the capacity of my steam box. I could easily make a longer box, but for occasional use I make a temporary extension by taping a plastic bag around one end of the box. For a long settee, steam and bend one end of each bow at a time. Since the center section of a settee is straight, this double steaming method also eliminates the need for special bending forms.

The center legs have no side splay. Since their rake matches the corner legs, they are about 3/8 inch shorter than the corner legs. It follows that the resultant angles for boring the center-leg mortises in the seat will be different than the angles for the corner legs. Bore and fit all four corner legs to the seat before beginning on the center legs. Use the fitted corner legs as a visual guide for aligning the center legs. The chart of resultant angles in the Appendix will also be useful.

Level the bench when all legs are in place, but before you fit the stretchers. Use a common height (measured from a flat bench top) for boring the mortises of all the stretchers.

The center stretcher is mortised to accept tenons of medial stretchers from either side of the chair. This requires using tenons less than 1 inch long or enlarging the swelling in the center of the stretcher. I make the tenons 15/16 inch long, with the center swelling 2 inches in diameter.

Experiment with the spindle spacing—the critical visual factor in a Windsor settee—before committing to boring mortises.

When assembling the bench section of a settee, I recommend a step-at-a-time gluing procedure. Before you start, label and tick mark all parts for position. Kerf the tenon ends of legs to accept wedges from the upper side of the bench. Begin by gluing one leg to one side stretcher. Then glue the opposite leg onto the same stretcher. From there, progress down the length of the undercarriage, gluing and reassembling the entire unit for each joint of the assembly.

Experiment with the spindle spacing on the bows before boring any of the bow mortises. The arm-bow holding fixtures (see Chapter 8) work very nicely with the arm-bow section of the settee. (You may want to make an extra fixture, so that you have two for holding the long back section in place.) I bend the spindles toward the ends of the back bow just slightly; some sack-back settees are made with considerably more spindle side flare (see fig. 16.5).

To make and fit the spindles, follow the steps described for the sack-back armchair in Chapter 13.

Fig. 16.5. Suggested spacing for sack-back settee spindles. The triangular areas at the ends of the long spindles "run wild"; the spacing between the long spindles is critical. Be careful to align the short spindles at both ends of the arm bow.

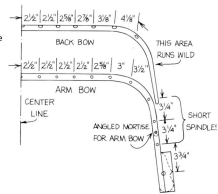

CHAPTER 17

English Windsor:
Double Hoop-Back Armchair

*The author's English-style Windsor combines
elements from several traditional styles.*

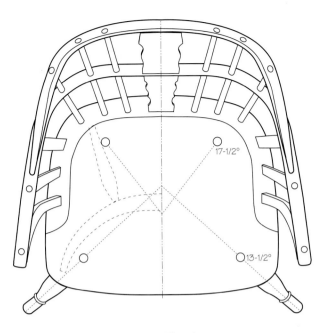

FIG. 17.1. Plan view

Scale: 1:8

FIG. 17.2. Front view

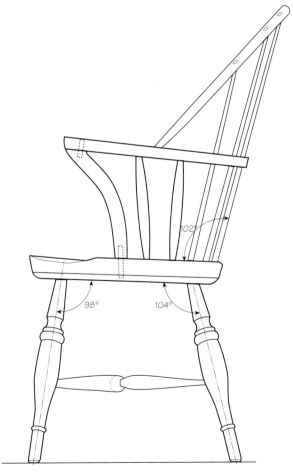

FIG. 17.3. Side view

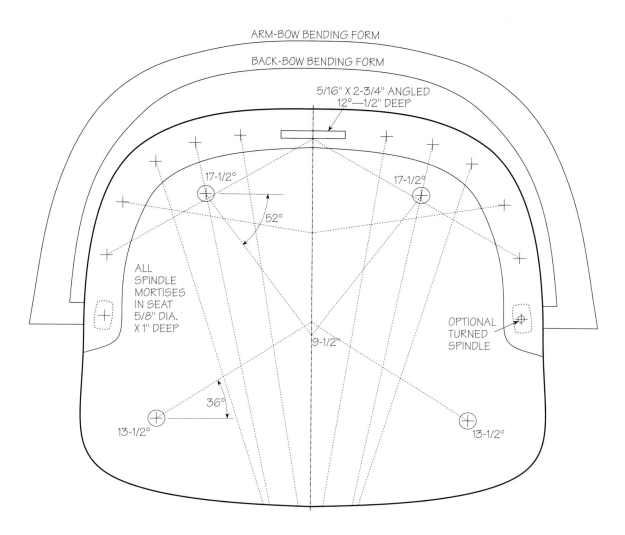

Fig. 17.4. Seat plan

Scale: 1:4

Scale: 1:2

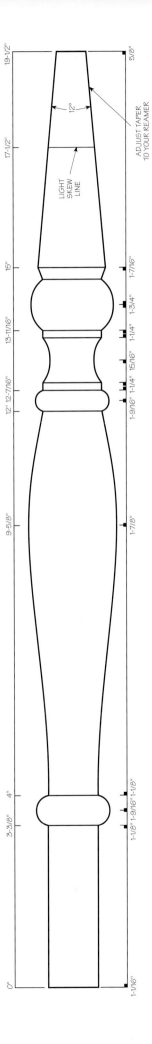

FIG. 17.5. Leg pattern for English ring-and-cove turnings

255

MATERIALS LIST: DOUBLE HOOP-BACK ARMCHAIR

Number of Pieces	Description	Rived Green Dimensions	Shaved Green Dimensions	Finish Dimensions
1	Seat plank	(sawed)	1-3/4" to 2" x 16-3/4" x 20-1/4"	1-5/8" to 1-7/8" x 16-1/2" x 20-1/4"
1	Back bow	1-3/4" sq x 50"+	1-1/8" x 1-1/4" x 45"+	Can be same
1	Arm bow	1-1/4" x 1-1/2" x 50"+	7/8" x 1-1/8" x 45"+	Can be same
4	Legs	2-1/2" sq x 22" rived (or) 2" sq x 22" sawn	1-7/8" major diameter	Can be same
2	Lateral stretchers	1-1/2" sq x 7"+	1-1/4" major diameter	Can be same
1	Crinoline stretcher	1-1/2" sq x 26"+	1-1/8" major diameter	Can be same
2	Ram's horn arm supports	1" x 1-1/2" x 13" rived (or) 1" x 2-1/2" x 12"+ sawed lumber	7/8" x 1-1/4" x 12"+	Can be same
4	Dowels			3/8" diameter
4	Short spindles	7/8" x 1-1/4" x 12"	5/8" x 7/8" x 12"	Can be same
6	Long spindles	7/8" sq x 21"	11/16" dia > 7/16" dia	5/8" dia > 3/8" dia
2	Splat blanks	n.a.	n.a.	Dressed 5/16" x 4" x 12"
16	Wedges	n.a.	n.a.	As required

Leg Angles (in degrees from 90) for the Double Hoop-Back Armchair

	Rake	Splay	Sighting	Resultant
Front	8	11	35.9	13.5
Rear	14	11	52.1	17.5

When I first began looking at English Windsors, it was almost impossible not to conclude that the American versions were superior. English Windsors appear less graceful and are certainly more quirky than their American counterparts. Their legs looked particularly strange, especially those with cabriole legs borrowed from Queen Anne furniture. On English Windsors the armrests end so abruptly they almost look sawed off. And I found the flat splat board in the center of the backrest in most cases jarring, especially those with fretwork that imitates a wagon wheel.

Not until I had the opportunity to spend some time in England did I begin to appreciate these traditional chairs. English Windsors are not made to a uniform standard of beauty. There are just too many styles, and too many variations of each. But I've discovered that many English Windsors have a sense of character lacking in the classic American styles. The differences are similar to comparing the slick perfection of Hollywood actors with the amazing array of characters in British movies. Like good friends, you must get acquainted with English Windsors before you can understand how wonderful these chairs can be.

I hope that the English-style Windsor in this chapter, which borrows traditional elements from a variety of English regional chairs and periods, will serve you as a satisfactorily pleasant introduction to the world of English Windsors.

BEFORE YOU BEGIN:
LOOKING AT ENGLISH WINDSORS

Perhaps the most prominent characteristic of English Windsors is the vertical back splat, a flat board fitted between the seat and back bows. Splats are found on some of the earliest English Windsors, always sawed with a decorative outline, often based on a vase or floral pattern. Usually, the interior of the splat is cut out to make a design, fretwork that can be the visual center of attraction of the chair. The inspiration for Windsor back splats most certainly derives from Queen Anne furniture, often considered the pinnacle of English furniture design.

The English-style Windsor in this chapter includes a splat, but I refrained from doing any interior fretwork. Instead, I selected a piece of cherry wood with an interesting figure. This is an example of where one's personal design taste becomes more important than following tradition. Actually, many English Windsors are made without a back splat, and the splats on very early English Windsors were often solid fruitwood panels without the fretwork.

More than a visual element, a back splat adds to the comfort of these chairs. One reason splats aren't found in American Windsors may be that they are not easy to make; they require a straight back section. As a contrast, the spindles of some American Windsors are slightly bent, with progressively more curvature toward the sides of the back bow.

The undercarriage of the English-style Windsor in this chapter is braced with a crinoline stretcher between the legs, as traditional on English Windsors as back splats, although "H" stretchers, like those found on most early American Windsors, are probably just as common. The crinoline style does a good job of stiffening the leg structure. The curved "cow's horn" harmonizes visually with the other curves of the chair, most notably the bows and outline of the seat.

The single-ring turning pattern used for the legs of my chair is seen on many English Windsors. There are infinite variations of this pattern and many other common turning styles.

English Windsors are built around a hardwood seat that is often thinner than the pine or poplar planks traditionally used for American Windsors. The shape is usually a rounded trapezoid, but a conservative version of a shield seat is also common. The Queen Anne influence dictates that the legs be mortised near the corners of the seat, where the plank is also thickest.

The bows on most English Windsors are considerably heavier than their American counterparts. One reason English Windsor bows look heavy is that they house the splat. More important, an English Windsor is supposed to look solid and stately.

The spindle mortises on English Windsor bows are usually blind joints rather than through mortises. Making tight blind mortises requires great precision and skill. (In some cases, wooden pins were driven through the bow to secure the spindles in place.) My chair does not abide by this custom. I don't find through joints with clearly visible wedges unaesthetic. They are certainly easier to make, and in most cases, they are stronger.

This chair also departs from English tradition with the lower than usual rake angle of its back bow, chosen for both appearance and strength. With the ends of the back bow mortised into the arm bow between the first and second short spindles, the rake angle is about 50 degrees. If you want to add an authentic detail to your version of this chair, locate the back-bow mortises farther back on the arm bow. This will require a different bending form, with a tight curve at the shoulders so that the ends of the bows are almost parallel with each other.

Compared to fine American Windsors, the front legs of a typical English Windsor have much less splay and rake in order to prevent their sticking out too far from the seat and getting in the way. In contrast, the rear legs of English Windsors often have more rake than their American counterparts. The contrast between the front and rear leg angles is a fine point in the design of these chairs.

Cabriole (Queen Anne) legs, though often identified with English Windsors, are actually fairly rare. Usually, these fancier Windsors combine two cabriole front legs with simple, turned back legs. The best examples look regal.

Using steel straps to bend the crinoline stretchers. The bent piece is considerably longer than the trim length of the stretcher.

Curved arm supports like those on the chair in this chapter are most often found on old English high-backs. These "ram's horn" arm supports are often damaged, repaired, or replaced on antique chairs that I've examined. Because of their curvature and angled position, they are difficult to attach to the seat and arm bow. The handholds at the ends of the arm bows of English Windsors are usually plain, almost stubby. In contrast, American Windsor chairmakers often concentrated their most elaborate ornamentation on this detail.

Most English Windsor chairs are stained, although some are finished with clear varnish. Some old chairs were painted; west-country chairs were often painted blue, green, or muddy red. The chair in this chapter was finished with an oil-varnish mixture, with paste wax for a top coat.

SELECTING MATERIALS

As you choose wood for your English-style Windsor, appearance should be a primary concern. My chair in the photos combines elm, red oak, and cherry. Gnarly grained elm is the prestige seat wood found in "best quality" English Windsors. Elm is chosen for its toughness—it almost never cracks—and for the wonderful grain patterns of flat-sawed elm boards. Oak, ash, yew, and sycamore are also used.

The seat is glued with the grain running side to side, using two carefully matched elm boards—one of two seats made from a mail-order elm plank 2 by 9 inches by 8 feet. The

wood was kiln dried and very hard. The bows are made from red oak. Elm, ash, and yew wood limbs are also traditional choices. The turnings are black cherry. Although beech, ash, and elm are more typical turning woods for English Windsors, fruitwoods (especially pear) and yew are found on many "better" English Windsors. The crinoline stretcher is red oak, selected for its bending quality. (On a newer version, I matched the crinoline-stretcher wood to the other turnings; all are cherry. I steamed the stretcher for one and a half hours, double the time for green wood, and used a bending strap. The straight-grained, air-dried cherry bent perfectly.)

Whether to use a crinoline stretcher or not is your option. Many English Windsors are made with conventional H-stretchers, and others use double-H stretchers. The double-H version, with two medial stretchers, is undoubtedly the strongest arrangement.

MAKING AN ENGLISH WINDSOR

Saddling the seat follows the procedures described in Chapter 8 on stick Windsors. Turning the rings on the legs requires concentration, but they are do-able by anyone who can make American double-baluster turnings. The leg tenons of English Windsors are usually, but not always, tapered. Bore mortises and fit the legs following procedures in Chapter 8.

Select a common height for boring the stretcher mortises. Determine the length of the crinoline stretcher by measuring between leg tangents at the mortise height (fig. 17.6). Measure the distance between the front legs at the tangent where the mortises will be bored. Add 1-7/8 inches for the two 15/16-inch-long tenons. You'll determine the lengths for the short lateral stretchers after fitting the crinoline stretcher to the front legs.

FIG. 17.6.
Crinoline-stretcher system. Make and fit the curved stretcher first, then take measurements for making the short lateral stretchers.

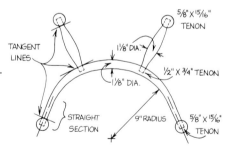

Bend the crinoline stretcher when it's octagonal in section, and 1-1/8 inches in thickness from end to end. Make the bending blank 12 to 15 inches longer than necessary. Don't pull the ends of the crinoline stretcher tight against the bending form. The divergent stretcher ends allow you to use the same bending form for chairs with a range of distances between the front legs.

Saw the crinoline stretcher to length. Taper the ends to 5/8 inch in thickness. Round the stretcher. Use a hollow auger or tenon former to make 5/8-inch diameter by 15/16-inch tenons at the ends. (You can also file and sand the tenons to shape.)

Bore mortises in the legs and fit the crinoline stretcher before turning the two short lateral stretchers. Measure the distance between the tangents of the crinoline stretcher and the rear posts. The tenon that is mortised into the crinoline stretcher is 1/2 inch in diameter by 3/4 inch. The rear tenon is 5/8 inch by 15/16 inch. Bore the required mortises, turn the lateral stretchers, and try a test fit.

When everything fits, kerf the leg tenons for wedges and glue the lower part of the chair together. I used liquid hide glue for the joints on this chair.

FITTING THE ARM BOW AND ARM SUPPORTS

Rive and shave both bows to a square-sided section. Because of their thickness, you'll need to use bending straps, described in Chapter 4.

Use the arm-bow holding fixtures to locate the arm bow in position (see Chapter 8). The back of the bow should form a 12-degree slouch angle to the seat.

For the chair in this chapter, the ram's horn arm supports were sawed from a section of an oak board that had some attractive curved grain. You can also use pieces of a surplus bent bow. If you use bent wood, you'll need to modify the shape of the arm support at the joint with the arm bow. (The reverse curve isn't possible.) A single curve is a style variation also found on traditional English Windsors.

Attaching the ram's horn arm supports between the seat and arm bow is one of the difficult steps in making this chair. The arm support rakes forward and splays out past the sides of the chair seat. Locate the arm supports equal distances from the center of the arm bow. Do not trim the arm bow to length until after the arm supports are fitted.

There are several ways to attach the arm support to the seat. The strongest joint is made by shaping the base of the arm support into a cylindrical or a tapered tenon. You then bore the required mortise, being very careful to find the proper sighting line and resultant angle, where the arm support meets the arm bow. (You could bend the arm bow *after* fitting both curved arm supports to the seat.)

The most common method for attaching these curved arm supports requires a half-lap mortise chopped into the side of the seat. The base of the arm support is cut with a small lap, so that the inner part mates with the surface of the seat. The arm support is then connected to the side of the seat with one or two dowels or countersunk wood screws. Lapped arm supports usually have little splay—they tend to be almost vertical from a front view.

Boring mortises for the crinoline stretcher tenons with the legs fitted to the chair seat

Detail of the English-style turnings and crinoline stretcher system

For the chair in this chapter, the arm supports were attached to the seat and arm bow with 7/16-inch-diameter hickory dowels. (I don't know if using dowels to attach bent arm supports was the practice for any of the old Windsors, but it's a technique used for repair work.) The arm bow was secured exactly in place using the horizontal arm-bow fixtures shown in Chapter 8. The ends of the arm supports were carefully scribed and sawed to mate with the seat and bottom of the arm bow. Dowel holes were drilled through the bottom of the seat and through the top of the arm bow. These were interesting drilling angles, with little room for error.

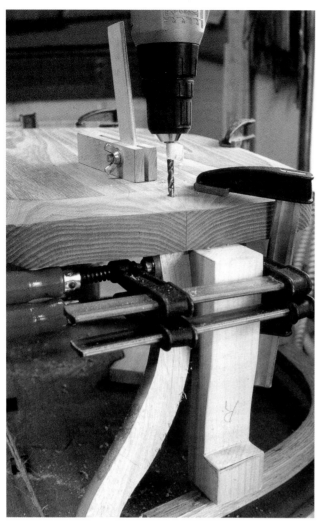

The ends of the curved arm supports are scribe fitted to the seat and bottom of the arm bow. The unit is clamped into position so that mortises can be bored for dowels, which hold the assembly together.

FITTING THE BACK BOW TO THE ARM BOW

The next hurdle is fitting the back bow to the arm bow, essentially the same procedure used to assemble an American sack-back Windsor but with two extra considerations.

Because the spindles on this chair are perfectly straight, the back bow must align with the spindle mortises of the arm bow and the seat deck. The flat (straight) splat is also mortised between the bows. The splat for this chair is made in two sections, which are let into shallow mortises chiseled into the bows and seat. The upper tenon of the upper splat fits into a mortise chopped in the bottom of the back bow (fig. 17.7).

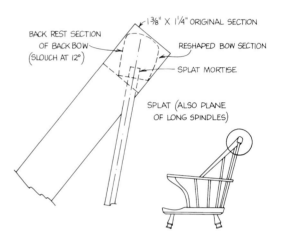

FIG. 17.7. Reshaping the upper section of the back bow to provide flats for the splat mortise and the sitter's comfort. Fair the altered section into the original shape at the sides of the bow.

The tricky part was securing the wiggly, off-balance arm bows in place to drill the holes. When a variety of clamps failed to solve this, I glued a triangular clamping block to the overhanging section of each arm support; these were still plain sawed pieces of oak, with no detailing or smoothing.. This provided a bearing surface for clamping the arm support to the arm bow. I also clamped the base of the arm support against the arm- bow holding fixture, which was still holding the arm bow in place.

Once everything was secure, I drilled the dowel holes with a hand-held electric drill. I then sawed off the glue blocks and finished shaping the visible surfaces of the arm supports. I inserted hardwood dowels into the holes but did not glue them at this time. Finishing the backrest requires disassembling the bows several times. If I use this system again, I'll saw the arm supports with the clamping blocks as single units. The joints of this chair are fine after two years' use.

The surface on the bottom of the back bow where the splat mortise is chopped must be made perpendicular to the splat. This requires reshaping the center section of the bow. The face of the back bow is also twisted, so that it's parallel to the splat and to the plane of the spindles. (If this wasn't done, the back bow would have a sharp frontal arris that would make the chair uncomfortable.) Reshaping the bow amounts to twisting the axis in the center of the backrest area. The amount of twist is regulated by the rake angle of the back bow. As the bow angle is lowered, you need more twist. (This is probably one reason why the back bow of an English double-bow Windsor is generally set at a much steeper angle than that of an American sack-back.)

Begin by mortising and fitting the back bow to the arm bow. Taper and round the ends of the back bow to fit the arm-bow mortises. Leave the center of the bow square in section until the fitting process is complete.

To determine the placement and angle for boring the mortises in the arm bow, sight a line down the back of both bows and the back of the chair seat. Select a mortise angle based on alignment of the bows with the seat.

Bore, ream, and fit the back bow. Determine where the bow needs shaping to create the flat underside for the splat and the flat front of the backrest. Clamp the back bow in a vise, or use a shaving horse, and work with a drawknife and spokeshave to shave smooth transitions between the backrest area and the tapered ends of the bow. You may need to use a rasp on the underside of the bow.

MAKING AND FITTING THE BACK SPLAT

The two-piece splat is fitted into shallow mortises chopped into the seat, arm, and back bow.

Design the splat as a single unit. To help with the planning, I also made a dummy splat from thin plywood that I could place against the bows on the chair.

Carefully determine the center line for the splat mortises on the seat, arm bow, and back bow. You should also determine the placement and spacing for the long spindles that are mortised at the sides of the splat.

When the spacing is set, saw the plywood dummy splat in half, then wedge it between the seat, arm bow, and back bow. Make sure that the spacing is good and that the bows line up with the back of the chair seat.

Lay out the splat mortises based on the spacing of the dummy splat. Disassemble both bows. The splat mortises are 5/16 inch wide and 5/16 inch deep. Set a sliding bevel to 12 degrees, which is the slouch angle of the backrest. Use a 1/4-inch-wide mortise chisel and a wide, flat chisel to chop the mortises. Follow the procedure described in Chapter 6 for mortising back slats on a ladder-back chair.

Saw the outline of the permanent splat, then crosscut the upper and lower sections, adding 5/16 inch at both ends of each splat to serve as tenons. Sand or file a slight chamfer at the leading edges of the tenons.

Test assemble the arm/back bow and splat unit.

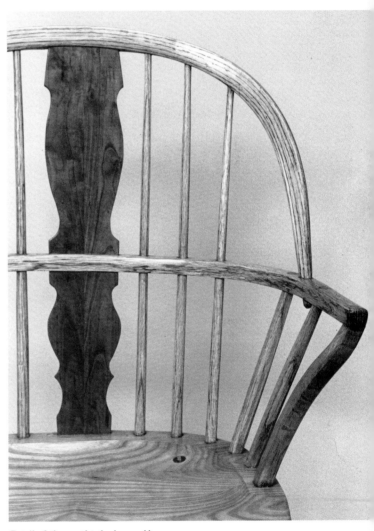

Detail of the complete back assembly

MAKING AND FITTING THE SPINDLES

The short arm-rest spindles on this chair have a flattened center section typical of old English Windsors. These spindles have a 5/8-inch-diameter tenon at the base, and a 1/2-inch-diameter tenon going into the arm bow. (These are diameters of kiln-dried equivalent spindles.) The center sections swell to a rectangular section 7/8 inch wide. The long backrest spindles taper from 5/8-inch-diameter tenons at the base to 3/8 inch at the back-bow mortises. The midsections of these round spindles are fitted through slightly tapered 1/2-inch mortises in the arm bow.

Set the spindles, dowels, or straight wires across the bows to determine the spindle spacing. Take measurements between the spindles on the left and right sides of the splat. Visual symmetry may require fudging the spacing. When the spacing is set, draw straight centerlines on the fronts of both bows. Then mark boring centers for the mortises on both bows and the seat. Use a straightedge to adjust the spindle centers into a straight line (see fig. 17.8).

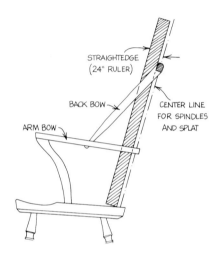

FIG. 17.8. Aligning spindle placements at the back bow, arm bow, and seat deck with a ruler. The spindles of English Windsors are almost always straight. Use a ruler to align spindle placements at the back bow, arm bow, and seat deck.

STRAIGHTEDGE (24" RULER)

BACK BOW

CENTER LINE FOR SPINDLES AND SPLAT

ARM BOW

I recommend boring all of the spindle mortises with both bows in place. Bore the back-bow mortises with a 3/8-inch-diameter bit, such as a powerbore, or an ordinary auger bit. (To prevent tearout, stop boring each hole when the lead of the bit begins to emerge through the bottom of the bow. Back bore all these mortises before going on to boring the arm bow.) To bore the arm-bow mortises, pass the shank of a spade-bit extension up through the 3/8-inch back-bow mortises. Attach a 1/2-inch powerbore bit to the extension. You can prevent bore-through damage to the arm bow by clamping a small wooden caul underneath each boring location. Use two coupled extensions and a 5/8-inch bit to bore the spindle mortises in the seat.

Fit the spindles to the seat and bow mortises. Use a rat-tail rasp to taper the arm-bow mortises for the center spindles just slightly, to match the taper of the long spindles.

Once everything fits, you can kerf the ends of the back bow and the upper spindle tenons that get wedges. Dress the shape and fine sand the ram's horn arm supports and the bows before the actual gluing.

Final assembly is the same as for any other Windsor chair.

Contemporary Windsors and Post-and-Rung Chairs

Ladder-back side chair. Red oak with hickory bark. Made by John D. Alexander Jr., Baltimore, Maryland.

Reproduction of a slant-back Shaker sidechair by Mark Taylor. The front and rear posts are raked at 8 degrees. This results in similar slouch in the back rest. Dimensions for the chair are from a Shaker original in John Kasay's book, The Book of Shaker Furniture.

High-back stick Windsor. Elm seat with red oak bow, comb, sticks, and legs. Made by John Brown, Newport, Pembrokeshire, Wales.

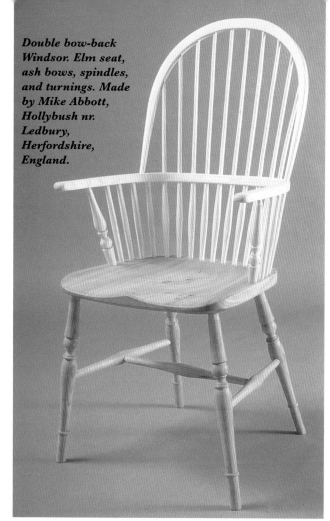

Double bow-back Windsor. Elm seat, ash bows, spindles, and turnings. Made by Mike Abbott, Hollybush nr. Ledbury, Herfordshire, England.

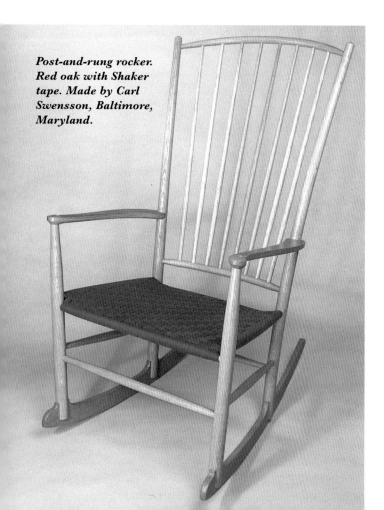

Post-and-rung rocker. Red oak with Shaker tape. Made by Carl Swensson, Baltimore, Maryland.

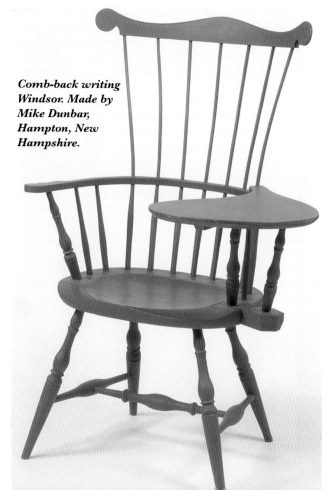

Comb-back writing Windsor. Made by Mike Dunbar, Hampton, New Hampshire.

Comb-back Windsor.
Made by Mario Rodriguez,
Warwick, New York.

High-back stick Windsor.
Painted hardwoods.
Made by Don Weber,
Mendocino, California.

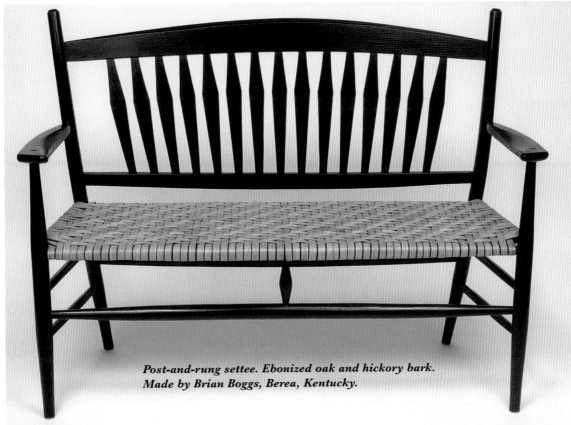

Post-and-rung settee. Ebonized oak and hickory bark.
Made by Brian Boggs, Berea, Kentucky.

Rod-back Windsor side chair. Made by Curtis Buchanan, Jonesboro, Tennessee.

Comb-back Windsor high chair. Made by Dave Sawyer, East Calais, Vermont.

Hybrid pass armchair and two post-and-rung tables. Chair based on Danish designer Hans Wegner's "Peacock chair," originally made in 1947. Made by Dan Stalzer, Ft. Bragg, California.

Part Five:
Equipping a Workshop

CHAPTER 18

A Shaving Horse

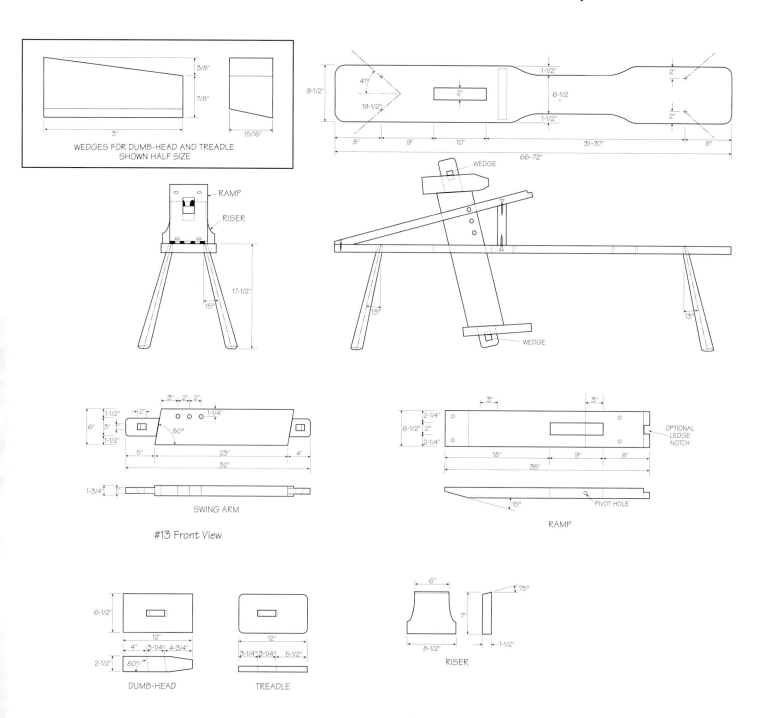

WEDGES FOR DUMB-HEAD AND TREADLE
SHOWN HALF SIZE

RAMP

RISER

WEDGE

WEDGE

SWING ARM

#13 Front View

RAMP

OPTIONAL
LEDGE
NOTCH

PIVOT HOLE

DUMB-HEAD

TREADLE

RISER

FIG. 18.1. Plans for a dumb-head shaving horse

Scale: 1:16

Part	Suggested Wood	Dimensions
Bench	Yellow pine or Douglas fir	1-1/2" x 9-1/2" x 66" to 72"
Ramp	Yellow pine or Douglas fir	1/1/2" x 6-1/2" x 35"
Riser	Yellow pine or Douglas fir	1-1/2" x 8-1/2" x 7
Swinging arm	Oak, ash, hard maple	1-3/4" x 5-3/4" x 32"
Dumb head	Oak, ash, hard maple	2-1/2" x 6-1/2" x 12"
Treadle*	Oak, ash, hard maple	1" x 6-1/2" x 12"
Head, treadle wedges	Oak, ash, hard maple	To fit tapered mortises
4 Legs	Oak, ash, hard maple	2" x 2" x 22"
4 Leg wedges	Oak, ash, hard maple	To fit leg kerfs
6 Wood screws		#8 x 1-3/4"
Steel bolt		1/2" x 8" to 10"

*A treadle made from solid-core birch plywood is less likely to split.

T hroughout this book I promote using tools and equipment that you can make in your own shop. Some, like the shaving horse and froe clubs, simply are not available through commercial suppliers. And often those that are available are not appropriate for chairmaking, especially on a small scale. An obvious advantage in making your own tools is saving money, but the time required may offset any saving. Always, though, you can count on a sense of real satisfaction when you make a tool that works properly.

SHAVING-HORSE DESIGN

The most important piece of shop equipment required for making the green-wood chairs in this book is a shaving horse. (In fact, workbenches with a screw vise were not commonly found in many workshops until the mid–nineteenth century.) Make your own shaving horse, scaled to your body, using materials from your locality.

Traditional shaving horses are of two basic types, each with its own following and both fine for chairmaking: the English shaving horse, sometimes called a bodger's bench, and the German *schnitzelbank*, sometimes called a "dumb-head" shaving horse. I started out using a schnitzelbank during my cooperage apprenticeship in the Swiss Alps and still use the basic design from Ruedi Kohler's cooperage shop.

The 1/8-inch scale plan (fig. 18.1) is for the basic shaving-horse design we use at Country Workshops. It's made from a combination of hardwoods (for strength) and softwoods (to save weight). Air-dried wood is suitable for all parts except the legs, which should be kiln dried. The plan is easy to modify in terms of size or materials.

Detail view of the Country Workshops dumb-head shaving horse

A shaving horse in use, from De Re Metallica, *a text on mining and metallurgy published in 1556*

While making a shaving horse isn't difficult, you should allow two full days for the project. Chopping the mortises and tenons for the swinging arm, dumb head, and treadle are the most time-consuming tasks. Boring and fitting the legs at uniform angles also takes some care.

The traditional way to make the dumb-head section of the swinging arm is to hew and sculpt it from a single hardwood timber, usually a green log. The top of the bulky dumb head can be drilled with holes to accept small tools and pencils. Very handy. Most of the shaving horses I make have a separate head secured by a mortise-and-tenon arrangement to the swinging arm. A third method is an imitation of the one-piece arm and dumb head made with two hardwood cheeks glued or bolted to the sides of the arm plank.

The bench can be shorter than 66 inches, but I prefer 72 inches — for working long rivings, such as Windsor bows or the back posts of rocking chairs. Any changes in the bench length should be made in the seating section. Make the front half following the dimensions in the plans.

BUILDING THE BENCH

Lay out centers for the legs and the dumb-head mortise in the bench. The narrow section in the center of the bench is designed to allow you to get a foot to the treadle without rubbing your inner thigh on the bench sides. Saw off the side slabs after you've test assembled the shaving horse.

You can make the large mortise for the swinging arm with a saber saw or by drilling a row of holes and then chopping with a large chisel.

The extension at the end of the ramp should be 4 to 5 inches past the point where the jaw closes on the ramp. (If it's shorter, the jaw won't hold long pieces securely in place.)

The legs can be shaved into an octagon or turned round. Octagonal legs are easily made with a drawknife. I prefer to use tapered tenons mated to mortises 1-3/8 inches in diameter at the bottom of the bench. This requires a large reamer. Lacking a reamer, make 1-inch-diameter cylindrical mortises and legs with sloped shoulders at the base of the 1-inch- diameter tenons.

Dry the legs thoroughly before shaping the tenons, which can be done with a drawknife and spokeshave. (Finish by sanding or filing to fit.) The quickest way to make the leg tenons is to turn them on a lathe.

Bore the leg mortises. The plan shows rake angles of 13 degrees and splay angles of 15 degrees. The sighting angle measured across the boring centers of the front or back legs is 40.5 degrees. The resultant boring angle is 19.5 degrees from plumb (vertical). Instructions for using sighting lines and resultant boring angles appear in Chapter 8 on stick Windsors.

Saw kerfs in the leg tenons. Position the legs with the rays in line with the length of the bench. Orient the wedge kerfs perpendicular to the length of the bench. Glue and wedge the legs in place.

Level the bench (see Chapter 6) and chamfer the bottoms of the legs, an important detail—legs are often broken when a shaving horse is dragged against a rough floor board or protruding floor nail.

Assemble the ramp and riser pieces. Bore the 9/16-inch-diameter bolt hole through the ramp before sawing or chopping the mortise. The ramp and riser are attached to the bench with two countersunk wood screws at each of the three connection points. I generally saw and chisel a ledge and center notch in the near end of the ramp, vestiges of a time when most woodworkers didn't have a workbench with a screw vise. The ledge and notch are used in conjunction with a breast bib to hold short pieces of wood for drawknife and spokeshave work.

Lay out and chop the mortises in the dumb head and treadle. Tenons on both ends of the swinging arm are angled 80 degrees and shouldered on four sides. To avoid cracking, the tenons must be long enough to have sufficient end grain beyond the wedges.

The wedge mortises that secure the dumb head and treadle to the swinging arm are 1 inch wide and tapered in height: Their outer walls slope 1/8 inch over the 1 inch width of the tenon. Undercut the lower walls below the dumb head or treadle. This helps the wedge pull the dumb head or treadle tight against the tenon shoulders.

Wedges must have an 80-degree angle at the base to match the angle of the dumb head and treadle and taper 1/8 inch per inch of length. They are 15/16 inch wide to fit easily through the 1-inch-wide mortises.

Square the sides and ends of the piece of wood for the dumb head. Careful layout is important here. Start making the mortise through the dumb head by drilling a row of 3/4-inch-diameter holes at an 80-degree angle. Use a chisel to remove the waste. Undercut the inner walls slightly; this helps in fitting the mortise over the tenon.

Chisel or saw the rolled surface at the bottom of the jaw. Put a 1/2-inch radius across the leading edge of the jaw, so that it won't leave an indention mark on the wood that it's gripping. Saw or chisel a small, inverted V-notch on the underside of the jaw on either the left or right jowl. You'll use this to hold square stock on edge when you begin to shave octagons.

Make the treadle following the steps for making the dumb head. Flat-sawed treadle stock is less likely to split than a nice piece of quarter-sawed wood. A plywood treadle is even stronger, if you can handle the inappropriate aesthetic.

Don't force the dumb head or treadle over the tenons. They could split. Locate any tight spots, and eliminate the problem.

Center the row of height-adjustment holes in the swinging arm 1-1/4 inches from the riser side of the plank. (The off-center holes cause the swinging arm to open automatically when you take your foot off the treadle.) The holes in the ramp and swinging arm are 9/16 inch in diameter.

The 1/2-inch steel pivot bolt can be an L-shaped masonry anchor bolt or a machine bolt with the threaded end hacksawed off. Chamfer the bolt end, so that it's easy to insert through the swinging arm when you change the jaw height.

Finally, saw the flanks from the midsection of the bench and radius the ends. Round off any sharp arris that will be uncomfortable pressing against your legs or when you move the shaving horse around the shop. I usually don't apply a finish.

CHAPTER 19

A Chairmaker's Workbench

FIG. 19.1. Plans for a chairmaker's workbench

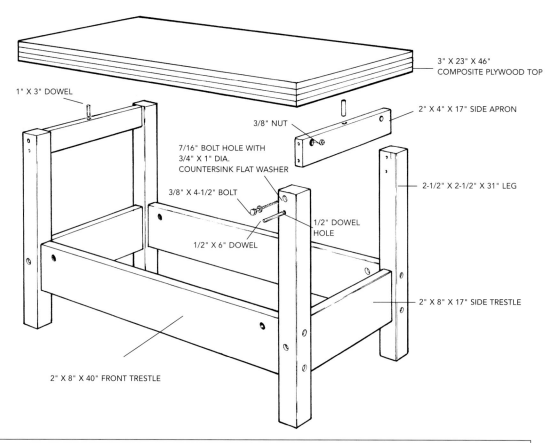

1" X 3" DOWEL

3" X 23" X 46" COMPOSITE PLYWOOD TOP

3/8" NUT

2" X 4" X 17" SIDE APRON

7/16" BOLT HOLE WITH 3/4" X 1" DIA. COUNTERSINK FLAT WASHER

3/8" X 4-1/2" BOLT

2-1/2" X 2-1/2" X 31" LEG

1/2" DOWEL HOLE

1/2" X 6" DOWEL

2" X 8" X 17" SIDE TRESTLE

2" X 8" X 40" FRONT TRESTLE

MATERIALS LIST: CHAIRMAKER'S WORKBENCH

Number of Pieces	Description	Dimensions
Frame		
4	Legs	2-1/2" sq x 31"*
2	Front trestles	1-1/2" x 7-1/2" x 40"
2	Side trestles	1-1/2" x 7-1/2" x 17"
2	Side aprons	1-1/2" x 3-1/2" x 17"
12	Bolts/nuts and washers	3/8" x 4"
4	Bolts/nuts and washers	3/8" x length required to bolt frame to floor
2	Hardwood dowels	1" x 3"
12	Hardwood dowels	1/2" x 4-1/2"
Tabletop		
1	Plywood sheet**	3/4" x 4' x 8'
or 4	Dry hardwood boards	1-1/2" x 6" x 48"
	Yellow glue	

* Heavier legs could be used, but 2-1/2" square is adequate. Leg length assumes that the tabletop will be 34 inches high and 3 inches thick. Adjust to your requirements and materials.

** I recommend birch cabinet plywood, but any solid core plywood will work.

A small, sturdy workbench designed to be located several feet from a wall. It is bolted to the floor and will not move when you're doing vigorous work, such as saddling a Windsor seat with an inshave.

The table top and jaws of the twin-screw vise are bored with holes to accept multiple round steel dogs. A wide range of shapes can be held in a variety of positions.

Detail of the butt-joint construction fastened with 3/8-inch bolts and captured nuts. The hole at the bottom of the post houses the captured nut that secures the post to the floor.

weather and humidity. Several rows of dog holes bored in the bench top hold round, steel bench dogs that can be pivoted so that their flat jaws make good contact with irregular shapes, such as a Windsor chair seat. The complete unit is very sturdy.

W hile a traditional joiner's workbench is a massive and impressive piece of shop equipment, it is not particularly suited to making chairs. The chairmaker's workbench in the photos and in figure 19.1 is the current version of a simplified workbench design that I have been making for more than twenty years. This one is just under four feet long, and the next version may be only three feet.

Inspired by work stations used by dentists, doctors, and mechanics, in the chairmaker's workbench utility rules over style. It was designed to be ideal for working on chairs, and also on large, carved bowls. Deep enough to hold an assembled chair on the bench top, its small overall size allows me to get to all parts of a Windsor chair seat without reclamping the stock.

The workbench is most useful if it's located at least 3 feet from the nearest wall, so that you can work on any side of a chair (or chair part) without repositioning it. Even the heaviest conventional workbench will migrate across the shop floor when you're doing vigorous drawknife and inshave work. This chairmaker's workbench is designed to be securely bolted to the shop floor. If anchoring to the floor isn't possible, the legs can be bolted to a full sheet of plywood, which you stand on while using the workbench.

The 3-inch-thick bench top, a lamination of four layers of 3/4-inch oak plywood, stays flat during changes in

The frame construction employs square-cut butt joints held together with ordinary bolts and nuts. For stability, the legs are located at the extreme corners of the bench top.

The workbench in the photos is fitted with two vises mounted inboard from the legs. On one side I've mounted a twin-screw vise that I made from a kit; it's designed so that a large Windsor chair seat can be secured between the screws. A chain links the two screws, which operate simultaneously. On the opposite side, I've mounted a conventional 9-inch-wide woodworker's bench vise.

A twin-screw vise that will securely hold the largest Windsor chair seats. This chain-linked vise is made from a kit. You can also make a wide vise with independent screws.

I used air-dried oak for the frame, purchased green from local saw mills at a very reasonable price. Ash, maple, hickory, beech, and birch are also suitable. If hardwood isn't available, consider using southern yellow pine or Douglas fir, both sold by lumber dealers. You could make the bench top from the same hardwoods, but the plywood version is easier to construct and less expensive.

While you could make the workbench with hand tools, this is one project that lends itself to using machinery. The butt joints require accurate, square cuts, most easily made with a table saw, chop saw, or sliding miter saw. You'll need a drill press if you opt for making the twin-screw vise.

MAKING THE FRAME

Stock for the legs, trestles, and aprons must be straight, flat, and square. Dress the parts as necessary. The width of the aprons and trestles holds the frame square. There is considerable latitude in sizing the other dimensions. Carefully saw all parts to length.

Use a 1-inch-diameter auger or forstner bit to bore holes for the cross nuts and countersinks for the bolts. Bore holes for the cross nuts through the full width of the posts: In the front trestles, 3 inches below the upper edge of the trestles; in the side trestles, 3 inches above the lower edge

of the trestles; and in the side aprons, centered on the width of the aprons. Countersinks for the bolt heads are 1 inch in diameter and 3/4 inch deep.

Use a 7/16- inch auger or twist bit to bore bolt holes through the posts and into the end grain of the trestles and side aprons. I use a drill press to bore bolt holes in the posts and a hand-held electric drill for boring the bolt holes through the end grain of the trestles and aprons. The provision for anchoring the legs to the floor uses similar holes for the frame's bolt and nut fasteners.

Bore a 1-inch-diameter hole 2 inches deep in the center of each side apron. Fit (don't glue) a 1-by-3-inch hardwood dowel in each hole. These large pegs secure the heavy bench top in place.

Test assemble the entire frame. Disassemble the frame and use a hand plane to chamfer the edges and the bottoms of the posts. Bolt the frame together.

Bore 1/2-by-4-inch dowel holes through the posts and into the end grain of the trestles and side aprons. Insert the 1/2-by-4-1/2-inch dowels. Do not glue. Chamfer the protruding 1/2 inch on each dowel. These dowels are non-structural; they simply prevent the trestles and aprons from twisting out of position.

MAKING THE BENCH TOP

Making a plywood bench top is easier than using solid wood, but there are some challenges and trade-offs. Plywood is easy to find, more stable during fluctuations in humidity, and at the 3-inch thickness does not require stiffening aprons between the front legs. The downside of using plywood is that the bench-top surface and edges will be less tough and resilient than if you'd used solid wood.

Making a Plywood Bench Top

Be sure to buy good quality plywood. The core material should be solid. White birch plywood is probably the best choice.

Use a circular saw or a table saw to rip the plywood sheet into four sections, each just under 23-7/8 inches wide. You'll trim the bench top to final dimensions after the plywood sheets are glued together.

You need a flat surface for gluing the pieces of plywood together. Several straight 2 by 4s placed on edge on an existing tabletop will work. If necessary, use thin wedges to make the 2-by-4s' top edges parallel. Sight across the top edges of the 2-by-4s, as if using a pair of winding sticks.

I recommend gluing two units of two sheets each, then gluing the resulting 1-1/2-inch-thick units together. Spread yellow glue over one entire surface of two quarter sheets of plywood. A toothed mastic spreader (made for flooring adhesives) works well for this. Use as many clamps as you can get around the perimeter of the glue job. Use wooden cauls approximately 1/2 by 1 by 2 inches between the clamp jaws and the plywood. You can press down the center of the glue sandwich with heavy weights or hold it down with several 24-inch-long 2 by 4s.

Once you've glued the plywood into a single unit, trim the edges of the bench top. You may want to plane or resaw the edges to slightly smaller dimensions. My plywood workbench is 23 inches wide and 46 inches long. Use a jointer or a hand plane to clean up the edges. Be sure to keep the edges straight and square in relation to the bench top.

I strengthened the edges of this plywood bench top by flooding the surface with marine epoxy. After the epoxy cured, I finished the edges by sanding. The resulting epoxy- impregnated oak and fir edges are tough and substantial.

Option: Making a Solid Hardwood Bench Top

Most of my earlier workbenches had oak or beech bench tops from 1-1/2 to 3-1/2 inches thick. To make a solid wood bench top you must have air-dried hardwood and the capability of jointing and thicknessing the planks. If possible, use quarter-sawed lumber, which is much more stable than flat or rift-sawed material. Wood movement from fluctuations in humidity can cause the bench top to warp or even split apart.

Cut the planks an inch or so longer than the trim length of the bench top. Joint and thickness the planks. Plank edges must be straight and square to the plank faces. Glue the planks together, following instructions for gluing up seat blanks in Chapter 8. You don't need dowels or biscuits between the planks—plain glue joints are stronger than the original wood. Do not run threaded steel rods through the edges of the tabletop. Bolted rods restrain wood movement, causing the tabletop to warp.

Finishing and Attaching the Bench Top to the Frame

Finish the frame with a penetrating oil or an oil/varnish blend, finishes also suitable for solid plank bench tops. Plywood bench tops should be finished with something tougher and more resistant to bruising, such as several coats of matte urethane varnish. Apply the same finish to the lower side of the bench top. Don't fine sand the bench-top surface, which would make it too slippery for woodworking.

Secure the bench top to the frame using dowels set into holes in the upper side of the side aprons and the underside of the bench top. This is the same simple system used to hold the bench tops of expensive joiners' workbenches made in Switzerland and Germany. The single dowels at each end allow the bench top to expand and contract with changes in humidity. Moving the workbench is also much easier, as the top and frame are carried independently.

Installing Vises

Mount a woodworker's bench vise to one face of the workbench. Buy a good quality cast-iron vise, or make one yourself (see fig. 19.2). The vise should be 9 to 12 inches wide, with the main screw 1 inch in diameter or larger. Conventional vises use two solid steel guide rods to keep the vise faces in alignment, these should also be at least 1 inch in diameter. Don't be impressed by the length of the screws and guide rods. You seldom need to open a bench vise more than 5 or 6 inches. A quick release is handy, but it may break or wear out long before the other parts are worn.

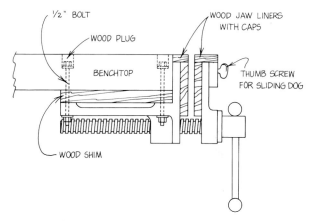

Fig. 19.2. A manufactured cast-iron bench vise mounted by hanging it from bolts through the top of the workbench, a much stronger technique than running lag screws into the bottom of the bench.

Cast-iron bench vises are commonly lag bolted to the bottom of a workbench. I prefer to hang vises using bolts, with heads and flat washers set into countersunk holes in the bench top (fig. 19.2). Cover the holes with removable wooden plugs. You may need to use thickness shims between the vise mounts and bottom of the bench top.

Wooden liners prevent the cast-iron vise jaws from marring surfaces of wood being held. The liners should include caps that cover the upper edges of the vise jaws. The simplest way to hold liners in place is to attach them to the vise jaws with white or yellow glue. When they need replacing, you can simply knock them off the jaws, since these glues are not intended for attaching wood to metal.

Constructing a Shop-Made Vise

I made the vise in figure 19.3 more than ten years ago as an experiment and to save money. Since then, Taiwanese vises have become available that sell for about the cost of the materials required to make the vise I designed. The shop-made vise is strong, does what needs doing, and affords some self-pride in the making.

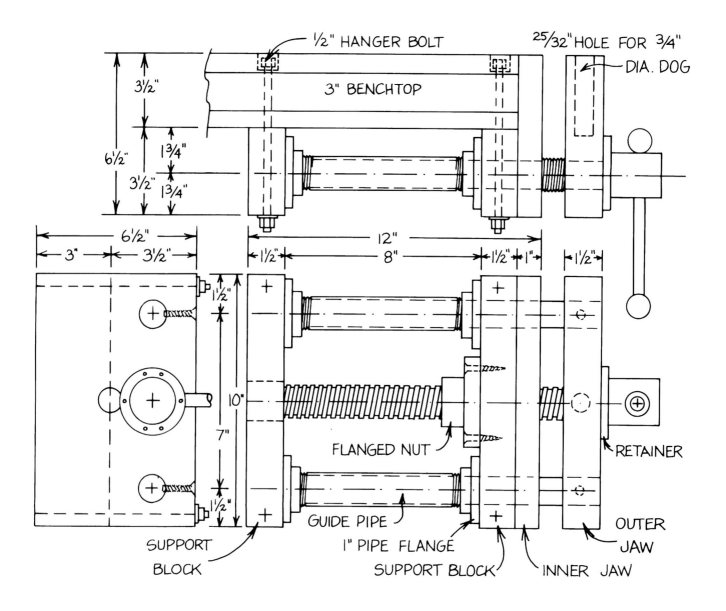

FIG. 19.3. Plans for a shop-made bench vise. The wooden jaws are made from any well-dried hardwood.

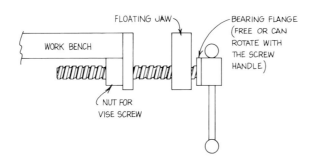

FIG. 19.4. A twin-screw vise with a floating front jaw. Unlike most vises, the bearing flange is not attached to the face of the front jaw.

This homemade vise has seen years of continuous service. It's made with an acme screw, and standard components available from plumbing and steel suppliers.

The screw, flanged nut, and retainer are made by several manufacturers and sold as a unit by various tool suppliers.

Machine the wooden jaws and support blocks from any dry hardwood. Have a plumbing shop cut and thread the guide pipes. Purchase guide rods from a steel supply house or a welding shop. The supplier can saw the solid steel rods to length.

The critical borings are the holes in the outer jaws that hold the steel guide rods. Screws driven through the

bottom of the outer jaws hold the guide rods in place. All other borings can be made slightly oversized. Align the guide pipes with their flanges very carefully.

The lower half of the inner jaw is glued to the forward support block that has the flanged nut for the vise screw mounted to its back side.

Hang the vise from the bench top with bolts, similar to the installation in figure 19.2.

You can bore one or two 25/32-inch-diameter holes in the top of the outer jaw to hold 3/4-inch-diameter bench dogs.

The twin-screw, chain-drive vise that I use was made from a kit available from mail-order tool suppliers. You can make a simpler version that may work just as well, although you'll have to tighten both screws separately (fig. 19.4). Make the screw holes through the outer jaw a little oversized so that you can turn one screw at a time without jamming the jaw.

For this version, the outer jaw floats on the two screws. (You pull it out after backing off the screws.) The jaw is closed by pressure from the inner flange on the handles. Unlike conventional vises, the handle flanges also float or rotate with the handle. The flanges are not attached to the face of the outer jaw. Ideally, this vise would be made with large wooden screws, but machined steel screws will work.

MATERIALS LIST: VISE

Number of Pieces	Description	Specifications
1	Outer jaw	1-1/2" x 6-1/2" x 10", dry hardwood*
1	Inner jaw	1" x 6-1/2" x 10", dry hardwood*
2	Support blocks	1-1/2" x 3-3/4" x 10", dry hardwood*
1	Threaded screw with matching flanged nut, retainer, and screw handle	
2	Solid steel guide rods	1" dia x 11-3/4" long
2	Guide pipes	1" inside dia x 8" long
4	Pipe flanges (for 1" inside dia pipe)	
	Wood screws for pipe flanges, flanged nut, retainer	
4	Hanger bolts/nuts, washers	1/2" x 6-1/2"**

* Adjust width for thickness of bench top and vise casting.

** Adjust length for depth of complete unit.

CHAPTER 20

Shop-Made Wood Kilns

A steel-drum kiln can be made in about an hour with components found around the workshop. The heat deflector between the lamp and wood rack redirects radiant heat throughout the chamber.

A consistent emphasis in this book has been on shaping wood while it is green and assembling chair parts when they have dried to optimum moisture contents for their particular functions. You don't need a special kiln to produce the proper moisture content. Often your workshop or home already provides a suitable drying environment— a rack above a water heater, furnace, or woodstove may do the job. The advantage of a kiln is having a known heat source independent of other household or shop functions. You can use an inexpensive, homemade kiln to speed up the drying process, and to achieve consistent results throughout the seasons.

AN OIL-DRUM KILN

In one kiln I've used, a 500-watt brooder lamp intended for raising chicks supplied the heat. The kiln body was a lidless, 55-gallon steel drum laid sideways across two sawhorses, with three large ventilation holes punched through the back end (the bottom of the drum). Chair rungs were set on a wooden rack several inches above the heat lamp, which faced upwards. I quickly learned that without a heat deflector between the heat source and the parts being dried, green rungs on the bottom of the rack would begin to char in less than an hour.

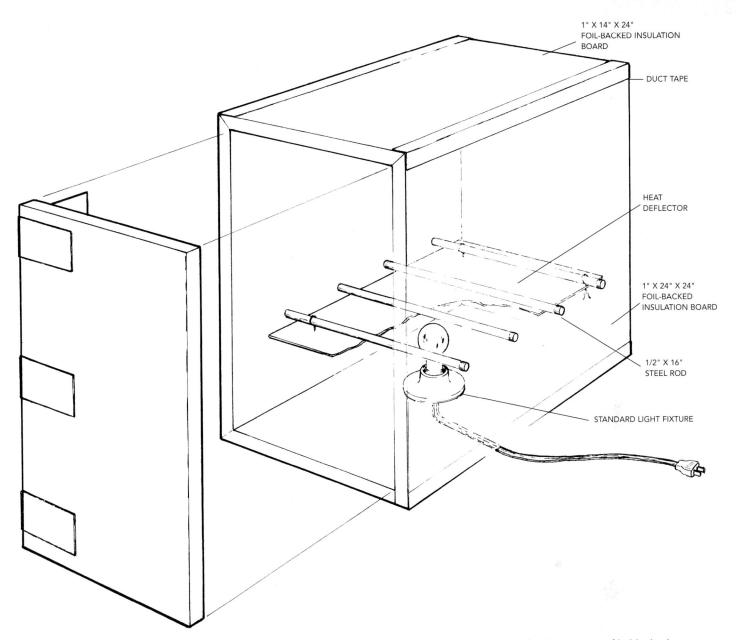

Fig. 20.1. A simple kiln made of foil-backed polystyrene panels and duct tape—more than adequate for drying rungs of ladder-back chairs

A sleeping bag draped over the oil drum served as insulation and an adjustable front door. (If the sleeping bag—or blanket—is removed, the kiln won't retain heat.) An inexpensive oven thermometer set on the wood rack monitored temperatures.

The oil-drum kiln served quite well for several years. Still, its rounded ceiling limited what could be loaded inside, and overall use of space was inefficient.

A POLYSTYRENE KILN

You can also make a kiln from 1-inch-thick foil-backed polystyrene panels (fig. 20.1). Duct tape joins the panels, hinges the door located at one end of the box, and holds the other end of the kiln closed. A porcelain lamp fixture and an ordinary light bulb provide the heat. Temperature

can be adjusted by leaving the door slightly open and by experimenting with different wattage light bulbs. (The door must be kept partly open to allow moisture to escape from the kiln.)

You must locate a metal deflector between the heat source and the wood being dried. Make a support for the deflector by punching several stiff metal wires through the kiln side walls.

THE COUNTRY WORKSHOPS KILN

I built our current kiln when Country Workshops decided to offer a course in making Windsor chairs. We needed something that could quickly dry many Windsor bows and spindles in one loading. The kiln is heated by a 3-foot-long 750-watt baseboard heater converted to operate at higher temperatures than the standard unit (fig. 20.2).

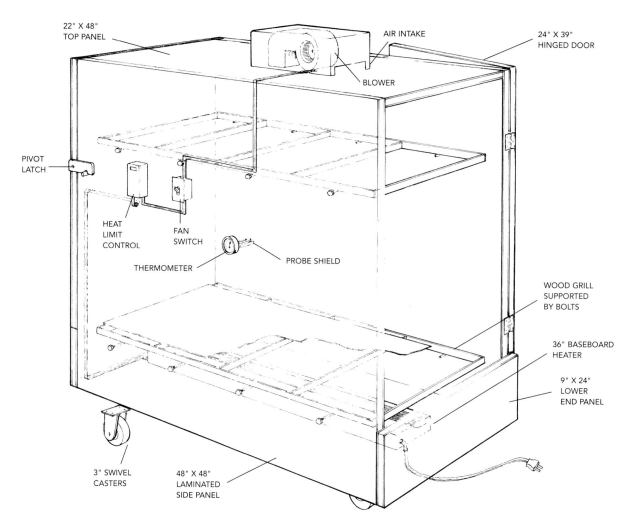

22" X 48"
TOP PANEL

AIR INTAKE

24" X 39"
HINGED DOOR

BLOWER

PIVOT
LATCH

HEAT
LIMIT
CONTROL

FAN
SWITCH

THERMOMETER

PROBE SHIELD

WOOD GRILL
SUPPORTED
BY BOLTS

36" BASEBOARD
HEATER

9" X 24"
LOWER
END PANEL

3" SWIVEL
CASTERS

48" X 48"
LAMINATED
SIDE PANEL

Fig. 20.2. Schematic for a kiln made from plywood and polystyrene panels. Each panel consists of a 3/4-by-1-1/2-inch frame, infilled with 3/4-inch-thick polystyrene sheets. The 1/4-inch plywood skins are tacked and glued to both sides of the frame.

I use the kiln year-round to dry chair parts, tool handles, and occasional small batches of lumber. My wife, Louise, uses it to dry vegetables, herbs, and flowers. I usually keep the temperature at about 90 degrees. In winter, the excess heat helps to keep my shop warm and prevents freezing damage to glues, finishes, and water stones.

The kiln is constructed with shop-made sandwich panels of 3/4-inch-thick rigid foam surrounded by 1/4-inch plywood. A simple frame made from 1 by 2s surrounds the foam panels and supports the plywood skin. The dimensions—2 feet wide, 4 feet long, and 4 feet high—came about as a best use of the plywood and foam panel sheets, but the size has proved excellent for drying chair parts. The panels are screwed together, with butt joints. At the bottom of each end, a 9-inch-wide panel is screwed in place to provide necessary rigidity. A metal heat deflector rests on the bottom rack, which is made of wood strips. The 39-inch-high doors are secured with conventional, square butt hinges. Door latches consist of a small steel strip that rotates on one roundhead screw, with a notch that slips over a second screw.

In addition to a heat source, the kiln uses a small C-frame blower mounted on top of the roof. I turn on the blower

when the kiln is fully loaded with wet wood or when I want to speed up drying without raising the temperature above 120 degrees. Usually I leave the blower off. I leave the doors slightly ajar for venting, a method that has worked so well I've never needed a more elaborate system.

Using a baseboard heater was more complicated than I had anticipated. Baseboard-heater thermostats are designed to be used within a control range of 50 to 90 degrees, and the wiring includes a safety shutoff device should the temperature go higher—I wanted to be able to run the kiln at temperatures up to 140 degrees. At a large commercial and industrial equipment supplier I found a heat-limit control made for forced-air furnaces that has a range of 50 to 300 degrees, with a stop that can be set semipermanently at lower temperatures. The limit switch has special contacts suitable for use on low-voltage circuits such as thermocouples and oil burners.

A friend who is an electrical engineer wired an inexpensive relay between the baseboard heater and the heat-limit control. Figure 20.3 shows the wiring diagram that he used.

You could build a similar kiln using the standard baseboard thermostat and an upper limit of 90 degrees. With the addition of a small fan, the kiln would be quite efficient.

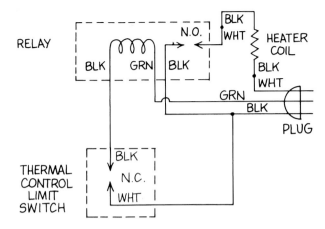

FIG. 20.3. Wiring diagram for the baseboard-heater wood kiln: *a*, a 115V circuit that consists of the relay coil and the limit switch (N.C.) of the temperature control; *b*, a 230V circuit that consists of the relay contacts (N.O.) and the baseboard-heater control. Note that the over-temperature control in the baseboard heater is disconnected and that the fan is a separate circuit but is grounded to the green wire on the 230V plug.

To constantly monitor the temperature, on one side of the kiln I permanently mounted a bi-metal dial thermometer that comes with a wall-mounting adapter and a screw fitting for a piece of pipe that protects the probe. The capped pipe is filled with grease, which serves as a heat transfer medium.

Racks in the kiln are supported by 1/4-by-2-1/2-inch bolts that extend into the interior (fig. 20.4). These bolts can be fitted to holes in the side walls at different heights. The removable racks are made of 3/4-inch-square wooden strips.

The interior surface of the kiln is painted with aluminum enamel paint, which serves as a moisture barrier (for the plywood) and heat reflector.

Safety and Homemade Wood Kilns

I usually operate Country Workshops' kilns at 90 to 100 degrees, and never above 140 degrees. Wood can begin to char at temperatures between 150 and 160 degrees. (I've seen green wood char from the heat of a 500-watt lamp in less than an hour.) Although commercial kiln operators use considerably higher temperatures, these kilns are low-tech devices that don't require specialized knowledge or drying methods.

If you make the polystyrene kiln in figure 20.1, be sure to check on the flash-point temperature for foam panels and other materials that you use. Then be very conservative in regulating the temperature.

Another safety consideration regards wiring, especially with heating units. Be sure to follow recommended guidelines. If you have any doubts, get qualified help.

A plywood kiln for drying Windsor bows, turnings, and spindles

CHAPTER 21

A Spring-Pole Lathe

A shop-made pole lathe can be used to turn ladder-back tenons, or for complete turnings of Windsors.

You can make all the turned parts of a post-and-rung or Windsor chair with a spring-pole lathe, which you can also use to turn bowls and plates up to 8 inches in diameter. Even if you prefer shaving parts for post-and-rung chairs, you still need an accurate way to make tenons. With a lathe you can produce cylindrical tenons of any size, including tapers. Purchasing a powered lathe just to make tenons would be extravagant, but you can make a pole lathe for almost no expense. A set of basic turning tools need not be costly.

A pole lathe is also an excellent tool for learning wood turning. It is low powered and the turning centers have no drive spurs—if you don't use the proper cutting techniques, the turning blank simply comes to a stop. You won't make nasty digs into the wood, and there is little chance that shattered turning stock will fly loose at high speed. And some turners simply enjoy pumping on a pole lathe. There is a special challenge in shaping a piece of rough wood into a uniform, useful object with basic cutting tools and your own energy.

Although I do most of my turning work at a motor-driven lathe, I also enjoy demonstrating and using a traditional pole lathe. The plans in this chapter are for a lathe that I first made in 1977. (A few details in the plans reflect improvements not incorporated in the lathe in the photographs.) This is just one of many ways to make a pole lathe, a rather refined version designed for long-term use in an indoor shop. The construction is based on mortise-and-tenon joinery throughout. Although my lathe is made from air-dried red oak, you can use almost any hardwood, and yellow pine is also appropriate. Feel free to adapt and modify. You can easily change the length, thickness, and width of the various parts.

Alternate construction concepts, along with detailed instructions on pole-lathe use, are included in Mike Abbott's book *Green Woodwork*. For a description of traditional turning with spring-pole and treadle lathes, I suggest reading Joseph Moxon's 1703 classic how-to book, *Mechanick Exercises; Or, the Doctrine of Handy Works*, now reprinted.

NOTES ON CONSTRUCTION

The tools you'll need for making the lathe are

- Tape measure or folding rule
- Combination square
- Rip saw
- Crosscut saw
- Brace with #4, 6, 8, 10, 12 augers
- 3/8-inch mortise chisel
- 5/8-inch firmer chisel
- 1-inch paring chisel
- Hammer and/or mallet

Careful layout and execution is required for mortise-and-tenon joinery. Use a sharp pencil and an accurate try square. Before you begin, joint and surface plane all components. The shoulders of the rectilinear tenons must be square to the length of the work stock. Ripsaw the tenon cheeks after crosscutting the shoulders. After sawing, use the paring chisel to flatten the tenon shoulders and cheeks.

The wedge mortises at the ends of the rails are 1/2 inch wide by 3 inches deep. These mortises should be laid out and executed before cutting the shouldered rail tenons that butt against the stiles.

Secure the foot-end tenons of the head and tail stiles to the feet by 1/2-inch-diameter hardwood dowels. Standard #8 (1/2-inch) augers are actually 33/64 inch in diameter; this doesn't matter if you shave your own dowels from rived hardwood. Offset the tenon dowel holes 1/16 inch in from the mortise dowel holes. Do not use machine-made hardware-store dowels, which tend to be weak and undersized. Point the dowel ends. The dowels will bend as they are driven through the offset holes, which pulls the feet tightly against the shoulders of the stile tenons. This is a standard joinery technique known as draw boring.

Begin the rectangular mortises by scoring the layout with a chisel. Use a brace and auger bits to drill out the center area. Bore from both sides of the mortise toward the center of the stock. Use chisels to chop and pare to the layout lines. Mortise walls can be undercut so that they are slightly concave instead of flat.

When my lathe was originally built, both feet were of equal length. I soon found that the head stile foot at the operator side of the lathe extended where I wanted to stand, so I sawed most of it off. This would not be a problem if you use the lathe standing on your right foot while pumping with your left. (A possible design improvement would be to construct the lathe with two movable puppets. With this arrangement, the turning stock could be centered on the rails, rather than worked from one end. Both stiles would terminate just above the rails.)

You'll need to improvise turning centers for the tail puppet and head stock. On my lathe, the head-stock center is a 4-inch lag screw, with threads at the lead end ground off, then filed to form a cone. You could also make the center from an overlength 1/2-inch-diameter bolt. Grind off the end threads for about 1 inch. Then grind a 45-degree cone at the end. Secure the head-stock center with washers and a nut.

For the tail puppet, you need a special center that screws in and out to tighten turning blanks in place. I used a 5/8-inch-diameter coarse-threaded screw (with sliding cross-handle) saved from a broken C-clamp. For this variation, drill a 9/16-inch-diameter hole through the tail puppet. Modify the leading threads on the screw to resemble a metal thread cutting tap. Use a triangular file to cut two grooves crossing the threads. This makes the cutters. Also, reduce the diameter of the first few rounds of

Fig. 21.1. Scale plans for making a spring-pole lathe using mortise-and-tenon joinery

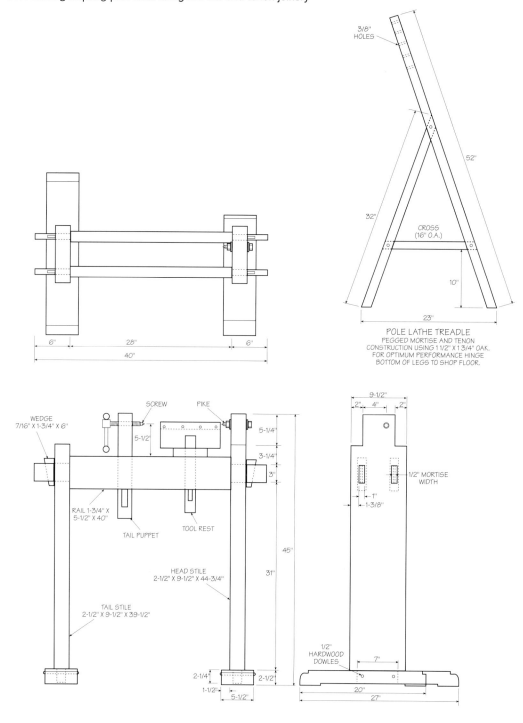

3/8"
HOLES

52"

32"

CROSS
(16" O.A.)

10"

23"

POLE LATHE TREADLE
PEGGED MORTISE AND TENON
CONSTRUCTION USING 1 1/2" X 1 3/4" OAK.
FOR OPTIMUM PERFORMANCE HINGE
BOTTOM OF LEGS TO SHOP FLOOR.

6"   28"   6"

40"

SCREW   PIKE

WEDGE
7/16" X 1-3/4" X 6"

5-1/2"

5-1/4"

3-1/4"

3"

RAIL 1-3/4" X
5-1/2" X 40"

TAIL PUPPET

TOOL REST

9-1/2"

2"   4"   2"

1/2" MORTISE
WIDTH

1"
1-3/8"

45"

31"

HEAD STILE
2-1/2" X 9-1/2" X 44-3/4"

TAIL STILE
2-1/2" X 9-1/2" X 39-1/2"

1/2"
HARDWOOD
DOWLES

7"

2-1/4"   2-1/2"

1-1/2"
5-1/2"

20"

27"

Scale: 1:16

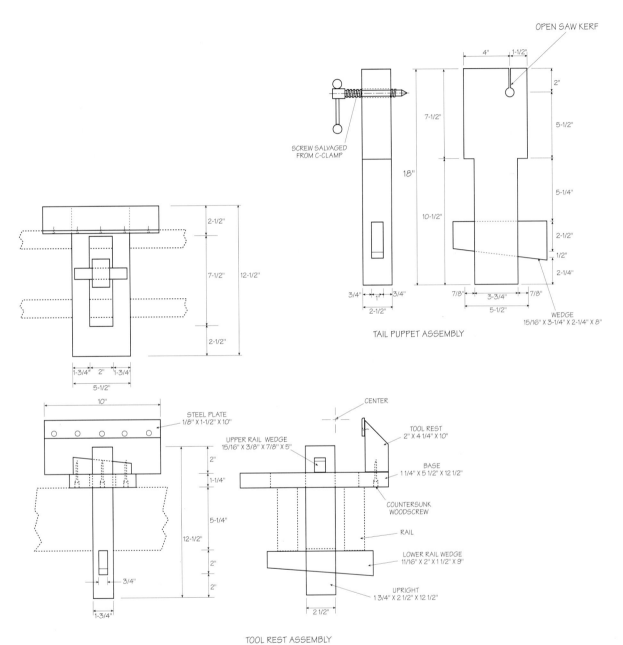

OPEN SAW KERF

SCREW SALVAGED
FROM C-CLAMP

4" 1-1/2"

2"

5-1/2"

7-1/2"

18"

5-1/4"

10-1/2"

2-1/2"

1/2"

2-1/4"

3/4" 1 3/4"

2-1/2"

7/8" 3-3/4" 7/8"

5-1/2"

WEDGE
15/16" X 3-1/4" X 2-1/4" X 8"

TAIL PUPPET ASSEMBLY

2-1/2"

7-1/2"

12-1/2"

2-1/2"

1-3/4" 2" 1-3/4"

5-1/2"

10"

STEEL PLATE
1/8" X 1-1/2" X 10"

2"

1-1/4"

5-1/4"

12-1/2"

2"

2"

3/4"

1-3/4"

CENTER

TOOL REST
2" X 4 1/4" X 10"

UPPER RAIL WEDGE
15/16" X 3/8" X 7/8" X 5"

BASE
1 1/4" X 5 1/2" X 12 1/2"

COUNTERSUNK
WOODSCREW

RAIL

LOWER RAIL WEDGE
11/16" X 2" X 1 1/2" X 9"

UPRIGHT
1 3/4" X 2 1/2" X 12 1/2"

2 1/2"

TOOL REST ASSEMBLY

Scale: 1:8

285

Materials List: Spring-Pole Lathe

Spring Pole

A springy sapling about 15 feet long

Lathe Frame and Bed

Head stile	2-1/2" x 9-1/2" x 44-3/4"
Tail stile	2-1/2" x 9-1/2" x 39-1/2"
Head foot	2-1/2" x 5-1/2" x 20"
Tail foot	2-1/2" x 5-1/2" x 27"
2 Rails	1-3/4" x 5-1/2" x 40"
4 Wedges	7/16" x 1-3/4" x 6"
4 Dowels	1/2" x 10"

Tail Puppet Assembly

Puppet	2-1/2" x 5-1/2" x 18"
Wedge	15/16" x 3-1/4" x 8"

Tool Rest Assembly

Base	1-1/4" x 5-1/2" x 12-1/2"
Upright	1-3/4" x 2-1/2" x 12-1/2"
Rest	2" x 4-1/4" x 10"
Wedge	11/16" x 2" x 9"
Wedge	15/16" x 1-3/8" x 5"

Treadle

1 piece	1-1/2" x 1-3/4" x 52"
1 piece	1-1/2" x 1-3/4" x 32"
1 piece	1-1/2" x 1-3/4" x 16"

Hardware

Tail puppet center

Head-stock center

Steel rest strip   1/8" x 1-1/2" x 10"

Screws to attach rest plate to tool rest and tool rest to base.

Lags or screws to attach lathe feet to shop floor or a piece of plywood.

threads. Rub some paraffin across the threads and begin cutting grooves in the screw hole in the tail puppet. The improvised cutter is not particularly efficient, but you only need to thread one hole, and it must match the screw from the C-clamp.

On my lathe, the wood threads for the tail-puppet screw were sometimes hard to turn, even using the sliding T-handle. The solution was cutting a saw kerf from the top of the puppet into the threaded hole, which not only reduces the grip of the wood around the screw but serves as an oil channel.

The most complex component is the tool-rest assembly, which is designed for flexibility in its use. This tool rest can be moved anywhere along the rails and adjusted close to the centers as a turning progresses. It can also be rotated for face-plate turning. The upper wedge could be eliminated if the upright is made with side cheeks that rest directly on the base.

Attach the tool rest to the base with three hefty screws. A steel strip is screwed to the vertical face. The top of the steel strip is 1/16 inch lower than the lathe centers. Slotted screw holes in the steel strip would allow for adjustment of the tool-rest height. You may want to raise the tool rest; this is a matter of personal preference.

The treadle consists of three oak timbers mortised and tenoned together to form an "A" configuration. Three 3/8-inch-diameter dowels hold the treadle together. One leg of the "A" is extended past the apex to accept the driving cord. Several holes in the extended leg are for adjusting the turning action for stock of varying diameters.

Installation

Pole-lathe installations tend to be customized for every situation. Begin by selecting a suitable spring pole. Mike Abbott says that the ideal pole is a coppice-grown ash sapling, 15 to 20 feet long, with a 2-1/2-inch butt tapering to 1-1/4 inch at the tip. But almost any springy sapling will work. I was surprised to find that a 12-foot tulip poplar sapling worked well, even after it had thoroughly dried.

The spring pole requires two attachment points. Secure the butt of the sapling either behind or in front of the lathe, with a second attachment point several feet from the butt. My lathe's pole is secured behind the lathe using wooden brackets nailed just below the ceiling of the shop. In another situation, I pinned the butt of a pole about four feet above the ground to a post outdoors. The pole passed through the upper portion of my shop window, with the tip end conveniently terminating just above the lathe.

You can use other springs instead of a long sapling. One traditional alternative is a wooden bow mounted horizontally above the lathe centers. With the drive cord tied to the middle of the bow string, the bow flexes as you push

The tool rest and foot treadle, as seen from in front of the lathe. The butt rest is the wood strip crossing the upper right-hand corner.

down on the treadle. In recent years, pole-lathe turners have learned that rubber bungee cords can be used for lathe springs. Experiment, and use what works.

With any lathe, vibration must be minimal, so you need to attach the lathe and treadle to the floor. Long wood screws (or lags) driven through the lathe feet work nicely. Two strips of leather tacked to the base of the treadle and the floor will allow for some flexibility as you pump. You can also screw the feet and treadle to a sheet of plywood, which you stand on when operating the lathe.

An optional refinement in the installation is a butt rest to lean against as you pump. This is a shallow ledge attached to a wall or other structure behind the lathe. A workbench stationed behind the lathe could serve this purpose. A butt rest can be horizontal, or tilted, as shown in Van Vliet's etching, *The Turner*, in Chapter 1.

Complete the installation by tying the drive cord to the spring and the treadle. Various kinds of cordage will work, but most pole-lathe turners use ordinary 1/8-inch nylon cord, which is flexible, strong, and inexpensive.

Using a Spring-Pole Lathe

Using a pole lathe is easier and more efficient than you might guess. Because of its relatively low power, you should practice with straight, preferably green turning stock. Freshly cut tulip poplar and soft maple are perfect. Avoid blanks that contain knots. A 12- to 15-inch blank about 2 inches across is good for practicing.

Properly sharpened tools are important. Due to the slow speed of a pole lathe, high-speed steel tools offer no particular advantage.

Use a drawknife to straighten, square up, and then shave the stock into an octagonal section. Indent center holes at the ends with an awl.

Fix the turning blank between the lathe centers. The drive cord should drop vertically to the right of the tool rest. Pass the cord in front of the billet (on the near or tool-rest side of the lathe). Wind the cord twice around the billet. Raise the treadle to a comfortable pumping height, then tie the cord around the end of the extension. **For safety, always wear eye protection when working at any lathe.**

Try the pumping action by itself for a few minutes. Press the treadle using an even rhythm, between one and two beats per second. Begin cutting with a roughing gouge. Hold the tool handle at a low angle. Gradually lower the bevel toward the reciprocating wood. The first cuts will be tentative as you cut into the uneven turning blank. You may want to retie the length of the drive cord to adjust the pumping action.

Cutting always occurs as you press down on the treadle. Immediately after each cut, lift the cutting end of the roughing gouge slightly by lowering the end of the handle. Work toward developing a rhythmic, pulsing action, where you engage the tool with each downward pump, followed by a slight retreat of the cutter as the blank reverses and the treadle returns to its starting position.

As turning progresses, and the blank becomes round, you should stop to relocate the tool rest as close as possible to the turned cylinder. Once you have the action working properly, you'll be shaving noodlelike strips off the cylinder.

Because the drive cord wraps around the stock that you're turning, you'll need to stop cutting before turning the far end of the stock. You can move the drive cord and tool rest to new locations, but most pole-lathe turners prefer to reverse the turning stock, leaving the tool rest in place. Back off the screw on the tail puppet, and then slip the blank out from the looped drive cord. Turn the blank end for end, then wind two loops of drive cord around it. There's no need to untie the drive cord at the end of the treadle extension.

As you practice, follow the standard rules for spindle turning. The bevel of the roughing gouge should rub against the stock, with the cutting angle kept as low as possible. Turn from large diameters to small diameters, so that you are always cutting into ascending fiber. Position the tool rest as close as possible to the turning stock.

When you have turned an even cylinder, you can smooth and refine the surface with a wide skew chisel. If the skew point bites into the wood, the turning just comes to a stop, with much less damage or risk than you would experience using a powered lathe.

Once you're comfortable with the pumping/pulsing action, you can begin turning ladder-back rung tenons or bamboo Windsor legs. Remember that sized tenons must be turned from dry wood.

Designing a Chair

You can do some designing during the process of constructing a chair. Here dowels are taped to a Windsor arm bow to experiment with spacing for spindles.

Although you can make a custom chair for a particular person's use, most chairs need to serve whoever happens to sit in them, and human bodies come in many shapes and sizes. You also need to consider the chair's intended use.

When I design a new chair or modify an existing pattern, I like to test it for a while. I've learned that first impressions regarding chair comfort do not always hold up. A chair that feels fine when you first sit down or for several minutes may feel much less comfortable after fifteen minutes or an hour. For instance, I tested my low-back stick Windsor with the add-on hand pieces for several months at our family dining table. Early on, I detected an area on the seat that would begin to press on my bottom after about fifteen minutes. The back crest looked fine and was comfortable as long as I was only slightly in contact with the back bow. But when I relaxed into the backrest, the upper

edge cut into my back. The chair went back into the shop. I slightly recontoured the bottom and rounded the back crest on the upper front edge, eliminating a handsome crisp arris in favor of comfort.

The amount of contouring of a saddled seat makes a significant difference in comfort. A deeply saddled Windsor seat may look spectacular but can cause discomfort if you have to sit in it for very long. Researchers who study seating have learned that it's important to be able to move around in a seat, and shallower contours allow more body movement.

Often, chair seats slope downward toward the back. On Windsors, it's important to distinguish between plank slope, which is easily measured and used during construction, and contour slope, the dipping shape of the hollow saddle. The sitter experiences the contoured slope, a design feature the chairmaker needs to take into account.

The amount of slope is a matter of personal preference and what you're doing while sitting in a chair. For sitting around and socializing, a fair amount of slope (with the back of the seat 3/4 to 1-1/2 inches lower than the front) could be comfortable and acceptable when you are actually leaning back, with your torso supported by the chair back. When working at a desk, especially if drawing or writing, you often lean over your work; the back support isn't a factor until you lean back and relax. In this case, the best seat may have no slope, or even slope slightly toward the front. Negative seat slope puts your feet flat on the floor, and you tend to sit straight. For dining, a chair with a level seat or very slight slope is appropriate. Too much slope on a dining or office chair puts abnormal stress on your lower back when you are not actually leaning into the backrest.

Seat height is also a consideration. My newly finished English-style double-hoop Windsor replaced the low-back stick Windsor in my testing station at our dining table. The seat of this chair is about 1-1/2 inches higher than the stick Windsor. The seat surface was fine, but for several weeks my feet didn't seem to contact the floor properly. Now that I'm used to this height, it feels comfortable. I discovered that I like sitting higher in relationship to the top of the dining table, that my arms, wrists, and hands feel better. I've also found that a higher seat requires a rounder edge at the seat front.

You can try out different seat heights and seat slopes without cutting up the legs of a chair. Placing boards or magazines on the floor in front of the seat will allow you to find out how a chair would feel if it were lowered. Shims can be placed under the chair legs to test for seat slope, back slouch, and modifications in seat height.

In all chairs, the backrest should form an obtuse slouch angle in relationship to the seat. Slouch the backrest between 8 and 15 degrees, depending on the chair's intended use.

Chair-leg length, rake, and splay angles determine the height and seat slope of a chair, in addition to the engineering tasks of resisting rocking and of supporting a seated person's weight.

Vernacular stick Windsors do not follow any particular rules regarding leg rake and splay angles. Some primitive chairs have legs with considerable rake, but no splay, and vice versa. Leg angles of English Windsors are determined partly by the thinness of the elm seat. When the center area is saddled, the legs must be positioned fairly close to the corners of the plank, where there is enough thickness for adequately deep mortises. The front legs of English Windsors can be fairly close to vertical. If there was much rake or splay, the angled legs would become obstacles around other pieces of furniture. The best American Windsors are known for dramatic leg angles combining a fair amount of rake and splay. Because the seat planks of American Windsors are thicker than their English counterparts, leg tenons can be mortised closer to the center parts of the seat.

Although one seldom looks at a chair from static side or front views in real life, these perspectives are useful in discussing and working with leg, bow, and spindle angles. Chairmakers commonly specify resultant (boring) angles beginning at 90 degrees, so that a bevel gauge can be set using angles on either side of plumb. Measurements of leg rake angles (from the side view) should be taken from the seat, not the floor. (Because the seat usually slopes, it is not parallel to the floor.) Although the rake of front and rear legs can be the same, chairmakers often rake the rear legs several degrees more than the front legs; this helps to prevent a chair from tipping backwards. Having less rake at the front legs also makes a chair more maneuverable, especially around table legs and nearby people. If you increase the seat slope of an existing chair by shortening the rear legs, the effective rake of front and rear legs relative to the floor changes; front legs angle farther forward (appearing to have more rake), while rear legs get closer to plumb.

Leg splay—the angle to the sides—is mostly a matter of personal taste. A Windsor with considerable fore and aft leg rake looks awkward if there is not a fair amount of side splay also.

USING WIRE-LEG MODEL CHAIRS TO APPROXIMATE LEG ANGLES

While writing this book, I found myself wanting to revise some of the leg angles that I've been using on Windsor chairs for the last ten years. I wanted front legs to have a bit less rake and splay, and I wanted rear legs to rake back more than I had been doing. I also wanted the leg angles of my Windsors to retain a feeling of dramatic flare. Drawing front and side views was a first step. But it's almost impossible to get a feeling of how these angled legs would look on a real chair from a drawing. I needed a practical way to experiment with leg angles—without producing a lot of strange chairs.

Half-scale wire models—quickly made and very useful for experimenting with the leg angles of Windsor chairs.

The method I developed uses simple, half-scale model stools that consist of a seat plank and four wire legs. I saw the seat planks to scale from 3/4-inch-thick scrap boards and shape them to approximate the intended chair. For legs I use straightened pieces of coat-hanger wire (1/8-inch steel rod would work better). I insert the leg wires in angled holes in the model seat planks that approximate the position of the leg holes in the full-size chairs.

With the model in an upright position, its legs contacting a work table, I experiment with different leg angles by bending the wire, and with different lengths by substituting wires or simply cutting bits off the ends of some wires. I factor in the slope of the seat plank at the same time. Once the legs and seat slope look right, I turn the model upside down and hold a flat plastic protractor against the wire legs to record sighting lines, resultant angles, front splay angles, and side rake angles—it's much easier than taking angles off a real chair. If there are differences in the wire angles of left and right legs, I make further adjustments or settle on an average.

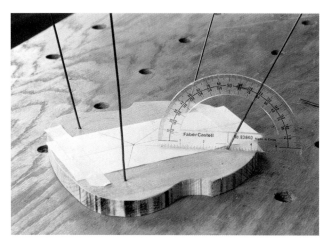

Record angles on paper taped across the bottom of the model seat, with a flat protractor positioned against a wire leg at the appropriate axis. Here, the resultant angle for the rear leg is 18 degrees.

I've learned that specific angles are less important than matching up pairs of front and rear legs, which should be symmetrical when viewed from front or rear and in alignment when viewed from the side. I draw the sighting lines and make notations on a piece of scrap paper taped to the bottom of the model seat. This allows me to develop different sets of angles using the same half-size model.

DRAWING A CHAIR

Scale front-, side-, and top-view drawings allow you to experiment with various proportions and angles before committing time to making a new chair. I also draw variations of details, such as turning patterns or hand ends of arm bows.

I made the original chair projections and turning drawings for this book using standard drafting techniques that I learned in junior high school in the midfifties. A full set of quarter-scale drawings usually fits on 14-by-17-inch drawing paper. Common drawing tools include

- 20-by-26-inch drawing board
- 14-by-17-inch translucent paper
- Tracing paper
- T-square
- 30-60 triangle
- Adjustable triangle
- Architect's scale
- Ordinary HB .5 and .7 mechanical lead pencils
- 180-degree clear plastic protractor (half-degree increments)
- 1/4-inch masking tape
- Straight-leg dividers
- Plastic circle templates
- Soft stick eraser
- Eraser shield

Drawings for a new chair often begin by taking tracings from drawings or specifications of an existing chair. For front-view angles, hold a protractor or sliding bevel gauge parallel to the front of the chair, regardless of the compound angle that the part may take. You can find sighting and resultant angles from existing chairs by drawing on a piece of cardboard folded or taped over the chair seat. Suspend a plumb line in front of your line of sight. Circle around the chair until the part you are sighting is in line with the plumb line. Visually project this line across the chair seat to locate the sighting point. Connect a line from the part to the sighting point. Find the resultant angle by setting a protractor or bevel gauge on the sighting line and against the part.

I usually begin drawings with front and side views. I find the locations of most details for the plan view from the front and side views. As the plan view comes together, I often make changes in the front and side views. I use straight-leg dividers to transfer measurements whenever a straight projection isn't possible.

The front view of the seat is the most difficult part of a chair drawing. A straight-on front view of a seat that slopes down at the back will include details of the bottom of the seat. The seat's upper surface is obscured by the slope. You can avoid this by drawing the seat dead level; seat slope is then accounted for by angling the floor line uphill toward the rear legs. (The sloped floor line takes getting used to.) Either convention will work; neither is entirely adequate.

New designs call for thoughtful consideration and, whenever possible, mock-ups. Drawings are not foolproof. My original drawing of the low-back stick Windsor with add-on crest and hand pieces showed the sticks in an arrangement that looked fine in front and side views. But in three dimensions, the sticks looked like a bunch of reeling drunks, as I discovered when I arranged straight wires in place to check the spacing. With some experimentation, I developed a stick spacing pattern that looked good from any perspective.

HOW TO USE THE TABLES

With basic drafting you can experiment with various rake and splay angles and you can project sighting lines onto the plan view. But you cannot rotate the drawing, as you would need to for finding resultant angles, which are used for boring compound angles. Another limitation of drawings is that error creeps in due to thickness of pencil lines, inaccurate placement of protractors, and so on—the human factor. These minute errors can accumulate, leading to an unacceptable degree of inaccuracy in the actual construction of a chair.

You can locate sighting lines on the seat plan of a Windsor by using rake and splay angles taken from side and front views. The sighting angle is formed between the sighting line and a line that connects the front legs or the back legs (app.1). The tables that follow allow you to determine (or experiment with) various sighting angles and resultant (boring) angles with mathematical accuracy. Sighting and resultant angles have been rounded to a single decimal point. In practice, you can round off to one-degree or half-degree units.

You can also use the tables to find sighting and resultant angles for spindles relative to a chair seat or a flat arm bow.

In both tables, rake and splay angles are always given in relationship to a 90-degree angle. For example, a rake angle of 15 degrees could be interpreted as 75 degrees (90 minus 15) or 105 degrees (90 plus 15). You must visualize the chair's geometry to determine if an angle is acute or obtuse. It's also important to remember that these angles are taken from a flat plane on the chair (usually the seat), not the floor.

The "Table of Sighting Angles" covers rake and splay angles between 0 and 30 degrees. The rake and splay angles can be taken from an existing chair, a drawing, or your imagination. You must use the proper rake and splay axis on this table. Sighting angles are always in relation to a connecting line that is perpendicular to the center line of

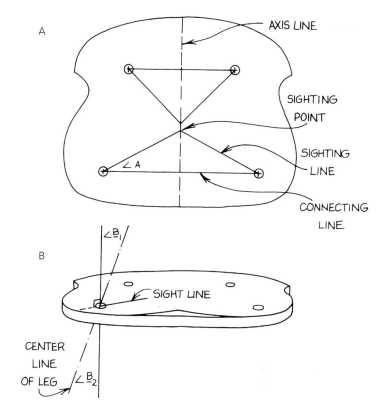

APP. 1. Terms used in describing chair geometry include: *a*, sighting lines (and sighting points), arrived at by establishing an angle that is measured from a connecting line perpendicular to the axis of the chair. You can find the sighting angle (angle A) using the rake and splay axis on the "Table of Sighting Angles"; *b*, angles B1 and B2 represent the resultant angle used to bore in plane with the sighting line. To find a resultant angle, refer to the "Table of Resultant Angles."

the chair (based on the fact that all chairs are bilaterally symmetrical).

The "Table of Resultant Angles" provides the actual tilt angle of a boring (leg or spindle). Resultant angles are always used in conjunction with sighting lines. This table is symmetrical; either axis can be used for rake or splay.

To use the charts:

Step 1. Find the sighting line. The sighting line is defined in terms of an angle relative to a line connecting both front posts or both rear posts. Examples: When rake is 12 degrees and splay is 7 degrees, the sighting line is 30 degrees from the connecting line. If rake and splay are equal, the sighting line is always 45 degrees from the connecting line.

Step 2. Find the resultant sighting angle. The resultant sighting angle is measured from 90 degrees when the leg is viewed perpendicular to the sighting line. Example: A leg that is perfectly plumb has a sighting angle of 0 degrees.

Table of Sighting Angles

(angle relative to a line connecting front posts or a line connecting back posts)

rake angle	splay angle 0	1	2	3	4	5	6	7	8	9	10	11	12	13	14	15	16
0	—	0.0	0.0	0.0	0.0	0.0	0.0	0.0	0.0	0.0	0.0	0.0	0.0	0.0	0.0	0.0	0.0
1	90.0	45.0	26.6	18.4	14.0	11.3	9.4	8.1	7.1	6.3	5.7	5.1	4.7	4.3	4.0	3.7	3.5
2	90.0	63.4	45.0	33.7	26.5	21.8	18.4	15.9	14.0	12.4	11.2	10.2	9.3	8.6	8.0	7.4	6.9
3	90.0	71.6	56.3	45.0	36.9	30.9	26.5	23.1	20.5	18.3	16.6	15.1	13.9	12.8	11.9	11.1	10.4
4	90.0	76.0	63.5	53.1	45.0	38.6	33.6	29.7	26.5	23.8	21.6	19.8	18.2	16.9	15.7	14.6	13.7
5	90.0	78.7	68.2	59.1	51.4	45.0	39.8	35.5	31.9	28.9	26.4	24.2	22.4	20.8	19.3	18.1	17.0
6	90.0	80.6	71.6	63.5	56.4	50.2	45.0	40.6	36.8	33.6	30.8	28.4	26.3	24.5	22.9	21.4	20.1
7	90.0	81.9	74.1	66.9	60.3	54.5	49.4	45.0	41.1	37.8	34.9	32.3	30.0	28.0	26.2	24.6	23.2
8	90.0	82.9	76.0	69.5	63.5	58.1	53.2	48.9	45.0	41.6	38.6	35.9	33.5	31.3	29.4	27.7	26.1
9	90.0	83.7	77.6	71.7	66.2	61.1	56.4	52.2	48.4	45.0	41.9	39.2	36.7	34.5	32.4	30.6	28.9
10	90.0	84.3	78.8	73.4	68.4	63.6	59.2	55.1	51.4	48.1	45.0	42.2	39.7	37.4	35.3	33.3	31.6
11	90.0	84.9	79.8	74.9	70.2	65.8	61.6	57.7	54.1	50.8	47.8	45.0	42.4	40.1	37.9	36.0	34.1
12	90.0	85.3	80.7	76.1	71.8	67.6	63.7	60.0	56.5	53.3	50.3	47.6	45.0	42.6	40.4	38.4	36.5
13	90.0	85.7	81.4	77.2	73.1	69.2	65.5	62.0	58.7	55.5	52.6	49.9	47.4	45.0	42.8	40.7	38.8
14	90.0	86.0	82.0	78.1	74.3	70.7	67.1	63.8	60.6	57.6	54.7	52.1	49.6	47.2	45.0	42.9	41.0
15	90.0	86.3	82.6	78.9	75.4	71.9	68.6	65.4	62.3	59.4	56.7	54.0	51.6	49.3	47.1	45.0	43.1
16	90.0	86.5	83.1	79.6	76.3	73.0	69.9	66.8	63.9	61.1	58.4	55.9	53.5	51.2	49.0	46.9	45.0
17	90.0	86.7	83.5	80.3	77.1	74.0	71.0	68.1	65.3	62.6	60.0	57.6	55.2	52.9	50.8	48.8	46.8
18	90.0	86.9	83.9	80.8	77.9	74.9	72.1	69.3	66.6	64.0	61.5	59.1	56.8	54.6	52.5	50.5	48.6
19	90.0	87.1	84.2	81.3	78.5	75.7	73.0	70.4	67.8	65.3	62.9	60.6	58.3	56.2	54.1	52.1	50.2
20	90.0	87.3	84.5	81.8	79.1	76.5	73.9	71.4	68.9	66.5	64.2	61.9	59.7	57.6	55.6	53.6	51.8
21	90.0	87.4	84.8	82.2	79.7	77.2	74.7	72.3	69.9	67.6	65.3	63.1	61.0	59.0	57.0	55.1	53.2
22	90.0	87.5	85.1	82.6	80.2	77.8	75.4	73.1	70.8	68.6	66.4	64.3	62.3	60.3	58.3	56.4	54.6
23	90.0	87.6	85.3	83.0	80.6	78.4	76.1	73.9	71.7	69.5	67.4	65.4	63.4	61.5	59.6	57.7	56.0
24	90.0	87.8	85.5	83.3	81.1	78.9	76.7	74.6	72.5	70.4	68.4	66.4	64.5	62.6	60.8	59.0	57.2
25	90.0	87.9	85.7	83.6	81.5	79.4	77.3	75.2	73.2	71.2	69.3	67.4	65.5	63.7	61.9	60.1	58.4
26	90.0	88.0	85.9	83.9	81.8	79.8	77.8	75.9	73.9	72.0	70.1	68.3	66.5	64.7	62.9	61.2	59.5
27	90.0	88.0	86.1	84.1	82.2	80.3	78.3	76.5	74.6	72.7	70.9	69.1	67.4	65.6	63.9	62.3	60.6
28	90.0	88.1	86.2	84.4	82.5	80.7	78.8	77.0	75.2	73.4	71.7	69.9	68.2	66.5	64.9	63.3	61.7
29	90.0	88.2	86.4	84.6	82.8	81.0	79.3	77.5	75.8	74.1	72.4	70.7	69.0	67.4	65.8	64.2	62.6
30	90.0	88.3	86.5	84.8	83.1	81.4	79.7	78.0	76.3	74.7	73.0	71.4	69.8	68.2	66.6	65.1	63.6

Table of Sighting Angles

(angle relative to a line connecting front posts or a line connecting back posts)

rake angle	splay angle 17	18	19	20	21	22	23	24	25	26	27	28	29	30
0	0.0	0.0	0.0	0.0	0.0	0.0	0.0	0.0	0.0	0.0	0.0	0.0	0.0	0.0
1	3.3	3.1	2.9	2.7	2.6	2.5	2.4	2.2	2.1	2.0	2.0	1.9	1.8	1.7
2	6.5	6.1	5.8	5.5	5.2	4.9	4.7	4.5	4.3	4.1	3.9	3.8	3.6	3.5
3	9.7	9.2	8.7	8.2	7.8	7.4	7.0	6.7	6.4	6.1	5.9	5.6	5.4	5.2
4	12.9	12.1	11.5	10.9	10.3	9.8	9.4	8.9	8.5	8.2	7.8	7.5	7.2	6.9
5	16.0	15.1	14.3	13.5	12.8	12.2	11.6	11.1	10.6	10.2	9.7	9.3	9.0	8.6
6	19.0	17.9	17.0	16.1	15.3	14.6	13.9	13.3	12.7	12.2	11.7	11.2	10.7	10.3
7	21.9	20.7	19.6	18.6	17.7	16.9	16.1	15.4	14.8	14.1	13.5	13.0	12.5	12.0
8	24.7	23.4	22.2	21.1	20.1	19.2	18.3	17.5	16.8	16.1	15.4	14.8	14.2	13.7
9	27.4	26.0	24.7	23.5	22.4	21.4	20.5	19.6	18.8	18.0	17.3	16.6	15.9	15.3
10	30.0	28.5	27.1	25.8	24.7	23.6	22.6	21.6	20.7	19.9	19.1	18.3	17.6	17.0
11	32.4	30.9	29.4	28.1	26.9	25.7	24.6	23.6	22.6	21.7	20.9	20.1	19.3	18.6
12	34.8	33.2	31.7	30.3	29.0	27.7	26.6	25.5	24.5	23.5	22.6	21.8	21.0	20.2
13	37.1	35.4	33.8	32.4	31.0	29.7	28.5	27.4	26.3	25.3	24.4	23.5	22.6	21.8
14	39.2	37.5	35.9	34.4	33.0	31.7	30.4	29.2	28.1	27.1	26.1	25.1	24.2	23.4
15	41.2	39.5	37.9	36.4	34.9	33.6	32.3	31.0	29.9	28.8	27.7	26.7	25.8	24.9
16	43.2	41.4	39.8	38.2	36.8	35.4	34.0	32.8	31.6	30.5	29.4	28.3	27.4	26.4
17	45.0	43.3	41.6	40.0	38.5	37.1	35.8	34.5	33.3	32.1	31.0	29.9	28.9	27.9
18	46.7	45.0	43.3	41.8	40.2	38.8	37.4	36.1	34.9	33.7	32.5	31.4	30.4	29.4
19	48.4	46.7	45.0	43.4	41.9	40.4	39.0	37.7	36.4	35.2	34.1	32.9	31.8	30.8
20	50.0	48.2	46.6	45.0	43.5	42.0	40.6	39.3	38.0	36.7	35.5	34.4	33.3	32.2
21	51.5	49.8	48.1	46.5	45.0	43.5	42.1	40.8	39.5	38.2	37.0	35.8	34.7	33.6
22	52.9	51.2	49.6	48.0	46.5	45.0	43.6	42.2	40.9	39.6	38.4	37.2	36.1	35.0
23	54.2	52.6	51.0	49.4	47.9	46.4	45.0	43.6	42.3	41.0	39.8	38.6	37.4	36.3
24	55.5	53.9	52.3	50.7	49.2	47.8	46.4	45.0	43.7	42.4	41.1	39.9	38.8	37.6
25	56.7	55.1	53.6	52.0	50.5	49.1	47.7	46.3	45.0	43.7	42.5	41.3	40.1	38.9
26	57.9	56.3	54.8	53.3	51.8	50.4	49.0	47.6	46.3	45.0	43.7	42.5	41.3	40.2
27	59.0	57.5	55.9	54.5	53.0	51.6	50.2	48.9	47.5	46.3	45.0	43.8	42.6	41.4
28	60.1	58.6	57.1	55.6	54.2	52.8	51.4	50.1	48.7	47.5	46.2	45.0	43.8	42.6
29	61.1	59.6	58.2	56.7	55.3	53.9	52.6	51.2	49.9	48.7	47.4	46.2	45.0	43.8
30	62.1	60.6	59.2	57.8	56.4	55.0	53.7	52.4	51.1	49.8	48.6	47.4	46.2	45.0

Table of Resultant Angles

(use either axis for rake or splay)

rake/splay	0	1	2	3	4	5	6	7	8	9	10	11	12	13	14	15	16
0	0.0	1.0	2.0	3.0	4.0	5.0	6.0	7.0	8.0	9.0	10.0	11.0	12.0	13.0	14.0	15.0	16.0
1	1.0	1.4	2.2	3.2	4.1	5.1	6.1	7.1	8.1	9.1	10.0	11.0	12.0	13.0	14.0	15.0	16.0
2	2.0	2.2	2.8	3.6	4.5	5.4	6.3	7.3	8.2	9.2	10.2	11.2	12.2	13.1	14.1	15.1	16.1
3	3.0	3.2	3.6	4.2	5.0	5.8	6.7	7.6	8.5	9.5	10.4	11.4	12.3	13.3	14.3	15.3	16.3
4	4.0	4.1	4.5	5.0	5.6	6.4	7.2	8.0	8.9	9.8	10.7	11.7	12.6	13.6	14.5	15.5	16.4
5	5.0	5.1	5.4	5.8	6.4	7.1	7.8	8.6	9.4	10.3	11.1	12.0	12.9	13.9	14.8	15.7	16.7
6	6.0	6.1	6.3	6.7	7.2	7.8	8.5	9.2	10.0	10.8	11.6	12.5	13.3	14.2	15.1	16.1	17.0
7	7.0	7.1	7.3	7.6	8.0	8.6	9.2	9.9	10.6	11.3	12.1	12.9	13.8	14.7	15.5	16.4	17.3
8	8.0	8.1	8.2	8.5	8.9	9.4	10.0	10.6	11.2	12.0	12.7	13.5	14.3	15.1	16.0	16.8	17.7
9	9.0	9.1	9.2	9.5	9.8	10.3	10.8	11.3	12.0	12.6	13.3	14.1	14.8	15.6	16.5	17.3	18.1
10	10.0	10.0	10.2	10.4	10.7	11.1	11.6	12.1	12.7	13.3	14.0	14.7	15.4	16.2	17.0	17.8	18.6
11	11.0	11.0	11.2	11.4	11.7	12.0	12.5	12.9	13.5	14.1	14.7	15.4	16.1	16.8	17.5	18.3	19.1
12	12.0	12.0	12.2	12.3	12.6	12.9	13.3	13.8	14.3	14.8	15.4	16.1	16.7	17.4	18.1	18.9	19.6
13	13.0	13.0	13.1	13.3	13.6	13.9	14.2	14.7	15.1	15.6	16.2	16.8	17.4	18.1	18.8	19.5	20.2
14	14.0	14.0	14.1	14.3	14.5	14.8	15.1	15.5	16.0	16.5	17.0	17.5	18.1	18.8	19.4	20.1	20.8
15	15.0	15.0	15.1	15.3	15.5	15.7	16.1	16.4	16.8	17.3	17.8	18.3	18.9	19.5	20.1	20.8	21.4
16	16.0	16.0	16.1	16.3	16.4	16.7	17.0	17.3	17.7	18.1	18.6	19.1	19.6	20.2	20.8	21.4	22.1
17	17.0	17.0	17.1	17.2	17.4	17.6	17.9	18.2	18.6	19.0	19.4	19.9	20.4	21.0	21.5	22.1	22.7
18	18.0	18.0	18.1	18.2	18.4	18.6	18.9	19.2	19.5	19.9	20.3	20.7	21.2	21.7	22.3	22.8	23.4
19	19.0	19.0	19.1	19.2	19.4	19.6	19.8	20.1	20.4	20.8	21.1	21.6	22.0	22.5	23.0	23.6	24.1
20	20.0	20.0	20.1	20.2	20.3	20.5	20.7	21.0	21.3	21.7	22.0	22.4	22.9	23.3	23.8	24.3	24.9
21	21.0	21.0	21.1	21.2	21.3	21.5	21.7	22.0	22.2	22.6	22.9	23.3	23.7	24.1	24.6	25.1	25.6
22	22.0	22.0	22.1	22.2	22.3	22.5	22.7	22.9	23.2	23.5	23.8	24.1	24.5	25.0	25.4	25.9	26.4
23	23.0	23.0	23.1	23.2	23.3	23.4	23.6	23.8	24.1	24.4	24.7	25.0	25.4	25.8	26.2	26.7	27.1
24	24.0	24.0	24.1	24.1	24.3	24.4	24.6	24.8	25.0	25.3	25.6	25.9	26.3	26.6	27.0	27.5	27.9
25	25.0	25.0	25.1	25.1	25.2	25.4	25.5	25.7	26.0	26.2	26.5	26.8	27.1	27.5	27.9	28.3	28.7
26	26.0	26.0	26.1	26.1	26.2	26.4	26.5	26.7	26.9	27.1	27.4	27.7	28.0	28.4	28.7	29.1	29.5
27	27.0	27.0	27.1	27.1	27.2	27.3	27.5	27.7	27.9	28.1	28.3	28.6	28.9	29.2	29.6	29.9	30.3
28	28.0	28.0	28.1	28.1	28.2	28.3	28.5	28.6	28.8	29.0	29.3	29.5	29.8	30.1	30.4	30.8	31.1
29	29.0	29.0	29.0	29.1	29.2	29.3	29.4	29.6	29.8	30.0	30.2	30.4	30.7	31.0	31.3	31.6	32.0
30	30.0	30.0	30.0	30.1	30.2	30.3	30.4	30.6	30.7	30.9	31.1	31.3	31.6	31.9	32.2	32.5	32.8

Table of Resultant Angles

(use either axis for rake or splay)

rake/splay	17	18	19	20	21	22	23	24	25	26	27	28	29	30
0	17.0	18.0	19.0	20.0	21.0	22.0	23.0	24.0	25.0	26.0	27.0	28.0	29.0	30.0
1	17.0	18.0	19.0	20.0	21.0	22.0	23.0	24.0	25.0	26.0	27.0	28.0	29.0	30.0
2	17.1	18.1	19.1	20.1	21.1	22.1	23.1	24.1	25.1	26.1	27.1	28.1	29.0	30.0
3	17.2	18.2	19.2	20.2	21.2	22.2	23.2	24.1	25.1	26.1	27.1	28.1	29.1	30.1
4	17.4	18.4	19.4	20.3	21.3	22.3	23.3	24.3	25.2	26.2	27.2	28.2	29.2	30.2
5	17.6	18.6	19.6	20.5	21.5	22.5	23.4	24.4	25.4	26.4	27.3	28.3	29.3	30.3
6	17.9	18.9	19.8	20.7	21.7	22.7	23.6	24.6	25.5	26.5	27.5	28.5	29.4	30.4
7	18.2	19.2	20.1	21.0	22.0	22.9	23.8	24.8	25.7	26.7	27.7	28.6	29.6	30.6
8	18.6	19.5	20.4	21.3	22.2	23.2	24.1	25.0	26.0	26.9	27.9	28.8	29.8	30.7
9	19.0	19.9	20.8	21.7	22.6	23.5	24.4	25.3	26.2	27.1	28.1	29.0	30.0	30.9
10	19.4	20.3	21.1	22.0	22.9	23.8	24.7	25.6	26.5	27.4	28.3	29.3	30.2	31.1
11	19.9	20.7	21.6	22.4	23.3	24.1	25.0	25.9	26.8	27.7	28.6	29.5	30.4	31.3
12	20.4	21.2	22.0	22.9	23.7	24.5	25.4	26.3	27.1	28.0	28.9	29.8	30.7	31.6
13	21.0	21.7	22.5	23.3	24.1	25.0	25.8	26.6	27.5	28.4	29.2	30.1	31.0	31.9
14	21.5	22.3	23.0	23.8	24.6	25.4	26.2	27.0	27.9	28.7	29.6	30.4	31.3	32.2
15	22.1	22.8	23.6	24.3	25.1	25.9	26.7	27.5	28.3	29.1	29.9	30.8	31.6	32.5
16	22.7	23.4	24.1	24.9	25.6	26.4	27.1	27.9	28.7	29.5	30.3	31.1	32.0	32.8
17	23.4	24.0	24.7	25.4	26.1	26.9	27.6	28.4	29.1	29.9	30.7	31.5	32.3	33.2
18	24.0	24.7	25.3	26.0	26.7	27.4	28.1	28.9	29.6	30.4	31.1	31.9	32.7	33.5
19	24.7	25.3	26.0	26.6	27.3	28.0	28.7	29.4	30.1	30.8	31.6	32.4	33.1	33.9
20	25.4	26.0	26.6	27.2	27.9	28.5	29.2	29.9	30.6	31.3	32.1	32.8	33.5	34.3
21	26.1	26.7	27.3	27.9	28.5	29.1	29.8	30.4	31.1	31.8	32.5	33.3	34.0	34.7
22	26.9	27.4	28.0	28.5	29.1	29.7	30.4	31.0	31.7	32.3	33.0	33.7	34.4	35.2
23	27.6	28.1	28.7	29.2	29.8	30.4	31.0	31.6	32.2	32.9	33.6	34.2	34.9	35.6
24	28.4	28.9	29.4	29.9	30.4	31.0	31.6	32.2	32.8	33.4	34.1	34.7	35.4	36.1
25	29.1	29.6	30.1	30.6	31.1	31.7	32.2	32.8	33.4	34.0	34.6	35.3	35.9	36.6
26	29.9	30.4	30.8	31.3	31.8	32.3	32.9	33.4	34.0	34.6	35.2	35.8	36.4	37.1
27	30.7	31.1	31.6	32.1	32.5	33.0	33.6	34.1	34.6	35.2	35.8	36.4	37.0	37.6
28	31.5	31.9	32.4	32.8	33.3	33.7	34.2	34.7	35.3	35.8	36.4	36.9	37.5	38.1
29	32.3	32.7	33.1	33.5	34.0	34.4	34.9	35.4	35.9	36.4	37.0	37.5	38.1	38.7
30	33.2	33.5	33.9	34.3	34.7	35.2	35.6	36.1	36.6	37.1	37.6	38.1	38.7	39.2

NOTES ON DESIGNING A ROCKER

Rocking chairs present unique challenges for chair designers and chairmakers. Chairs for relaxing, reading, knitting, and enjoying life, rockers must be very, very comfortable.

The actual rockers must have identical curves, or the chair will walk across the floor as it's used. The curves must also be perfectly parallel to each other. Rocker radius affects speed of rocking. Large-radius rockers rock faster than rockers with a smaller radius. Rockers are generally longer than necessary; the extension behind the rear chair legs serves as a psychological assurance that the rocker won't tip over backwards.

The sitter's center of gravity in relation to the seat and the rockers affects the static resting point of the chair. If that center of gravity is too far forward, the rocking chair will want to tip forward; you have to use your feet and legs to counteract the sense that you're about to fall on your face. When the center of gravity is too far backwards, a sitter also feels unsafe.

Seat slope and back slouch affect the placement of a sitter's center of gravity over the rockers. If the backrest doesn't have enough slouch, you may find yourself sliding forward to get comfortable. The center of gravity shifts forward, and the rocker tries to nosedive.

Rockers have short legs to compensate for the rise of the rockers. Leg lengths can be adjusted to modify seat slope, back slouch, and balance of the chair itself. When you're sitting comfortably on a rocking chair, your feet may be placed somewhat forward compared to sitting in most other chairs, but your legs must be relaxed.

ENLARGED PLANS AVAILABLE

The producers of *The Chairmaker's Workshop* are pleased to offer a special Plans Package, containing 1:4 scale projections for the eleven chairs shown in this book, enlarged and ready to use in your shop; plus full-sized patterns for Windsor chair seats, Windsor bow bending forms, and Windsor turnings.

For each Plans Package send a check or money order made payable to Lark Books for $16.95 plus $4.95 postage and handling (in Canada, $23.95 plus $4.95 postage and handling) to:

Chairmaker's Workshop Plans Package
c/o Lark Books
P.O. Box 2580
Asheville, North Carolina, U.S.A. 28802-2580

Please allow 2-3 weeks for delivery. Your satisfaction is fully guaranteed.

Glossary of Tools, Chairs, and Woodworking Terms

Air dried. Wood that has attained an equilibrium moisture content (e.m.c.) with the environment. Fully air-dried wood may reach a moisture content of 10 to 20 percent.

Alligator chuck. Two-piece bit-brace chuck that pivots at one end. Used mainly for auger bits having a tapered square lug at the attachment end.

Arris. Edge formed by the junction of two planes.

Ascending grain. Wood fiber (grain pattern) that runs up into a progressing cut.

Auger bit. Common boring tool used with a bit brace. The cutting end has a tapered lead screw, two cutters, and two scoring nickers; the shank is surrounded by a spiral that carries away shavings. The traditional shank end, for use with a bit brace, is a tapered square lug.

Balloon-back. Bow-back Windsor with the lower portion of the bow pinched in (taking a reverse curve) before entering the seat deck.

Baluster-and-ring turning. Common name for a fancy turning style commonly found on early American Windsor chairs. Typically combines two vase-shaped balusters with a ring and tapered cone at the bottom end. Also called "double baluster."

Bamboo turning. A simple American Windsor turning style based on nodes of bamboo. Dated beginning about 1790. Also called "double bobbin."

Bast. The inner, soft layer (phloem) of tree bark.

Bead. A positive (convex) semicircular form in spindle turning.

Bench dog. Square- or round-sectioned device that fits into matching mortises in the top of a workbench. Usually used in conjunction with a vise dog. Dogs can be set at various heights above the surface to help secure work in place.

Bending strap. Steel strap that is placed along the convex side of the piece of wood to be bent. Strap ends are held in place by stops located at both ends of the wood.

Bevel. (1) Angled facet that forms the cutting edge of a tool. Bevels can be flat, hollow ground, or rolled (convex). (2) Any chamfer.

Billet. Small riving, the result of riving larger bolts.

Bolt. Sizable piece of a log formed by riving.

Bound water. Water within the cell wall of wood. Loss of bound water results in dimensional shrinkage.

Bow-back Windsor. Windsor side chair with a back support consisting of a single, looped bow having both ends mortised into the plank seat. Five to eleven vertical spindles fill in the backrest area. Sometimes called a "loop-back" Windsor. An English bow-back is similar to an American sack-back.

Brace or **bit brace.** Hand-held boring tool that consists of a pommel, crank, and chuck, usually used with auger bits or spoon bits, but adaptable to other boring devices.

Brake. English country-craft term for any simple holding device. Example: a pair of narrow forked branches, useful for holding stock when riving chair parts.

Burr or **wire edge.** Minute metal flap formed on the opposite side of an edge during grinding or honing that indicates that abrasion has taken place at the arris.

Cage. Rung section of a post-and-rung chair frame.

Cambium. The layer of cells on a tree stem that forms the boundary between bark and wood. Leaves, pith, and cambium are the only growing part of the stem.

Cane. Chair-seat material that consists of thin strips from the outer layer of rattan vines. Cane is usually woven in an octagonal pattern on a flat chair frame.

Cant hook. Strong wooden bar fitted with a curved iron arm and a hook at one end, used to lever logs and heavy timbers.

Case-hardened. Condition in which the exterior layers of a piece of wood are considerably drier than the interior layers. Caused by drying wood too rapidly.

Cat face. Scar on the bark surface that reflects the presence of a knot within the wood.

Cathedral or **onion rings.** The growth-ring pattern on the sides of a board.

Caul. Plate or pad (often scrap wood) used as a spacer between clamp jaws and the item being clamped.

Chairmaker's shave or **travisher.** Spokeshave with a sole that curves gently from handle to handle, used to finish the saddling of Windsor seats.

Chip breaker or **cap iron.** Secondary blade fitted above and behind the cutting edge of some plane and spokeshave irons.

Chord. Straight line intersecting two points of a curve or circle.

Clearance angle. Angle between the lower face of a blade and the wood being cut.

Comb. Curved, horizontal piece of wood that connects the spindles of a comb-back Windsor.

Comb-back Windsor or **high-back Windsor.** Tall Windsor armchair having a horizontal arm bow with spindles passing through the back section that terminate in a horizontal comb.

Continuous-arm or **continuous-bow Windsor.** Windsor armchair whose single bow forms armrests and a raised back section. Originally based on the French *bergere* chair.

Cove. A negative (concave) semicircular form in spindle turning.

Crest rail. Low addition to the backrest area on the bow of a low-back Windsor. Can be used as a splice on pieced bows and increases comfort of the chair.

Cutting angle or **rake angle.** Angle between the upper face of a blade and the wood being cut. The cutting angle equals the included blade angle plus the clearance angle.

Deck or **island.** Flat area on the back half of a Windsor seat that houses mortises for the spindles.

Descending grain. Wood fiber that runs downwards into a progressing cut.

Dial gauge. Machinist's caliper that uses a dial readout in hundredths or thousandths of an inch, useful for exact measurements of cylindrical tenons and mortises.

Differential shrinkage. The different rates of wood shrinkage parallel with the rays compared with shrinkage tangent to the growth rings.

Diffuse porous. Hardwood species in which pores are approximately the same size and distributed evenly across each growth ring. Examples: maple, birch, and beech.

Double-bobbin turning. *See* bamboo turning.

Double bow-back Windsor. English equivalent of an American sack-back Windsor.

Drawknife. Chairmaker's cutting tool that consists of an essentially straight blade, usually 8 to 12 inches long, with perpendicular handles at each end.

Equilibrium moisture content (e.m.c.). Moisture content (m.c.) of a piece of wood after full adjustment to environmental humidity and temperature.

End grain. A wood surface consisting of exposed cross-cut fibers.

Extractives. Compounds deposited in wood during the transition from sapwood to heartwood that give heartwood its dark color, and sometimes impart decay and insect resistance.

Fan-back Windsor. Late eighteenth-century side chair whose back consists of a fanlike array of long spindles capped with a comb. A structurally weak but aesthetically pleasing design.

Felling. Cutting or harvesting a standing tree.

Fiber saturation point. Point at which wood-cell walls are fully saturated with bound water but the cell cavities are empty of free water.

Flat sawed. Also plain sawed, slash grained. Pieces of lumber with the annual rings intersecting the surface at less than 45 degrees.

Flitch sawed or **through-and-through sawed.** Sawed lumber retaining the original waney bark edges of the log. Preferred for resawing chair parts because pieces can be aligned with the growth rings.

Forstner bit. Specialty wood-cutting bit that rides on semicircular spurs; it makes a clean, flat-bottomed hole and can be used at extreme angles with a drill press.

Free water. Moisture within the cell cavities of wood, not in the cell walls, whose loss does not result in appreciable shrinkage.

Froe. Also lath axe, splitting knife. A riving tool with a straight blade (usually 8 to 12 inches long) and a perpendicular handle.

Froe club. Narrow, hardwood club used to strike the back of a froe blade.

Frog. The angled section within a plane or spokeshave body that supports the blade.

Glut. Large wooden splitting wedge, usually shop made.

Green woodworking. An approach to woodworking that takes advantage of the structural qualities of freshly felled wood, including use of rived parts with little grain run out, easy cutting with hand tools, and superior bending characteristics. Green-worked wood is dried to appropriate moisture content before assembly of structural members, such as chair parts.

Growth ring or **annual ring.** Layer of wood cells added to a tree trunk or stem during one growing season.

Head stock. The stationary puppet housing the pulleys and driving center of a powered lathe.

Heartwood. The inner core of a tree trunk or stem that no longer conducts sap. While not alive, heartwood serves as a skeletal support for the living tree. Sometimes heartwood is decay and/or insect resistant.

High-back Windsor. English equivalent of an American comb-back Windsor.

Hollow auger. Tool used to form cylindrical tenons, such as those on the ends of rungs.

Hollow grind. Slight concavity across the width of a bevel caused by grinding on the rim of a turning grindstone.

Hollowing adze. Cutting tool whose blade is set at a right angle to the handle, used to rough out the upper section of Windsor seats.

Honeycombing. Checks in the interior of a piece of wood, usually caused by case-hardening during rapid drying.

Honing. The second step in sharpening, between shaping (grinding) and polishing; employs grits with 800 to 1,200 mesh.

Hygroscopic. Ability of a material to lose or gain moisture content with fluctuations in environmental humidity.

Included angle. Angle formed by the two facets of a cutting edge.

Inshave. Deeply dished drawknife used to sculpt the saddled section of Windsor chair seats.

Iron. The blade of such tools as a plane or spokeshave.

Kerf. Slot formed by a saw.

Kiln dried or **hot-air dried.** Wood dryness below the moisture content attainable by air drying, usually 6 to 8 percent m.c. Kiln-dried wood will pick up moisture whenever it is in a moisture-bearing environment.

Linseed oil. A reactive finish made from the seeds of flax plants.

Loop-back Windsor. American bow-back Windsor.

Low-back Windsor. Windsor with a single horizontal bow that supports armrests and the back section. Also called a "captain's chair."

Maul. Wooden club, used for splitting.

Micro-bevel. Narrow subbevel immediately behind an edge. The included angle of a micro-bevel will be a few degrees greater than the bevel angle.

Mineral spirits or **paint thinner.** Standard solvent for oil-based paints and varnishes.

Moisture content (m.c.). The percentage of moisture in a piece of wood compared to the same piece when it is thoroughly dried.

Mortise. Round or rectangular cavity that houses a tenon or back slat.

Outside caliper. Compasslike tool with curved legs, for taking or transferring measurements on the outside of a turning.

Peavey. Log-moving tool similar to a cant hook, with a spike at the end instead of a hook.

Pith. The first year's growth of a tree stem, found approximately in the center of a tree trunk or branch.

Plain sawed. *See* flat sawed.

Point fence. Band-saw fence that consists of a rounded block of wood, located on the saw table with the tangent spaced at the desired distance from the saw blade.

Pommel. The high point at the front center of a saddled Windsor seat.

Post-and-rung chair. Chair style that consists of vertical posts and horizontal rungs. The continuous rear posts also form the supports for the backrest, which can consist of slats or spindles. The seat, usually woven, is often trapezoidal in plan.

Puppet or **stock.** Vertical member of a lathe that houses either of the two lathe centers. Usually the dead center.

Quarter sawed. Also vertical grain, edge grain. Sawed pieces in which the growth rings form an angle of 45 degrees or more to the wood surface—ideally, close to 90 degrees.

Racking. Force applied fore and aft to a chair.

Radial. A hypothetical plane that radiates from the pith outwards toward the bark.

Rake. The angle fore and aft (as seen from a side view) of chair legs, and sometimes other members. Often measured in degrees more or less than a right angle.

Ray. Cluster of wood cells arranged radially. Rays give quarter-sawed or split wood its distinctive fish-scale appearance.

Reaction wood. Distorted wood formed in leaning trunks and branches of trees that dries unpredictably, often twisting and cracking.

Reamer or **taper reamer.** A cone-shaped cutting tool used to convert a cylindrical mortise into a conelike configuration.

Resaw. To rip lumber into narrower pieces.

Resin or **pitch.** Translucent, sticky material secreted in canals or pockets in the wood of various conifers, particularly eastern white pine.

Resultant angle. The lean angle of a cylinder (usually a chair part or drill shaft) in line with a sighting angle. Often measured in degrees more or less than a right angle.

Rift sawed. Sawed pieces whose annual rings intersect the surface at about 45 degrees.

Ring-porous. Hardwood species that develop relatively large pores during early annual growth and much smaller pores later in the season. Examples: oak, ash, hickory, and elm. Except elm, these are tough, coarse-fiber woods, excellent for riving and shaving.

Rive. To split wood with maximum control of thickness, used mostly with ring-porous hardwoods.

Rod-back Windsor. Variation of a fan-back, with one or two rodlike bows connecting the upper ends of the spindles.

Rouging gouge. Large, square-nosed gouge used by turners to convert square stock and rivings into a cylindrical section; also used for shaping bamboo turnings.

Runout or **grain slope.** Grain deviation across a board; measured as a ratio of cross distance to length, such as 1 inch in 12 inches.

Rush. Natural, grasslike fiber used to weave post-and-rung chair seating. Examples: cattail and bulrush. "Fiber rush" is an imitation made of twisted brown paper.

Sack-back Windsor. American Windsor armchair with a horizontal arm bow (bent, or laminated), a supplementary back bow mortised into the arm bow, and—usually—a wide, shallow oval seat.

Saddling. Carving the upper side of a Windsor seat.

Sapwood. The outer growth rings; the physiologically active part of a living tree. Usually lighter than heartwood and lacks decay resistance.

Scratch beader. Simple tool used to scratch a decorative bead on D-section Windsor bows.

Settee. Wide chair for two or more persons.

Shaker tape. Cloth tape the Shakers used for seating chairs sold to the public.

Shaving horse. Wood-holding device based on a low bench on which the woodworker sits; a foot-operated swinging arm acts as a clamp.

Sighting angle or **offset angle.** Angle between a sighting line and two specified points, usually the centers of both front legs or both rear legs of a chair.

Sighting line. Line across a flat surface (such as a Windsor chair seat) that indicates the leaning direction of an angled cylinder (the resultant angle), usually a chair part or drill shaft.

Sighting point. Any specified point on a sighting line.

Skew chisel. Turner's chisel with an angled cutting edge and a symmetrical bevel used to take fine cuts, especially beads and tapers.

Skewing cut. Using a drawknife, spokeshave, chisel, or plane at an angle, instead of perpendicular to the cutting edge. This lowers the effective cutting angle, resulting in a finer surface.

Slicing cut. Shifting a tool's cutting edge from one side to another during a cut, with the same effect as skewing.

Slope. Angle of a seat from front to back.

Slouch. Angle of a seat back from vertical.

Sloyd. Swedish term for "handcraft."

Spindle. Slender, cylindrical chair part that supports the back and armrest bows of Windsor chairs. Also, a vertical member mortised between horizontal rails in the backrest of some post-and-rung chairs.

Spindle gouge. Turning gouge sharpened with a "fingernail" cutting edge, for cutting beads, coves, and balusters.

Splat. Flat, thin board, usually mortised vertically into the center area of the backs of English Windsors and often sawed with elaborate shapes and interior cutouts called "fretwork."

Splay. The angle of chair parts (usually legs or spindles) to either side of a chair, as seen from a front or rear view. Often specified in degrees more or less than perpendicular.

Spofford brace. Simple bit brace that employs a split steel chuck tightened with a wing bolt.

Spokeshave. Cutting tool consisting of two in-line handles with a small, planelike cutter mounted in the center.

Spoonbit or **chairmaker's bit.** Gouge-shaped wood bit with a rounded nose at the front.

Stick Windsor. Simple Windsor chair, often with shaved legs and no stretcher system.

Sticks. Chair parts that are roughly cylindrical. Also, bow and comb supports on Windsors when they are shaved, instead of turned. Post-and-rung chairs are sometimes called "stick chairs."

Stock. *See* puppet.

Stretchers. Horizontal components that connect and strengthen chair legs. Medial stretchers connect the midpoints of left and right side stretchers on a Windsor with an "H" stretcher pattern.

Tail stock. Vertical member of a lathe that can be moved along the ways to secure wood of different lengths.

Tapering plane. Tenon former with the blade set at an angle for making conical tenons. A matching reamer must be used to make the tapered mortise.

Tenon. Rectangular or cylindrical projection made to fit into a matching mortise. Used in mortise-and-tenon construction for many chair joints. Cylindrical tenons can often be made on a lathe.

Tenon former or **hollow auger.** A cutting tool for making cylindrical tenons.

Throat. Slot on the sole of a plane or spokeshave where the blade protrudes and through which shavings are ejected.

Through-and-through. *See* flitch sawed.

Travisher. *See* chairmaker's shave.

Tung oil. Oil finish expressed from tung nuts.

Universal chuck. Bit-brace chuck whose two pivoting jaws can hold bits with parallel-sided shanks in addition to the traditional tapered square-lug shank.

Waney. Sawed lumber with its natural (bark) edge intact, produced by flitch sawing.

Warp. In weaving a chair seat, the initial strands wrapped around the front and rear rungs.

Ways. The bed rails for a lathe.

Weft. In weaving a chair seat, the strands woven across the weft (from side rung to side rung).

Windsor chair. Chair form based on a solid wood seat, with independent leg and back-support systems.

Wire edge. *See* burr.

Henderson Mullens was turning chair parts on this pole lathe in rural Kentucky, about 1930.

CHAIRMAKING HISTORY

Andrews, Edward Deming, and Andrews, Faith. *Shaker Furniture.* New Haven, Conn.: Yale University Press, 1937; reprint, New York: Dover, 1964.

Cotton, Bernard D. *The English Regional Chair.* Woodbridge, Suffolk, U.K.: Antique Collector's Club Ltd., 1990.

Edlin, Herbert L. *Woodland Crafts in Britain.* Newton Abbot, Devon, U.K.: David and Charles, 1949.

Evans, Nancy Goyne. "A History and Background of English Windsor Furniture." In *Furniture History,* vol. 10. London: Furniture History Society, 1979.

_____. *American Windsor Chairs.* New York: Hudson Hills, 1996.

Forman, Benno. *American Seating Furniture, 1630-1730.* New York: Norton, 1988.

Jenkins, J. Geraint. *Traditional Country Craftsmen.* London: Routledge and Kegan Paul, 1965.

Kassay, John. *The Book of Shaker Furniture.* Amherst, Mass.: University of Massachusetts Press, 1980.

Kinmonth, Claudia. *Irish Country Furniture, 1700-1950.* New Haven, Conn.: Yale University Press, 1993.

Nutting, Wallace. *A Windsor Handbook.* Boston: Old America, 1917; reprint, Rutland, Vt.: Tuttle, 1973.

Santore, Charles. *The Windsor Style in America.* Philadelphia: Running Press, 1981; reprint, Mendham, N.J.: Astragal, 1994.

Shaw-Smith, David. *Ireland's Traditional Crafts.* London: Thames and Hudson, 1984.

Sparkes, Ivan G. *English Windsor Chairs.* Bucks, U.K.: Shire, n.d.

MAKING CHAIRS

Alexander, John D., Jr. *Make a Chair from a Tree.* Newtown, Conn.: Taunton, 1978; reprint, Mendham, N.J.: Astragal, 1994.

Brown, John. *Welsh Stick Chairs.* Fresno, Calif.: Linden, 1990.

Dunbar, Michael. *Make a Windsor Chair.* Newtown, Conn.: Taunton, 1984.

Hill, Jack. *Country Chair Making.* Newton Abbot, Devon, U.K.: David and Charles, 1993.

GREEN WOODWORKING TECHNIQUES, FINISHING, AND TURNING

Abbott, Mike. *Green Woodwork.* Lewes, East Sussex, U.K.: Guild of Master Craftsmen, 1989.

Conover, Ernie. *The Lathe Book.* Newtown, Conn.: Taunton, 1993.

Dent, D. Douglas. *Professional Timber Falling.* Beaverton, Ore.: Dent, 1974.

Dresdner, Michael. *The Woodfinishing Book.* Newtown, Conn.: Taunton, 1992.

Fine Woodworking on Bending Wood. Newtown, Conn.: Taunton, 1983.

Fine Woodworking on Chairs and Beds. Newtown, Conn.: Taunton, 1986.

Fine Woodworking on Wood and How to Dry It. Newtown, Conn.: Taunton, 1986.

Flexner, Bob. *Understanding Wood Finishing.* Emmaus, Pa.: Rodale, 1994.

Holdstock, Ricky. *Seat Weaving.* Lewes, East Sussex, U.K.: Guild of Master Craftsmen, 1994.

Langsner, Drew. *Country Woodcraft.* Emmaus, Pa.: Rodale, 1978.

_____. *Green Woodworking.* Rev. ed. Asheville, N.C.: Lark, 1995.

Moxon, Joseph. *Mechanick Exercises.* Reprint of the 1703 edition. Mendham, N.J.: Astragal, 1994.

Raffan, Richard. *Turning Wood.* Newtown, Conn.: Taunton, 1985.

Rowley, Keith. *Woodturning: A Foundation Course.* Lewes, East Sussex, U.K.: Guild of Master Craftsmen, 1990.

TOOLS AND SHARPENING

Lee, Leonard. *The Complete Guide to Sharpening.* Newtown, Conn.: Taunton, 1995.

Miller, Warren. *Crosscut Saw Manual.* Washington, D.C.: Government Printing Office, no date. Stock number 001-001-00434-1.

Salamon, R. A. *Dictionary of Woodworking Tools.* London: Allen and Unwin, 1975; reprint, Newtown, Conn.: Taunton, 1990.

TREE IDENTIFICATION AND WOOD SCIENCE

Gordon, J. E. *The New Science of Strong Materials.* New York: Walker, 1968.

Hoadley, R. Bruce. *Identifying Wood.* Newtown, Conn.: Taunton, 1990.

_____. *Understanding Wood.* Newtown, Conn.: Taunton, 1980.

Little, Elbert L. *The Audubon Society Field Guide to North American Trees.* 2 vols. New York: Knopf, 1980.

U.S. Department of Agriculture. *Properties, Selection, and Suitability of Woods for Woodworking.* Madison, Wis.: Forest Products Laboratory, n.d.

_____. *Silvics of Forest Trees of the United States.* Agriculture Handbook No. 271. Washington, D.C.: Government Printing Office, 1965.)

_____. *Wood Handbook.* Madison, Wis.: Forest Products Laboratory, 1974; reprint, *The Encyclopedia of Wood.* New York: Sterling, 1980.

U.S. Department of the Navy. *Wood: A Manual for its Use as a Shipbuilding Material.* Washington, D.C., 1945; reprint, Kingston, Mass: Teaparty, 1983.

Index